# LNER STANDARD GRESLEY CARRIAGES

## MICHAEL HARRIS

Mallard BOOKS,
Ottershaw, Surrey

# PREFACE

To all the LNER men and women
who designed, built and maintained
the coaching stock of their Company

LNER Standard Gresley Carriages
© Michael Harris and Mallard Books 1998

First published in 1998

ISBN 0 9532896 0 5

Published by Mallard Books, 22 Crofton Close, Ottershaw,
Chertsey, Surrey KT16 0LR
Telephone and fax: 01932 873105

Designed by Robert Wilcockson

Printed by Ian Allan Printing, Riverdene, Molesey Road, Hersham,
Surrey KT12 4RG

## Publisher's Note

*LNER Standard Gresley Carriages* is primarily concerned with the new designs
of Gresley teak-bodies carriages that were
introduced between 1923 and 1931, but built in
quantity until the early part of World War 2
and forming the vast majority of LNER-built
carriages.

The later designs of vehicle, special train
sets and postwar LNER-design carriages will
feature in another book in our list, depending
of course on the success of this volume.

Our intention is that the main outlet for
our books will be through the specialist transport bookshops and we will not offer this or
other titles at discounted rates to book clubs.

**T**HIS book is concerned with the Gresley teak-bodied standard
designs of coaches and vans introduced from 1923, and built,
in some cases, as late as the early years of World War 2. It also
includes a sprinkling of other types, such as the all-steel coaches and vans built in 1927/8, the 'Super Firsts', and one or two other vehicles. Effectively, this volume comes to an end in 1931, so far as new
designs of coaches and vans are concerned. Not covered are those new
designs produced after 1931, not least the stock for the LNER's high-
speed trains, such as the 'Silver Jubilee' and 'Coronation', as well as the so-
called 'end-door' types of vestibuled stock, steel-panelled coaches for general service, and all postwar coaches and vans to LNER design, and the
non-common user stock.

So far as illustrations are concerned, the book has as its basis the
Diagrams issued by the LNER from 1927, and normally encountered in
bound form, sometimes amounting to three volumes, with the Diagrams
listed from 1 upwards to 376. These are featured in this book.

A few words of explanation are due. The Diagrams were not engineering drawings in the true sense at all, but produced for the operators
of the vehicles. They are generally accurate so far as the <u>overall</u> propor-
tions of the vehicles are concerned, and portray the operating characteristics of the vehicles faithfully. But the Diagram drawings lack underframe
detail, as well as various fittings on the roof and ends. They were also not
updated for those designs that continued to be manufactured into the
mid/late 1930s, by which time coaches were being built with welded
underframes with angle-iron trussing, intermediate armrests, and various
other improvements. That means, for example, that the Diagram appearing of, say, a Diagram 115 coach is representative only of the earlier vehicles built to this design. In defence of the LNER, it must be said that the
quality and consistency of the Diagram drawings are better than those
emanating from the LMS and GWR. It is best to keep quiet about those
produced by the SR which are so crude as to be almost unbelievable!

Where possible, the photographs are a mixture of official shots, and
of those of vehicles in service in BR days. It hardly needs to be said that
the pristine state of the newly outshopped coach in the glory of glowing
varnished teak, white roof and teak-colour painted underframe lasted a
relatively short time. Some vehicles received special cleaning attention
but the varnish soon dulled, and the tones of the woodwork darkened.
The photographs from BR days are useful for showing some of the detail
that tended to be lost by the official photographers' penchant for broad-
side views, with the result that the features of the panelling, beading and
fittings were seldom clear.

The book is arranged in order of vehicle types rather than in chrono-
logical order, for the reason that it seemed helpful to be able to compare
the various designs of, say, vestibuled brake thirds, or articulated coaches.
Apart from coaches built for the LNER, the handful of designs of coaches
built for the Cheshire Lines Committee to Gresley designs are included.

*Michael Harris*

Ottershaw,
Surrey
April 1998

# CONTENTS

# INTRODUCTION

THE LNER was unique among the Big Four companies in that standard designs of vestibuled and non-vestibuled coaches were produced very soon after Grouping and effectively remained in production for some 20 years. By the outbreak of World War 2, the other Big Four companies' standard stock was very different in outward appearance from what had been built in the aftermath of Grouping, from 1923. 'Outward appearance' is a qualification used for good reason, for though the sleeker, steel-panelled stock built by the LMS and GWR in 1939 looked more modern, its general specification was not all that different from the designs of two decades before. The body framing remained wooden-framed and was built separately from the underframe and bogies which again represented no real advance on what had become commonplace on British railways by 1923.

In the case of the LNER, the last general service teak-bodied coaches entering service in the early years of World War 2 were little different from those built by Doncaster and York Works for the 'Flying Scotsman' in 1914. Having said that the LNER standard designs were 'effectively' in production for some 20 years, it is worth pointing out that the original designs had been supplanted on front-line service by a range of more modern designs, most of these, it is true, being similarly teak-panelled. Steel-panelled stock was used either for the prestige 'high-speed trains' (the title accorded to the 'Silver Jubilee', 'Coronation' and 'West Riding Limited' by the LNER management) and for the secondary stock, used on semi-fast or stopping trains.

What do we mean by Standard stock? Being pedantic, few coaches built to standard designs could really be said to be 'Standard' until production lines were set up in the 1980s and 1990s for jig-building of vehi-

cles to close tolerances. There were variations in dimensions as between individual vehicles (engineering tolerances were hardly in the range of 'ten-thou' in the railway workshops until the 1960s) and as between different batches. Some of these variations will be alluded to during the course of description of the various designs.

Also, there were differing interpretations of design features or fittings as between Doncaster, York and the other LNER carriage-building workshops. Some of these departures were trivial and derived from pre-1923 loyalties, reinforced by the LNER's 1923 company organisation of decentralised management. This provided for each works to be under the control of an individual Area or section, these being based on the pre-Grouping companies. So, yes, there were 'Standard' designs of coaching stock, but the vehicles themselves were not necessarily standard, meaning identical, when it came to dimensions, details of panelling, fittings and the like.

## GENESIS

The LNER Gresley standard designs of coaching stock had their origins in H. N. Gresley's practice for the Great Northern Railway and the East Coast (and Great Northern/North Eastern) Joint Stock. Gresley joined the GNR as carriage and wagon superintendent in 1905 and, almost immediately, brought the company up to date so far as its passenger stock was concerned. In came elliptical-roofed bodies, modern, all-steel underframes, electric lighting and contemporary taste for the interior decor. The pioneering stock embodying these features was that built for the Sheffield (and Manchester) expresses in 1906, and the new principles were quickly introduced for the East Coast Joint Stock (ECJS) vehicles built at Doncaster, as well as influencing the design of those built at

Epitomising the prewar LNER, the 2.20pm Manchester London Road-Marylebone stands at Nottingham Victoria on 17 July 1937. The engine is 'B17' 4-6-0 No 2869 *Barnsley*, and the leading coach a brake third to Diagram 40, one of the vehicles transferred in the mid-1930s from East Coast stock to the Great Central Area.

The North Eastern Area used non-vestibuled stock extensively on main line trains as late as the mid/late 1930s. A recently outshopped Diagram 56 or 57 third is behind the tender of 'C7' Atlantic No 2172 as it passes York shed with a Newcastle express.

York, too. Similarly changed were the coaches for the Great Northern/North Eastern Joint Stock where the NER's slab-sided body-work was also discarded in favour of the Gresley/Doncaster standard of tumblehome sides and the roofs curving down at each end.

For the time being, the coaches built for the GNR and ECJS were of varying overall dimensions and ran on pressed-steel bogies. By the outbreak of World War I, a length over the body ends of 61ft 6in was becoming standard for the GNR vestibuled carriages which ran on compound-bolster bogies whose design was the outcome of collaboration between Spencer, Moulton, of suspension fame, and Gresley. These complicated and somewhat expensive to maintain bogies became another Gresley/LNER trademark on account of their good riding characteristics. They outlived the production of Gresley teak-bodied coaches and, indeed, continued to be used by BR, for electric multiple units into the 1960s, and some remain at work.

The coaches put into service after World War I by the GNR, and for the ECJS fleet, were generally very similar to those built as LNER standard stock after 1923, and are easily mistaken at first sight in photographs. Although it was likely that once Gresley was appointed as chief mechanical engineer of the LNER the company's coaching stock would follow his principles, the new coaches were by no means identical in detail to those built for the GNR and ECJS. How the standard designs were evolved is the subject of a succeeding section of this Introduction.

If the 1939 general service LNER teak-bodied coach was at first sight little advance on that built in 1907 or 1922, the general specification had undergone a number of changes, not all for the better. When there was debate in LNER days about the cost of an individual Carriage Building Programme, the result was often that Gresley proposed that savings could be made in production costs. Corners were cut to some extent by reducing the quality of specifications, and inferior materials were gradually introduced. Such economies were probably unavoidable but the one constant was the use of teak panelling for the bodywork. Varnished teak was the livery of the LNER (and the GNR and ECJS before it) and tradition was not sacrificed easily.

## EARLY DAYS OF GROUPING

Gresley was not appointed CME of the LNER until February 1923, once the company had came into active existence. While it took some time for a policy to be evolved for locomotives, matters moved swiftly on the carriage and wagon side and, as early as the spring of 1923, principles and practice for the new standard coaches were being established.

At the very first meetings of the LNER superintendents and passenger managers, as early as those of January and February 1923, it was recommended that all new passenger stock should be electrically-lit and that, subject to inspection by the LNER directors of some newly shopped specimen vehicles, varnished teak was the preferred livery, (regrettably)

without the company coat-of-arms, and with the class of accommodation denoted by a numeral displayed on the door bottom panels.

At first, there was less concern about appearance and materials than dimensions, braking systems, gangways and couplings. After all, these were major influences in the production of standard vehicles. In the meantime, and under the 1923 Carriage Building Programme, coaches were built to existing designs of the pre-Grouping companies, generally to fulfil orders placed before Grouping. Under this, and the next couple of Carriage Building Programmes, there was limited construction of existing (or slightly modified) designs for other Areas, eg North Eastern Railway types were ordered for the Southern Scottish Area and for the Great Eastern section. The Building Programme for 1923 was really a tidying-up process, with the addition of sleeping cars urgently needed to update the East Coast stock fleet. The first real LNER Carriage Building Programme, and the one to feature the standard designs, was that for 1924.

## HOW THE LNER WAS ORGANISED

At this juncture, it is important to remind the reader of the way in which the LNER organised itself, not least because this determined much of its coaching stock practice. The headquarters of the company was at Marylebone station, London, but day to day management was devolved to the four divisional general managers, each being in charge of an Area, with the Southern Area being sub-divided.

This structure comprised the following entities:

**Southern Area**
> Western section, comprising the territory and operations of the former Great Northern and Great Central Railways
>
> Eastern section, comprising the territory and operations of the former Great Eastern Railway

**North Eastern Area**, comprising the territory and operations of the former North Eastern Railway (recently having merged with the Hull & Barnsley Railway)

**Southern Scottish Area**, comprising the territory and operations of the former North British Railway

**Northern Scottish Area**, comprising the territory and operations of the former Great North of Scotland Railway. The NSA later amalgamated with the SSA.

While the chief mechanical engineer was responsible for the design and construction of the locomotives, coaches and wagons coming under his care, he was not responsible for specifying the *types* to be ordered to meet commercial requirements. That was left to the individual Areas or sections, whose divisional general manager reported to the chief general manager and was usually represented in discussions about coaching stock by the passenger managers. What they specified – as a result of the deliberations of the Superintendents' and Passenger Managers Committee – formed the annual carriage building programme, providing this met with the approval of the chief general manager and the necessary headquarters' committees of the LNER, principally the Locomotive and Traffic Committees.

So the initiative for specifying the *types* of coaching stock lay with the operating and commercial people, not with Gresley and his department. The engineers' remit was to undertake the design and construction of the vehicles, and possibly there were a number of features which were not to the liking of the engineers. The driving force was provided by the combination of Gresley and Ralph Wedgwood, the general manager, who worked closely together, backed by their very able staffs. In the search for new designs and ideas, the commercial requirements were quickly met by engineering ingenuity.

When it came to the building programme and the case for constructing new vehicles, the impetus originated with the chief mechanical engineer, in what at first sight was a negative direction. He was responsible for putting forward a programme for breaking-up over-age or otherwise redundant coaches during the coming year. In replacement of these, the superintendents and passenger managers set out their proposals for new carriages which usually had the effect of 'cascading' vehicles, to replace those scheduled for condemnation.

## THE STANDARD DESIGNS OF 1923

While the CME's offices were located at Kings Cross station, the design work on the Standard coaches was undertaken in the Darlington drawing office, under the control of the assistant CME, A. C. Stamer.

In April 1923, the Traffic Committee recommended that Pullman gangways should be used for complete sets of coaches but that, for the present, the policy of the constituent companies should be followed as regards the fitting of gangways, the GER-type British Standard gangway having been adopted in December 1923 as the preferred type; after further tests, the NER-type was chosen in early 1924.

Kings Cross informed Darlington in June 1923 that the partition-to-partition dimensions of the first-class compartments should be 7ft 6in and the third-class, 6ft 3in. With these dimensions, work went ahead with designs for coaches on 52ft (later changed to 51ft) and 60ft underframes, the size of the lavatories being dependent on the remaining space left once the required number of compartments had been accommodated within the body length. Width over the body mouldings was originally to be 8ft 6in, but Kings Cross agreed with Stamer that this dimension should be 8ft 9in (9ft over the body-side handles). First-class seating would be three-a-side, and third-class, four-a-side. All windows were to have square corners, to which Stamer objected and expressed the former NER's preference for radiussed corners to windows. But square windows were to be the standard.

For their part, the SPMs recommended that the interior fittings of ECJS vehicles should be adopted as standard for the new vehicles, and that, other than in brake compartments, inside door handles should be provided in suburban stock only. These recommendations were duly followed.

In August 1923, a meeting was held on rolling stock policy at Kings Cross, with O. V. S. Bulleid, personal assistant to Gresley, as chairman. Darlington was instructed that all brake ends and full brakes were to have glazed lights (windows) at cant-rail level; hit and miss ventilators were to be fitted to the doors above the droplights (fanlights above the quarterlights, and also above the droplights, were a feature of the Gresley GNR coaches); guard's duckets (lookouts) should be of a faceted design, and there should be no continuous stepboard below the side doors.

As the first year of Grouping proceeded, the designs for Standard coaches were produced at Darlington where the drawing office must have been hard-pressed to turn out the drawings. At first, the designs were listed as 'proposed'. Fortunately, the drawing office register has survived and so it is interesting to note the progress of the draughtsman's efforts.

| Drawing No | Date | Description |
|---|---|---|
| 11784 | 2 May 1923 | Section of proposed standard carriage |
| 11785 | May 1923 | Proposed vestibuled third on 60ft underframe |
| 11786 | May 1923 | Proposed vestibuled third on 52ft underframe |
| 11787 | May 1923 | Proposed vestibuled composite on 60ft underframe |
| 11788 | May 1923 | Proposed vestibuled composite on 52ft underframe |
| 11789 | May 1923 | Proposed vestibuled brake composite on 60ft underframe |
| 11790 | May 1923 | Proposed vestibuled brake composite on 52ft underframe |
| 11791 | May 1923 | Proposed vestibuled brake third on 60ft underframe |
| 11792 | May 1923 | Proposed vestibuled brake third on 52ft underframe |
| 11855• | June 1923 | Proposed vestibuled first on 60ft underframe |
| 11856 | June 1923 | Proposed vestibuled first on 52ft underframe |
| 11857• | June 1923 | Proposed vestibuled third on 60ft underframe |
| 11858 | June 1923 | Proposed vestibuled third on 52ft underframe |
| 11859• | June 1923 | Proposed vestibuled composite on 60ft underframe ¶ |

¶drawing modified with coupé compartment as third-class rather than first-class.

| Drawing No | Date | Description |
|---|---|---|
| 11860 | June 1923 | Proposed vestibuled composite on 52ft underframe |
| 11861 | June 1923 | Proposed vestibuled brake composite on 60ft underframe |
| 11862 | June 1923 | Proposed vestibuled brake composite on 52ft underframe |
| 11863 | June 1923 | Proposed vestibuled brake third on 60ft underframe |
| 11864 | June 1923 | Proposed vestibuled brake third on 52ft underframe |
| 11992• | November 1923 | Proposed composite sleeping car |
| 11995 | November 1923 | Proposed non-vestibuled full brake on 51ft underframe |
| 11996 | November 1923 | Proposed non-vestibuled full brake on 60ft underframe |
| 11998• | December 1923 | Proposed vestibuled composite (2½ first, 4 third-class) on 60ft underframe |
| 11999• | December 1923 | Proposed vestibuled locker composite (2½ first, 4 third-class) on 60ft underframe* |
| 12004 | December 1923 | Proposed vestibuled full brake on 51ft underframe |
| 12005 | December 1923 | Proposed vestibuled full brake on 60ft underframe |
| 12006• | December 1923 | Proposed vestibuled brake composite on 60ft underframe |
| 12007• | December 1923 | Proposed vestibuled brake third on 60ft underframe |
| 12008 | December 1923 | Proposed vestibuled full brake on 60ft underframe |
| 12009• | December 1923 | Proposed vestibuled brake first on 60ft underframe |
| 12010 | December 1923 | Proposed vestibuled full brake on 51ft underframe |
| 12028 | 31 Dec 1923 | Proposed sleeping car |
| 12029 | January 1924 | Proposed open first on 60ft underframe |
| 12030 | January 1924 | Proposed open third on 60ft underframe |

These drawings were generally referred to with the addition of a 'D' suffix to denote Darlington eg, 12030D.

Most of the above drawings were confirmed in December 1923, and duly signed by the SPMs, those definitely recorded as such being denoted by • Some of the drawings were modified in response to the requests of the commercial managers.

A range of drawings for non-vestibuled stock was produced by Doncaster drawing office.

| Drawing No | Description |
|---|---|
| 4417 | Third |
| 4420 | Brake third |
| 4448 | Composite (four first, three third compts) |
| 4591 | First |

Doncaster also produced drawings for the articulated – and other – restaurant cars

| | |
|---|---|
| 4580 | Triplet restaurant cars |
| 4673 | Restaurant first |
| 4674 | Restaurant third |
| 4675 | Restaurant pantry third |

These drawings were generally referred to with the addition of a 'N' suffix to denote Doncaster eg, 4448N.

It should be noted that these drawings were not the full general arrangement drawings but merely diagrams showing the general plan of the vehicle. They are of significance as the number references were used in official discussions until the well-known Diagram numbers were introduced in the late 1920s.

By December 1923, work on the various standard coach designs had been concluded, and the SPMs initialled their consent to a number of drawings. The previous month, the SPMs had provisionally recommended that, until there had been a conclusive review of the LNER's loading gauge restrictions, vehicles should be built to an overall width of 9ft (8ft 6in only for the van section of brake vehicles) and to lengths of 51ft (vestibuled stock) and 60ft (non-vestibuled). The 51ft non-vestibuled stock was to be

On the Great Eastern section, dual-fitted coaches continued to be built for outer suburban use into the mid-1930s. A rake of non-vestibuled stock, with a Diagram 56/57 third leading, forms an express from Liverpool St-Clacton/Walton, photographed near Brentwood c 1930 behind 'D16/2' 4-4-0 No 8785.

built to a height of 12ft 10in to enable it to work over the Widened Lines. All other standard LNER elliptical roofed stock – and most stock over 52ft over the headstocks – was barred from working over the Widened Lines, at least in earlier days.

The exceptions to these standards comprised the vestibuled stock for the Great Eastern section which would be built on the 51ft underframe, in order to suit the restricted length at Liverpool Street station platforms. Other non-standard length vehicles, but featuring the familiar Gresley LNER outline, comprised some non-vestibuled firsts and thirds built at Dukinfield for the GC section. These made use of underframes of Great Central Railway design recovered from ambulance train vehicles.

For non-vestibuled stock, other than the suburban trains which are dealt with under the Type Descriptions, compartment partition to partition dimensions were maintained as closely as possible to 7ft 3in for the first-class and 6ft 2in for the third-class. Van compartments up to 17ft long had one pair of doors each side, those over 17ft having two pairs of doors, with a guard's door in addition in each case. The guard's seat and hand brake were normally at the far end.

## THE STANDARDS EVOLVE

Originally, it was intended to build restaurant sets comprising either a restaurant pantry third and restaurant first, or a kitchen car serving an open first and an open third. At a meeting of rolling stock controllers held at York in November 1923, the CME's representative put forward an alternative proposal, for articulated restaurant car triplets, with either gas or electric cooking equipment, the latter finding favour with the SPMs following a trial run between Kings Cross and Darlington in late 1923, possibly with the quintuplet set which had been put into service by the GNR during 1921. The case for the triplets was established because they reduced the number of catering vehicles required for East Coast service.

Subject to the engineer's approval, the non-articulated restaurant cars – firsts, composite, third and third pantry – were to be of 65ft length over the headstocks. Such approval must have been withheld because early in 1924 it was decided that non-articulated restaurant cars would be built on the 60ft underframe.

As the discussion on the 1924 CBP continued during late 1923/early 1924, the details of the basic designs of LNER standard passenger coaches were finalised. There were to be no composite restaurant cars at this stage, and the first-class restaurant cars and third-class pantry cars were to be based on GNR designs; a stack of shelves for luggage would not be provided in either the first-class or third-class open coaches – instead there were to be net racks above seats and space under seats for stowing luggage; the large side windows in restaurant cars and open vehicles would be glass-louvred, to the design of fitting used by the NER; most brake vehicles would not have windows in the body ends, as had been favoured by the NER in particular, an exception being made for non-vestibuled brakes; full brakes would have three pairs of double doors each

side and one single (60ft vans), and two pairs and one single (51ft vans); brake vans would not – after all – be fitted with duckets.

Most of these principles were maintained for the standard coaches in the ensuing 20 years.

For a short period in 1923, new stock for the Great Eastern section, other than suburban stock which was Westinghouse fitted only, was specified to be dual-fitted, as were carriage trucks ordered by the Great Central section. In the 1924 CBP, dual-fitted stock was built for the North Eastern Area, with the exception of the set for the Newcastle-South Wales express which was vacuum only. Also, a series of vestibuled coaches fitted with vacuum only had been allocated to the Northern Scottish Area. For the 1925 CBP, it was agreed that all vestibuled vehicles should have Pullman gangways and that vacuum braking should be fitted to all vehicles, other than those for the Northern Scottish Area which would be dual-fitted, as would the non-vestibuled stock being supplied to the North Eastern Area, and the Great Eastern section.

## UNDERFRAMES AND RUNNING GEAR

Of the two standard lengths for underframes, the 60ft type with buckeye couplers was specified for vestibuled stock (except for general service stock on the GE section), and the 51ft type with screw couplings for non-vestibuled stock. Vestibuled stock (other than in set trains) for general service on the GE section was built on 51ft underframes with buckeye couplers.

The buffers of the 60ft underframe measured 1ft 9in from headstocks to buffer face, with the buffers in the extended position, 1ft 0¼in when pushed-in. The buffers on the 51ft underframes used for non-vestibuled stock measured 1ft 10in.

## BOGIES

Bogie designs were standardised in 1923, principally on the compound-bolster Gresley Spencer Moulton bogie with outside solebars, pressed steel side frames and bolsters, cast iron centre and side castings, and gunmetal bearings.

For a short time, the 8ft single wheelbase, pressed steel bogie with inside solebars was used for bogie brake vans.

### Standard types of compound bolster bogie

| Use | Wheelbase | Max load on pivot | Journals* | Drawing No |
|---|---|---|---|---|
| Passenger carriages – not exceeding 35 tons weight – 1914 Light Type | 8ft 6in | 12 tons | 8in + 4in | 1367N |
| Vehicles with a tare weight over 35 tons or articulated stock – 1921 Heavy Type | 8ft 6in | 18 tons | 10in + 5in | 3378N |
| Heavy Type for GE section suburban stock | 8ft | 18 tons | 10in + 5in | 6405N |

* The larger journals had a higher tin content in the white metal when used for main line stock

## BODY CONSTRUCTION

The standard vestibuled carriages were characterised by their teak panelled bodywork, with the roof sloping down at each end, and bowed body ends. Pullman-type gangways, buckeye couplers and retractable buffers were fitted to all, except for a limited number of carriages used

Diagram of the buckeye automatic coupler on standard LNER coaches, as reproduced in the company's Appendix to General Rules and Regulations.

List of parts numbered: 1. Knuckle; 2. Knuckle pin; 3. Emergency coupling pin; 4. Slot for emergency coupling; 5. Holes in knuckle for emergency coupling pin; 6. Knuckle tongue; 7. Vertical lock; 8. Uncoupling lever; 9. Coupler support pin; 10. Pivot pin; 11. Uncoupling chain; 12. Emergency link coupling; 13. Coupler head; 14. Headstock hook; 15. Buffer saddle.

Over the years, the design of the fittings was improved. On more modern vehicles, items 3, 12 and 15 were fixed on the headstock, and not allowed to hang.

To change the side buffers from the 'short' to the 'long' position, the shunter pulled out the buffers as far as they would come, and placed the saddles flat on the buffer spindles. To change to 'short' position, the saddles were removed and the buffers pushed back as far as they would go. The buffers of vestibuled coaches had a flat top to the buffer face so as to clear the bowed end of the coach body.

To couple buckeyed vehicles together, the buffers were in the 'short' position, and the vestibule shields removed. The couplers were secured in the position as in the illustration, and the knuckle of the coupler head of one of the vehicles opened by pulling the uncoupling chain which operated the lock. The knuckle of the other coach was kept closed, except when the vehicles were to be coupled on a curve in which case both knuckles were usually opened. The vehicle to be coupled was brought up steadily against the stationary vehicle and, when the vestibules were compressed sufficiently, the coupler knuckle closed, and the lock dropped. Buckeye fitted coaches were coupled to screw-coupled coaches with the buffers in the 'long' position, lowering the coupler head, and placing the screw coupling shackle on the buckeye hook. The vestibule of the screw coupled coach with the British Standard pattern needed to be fitted with an adaptor to couple successfully with a Pullman vestibule. Some LNER buckeye-fitted coaches were fitted with BS vestibules.

on through workings in trains of LMS stock, as a result of which they had British Standard gangways. At first, duckets (guard's lookouts) were not fitted to brake compartments.

| Dimensions | Vestibuled stock* | Non-vestibuled stock |
|---|---|---|
| Body over end mouldings | 61ft 6in | 51ft 1½in |
| Distance between bogie centres | 43ft 0in | 35ft 0in |
| Width over body mouldings | 8ft 9in | 8ft 9in |
| Width overall | 9ft | 9ft |

*Other than GE section general service stock

As to the materials used, all body framing comprised best quality Moulmein or Rangoon teak, with the exception of the cross-bearers and long floor-bearers which were oak, and the cant-rails which were pitch-pine. The roof boards were of ⅞in red deal, and 1¼in red deal boards, transversely placed, were used for the floor. The roofsticks were steel bars, of rolled channel section.

The body framing was fitted together with tenons and mortises, and bound with iron and steel knees. The body panelling – ⅜in teak – was secured by copper pins, and each panel was fastened with glued softwood blocks. The body cushions were india-rubber. Half-round wooden beading or mouldings were arranged to give square-cornered panels on the body sides. The roof boards were covered with raw roofing canvas once they had been painted, then filled with putty, and a layer of thick white lead and boiled oil was applied using a brush. The canvas was nailed down on top of this and left for fourteen days. The cornice was teak, and the rainstrip of pitch-pine with a zinc water shoot.

The Pullman gangways were covered with three-ply canvas and india-rubber.

As to the interior, the corridor partition, doors, panels and mouldings were of teak. The interior finishes of the Standard vestibuled stock followed the East Coast Joint stock practice of darkened and polished teak in the first-class, and natural teak in the third-class, bodied up with polish and given one coat of varnish. Until the mid-1930s the interior panelling of non-vestibuled stock comprised varnished and polished teak.

The compartment doors in vestibuled coaches had balanced frameless droplights. The inside of the roof, and partitions above the cornice level, were covered in millboard. Hardboard or millboard was used for the lavatory panelling (earlier first-class lavatories had vitrolite panels) above the lower, matchboarded teak, the latter also being used in the compartments to waist height. The ceiling comprised painted millboard.

White enamel was used for the compartment panelling above the luggage racks, ceilings were finished in flat white paint, and brake compartments were painted light-stone on the sides and ends, with a white ceiling.

As agreed in November 1923, standard metal fittings in carriages were of polished brass or, less frequently, were stainless steel in the first-class, and dark oxidised brass in the third-class. Double parcels racks were fitted in the first-class. Hat pegs were provided in first-class compartments,

discontinued in non-vestibuled stock after 1926. Each smoking compartment had four ashtrays. Two portable tables were provided in each vestibuled vehicle except brake firsts and thirds which had one only. Tables were fixed in open firsts, open thirds and brake open thirds.

One mirror was provided per compartment, with framed scenic prints in the first-class, and framed advertisements in the third-class.

Blue cloth upholstery in first-class compartments, crimson and black rep in the third-class. Green leather upholstery was used for seating in first-class restaurant cars.

The floors in the compartments and corridors were covered in ¼in thick dark cork lino, with a Wilton rug fitted in the first-class. The lavatory floors were covered in Korkoid, those in the brake compartment had Decolite with oak flooring at the luggage doorway.

As built, the interior finish of the first-class compartments in the GN suburban quad arts consisted of varnished teak to cant-rail level, white enamel above, and with a wire and horsehair foundation for the seats which were covered with blue cloth. There was a blue/grey mat on the floor. In the other classes, the interior was varnished teak or painted teak colour to cant-rail level, white paint was used above. The seat-backs had no springs, and brown and gold rep was used as upholstery in the second-class, and crimson and black pile in the third-class.

### Heating

There was one heater per compartment, placed under the left-hand seat (as seen from the corridor), with passenger control. Heat was regulated by a thermostat which tended to shut off the heat before the maximum temperature was reached.

### Lighting

Four corner lights under the control of passengers for all first-class and third-class vestibuled stock. Four single lights, one in each corner, and a fifth in the centre of the ceiling, were provided in first-class non-vestibuled coaches.

The first-class lighting in each compartment of the GN suburban quad arts comprised four lamps in an enclosed fitting, the other classes had three lamps per compartment.

# SUBSEQUENT CHANGES TO THE LNER STANDARD COACH DESIGNS

## Braking

A programme was adopted for the unification of braking systems in March 1928. In the North Eastern Area, loose, air-braked stock was first to be converted to dual braking, then to vacuum only. Set trains were to be converted to vacuum. On the GE section, air-braked stock was to be converted to vacuum where it was required to work with vacuum fitted stock. Suburban sets were to remain air braked. In the Scottish Areas, air-braked stock was to be converted to vacuum at the earliest opportunity. New stock to be built during 1928 was to be fitted with dual braking, where appropriate. All common user stock was to be dealt with on a line basis.

## Underframes

The development of a 65ft underframe in 1930/1 led to the general adoption of angle-section, rigid trussing for the shorter underframes as well, in place of the bar sections and turn-buckle adjustment. The camber usually applied to underframes was altered as a result.

Welded underframes were introduced in the 1930s. The first carriage so constructed was an open third on Dia 27A, No 21308 built in February 1934. This resulted in a gradual change to welded underframes. One benefit was a saving in weight: the Dia 186 open thirds with all-welded underframes were 1 ton lighter than those with riveted frames.

## Bogies

Variants to the standard 8ft 6in compound bolster design were introduced over the years. From 1929, the main crossbars in the heavy type standard 8ft and 8ft 6in bogies were made thicker. This followed the inclusion of strengthening angles from 1927, a response to an incidence of cracking at the bottom flange of the crossbar.

The compound bolster bogie was expensive to manufacture and, in 1927, it was decided to produce a simplified version of the Heavy Type bogie. The set of swing links carrying the inner bolster was eliminated, the bolster instead being carried in a steel casting supported on the outer bolster springs. But side control was found to be inferior on test. Neither this, nor the similar Light Type bogie produced in 1930 were built in quantity. Both were manufactured by Metro-Cammell, and were generally referred to as 'Metro' bogies.

### 'Metro' bogie types

| Duty | Wheelbase | Pivot Weight | Journals | Drawing | No/Notes |
|---|---|---|---|---|---|
| Alternative Heavy Type - 1927 single bolster | 8ft | 18½tons | 10in + 5in | 44841 | Met-Cam built |
| Alternative Light Type - 1930 single bolster | 8ft | 12½tons | 9½in + 4¼in | 6776N | Met-Cam built |

The non-vestibuled stock built for the Liverpool Street-Ilford services in 1935/6 was uniquely equipped with GER-type 8ft wheelbase bogies with inside solebars.

## Body construction

In 1922, a committee had been set up to review the adoption of a standard loading gauge for the forthcoming LNER group. It took until late 1925 for the committee to produce its recommendations, and a programme of work was approved in early 1926 for the easing of loading gauge restrictions at various locations on the LNER, principally in the North Eastern and Southern Scottish Areas. Until then, there were restrictions on the use of vehicles of a greater width than 8ft 9in over the body, and 9ft overall.

Gresley vestibuled stock compared: (bottom) is Diagram 23 third E 12020 E (built in March 1925 as 10043J, then renumbered 1024 in May 1927, and to the SSA as 31156 in June 1936) seen from the corridor side. This early Gresley LNER coach has the bar trussing with turn-buckle adjustment. When photographed on 7 July 1952, it remained in varnished teak finish, by then without lining-out, and with the BR serial applied in Gill Sans transfers. It is formed in an up express leaving Ipswich behind 'B12/3' 4-6-0 No 61514.

(right) is a Diagram 127 brake composite, from the compartment side. It, too, retains its varnished teak finish, as late as July 1953, with BR lettering and class transfers. This design was built from the start with the angle-iron trussing. Note the cant-rail glass lights in the brake compartment, and the double set of doors to the luggage/brake compartment. The LNER Diagram drawings have the disadvantage of showing the corridor side only of vestibuled coaches. The coach is in a Skegness-Leicester train approaching Barkston East Junction, and 'B1' 4-6-0 No 61188 is the motive power.

With the assumption that the necessary civil engineering works would be carried out during 1926, provision was made in the CBP for 1927 for coaches to be built to a body width of 9ft, and 9ft 3in over the handles. This resulted in the introduction of new designs to the increased width in replacement of most of the 1923 standard types of vestibuled and non-vestibuled coaches. But there continued to be restrictions on the use of Standard stock on lines such as Newcastle-Carlisle, and elsewhere.

Late in 1928, Ralph Wedgwood, chief general manager, wrote to the Locomotive and Traffic Committees to say that 'there were good reasons for constructing restaurant and sleeping cars to an overall body width of 9ft 3in'. This dimension would be acceptable, providing that the end entrance doors of such coaches were recessed, so that, with the door handles fitted, the width did not exceed 9ft 3in over the waist rail, and over the door handles. To accommodate vehicles to this dimension, limited alterations were carried out at locations such as in Ipswich and Penmanshiel Tunnels, and at Newcastle Central station.

In June 1927, Gresley issued an instruction that in future restaurant and kitchen cars were to be built with teak cant-rails.

When the LNER was considering the acceleration of main line trains in the late 1920s, it was noted that trains were delayed at station stops because men had to climb on to the roofs of coaches to fill lavatory and kitchen water tanks. Gresley was asked to find a solution, and the result was that steel pipes were provided, to run from the lower part of the vehicle body end, on each side, to the water tanks on the roof. Flexible pipes from the platform water supply, or from bowsers, were slipped over nozzles on the pipes on the vehicle ends, and the tanks were seen to be full when water gushed from the pipe on the other side of the coach.

At first, the standard stock was not built with duckets but, in September 1928, came the instruction that: 'in future, duckets to be fitted to each guard's seat in all new vans and brake compartments.'

From 1933, stepboards were fitted at the doorways of brake vans and commode handles were introduced, until then not generally used on Standard stock.

From April 1935, as part of the cost savings in construction then being implemented, all vehicles were built with the bottomsides direct on the solebar, and body cushions were dispensed with. The construction of the floors was also changed and reduced in specification, except in the case of restaurant cars and first-class sleeping cars.

Vestibule shields were mandatory for the front and rear vehicles of a train, except where the front vehicle was coupled to a locomotive with a corridor tender and the buckeye coupler was used. Non-standard shields were used for TPO vans.

## INTERIOR FITTINGS, LIGHTING HEATING AND SEATING – changes in subsequent years

### Seating

Hinged armrests and headrests were introduced for new first-class carriages after November 1928. From 1930, some special East Coast vehicles seated two-a-side in the first-class, and three-a-side in the third-class. Three-a-side seating with armrests was introduced for third-class on selected services from 1932-4, thereafter generally. Older vehicles were converted to three-a-side after 1936. During World War 2, the armrests in third-class vestibule coaches were fixed in the upright position and the seating was four-a-side.

Open thirds were designed to sit two passengers to the larger seat in the Dia 27 series vehicles and one on the other side when used as dining cars but, in general use, three passengers to the larger seat.

Bucket seats, first introduced with the Tourist stock, were fitted to the teak-bodied Tourist Open Thirds and Brake Opens on Dias 186/196/216/217 but such seats proved unpopular with passengers. They began to be replaced in early postwar days by conventional seats. This may have been encouraged by the official accident report into a train fire in April 1941, the seats being cited as a contributory cause in that there was a space between the seats and the body sides which was something of a dust-trap. Schoolboys travelling on a down East Coast train had been flicking lighted matches at each other, one of the matches seeming to have lodged in one

of the dust-traps in the open third in which they were travelling. An initial fire was soon out of control, unhappily resulting in the deaths of six boys, their carriage and the adjoining one being burnt to the frames. The seat design was not in itself blamed although the accident report suggested that the Rexine seat-back covering encouraged the spread of flame.

### Lighting

Through lighting control, with control from the guard's compartment and through cable connections between coaches, was introduced from the 1929 CBP, with the exception of vehicles built for the North Eastern Area; all new LNER coaches had through lighting control as from 1933. Four shoulder or reading lights per compartment were provided in first-class compartments from 1934, and in the third-class from 1938, in addition to one lamp in the ceiling (later two lamps in some first-class compartments); this was accompanied by the provision of larger dynamos in the lighting equipment. The shoulder-lights had plastic shades and separate switches.

Certain semi-open firsts and vestibule firsts were fitted with bracket light fittings with shaded bulbs.

### Heating

From 1927, after public complaints of inadequate heating, improved heaters were fitted in compartments and, from 1930, larger diameter pipes were used in restaurant cars.

Gresley appreciated the limitations of steam heating and went so far as experimenting with electric heating before introducing pressure ventilation. Interest in electric heating led to the development of pressure ventilation, initially from 1930 with the Thermotank system, the fans, filters and heating unit being located in a cupboard next to the lavatory. Such equipment was used in the 'super firsts' Dias 147/156, and the first-class sleeping cars. From the main unit, air was circulated through trunking running above the corridor ceiling, with ducts into each compartment. No steam heating was provided in these vehicles as first operated but it was soon found that steam heating was also required to heat the carriage sufficiently before the train departed, and 30 minutes was the usual allowance for pre-heating.

Stone's fully automatic pressure ventilation system was adopted from 1934 in the set of standard coaches forming the 8.15am Newcastle-Kings Cross and 5.30pm return. The equipment containing the air filters, heater, fan and motor and master thermostat for 'winter' or 'summer' working was mounted on the underframe of each of the carriages, the power supply coming from the train lighting equipment. The equipment could be switched on at a control box mounted either on the vehicle end, or in the brake compartment.

The vehicles in the Newcastle set were corridor third No 168, Dia 115; open third No 175, Dia 27A; corridor first No 1138, Dia 173 (not described in this book); semi-open first No 1139, Dia 172 (not described in this book) and restaurant triplet set Nos 16441-3. Dias 12-14.

### Vestibuled coach interiors
### General

As a result of a passenger's adverse comment at the drabness of the standard interior finish introduced in 1923, a number of changes were made in new stock built from the late 1920s. New, lighter coloured upholstery was introduced from 1928, there was a reduction in the amount of polished wood surfaces within compartments and a commensurate increase in the area of white paint, the designs of light fittings, window blind boxes and mouldings were simplified from 1927, and the flooring was improved.

Typical of vehicles with the 'improved finish' were those comprising the two sets built in 1929 for the Liverpool St-Cromer service. The first-class compartments had polished teak panelling, polished brass fittings and velvet moquette, the armrests being trimmed in dark-blue Morocco leather. There were four reading lamps to each compartment. The third-class had the lighter teak panelling, offset by teak-painted metal fittings, and fawn rep upholstery with brown piping and armrests. Each compartment had a single light fitting with four bulbs enclosed by a frosted-glass globe shade. The first-class restaurant car had mahogany panelling, with a patterned,

painted millboard coving and ceiling. The seats were upholstered in green buffalo hide, green Morocco leather was used for covering the table tops, there were green cloth curtains, a rose-coloured carpet, brass parcel racks, a table lamp to each table, and a clock. The open thirds used for dining followed the scheme of the side-corridor coaches, except that the parcel racks were of polished brass, the seat ends were of painted cast aluminium, and the tables were covered in brown leathercloth.

Subsequent changes included the provision of increased knee-space in compartments from 1932, improved light fittings, and the use of teak-colour painted interior metalwork in place of polished metal finishes. Third-class parcel racks were made up of die-cast aluminium brackets with teak front rails. The door handles and corridor window rails continued to be of polished brass, except for restaurant firsts, sleeping cars and corridor firsts for which chrome plating was used.

Stock for the East Coast was usually to a higher specification and often included refinements not to be found in the standard stock built for the Areas. Features included vestibule mats, cushions and hassocks in the first-class, and roller towels in the lavatories.

### Interior panelling, wall finishes, use of Rexine

The standard specification for interior finishes that has been described remained more or less the same throughout the 1930s, except that in due course corridor partitions and doors were simplified in design, and panelled in plywood.

Painted surfaces in the compartments and saloons were increasingly replaced by Rexine from the early 1930s. This new material, a type of leathercloth comprising a cloth fabric coated with nitro-cellulose, was preferred to painted finishes because it resisted scuffing better. Rexine was used to a major extent after about 1935. Usual colour schemes were ivory Rexine for ceilings in the first-class, cream in the third-class, dove-grey for the wall covering in the first-class compartments, and brown in the third-class. Peach-coloured Rexine was used in the immediate prewar period, for first and third-class vestibuled stock but brown schemes were retained in open stock.

In the late 1930s, Bakelite frames were used for mirrors, and for picture/advertising frames in compartments.

Above: **View along the interior corridor in the first-class section of a non-vestibuled coach of the mid-1930s, possibly one of the articulated twins.**

Left: **Interior of a TTO open third with high-backed in place of bucket seats, and probably one of those to Diagram 302, built in 1939. Note the darkened light-bulbs for wartime travel. The walls are lined with brown Rexine, and the upholstery is in shades of brown and orange.**

### Upholstery

Until 1932, the standard upholstery materials were first-class, velvet moquette; third-class, fawn rep with brown buttons and piping and brown armrests, except for suburban stock where crimson and black pile was used. First-class restaurant car seating was upholstered in leather, the third-class in moquette. First-class blinds were maroon rep, altered to Rexine from 1930; third-class blinds were jasper, later brown Rexine. The armrests, inner head-rest rolls and arm-slings in the first-class were covered or made of dark-blue Morocco leather.

Rubber flooring was used in the early standard first-class restaurant cars, and for the corridors in some coaches but was increasingly replaced by cork lino with parquet pattern lino down the aisles, and by carpeting.

From 1932, Gresley instructed that the standard upholstery materials used from the late 1920s must be 'gradually eliminated'. For the future, first-class coaches, except end-door firsts, were to have floral-patterned moquette; third-class coaches with intermediate armrests, 'special' brown moquette; third-class without armrests, ordinary brown moquette; composite and third-class sleeping cars, blue moquette in the third-class. Second-class upholstery was generally blue and brown in colour. Armrests were trimmed in Morocco leather.

Materials for use in restaurant cars and the end-door firsts, not to mention special stock, were to be referred to Gresley for approval. A velvet material, usually with an Art Deco pattern, was used for the first-class upholstery of prestige stock in the late 1930s. The teak bodied Tourist third opens were upholstered in material with Art Deco patterns, chiefly in orange and brown colours.

Antimacassars were affixed to the backs of all first-class seats in vestibuled vehicles working in regular and relief trains as from 1934, previously the various Areas having different rules, some supplying antimacassars in dining cars or main line trains only.

From the early 1930s, non-vestibuled stock had veneered blockboard for the partitions, with Rexine used on the side walls, and teak frames for mirrors and system maps, advertisements or pictures above the seat backs. The familiar black and crimson pile upholstery, to take the third-class as the example, was relieved by compartment side armrests trimmed in leathercloth, and with blinds of the same material, or Rexine, usually in brown. The increasing use of Rexine for compartment interior finishes perpetuated previous colour schemes; typical were the ivory ceiling and brown side walls to be found in the Dia 204 seconds in the Ilford sets.

## LIVERIES AND FINISHES – standard carriages

### Teak panelled stock

Each carriage varied in appearance, despite careful matching of the teak body panels, and the varnished finish relied on the natural textures and colourings of the teak. Successive coats of varnish changed the overall colouring and the varnish itself faded or mellowed with age. Teak panelled stock normally went for shopping every three years to receive a fresh coat of varnish. In the course of time, older vehicles assumed a darker colour with the process of successive varnishing and staining in everyday service.

### Bodyside varnishing, lining out and transfers

A standard procedure for varnishing teak-panelled stock was based on the methods in use at the works and agreed at a meeting held at Kings Cross on 14 August 1923 and chaired by Bulleid.

In specifications issued to manufacturers for the purpose of tendering for new stock, the LNER described its standard livery as follows:

'Exterior of body sides and ends to be painted (! – *author's comment*) in varnished teak, and lined out in primrose bordered with a fine red line.'

Non-vestibuled stock was subject to the same finish, except that lining out was generally in primrose only on the mouldings. The quad arts were turned out in unlined varnished teak, with white roofs, all the articulated suburban sets being devoid of any lining in later days although, when new, the quint art sets were described as being lined out fully, in primrose and red. Lining out was officially abandoned for all stock as from November 1941. The ends of non-vestibuled carriages were painted plain black after October 1925.

The process of applying the varnished teak finish was as follows:
1. One coat of gold size.
2. One coat of preparing varnish.
3. As 2, rubbed in while wet.
4. Stopping up, then sandpapered.
5. One coat of preparing varnish rubbed in while wet.
6. One coat of preparing varnish. Holes stopped up.
7. When surface hard, faced down with pumice-stone and water.
8. Lining out, primrose two coats, fine line red.
9. Varnish transfer panels.
10. Putty and touch up cornice, hinges etc.
11-14. two coats of preparing varnish, two coats finishing varnish.
15. Flat down with pumice dust and water.
16/17. Two coats of finishing varnish.
18. Exterior touched up.

All vestibuled stock was lined on bodyside and bodyend mouldings and upright casings with a ⅜in primrose line edged both sides with a ¹⁄₁₆in red line – stage 8 in the above procedure. In practice, widths varied with ¼in primrose, and/or ⅛in red lines. The terminations of these lines had a small arrow-like head which in later days, at least, was a transfer. The lining out was done with a long-haired pencil brush held between the finger and thumb and placed on the centre of the moulding. No other aid was employed.

Exposed internal chains and indication discs of the passenger communication cord system were painted red and the bodyend boxes were black.

### Roofs

Nearly all vehicles had deal-boarded roofs with canvas covering. The roof was painted two or three coats of white lead paint and the cornices remained in teak finish. After November 1941, roofs were painted in bauxite, some later in grey, the latter of a shade similar to that used in BR days.

The three Diagram 66 non-vestibuled brake thirds at the front of this up empty stock train are allocated to the Southern Scottish Area and, having been outshopped or perhaps when new, are seen near Goswick (scene of an unhappy accident in 1947) with 'C6' Atlantic No 742. The date is 1928. The brilliance of the freshly painted roofs is noticeable.

Newly outshopped London suburban quad art train No 78 has been pur-loined for an evening excursion to Mablethorpe, seen leaving Mansfield Road Tunnel and entering Nottingham Victoria station on 22 August 1937. The use of these trains on such duties was not unusual, despite their lack of lavatories. The engine is 'J6' 0-6-0 No 3628.

## Underframes and running gear

Carriage solebars, headstocks, buffer shanks and sleeves were painted in teak paint and varnished. Wheel centres were also in the same colour, unvarnished. Solebar nuts, at least in earlier days, were picked out in green. The teak paint was a mixture of not less than 80% zinc oxide and linseed oil.

The pine stepboards were painted black. The underframes, bogies, drawgear, brakework and buffer heads were black. Wheel rims and axles were painted white. Wartime finishes standardised in November 1941 dictated that the whole underframe, bogies, wheels and axles were to be painted black lacquer.

Underframe lettering was picked out in white.

## Lettering and numbering

Letters and numbers were gold leaf transfers with each letter or numeral shaded to the left and below in red, pink and white, and back-shaded to the right and below in black and brown.

The letters (LNER) and carriage stock number were 4in high and 5in over the gold in width. Until 1928 the 'LNER' was placed, to quote, 'as near the centre as practicable on the waist panel on both sides of the body'. After that date the 'LNER' was moved to the furthest left position on each side of the body. In all cases, from July 1925 the vehicle number was positioned on the waist panel at the opposite right-hand end of the body to the 'LNER'. From April 1925, the decision was taken to discontinue the suffix lettering to the running number, but while used their dimensions were 2½in by 3in.

Guard's compartments were lettered 'Guard' in transfer letters 2⅜in by 3in over the gold on the waist panel of the doors on both sides of the body. Carriages in the Cheshire Lines Committee fleet received standard type transfers with 'CLC' in place of the 'LNER'.

Class designations (1, 2, 3) were numerals 7in high over the gold (9in over the shading) to the same elaborate shading as letters and numerals and were placed on the lower panels of the doors. Special vehicles were designated 'Restaurant Car' or 'Sleeping Car' with lettering of the same size as the class numerals. The title 'Sleeping Carriage' was officially discontinued after September 1925.

The LNER maintained second-class on the GN/GE sections' suburban

services until withdrawal with effect from 1 January 1938. After 6 October 1941, first-class accommodation was discontinued on local services originating within the London area.

The figure '3' denoting third-class accommodation was abolished from July 1940, the '2' designation ending with the abolition of that class in the London suburban area from 1938. Although the withdrawal of the Continental boat trains occurred immediately before the outbreak of World War 2, the vehicles designated second-class are not recorded as being reclassified third-class until 1942/3.

From November 1940 a transfer figure '1' was applied to the windows of first-class compartments. Other wartime changes included the abbreviation of 'LNER' on the body sides to 'NE' and this lasted until January 1946, after which the positions of the 'LNER' and running number were moved inwards on the bodyside. In the 1947/8 period, a number of carriages appeared with the running number in sans-serif characters, before and after nationalisation.

One feature of the body ends was a plate giving details of length over headstocks, width over body, maximum width over projections and weight. Before 1934 the plate also gave the height of the centre of the roof from rail, and the number of seats. The LNER standard telegraphic codes were not painted on vehicle ends – in white – until at least 1942. A full list of the telegraphic codes is given elsewhere in this book.

## Interior details/notices

Internal designations were as follows: non-vestibuled stock had 7in class numerals on the lower inside door panels in black-shaded primrose transfers. The running number and class designation were 1in black-shaded gold transfers affixed to door garnish rails. The running number was written in 4in black numerals on the body end of the brake compartments or full brake, but this was discontinued after 1935. 'Toilet' was a transfer in white-shaded black script on the appropriate door.

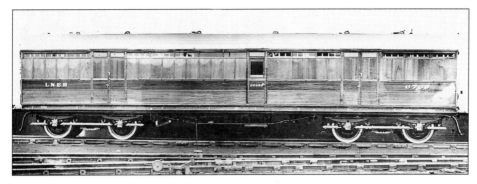

This picture of non-vestibuled full brake No 6768 (Diagram 129, later No 70259) is of poor quality, but of relevance for showing the effect of a newly built or outshopped vehicle, with the teak panelling revealing its grain and the brightness of the freshly worked wood.

There was a variety of Ivorine notices placed in LNER carriages instructing or admonishing passengers, as well as red transfer panels with similar edicts.

The standard interior notices included the following:

*Transfers*

'This rack not to be used for heavy or bulky items' (On luggage rack)

'Warning to passengers. Dangerous to put head outside the window' (On door immediately above droplight)

'Gentlemen please lift the lid' (On wc seat)

'Alarm Signal'

*Ivorine notices*

'For first class passengers only'

'LNER In case of emergency, rescue tools and appliances, fire extinguishers, and First Aid requisites will be found in the Guard's Compartment. Fire extinguishers are also provided in Restaurant and Sleeping Cars'

'Passengers are requested not to use the lavatories while the trains are standing at stations'

'LNER Bags, portmanteaus, or other articles etc'

'Passengers' luggage must not be placed in the corridors or vestibules. The Company's staff have instructions to remove to the Guard's van passengers' luggage left in corridors or vestibules'

A map of the LNER system was placed in such spaces as suitable, but they were removed from corridors after 1925. Advertising panels were to be found – at times – in all but dining cars and the first-class compartments of East Coast stock and Continental boat trains.

Labels for windows denoting 'Smoking' in blue were introduced in 1925. A 'Smoking Prohibited' label began to be applied from 1930, replaced by a red triangular label the following year. In 1933 a profitable contract was concluded with Imperial Tobacco for 'Smoking' labels to appear in windows. On expiry of the contract in 1942 it was decided that only 'No Smoking' labels should be displayed on carriage windows.

### Destination and similar boards

Generally introduced from 1927, the roof-mounted destination boards had black characters 4in high on a white ground, the original block lettering changing to Gill Sans after 1935. Similar lettering was used for named trains and boards 8ft in length were used.

The official instruction was that all regular passenger trains except workmen's trains must bear destination boards, excepting the strengthening coaches added to a diagrammed set of coaches. These boards were in white with 2 in or 2½in lettering in black. Generally end and centre vehicles carried the boards. Some Inner Suburban trains carried similar boards but many sets had roller blind indicators. In postwar days the carriage identification plates were placed in the small destination brackets fixed to the cornice and they were painted standard LNER dark-blue, with white characters.

### BR liveries

From March 1949, the carmine and cream livery became the BR standard. There were some variations in the styles used, particularly as regards lettering and numerals. One characteristic feature of the Gresley teak bodied stock in this livery was the absence of the carmine band just under the cant-rail which was otherwise part of this livery scheme. In general, the teak panelled stock literally took the carmine and cream, and later maroon, BR liveries very badly. The panelling had to be primed with gold size to prevent condensation from coming out through the panels.

Some teak-bodied full brakes survived to be painted in the all-blue BR livery from 1966, and the grey and blue livery was carried by a limited number of buffet and sleeping cars.

In BR days, the full brakes were generally painted in one colour only, but some of the vestibuled brakes wore the carmine and cream livery, such as Diagram 113 E 70182 E (No 5214 of 1929). The identity of this train of vestibuled stock photographed at Darlington Bank Top in 1956 is unknown, the engine being post-Grouping 'A5' 4-6-2T No 69842.

# RUNNING NUMBERS AND DIAGRAMS

## LNER NUMBERING SCHEMES 1923-1925

In January 1923, it was decided that there would be no central control of passenger rolling stock, with the consequence that the individual sections or Areas would be responsible for their own stock and, as a result, would maintain their own number series.

Instructions were issued by the chief mechanical engineer during April 1923 concerning the numbering of coaching stock taken into the new organisation. All vehicles would retain their pre-Grouping numbers but a suffix letter would be added to denote the section to which they were allocated, and which would be responsible for their maintenance.

New stock, both to the constituent companies' own designs, and where built to the design of another constituent, was numbered in the existing series. The suffixes allocated were: East Coast stock – J; North Eastern Railway/Area – Y; North British Railway/Southern Scottish Area – B; Great Northern Railway/section – N; Great Central Railway/section – C; Great Eastern Railway/section – E; Great North of Scotland Railway/Northern Scottish Area – S.

In April 1924, it was decided by the chief mechanical engineer's office that new carriages to the LNER standard designs should be numbered in their own series from 10000 upwards. A suffix letter denoted the Area/section to which they were allocated, using the suffix letters that had been applied to pre-Grouping vehicles. East Coast stock carried 'J' suffixes.

As to examples, the vehicles forming the GE section Continental boat sets were numbered 10000E etc, the main series of East Coast thirds 10019J-49J, and non-vestibuled vehicles for the Southern Scottish Area, 10263B-6B and so on. The scheme made no distinction as between types or sections and Areas, and had no real logic. There remains some confusion as to the complete application of the scheme, as some vehicles that by rights should have received 100xx numbers did not while others did not actually carry the numbers although referred to as having them in official documents. By the spring of 1925 numbers were being allocated to GE section quintuplets in the range from 10362E up to 106xxE.

In April 1925 a new numbering scheme was introduced by the LNER and the 100xx serials were discontinued. The renumbering of these vehicles into the replacement series continued until 1930.

A Coaching Rolling Stock Controllers sub-Committee reported to the LNER Board in 1924 as follows:

Numbering should give a clear indication to working staff as to the section to which the coach is allocated.

There is a separate number range for: 1. Coaches; 2. Vans; 3. Horseboxes and special cattle vans; 4. Carriage trucks.

## LNER NUMBERING SCHEME 1925-43

The new scheme was introduced in April 1925, and dispensed with the application of suffixes to denote owning Areas or sections, as well as the use of the 100xx series of numbers.

From now onwards, the owning Area or section was denoted by the first digit in the number, this prefix being added to the existing number. This was in similar manner to the locomotive numbering scheme brought in from early 1924 and the effect was as follows:

| Section/Area | April 1923 numbers | April 1925 numbers |
|---|---|---|
| East Coast | 12J/123J | 112/1123 |
| North Eastern | 12Y/123Y/1123Y | 212/2123/21123 |
| Southern Scottish | 12B/123B/1123B | 312/3123/31123 |
| Great Northern | 12N/123N/1123N | 412/4123/41123 |
| Great Central | 12C/123C/1123C | 512/5123/51123 |
| Great Eastern | 12E/123E/1123E | 612/6123/61123 |
| Northern Scottish | 12S/123S | 712/7123 |

The numbers shown above are only for the purposes of illustration.

New standard stock was allocated the lowest available number in the various three, four and five-digit series, but other isolated blocks of numbers were used in the five-digit ranges. Individual numbers generally gave no indication of the age of the vehicle. Numbers were reused so that destroyed or transferred vehicles' numbers might be allocated to their replacements.

The new scheme included four separate ranges of numbers:
1. Carriages.
2. Passenger brake vans.
3. Non-common user vans.
4. Horseboxes and special cattle vans.
5. Carriage trucks.

The separate series allocated to carriages and to passenger brake vans meant that there was duplication of numbers, as indeed there was with ranges 3-5 above!

Some mention must be made of the Stratford-inspired renumbering which came into effect for GE section stock early in 1926. Although each class of GER carriage had its own series of running numbers starting from 1, the renumbering scheme devised at Stratford ensured that all passenger-carrying stock had a unique LNER running number. One effect of this was to ensure that no LNER number bore any resemblance to its pre-Grouping number! However, the scheme was splendidly logical and grouped different classes of stock in separate blocks of numbers, being generally arranged in order of the building date.

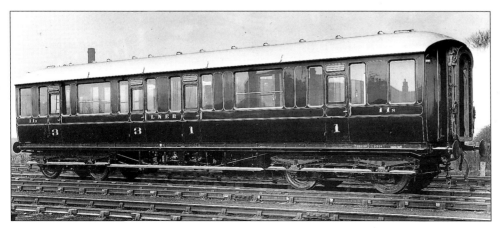

The April 1923 numbering scheme merely added the owning Area or section suffix letter to the pre-Grouping series number. New stock took vacant numbers in the old series such as No 11s, a 50ft 6in dual-fitted vestibuled composite of modified North Eastern Railway design, built for the Northern Scottish Area in 1924. The vehicle has a painted finish, with the panels and mouldings lined out. No 11s became 7877 under the 1925 renumbering. To Darlington drawing 11758, this coach was allocated **GNS Diagram number 77S.**

Vehicles transferred from one Area or section to another were renumbered in the case of almost all standard LNER vehicles and usually – although not always – with pre-Grouping stock. Vehicles transferred from the East Coast stock to Areas or sections were renumbered. Sometimes vehicles were renumbered by the sections, for instance, the GE section renumbered Dia 27 open thirds used for dining from 61xxx to 61xx, and restaurant cars from 61xx to 6xx. The Southern Scottish Area renumbered carriages transferred from first-class to composite.

The full range of numbers for carriages and passenger brake vans was as follows:

### East Coast stock
Carriages: 10-19; 100-199; 1000-1999. Also 16431-16533. Nos 16431-3/41-3, and possibly 16451-3/61-3/71-3, were originally numbered 6431-3J/41-3J etc. Vans: 10-19; 100-199; 1000-50.

### North Eastern Area
Carriages: 20-29; 200-299; 2000-2999; 20000-26179. Vans: 20-29; 200-299; 2000-2500.

### Southern Scottish Area
Carriages: 30-39; 300-399; 3000-3999; 30000-33000. Vans: 30-39; 300-399; 3000-3200.

### Southern Area – Great Northern section
Carriages: 40- 49; 400-499; 4000-4999; 40000-49419. Vans: 40-49; 400-499; 4000-4375.

### Southern Area – Great Central section
Carriages: 50-59; 500-599; 5000-5999; 50000-59349. Vans: 50-59; 500-599; 5000-5482.

### Southern Area – Great Eastern section
Carriages: 60-69; 600-699; 6000-6999; 60000-65369. Vans: 60-69; 600-699; 6000-6999; 60000-60023.

### Northern Scottish Area
Carriages: 70-79; 700-799; 7000-7963. Vans: 70-79; 700-799, 7000-7159.

When the LNER took over responsibility for passenger stock from the Midland & Great Northern Joint line after October 1936, all vehicles, carriages, vans, CCTs and horseboxes were given numbers in a new 8xxxx series but remained with M&GN lettering. In BR days, these carriages were renumbered within the GE pre-Grouping range with numbers in the 6xxxx series.

Vehicles belonging to the Cheshire Lines Committee stock are described in this volume. The number series for CLC stock extended from 1-724, including those transferred to the CLC from the LNER, and new construction up to 1937, the last built being Nos 700-24. When the London Midland Region took over responsibility for the operation of the CLC lines in 1949, the inherited coaching stock was eventually renumbered within the main LMS scheme, employing blank number ranges. Exceptions were the articulated twins built in 1937 which were given numbers in the 60xxx range, this having been used by the LMS for its own articulated non-vestibuled stock.

## LNER NUMBERING SCHEME FROM 1943

In March 1939 the CGM met the Area Managers and the central distribution of passenger rolling stock was contemplated, in a similar manner to the central control of freight stock introduced previously on the LNER. Not all the Areas were in favour, and the outbreak of World War 2 delayed further development until an all-line operating organisation was set up during 1941, with a Central Coaching Stock Control Office located at York.

The new Control Office issued new general instructions relating to the control and distribution of coaching rolling stock, and these supplanted Area-based directives that had applied since 1923. On and from 28 April 1941, all passenger coaching vehicles, including vans, were controlled from this office. Excluded were non-common user vehicles.

From that date in 1941, the Area control of vehicles ceased, and the instructions advised that 'Notwithstanding their "Area" numbering, all vehicles except East Coast Stock will be used indiscriminately, unless definite instructions to the contrary are issued. Regular train sets will, for the present, be formed in each Area as far as possible of vehicles from the stock of that Area'.

As far as East Coast vehicles were concerned, the instructions read: 'East Coast vehicles (the initial number of which is always "1") are provided for working on the main line between London, York, Newcastle, Edinburgh and beyond. They must not be used on other sections of the line except on direct instructions from the District Superintendent.'

With the implementation of the new control arrangements, proposals were submitted in March 1942 for a new all-line system of numbering for coaching stock vehicles. A final plan was submitted under the joint names of the chief mechanical engineer, the rolling stock controller and the chairman of the SPM Committee, and this received final approval in November 1942.

Under the new scheme, generally referred to in this book as the 1943 renumbering, LNER standard carriages and passenger brake vans were renumbered by type and the new numbers were allocated in order of the vehicles' diagram numbers and, within the range allocated to the diagram number, in the order North Eastern, Southern Scottish, Great Northern, Great Central, Great Eastern, Northern Scottish and East Coast. Pre-Grouping carriages – and the exceptions noted below! – retained their old numbers. Unlike the renumbering of the company's locomotives, there was no set day for the new numbering to be applied; the process began in 1943 but some vehicles retained their old numbers until early BR days. East Coast vehicles retained their numbers, except as indicated below, new East Coast stock taking 1xx and 1xxx series numbers, also 10-19 in the case of vans.

The numbering blocks were as follows:

| Type | Series range | Highest number in 1954 |
| --- | --- | --- |
| **VESTIBULED STOCK** | | |
| East Coast* carriages | 100-199 | 157 |
| | 1000-1999 | 1998 |
| vans | 10-19 | 19 |
| | 100-199 | 193 |
| | 1000-1020 | 1012 |

*The triplet restaurant cars numbered in the range 16431-16533 were renumbered 1401-33.

| | | |
| --- | --- | --- |
| **Catering vehicles** | 9000-9370 | 9217 |
| **Composite brakes** | 10000-10370 | 10174 |
| **Firsts and first brakes** | 11000-11370 | 11189 |
| **Thirds** | 12000-14225 | 13985 |
| **Third brakes** | 16000-17112 | 16873 |
| **Composites** | 18000-18741 | 18517 |
| **Passenger brake vans – vestibuled and non-vestibuled, TPO vans** | | |
| | 70000-70999 | 70767 |

Motor car vans converted from passenger stock in BR days were numbered 71000-71099

## NON-VESTIBULED CARRIAGES

| | | |
| --- | --- | --- |
| **Composite brakes** | 80000-80741 | 80421 |
| **Firsts and first brakes** | 81000-81370 | 81084 |
| **Thirds** | 82000-83112 | 82905 |
| **Third brakes** | 86000-87483 | 87333 |
| **Composites** | 88000-88741 | 88616 |

Gaps were sometimes – although not always – left in the blocks of numbers where vehicles had been lost to enemy action.

This was the overall series but the former indication by Areas and sections was not to disappear completely. Although there were blocks of numbers allocated in the main scheme for 'short' vehicles (these being the

vestibuled carriages on 51ft underframes) for some reason these were not taken up. The result was that the following retained their 1923-43 scheme numbers:

**Open thirds Dia 26** 23801/2 At least these were to all intents and purposes pre-Grouping vehicles!

**Composites Dia 190** 42759-66

**All vestibuled GE 'short' carriages** 6452-6/8/9/61-5/84, 6990/1, 60500-98/600-3, 61634-46/97-704/14-93, 61867-81, 61957-74, 62549-70/98-623/30-49/55-65, 62748-84, 63291-319, 63801/10-30/7-52/65/6/71-86, 63967-94.

In addition, electric multiple units built in LNER days or to LNER designs were allocated numbers in the old Areas/sections ranges. The Tyneside stock was renumbered from its former 24xxx series to 29xxx, the Manchester-Glossop/Hadfield units took 'Great Central' numbers 59401-8, 59501-8, 59601-8, and the Liverpool Street-Shenfield stock 'Great Eastern' numbers 65201-92, 65401-92 and 65601-92.

Under the 1943 renumbering, the Tyneside stock originally had been allocated numbers in the 8xxxx series: 80222-89, 82452-82511 for the passenger vehicles and the luggage vans, 70552/3.

After nationalisation, LNER carriages and vans appeared from late 1948 with a prefix 'E' only to their numbers – for example, E1234. With the introduction of the BR Standard stock, a suffix was added to the numbers of all earlier stock to indicate the Region responsible for its maintenance, with the result that the vehicle in this example now became E1234E. From 1951, the Scottish Region received its own allocation of passenger stock so that former LNER vehicles in that Region's stock became, for example, SC1234E. LNER vehicles reallocated to another Region became, for example, M13927E. Other changes affecting ex-LNER vehicles in the 1960s included the use of a 'GE' prefix for vehicles allocated to the Great Eastern Line of the Eastern Region, and a 'NE' prefix for those allocated to the North Eastern Region.

## DIAGRAMS

At first, the LNER standard vehicles seem to have been referred to by the drawing number for the particular type, eg 11857D or 4673N where D=Darlington and N=Doncaster drawing offices. From 1923, at first the individual Areas or sections seem to have added the new LNER standard designs to the existing diagram books maintained by the Area/section's drawing office. This led to some silly results as, for example, the GN section allocated a variety of third-class vehicles Diagram numbers starting at 248, this having been the page number in the GNR diagram book with thirds/open thirds. As a result, suffixes were applied so that 248Y described pantry thirds, and 248W, vestibuled thirds.

A separate Diagram book continued to be maintained for the East Coast stock with numbers allocated from 1 upwards, each diagram being allocated a page in the book. A new book of diagrams had been introduced in 1908. Numbers ranged between 1 and 82 at 1923. After Grouping, new standard LNER designs were allocated diagram numbers in the ECJS 1908 book until c 1930, although also listed under an LNER allocated diagram in the LNER diagram book. Examples are: 39D for LNER Diagram 43, and 74A for LNER Diagram 20.

During 1927, the chief mechanical engineer produced a diagram book for LNER standard carriages and vans (including milk tanks, steam and diesel railcars and electric multiple units) which was issued after incorporating comments from the SPMs. This diagram book began with Diagram 1 and numbers were progressively added over the years, a new number being allocated to each new design, until there were three volumes of diagrams, the highest numbered diagram being 376, this covering the conversion of vehicles in 1956.

Some conversions were covered by new diagrams, some were not. Sometimes updated designs were allocated a new number, in other cases a suffix was applied, eg 27A and 27C. Even so, the diagram number was not universally used as a reference, the Carriage Working books usually referring to vehicles by number series, eg the GN section book talked of '1440 series' when describing Dia 115 thirds because this was the number series of a batch of this type built in 1934.

A period piece from 1957: 'E4' 2-4-0 No 62789 was working the Mildenhall branch. and is seen leaving Barnwell Junction. The leading coach is one of the vestibuled composites of modified NER design built for the GE section in 1924/5, and is E 63773E, this number replacing the original 871E. To NER Diagram 249, the type was known on the GE section as Diagram 14600-249E. Note the Gresley bogies, and the teak paint livery, shared also by the companion ex-GER brake.

# LNER TELEGRAPHIC CODES FOR COACHING STOCK

The LNER's coaching stock telegraphic code was widely used in official communications, particularly on the railway telegraph, but was not painted on the vehicles themselves until after 1942.

The exact date of its introduction is unknown but a general instruction relating to the distribution of rolling stock, issued by York in February 1928, precedes the listing of the codes by saying that 'The new telegraphic code for coaching rolling stock...has been compiled for use at all LNER stations and must be used in all telegraphic and telephonic advices...' Many aspects of the code had been used by the Great Eastern Railway.

The basic code for vacuum braked, bogie stock was as follows, as at April 1941, being supplemented by suffixes after the basic code to specify particular stock. Earlier codes from 1928 et seq are shown where applicable.

| Saloons | | |
|---|---|---|
| | First-class | SF |
| | Third-class | ST |
| | Invalid | SI |

| Vestibuled carriages | | |
|---|---|---|
| Catering vehicles | First kitchen | RF |
| | Composite kitchen | RC |
| | Either class kitchen | RU |
| | Third kitchen | RT |
| | Triplet set | RTS |
| | Pantry third | RTP |
| | Buffet car | RB |
| | (Buffet car Tourist stock | TRB*) |
| | Kitchen only | RK |
| Sleeping cars | First-class | SLF |
| | First-class (twin) | SLFT |
| | Composite | SLC |
| | Composite (twin) | SLCT |
| | Third-class | SLT |
| Open stock | First-class | FO |
| | Composite | CO |
| | Third-class | TOV (TO – 1928) |
| | Third-class brake | BTO |
| | Semi-open first | Semi FO |
| | Second-class | SO |

| | | |
|---|---|---|
| Tourist stock (bucket seats) | Third open | TTO |
| (teak-bodied) | Brake third open | TBTO |
| Tourist stock | Twin third open | TT |
| (green and cream painted) | Brake third open | TBT |
| Vestibuled stock | First-class | FKL |
| | First-class brake | BFKL |
| | Second-class | SKL |
| | Composite | CKL |
| | Composite locker | CG |
| | Composite brake | BCKL |
| | Third-class | TKL |
| | Third-class locker | TG |
| | Third-class brake | BTKL |

| Non-vestibuled stock | | |
|---|---|---|
| | First-class | F |
| | First-class (lavatory) | FL |
| | First-class brake | BF |
| | First-class brake (lavatory) | BFL |
| | Composite | C |
| | Composite (lavatory) | CL |
| | Composite brake | BC |
| | Composite brake (lavatory) | BCL |
| | Second-class | S |
| | Third-class | T |
| | Third-class (lavatory) | TL |
| | Third-class brake | BT |
| | Third-class brake (lavatory) | BTL |

| Articulated stock | | |
|---|---|---|
| | This was referred to by the prefix of the word 'Twin', 'Triple', 'Quad', 'Quint', as appropriate. | |

| Post Office vehicles | | |
|---|---|---|
| | PO sorting van | POS |
| | PO tender | POT |

| Passenger vans (brake vans) | Brake van | V |
|---|---|---|
| | | BV – 1935 |
| | | B – 1941 |
| | Milk van | M |
| | Pigeon van | P |
| | Miscellaneous traffic van | MTV |

| Railcars | Steam | RLS |
|---|---|---|
| | Petrol | RLP |
| | Diesel | RLD |

| The various suffixes added were as follows: | Dual brake fitted | D |
|---|---|---|
| | Westinghouse air brake | W |
| | Pullman vestibule | PV, (PG in BR days) |
| | British Standard vestibule | BS |
| | BS with Pullman adaptors | A |
| | Vestibule – type not specified | V |
| | Locker | G |

Thus an open first, with dual brake and BS gangway would be FODBS

Earlier suffixes were: SH Steam heater fitted; E Electric lighting; IG Incandescent gas; SLIP Slip carriage.

Six-wheeled passenger stock was denoted by an X as a prefix, eg XF, XC, XT. Four-wheeled passenger stock used the Y prefix.

Notes: * code shown in NEA telegraphic list of July 1935, possibly applicable to this Area only.

| Codes as used in BR days: | |
|---|---|
| Bogie (without gangways) B | |
| Bogie (with gangways) | BG |
| For racing pigeon traffic (braked) | BPBGP |
| Milk van (braked) | BM |
| Four-wheeled | BY |
| Six-wheeled | BZ |

| Miscellaneous vans | Parcels and miscellaneous vans | PMV |
|---|---|---|

| Later BR codes for vehicles featured in this book were: | Kitchen buffet car | RKB |
|---|---|---|
| | Cafeteria car | CAF |
| | Restaurant cafeteria car | RCAF |
| | First-class (loose chairs) | RFO |
| | Third-class (loose chairs) | RTO |

In LNER, and BR Eastern/North Eastern Region publications, when it was necessary to specify a particular number of first and third-class seats this was done as follows:

| Lavatory composite with 4 first, 3 third class compartments | CL (4 – 3) |
|---|---|
| Brake third with 3 compartments | BT (3) |
| Open third with 48 seats | TOV (48) |

# TYPE DESCRIPTIONS

In the sections which follow, the coverage of the various types is in the order:

## 61ft 6in GENERAL SERVICE COACHES
**Vestibuled/open stock:**
Open firsts
Vestibuled firsts
Semi-corridor firsts
Open seconds
Vestibuled second
Open third
Tourist open third
Vestibuled third
Vestibuled composite
Vestibuled brake first
Vestibuled brake second
Brake open third
Vestibuled brake third
Vestibuled brake composite

## 52ft 6in GENERAL SERVICE VESTIBULED COACHES:
Open first
Vestibuled first
Vestibuled third
Open third
Vestibuled third
Vestibuled composite
Open brake third
Vestibuled brake third

## NON-VESTIBULED COACHES:
First
Second
Third
Composite
Lavatory composite
Brake third
Brake composite

## ARTICULATED TWINS/QUADRUPLETS/QUINTUPLETS:
Twins
Quadruplets
Quintuplets

## CATERING VEHICLES:
Restaurant cars
Pantry third
Triplet

## SLEEPING CARS:
First
Third
Composite
Twin

## SPECIAL VEHICLES:
Open thirds to GER design
All-steel open thirds
'Toilet thirds' for 'Flying Scotsman'
'Super firsts' for East Coast stock

## NON-PASSENGER STOCK:
Vestibuled
Non-vestibuled
Non-bogie
TPO van

**A GC section express hauled by 'A1' Pacific No 4474 *Victor Wild* is seen near Calvert in May 1939. The leading coaches are brake composite No 51866 (Diagram 175, built 1937, and later 10112) and third No 52281 (Diagram 115, built 1937, and later 12640).**

**Notes on the format of and codes used in the listing of vehicles under each type in the Type Descriptions' sections:**

**General**

All vehicles are to LNER diagrams unless otherwise shown. * following a diagram number indicates that other vehicles were built to this diagram in some other year.

After 1923, the bodies of articulated sets were generally on different diagrams, from 1935 the complete set was usually on one diagram.

| Column No | Heading in table | Notes |
|---|---|---|
| 1. | **Diag No** | The post-1928 LNER Carriage Diagram Number – for details see the section Running Numbers and Diagram Numbers |
| 2. | **CBP Year** | The date given is the Carriage Building Programme under which the vehicles were ordered. |
| | | From 1925, these were for the 12 months ending on 31 March of the following year, eg the CBP was shown as 1926/7. The Depression resulted in the CBP for 1931/2 extended to 15 months, then to 21 months – to 31 December 1932 – and the attenuated 1933 CBP began on 1 January 1933. For 1935, it was decided to draw up a supplementary programme, and as a result the CBP was extended to cover the two-year period 1935/6. |
| | | Those vehicles ordered in January 1936 under the Government assistance programme to the main line railways are indicated by the symbol #. Those in the Special 1935/6 programme are shown by the symbol • |
| 3. | **Order No** | Official LNER order number. |
| 4. | **Compts/seats** | These are shown as 4 : 32 etc where 4 denotes the number of compartments and 32 the number of seats. |
| | | † as a suffix denotes seating in open saloons, by number of saloons. |
| | | Composite vehicles are shown as 2/5 : 14/48 where 2 is the number of first-class compartments, 5 the number of third-class. A coupé compartment is shown as ½ |
| 5. | **Built at** | The following codes are used: **LNER works**: DK Dukinfield; DL Darlington: SF Stratford; YK York. **Contractors**: BHM Birmingham Railway Carriage and Wagon Co; CL Clayton Wagon Co; CM Cammell-Laird, later absorbed into Metropolitan Cammell; CR Cravens; GLO Gloucester RC & W Co Ltd; HN Hurst Nelson & Co Ltd; MET Metropolitan CW & Finance Co Ltd, later absorbed into Metropolitan Cammell; MID Midland RC & W Co Ltd; M-C Metropolitan Cammell Carriage Wagon & Finance Co Ltd; RYP R. Y. Pickering & Co Ltd. |
| 6. | **Original number/changes** | The number first shown is that allocated when new. Subsequent numbering is shown by brackets – (1234) for the first change of numbers, [5678] for the second change of number or for subsequent changes, as appropriate. |
| 7. | **1943 number** | The numbers in column 7 are those allocated under the 1943 scheme and were carried until withdrawal. |
| | | Under the BR scheme, prefixes were allocated according to Regional allocation, eg E for Eastern/North Eastern Region, SC for Scottish Region. The Region responsible for maintenance was denoted by a suffix, eg E. Therefore, a typical example would be LNER 13685 which became E13685E. |
| | | Some vehicles, principally those remaining in the East Coast fleet, retained their numbers, and in such cases the numbers are repeated |
| | **Notes** | ≠ Dual brake fitted as built, ie with air and vacuum braking. |
| | | §§ Vehicle with gas cooking equipment. |
| | | BS gangways – vehicle with British Standard gangways. |
| | | LH left-handed brakes as built, otherwise RH – right-handed. |
| | | DEA destroyed by enemy action in World War 2 and withdrawn. |
| | | W/O written off as a result of the accident/fire etc indicated if the location is known. |
| | | Accident replacement – vehicle built to replace vehicle written-off in an accident or destroyed by fire. |
| | | Trans – vehicle transferred from East Coast to Area or section stock, or between Areas and sections. |

# 61ft 6in GENERAL SERVICE COACHES
## Vestibuled/open stock

## Open firsts: (FO)

Almost all these vehicles were built for identified specific services, usually to provide at-seat dining seats.

### DIAGRAM 3

One of the original 1923 types, but to the 9ft 3in width, and referred to by Stratford – where they were built under the 1924/5 CBP – by different drawing Nos for the two vehicles, 10008E as 24309aE and 10009E as 24310aE. Otherwise similar to Diag 4 except that the body panelling was different.

The two vehicles were built for the vacuum braked 'Hook Continental' and Antwerp boat train sets respectively, and were used with the restaurant cars for dining accommodation. Transferred away from the GE section under 1935/6 CBP with the arrival of new vehicles for the 'Hook Continental'.

### DIAGRAM 4

One of the original 1923 designs, drawing No 12029D. Both these and the Dia 3 vehicles had the glass louvred windows, and one lavatory only.

First opens were not the usual choice for the East Coast and the two 1924/5 vehicles were built to replace four vestibuled firsts being withdrawn. The East Coast preference was for a restaurant kitchen car working with a pantry third. The NEA vehicle was built for the vacuum braked Newcastle-Swansea set, at that time uniquely so equipped for this Area.

Diagram 4 open first No 1221 (built Doncaster 1925, and later 11036). Although built in 1925, it was outshopped at the end of the year, and so has a new series number. Compare the lettering and numbering style with that in the photograph reproduced on page 17 of No 10005Y.

### DIAGRAM 218

A one-off, basically an updated Dia 3 but with luxurious 1 + 1 movable armchairs for seating, and with unusual grey-blue interior decor. Used for dining and ran with a restaurant kitchen first on one side, and a semi-open first (to Dia 219) on the other. Two lavatories, with electric immersion heaters for wash-basins.

Included in the combined Hook of Holland/Antwerp boat train introduced on 3 May 1936.

### DIAGRAM 262

First-class cars for general service with 2 + 1 seating and one lavatory only; referred to as updated Dia 4 design.

1936 GC section cars for boat specials, eg Marylebone-Immingham, the East Coast cars for 'additional traffic'. 1938 GN section cars for 'Leeds Flyer'. The 1938/9 East Coast examples were straight replacements for old stock transferred to the Areas.

### LIST OF VESTIBULED OPEN FIRSTS:

| Diag No | CBP | Order No | Compts/ seats | Built | Original number/changes | 1943 number |
|---------|------|----------|---------------|-------|--------------------------|-------------|
| **Built 1925** | | | | | | |
| 4 | 1924/5 | 68 | 2† 42 | DR | 1220/1 | 11035/6 |
| | | | | | 10005Y (21509) | 11034 |
| 3 | 1924/5 | 59 | 2† 42 | SF | 10008E (688) | 11033 |
| | | | | | [52101] | |
| | | 60 | | | 10009E (689) | 11032 |
| | | | | | [31890] | |

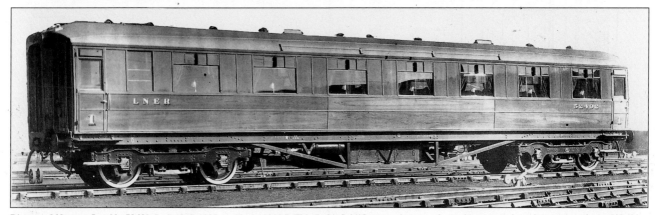

Diagram 262 open first No 52402 (built York 1936, and later 11124). This Dukinfield/Gorton photograph would seem to have been taken during World War 2, by which time roofs were no longer being painted white, and the lining out was omitted from the beading.

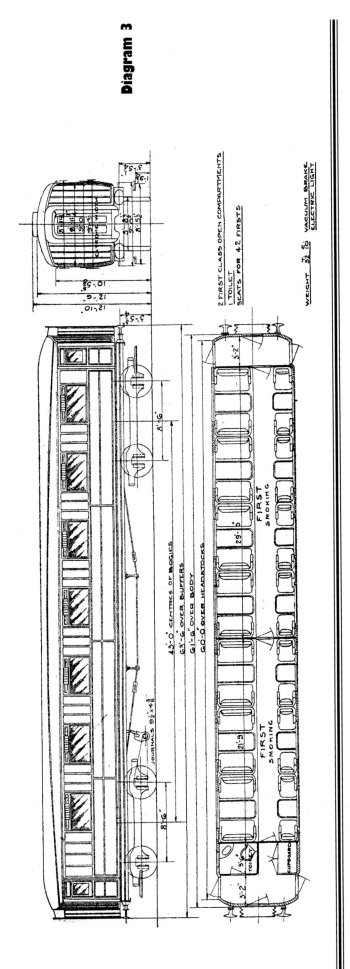

**Diagram 3**

2 FIRST CLASS OPEN COMPARTMENTS
1 TOILET
SEATS FOR 42 FIRSTS

VACUUM BRAKE
ELECTRIC LIGHT

WEIGHT 32.0

43'-0 CENTRES OF BOGIES
63'-6 OVER BUFFERS
61'-6 OVER BODY
60'-0 OVER HEADSTOCKS

JOURNALS 9½ x 4¾

FIRST
SMOKING

FIRST
SMOKING

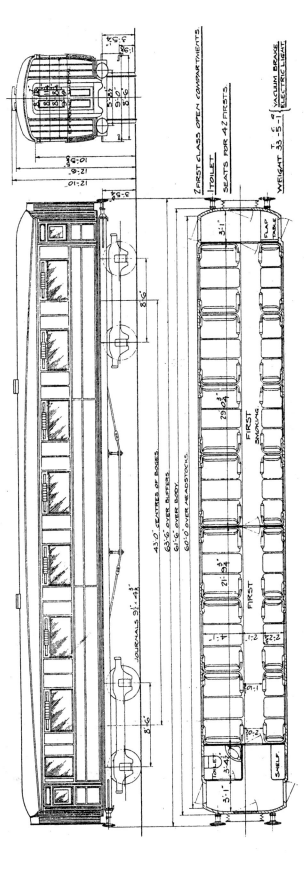

**Diagram 4**

2 FIRST CLASS OPEN COMPARTMENTS
1 TOILET
SEATS FOR 42 FIRSTS

WEIGHT T. C. Q.
33 -5 -1

VACUUM BRAKE
ELECTRIC LIGHT

43'-0 CENTRES OF BOGIES
63'-6 OVER BUFFERS
61'-6 OVER BODY
60'-0 OVER HEADSTOCKS

JOURNALS 9½ x 4¾

FIRST
SMOKING

FIRST

TOILET

SHELF

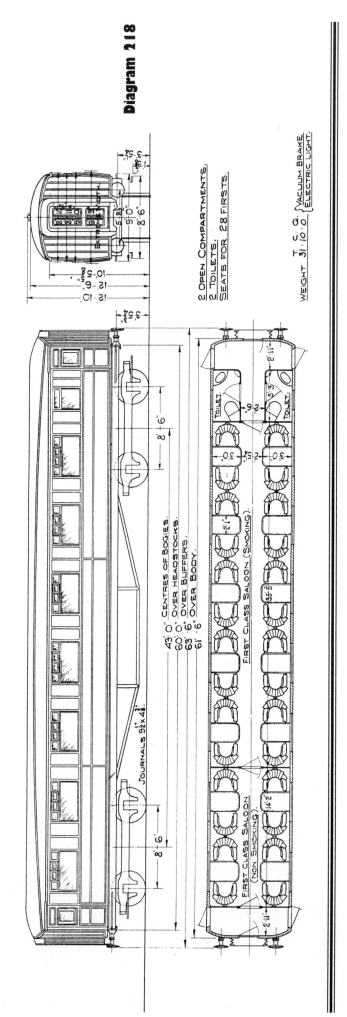

**Diagram 218**

2 OPEN COMPARTMENTS.
2 TOILETS;
SEATS FOR 28 FIRSTS.

WEIGHT T.C.Q. 31·10·0 { VACUUM BRAKE
{ ELECTRIC LIGHT.

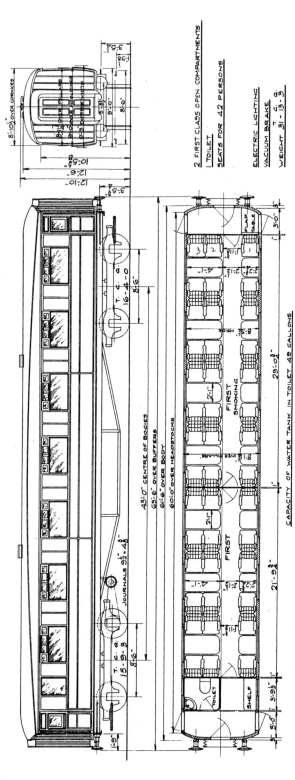

**Diagram 262**

2 FIRST CLASS OPEN COMPARTMENTS

1 TOILET

SEATS FOR 42 PERSONS

ELECTRIC LIGHTING

VACUUM BRAKE
WEIGHT T.C.Q. 31·13·3

*Built 1936*

| Diag No | CBP | Order No | Compts/seats | Built | Original number/changes | 1943 number |
|---|---|---|---|---|---|---|
| 262* | 1935/6 | 616 | 2†42 | YK | 1473 | 11127 |
|  |  | 692 |  |  | 52402/3 | 11124/5 |
|  |  |  |  |  | 1588 (1704) | 11128 |
|  |  |  |  |  | Renumbered 1938 |  |
| 218 | 1935/6 | 649 | 2†28 | YK | 689 (6491) | 11107 |

*Built 1938*

| 262* | 1937 | 765 | 2†42 | YK | 41251/2 | 11122/3 |
|---|---|---|---|---|---|---|

*Built 1939*

| 262* | 1938 | 857 | 2†42 | YK | 24485/6 | 11120/1 |
|---|---|---|---|---|---|---|
|  |  |  |  |  | 6488 | 11126 |
|  |  |  |  |  | 1862 | 11129 |

*Built 1940*

| 262* | 1939 | 951 | 2†42 | YK | 1863/4 | 11130/1864 |
|---|---|---|---|---|---|---|

The following vehicles were allocated to Scottish Region stock after 1949, and the number prefixed by SC: 11032, 11120/4.

# Vestibuled firsts: (FK)

## DIAGRAM 1

A 9ft 3in width, seven-compartment design originally built for the two GE section Continental boat sets of 1925. However, with the clearance for general use of 9ft 3in vehicles, the Diagram was adopted as the standard side-corridor design and replaced Diagram 2. It remained in limited production until 1939, by which time the coaches specified to this Diagram were being constructed with rigid trussing and welded underframes.

Six of the type were built in 1930 by Cravens, as part of an order placed with this and other contractors for 62 vehicles for the Southern Scottish section, and were formed in six, seven-coach vestibuled sets with four Diagram 115 thirds and two Diagram 114 brake thirds, for use on Edinburgh-Glasgow expresses, and between Perth, Edinburgh and York.

After the introduction of the end-door firsts, the requirement for the earlier layout was limited.

## DIAGRAM 2

The 1923 standard design, on Drawing 11855D, to 9ft width, limited to just two batches before the design was superseded by Diagram 1.

## LIST OF VESTIBULED FIRSTS (FKs):

| Diag No | CBP | Order No | Compts/seats | Built | Original number/changes | 1943 number |
|---|---|---|---|---|---|---|
| *Built 1925* |  |  |  |  |  |  |
| 1* | 1924/5 | 59 | 7:42 | SF | 10000/1E (6441/2) [4146/7] | 11016/7 Continental |
|  |  | 60 |  |  | 10002-4E (6443-5) | 11022-4 Continental boat set |
| *Built 1926* |  |  |  |  |  |  |
| 2* | 1925/6 | 109 | 7:42 | DR | 51651/2 | 11029/30 |
| *Built 1927* |  |  |  |  |  |  |
| 2* | 1925/6 | 109 | 7:42 | DR | 1130/1 (4151, 52048) | 11028/31 Trans 1930 |
| *Built 1928* |  |  |  |  |  |  |
| 1* | 1928/9 | 245 | 7:42 | YK | 441 / 31940-3 | 11015 / 11011-4 |
| *Built 1930* |  |  |  |  |  |  |
| 1* | 1929/30 | 308 | 7:42 | DR | 31869/76/82 | 11002/3/6 |
|  |  |  |  | CR | 31879/80/5/91, 31906/16 | 11004/5/7-10 |
| *Built 1931* |  |  |  |  |  |  |
| 1* | 1930/1 | - | 7:42 | CR | 22356/7 | 11000/1 |
| *Built 1935* |  |  |  |  |  |  |
| 1* | 1935/6 | 615 | 7:42 | YK | 52401 | 11021 |
| *Built 1936* |  |  |  |  |  |  |
| 1* | 1935/6 | 615 | 7:42 | YK | 6467 | 11025 Continental boat set |
| *Built 1937* |  |  |  |  |  |  |
| 1* | 1937 | 764 | 7:42 | YK | 41241-3 | 11018-20 |
| *Built 1939* |  |  |  |  |  |  |
| 1* | 1939 | 956 | 7:42 | DR | 6489/90 | 11026/7 |

The following vehicles were allocated to Scottish Region stock after 1949, and the number prefixed by SC: 11002-4/12/6/7/26/7.

# Semi-open firsts: (Semi FO)

This described a coach with the combination of side-corridor compartments and a saloon with fixed tables for dining accommodation. The type was first used for East Coast Joint Stock from the 1900s where the open accommodation proved unpopular with passengers. No doubt draughts were the problem.

The leading proponent in post-Grouping days was the GN section which used them on trains such as the 5.45/5.50pm Kings Cross-Leeds, working with a restaurant first to provide additional capacity (18 seats) for at-seat dining service. One senior passenger manager recalls that, even in the late 1950s, 'they were treated like gold dust as there was no suitable alternative and, if they were not available for trains such as the 'North Briton' or 'Master Cutler', two coaches had to be put in the formation.'

## DIAGRAM 5

Introduced by the time that the 9ft 3in width was acceptable for general service and to a drawing produced at Doncaster for the 1926/7 CBP.

One of the more notable Diagram 5 cars was No 21254, built in 1930/1 for the 9am Leeds-Glasgow and 4pm return in which it ran next to the Diagram 145 restaurant third. This was regarded as a prestigious set and received special attention for external cleaning.

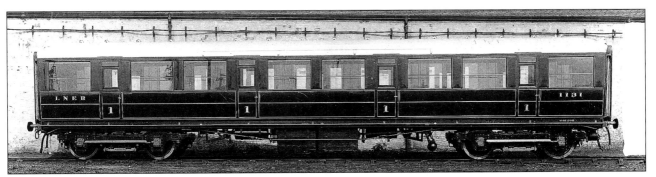

Diagram 2 vestibule first No 1131 (built Doncaster 1927, transferred to the GC section as 52048 in 1930, and becoming 11031 under the 1943 renumbering).

## Diagram 1

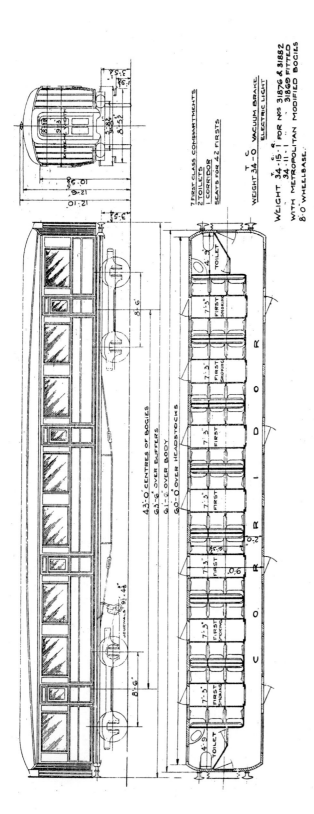

43'-0" CENTRES OF BOGIES
63'-6" OVER BUFFERS
61'-6" OVER BODY
60'-0" OVER HEADSTOCKS

JOURNALS 9½"×4½"

7 FIRST CLASS COMPARTMENTS
2 TOILETS
1 CORRIDOR
SEATS FOR 42 FIRSTS

T. C.    VACUUM BRAKE
WEIGHT 34-0    ELECTRIC LIGHT

WEIGHT 34-15-1 FOR Nos 31876 & 31882
        34-11-1 31869 FITTED
WITH METROPOLITAN MODIFIED BOGIES
8'-0" WHEELBASE.

## Diagram 2

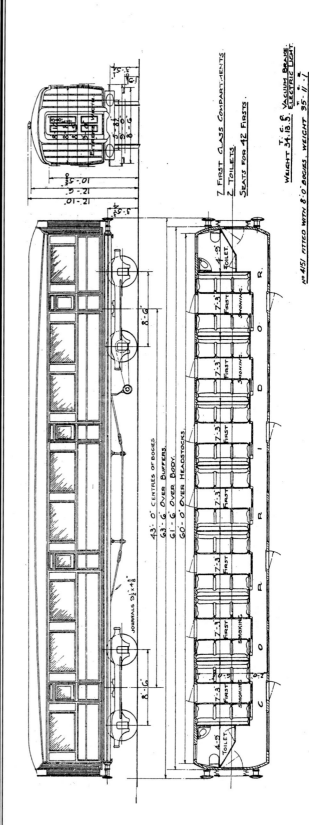

43'-0" CENTRES OF BOGIES
63'-6" OVER BUFFERS
61'-6" OVER BODY.
60'-0" OVER HEADSTOCKS.

JOURNALS 9½"×4½"

7 FIRST CLASS COMPARTMENTS
2 TOILETS
SEATS FOR 42 FIRSTS

T. C.  B. VACUUM BRAKE.
WEIGHT 34.18.5. ELECTRIC LIGHT.

No 4151 FITTED WITH 8'-0" BOGIES. WEIGHT 35-11-1.

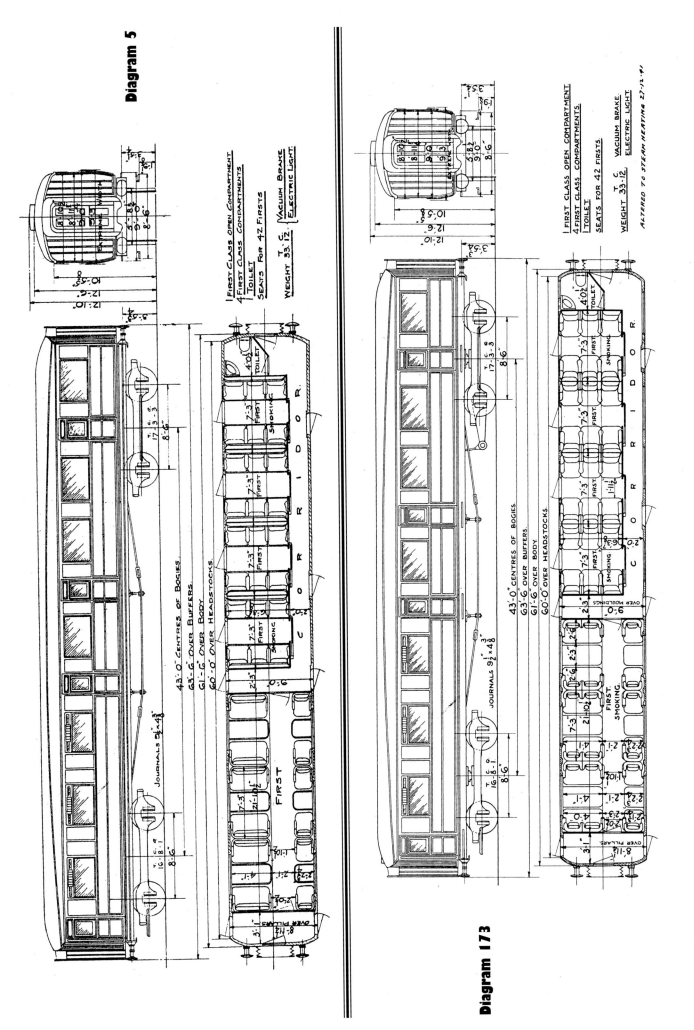

**Diagram 5**

1 FIRST CLASS OPEN COMPARTMENT
4 FIRST CLASS COMPARTMENTS
1 TOILET
SEATS FOR 42 FIRSTS

T.C.
VACUUM BRAKE
WEIGHT 33.12
ELECTRIC LIGHT

**Diagram 173**

1 FIRST CLASS OPEN COMPARTMENT
4 FIRST CLASS COMPARTMENTS
1 TOILET
SEATS FOR 42 FIRSTS

T.C.
VACUUM BRAKE
WEIGHT 33.12
ELECTRIC LIGHT

ALTERED TO STEAM HEATING 27.12.41

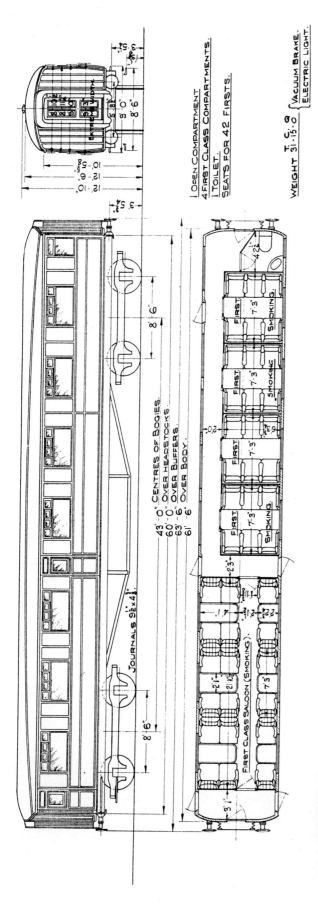

Diagram 219

## DIAGRAM 173

Seemingly virtually identical to Dia 5, except for the type of saloon seating.

A single vehicle built in 1933 for the 8am Newcastle-Kings Cross and 5.30pm return, working with the triplet restaurant car set, the stock for this train being in the East Coast fleet. No 1138 was taken out of the set when its working was changed with the introduction of the 'Silver Jubilee'. Fitted with pressure ventilation equipment from 1934-41.

## DIAGRAM 219

To the same seating capacity as the earlier Diagrams but differently 'handed', built on a welded underframe, and with the deep, sliding ventilators in place of the glass louvred variety used for earlier vehicles of this type. Strictly speaking, these coaches belong to the 'end door' category as there were no outside doors to the compartments.

The first-built of this type was for the 1936 'Hook/Antwerp' boat set mentioned in respect to Diagram 218, working next to that car. The GN section cars were for Leeds Flyer, and the NEA example was for Leeds-Glasgow working, later the 'North Briton'.

### LIST OF SEMI-OPEN FIRSTS (SEMI FOs):

| Diag No | CBP | Order No | Compts/ seats | Built | Original number/changes | 1943 number |
|---|---|---|---|---|---|---|
| **Built 1928** | | | | | | |
| 5* | 1926/7 | 151 | 5† 42 | DR | 4231/2/4 | 11039-41 |
| **Built 1930** | | | | | | |
| 5* | 1930/1 | 377 | 5† 42 | YK | 4100 | 11038 |
| **Built 1931** | | | | | | |
| 5* | 1930/1 | 377 | 5† 42 | YK | 21254 | 11037 Leeds-Glasgow set |
| **Built 1933** | | | | | | |
| 173 | 1933 | 486 | 5† 42 | DR | 1138 | 11104 PV |
| **Built 1936** | | | | | | |
| 219* | 1935/6 | 648 | 5† 42 | YK | 6468 | 11113 Continental boat set |
| | 1935/6 | 657 | | YK | 4101 | 11109 |
| **Built 1938** | | | | | | |
| 219* | 1937 | 766 | 5† 42 | YK | 41261-3 24289 | 11110-2 11108 |

The following vehicles were allocated to Scottish Region stock after 1949, and the number prefixed by SC: 11039, 11104, 11113

# Open seconds: (SO)

Second-class was retained by the LNER for GN/GE sections' London sub-urban services and for the Liverpool St-Harwich Parkeston Quay Continental boat trains. The boat trains were withdrawn two days before the outbreak of World War 2, but the vehicles designated second-class are not officially recorded as being reclassified third-class until 1942/3.

The seating in second-class vehicles was the same as for third-class, but there were minor differences in interior decor. On reclassification, the vehicles concerned were reallocated to the Diagram numbers of the corresponding third-class designs.

## DIAGRAM 22

The four coaches on this Diagram were built for the Hook of Holland and Antwerp boat trains. At first sight, they were very similar to the Diagram 27 vehicles, but were of 9ft 3in width, and with different body panelling, with the interior divided into two saloons, and devoid of lava-tories. They were intended to provide dining accommodation and Nos 695/6 were lettered as restaurant cars.

With the arrival in 1936 of a new set of coaches for the 'Hook

Diagram 5 semi-open first No 4234 (built Doncaster 1928, and later 11041). The print has suffered during developing, but shows well the effect of these half-open, half side-corridor coaches. Note the table-lamps in the saloon, and also the metal-framed ventilators left unpainted. Some vehicles had the ventilators painted, but there was no apparent rule.

Continental', two of Diagram 22 were rebuilt with one lavatory, and reduced to 46 seats, redesignated Dia 225, and transferred to the North Eastern Area as open thirds.

## DIAGRAM 27B

Apart from their designation as second-class, the vehicles on this Diagram were identical to third-class Diagram 27A to which they were transferred in 1942. Lettered Restaurant Car.

## LIST OF OPEN SECONDS (SOs):

| Diag No | CBP | Order No | Compts/ seats | Built | Original number/ changes | 1943 number |
|---|---|---|---|---|---|---|
| **Built 1925** | | | | | | |
| 22 | 1924/5 | 59 | 2† 48 | SF | 10014/5E (695/6) | 12000/1 Continental boat set |
| | | 60 | | | 10016/7E (6986/7) [2275/92]¶ | 13673/4 Continental boat set ¶Later converted to Dia 225 |
| **Built 1930** | | | | | | |
| 27B | 1929/30 | 311 | 2† 48 | YK | 697¶ | 12201 ¶Became open third on Dia 27A, 1942. |
| **Built 1935** | | | | | | |
| 27B* | 1935/6 | 651 | 2† 48 | YK | 698¶, 6994 | 12202/3 ¶ Lettered RC Became open thirds on Dia 27A in 1942. |

# Vestibuled second: (SK)

## DIAGRAM 21

Built for the 1925 Continental boat trains and the 9ft 3in wide version of Diagram 23, but with three-a-side seating, in view of their second-class designation.

## DIAGRAM 115

The standard 9ft 3in width vestibule third-class coach design (see vestibule third) but in any case practically identical to Diagram 21.

These two coaches were built in 1936 for the Hook/Antwerp boat train set which replaced the 1925 set and the Diagram 21 vehicles.

## LIST OF VESTIBULE SECONDS (SKLs):

| Diag No | CBP | Order No | Compts/ seats | Built | Original number/ changes | 1943 number |
|---|---|---|---|---|---|---|
| **Built 1925** | | | | | | |
| 21 | 1924/5 | 59 | 8: 48 | SF | 10011E (6983) [2273] | 12244 Continental boat set |
| | | 60 | | | 10012E (6984) [4172] | — |
| | | | | | 6985 | 12686 2273, 6985 later on Dia 115 |
| **Built 1936** | | | | | | |
| 115 | 1935/6 | 647 | 8: 48 | YK | 6992, 6993 (61997) | 12687, 12705 Continental boat set Both thirds after 1942. |

Diagram 27B open second No 697 (built York 1930, and No 12201 under the 1943 renumbering, by which time it had become an open third). Lettered restaurant car but this was later removed. York photograph dated April 1930.

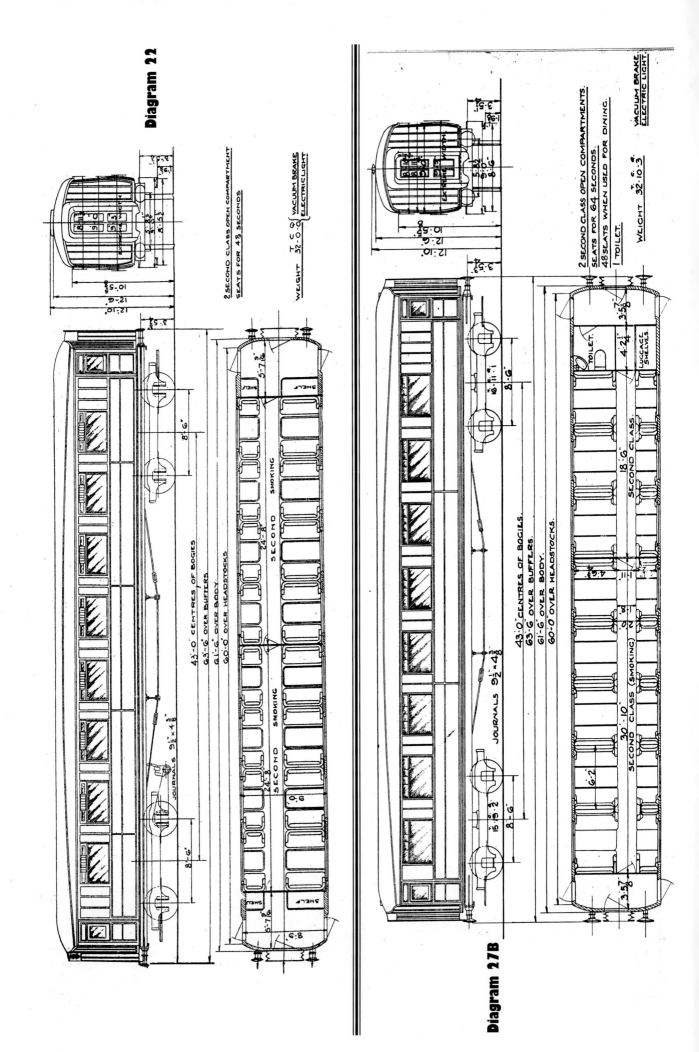

**Diagram 22**

2 SECOND CLASS OPEN COMPARTMENT
SEATS FOR 48 SECONDS

WEIGHT T.C.Q. 32-0-0 { VACUUM BRAKE
ELECTRIC LIGHT

43'-0" CENTRES OF BOGIES
63'-6" OVER BUFFERS
61'-6" OVER BODY
60'-0" OVER HEADSTOCKS

JOURNALS 9½ × 4⅜

SECOND SMOKING
SECOND SMOKING

SHELF

**Diagram 27B**

2 SECOND CLASS OPEN COMPARTMENTS.
SEATS FOR 64 SECONDS.
48 SEATS WHEN USED FOR DINING.
1 TOILET.

WEIGHT T.C.Q. 32-10-3 { VACUUM BRAKE.
ELECTRIC LIGHT.

43'-0" CENTRES OF BOGILS.
63'-6" OVER BUFFLRS.
61'-6" OVER BODY.
60'-0" OVER HEADSTOCKS.

JOURNALS 9½ × 4⅜

TOILET.
LUGGAGE SHELVES.
SECOND CLASS.
SECOND CLASS (SMOKING)

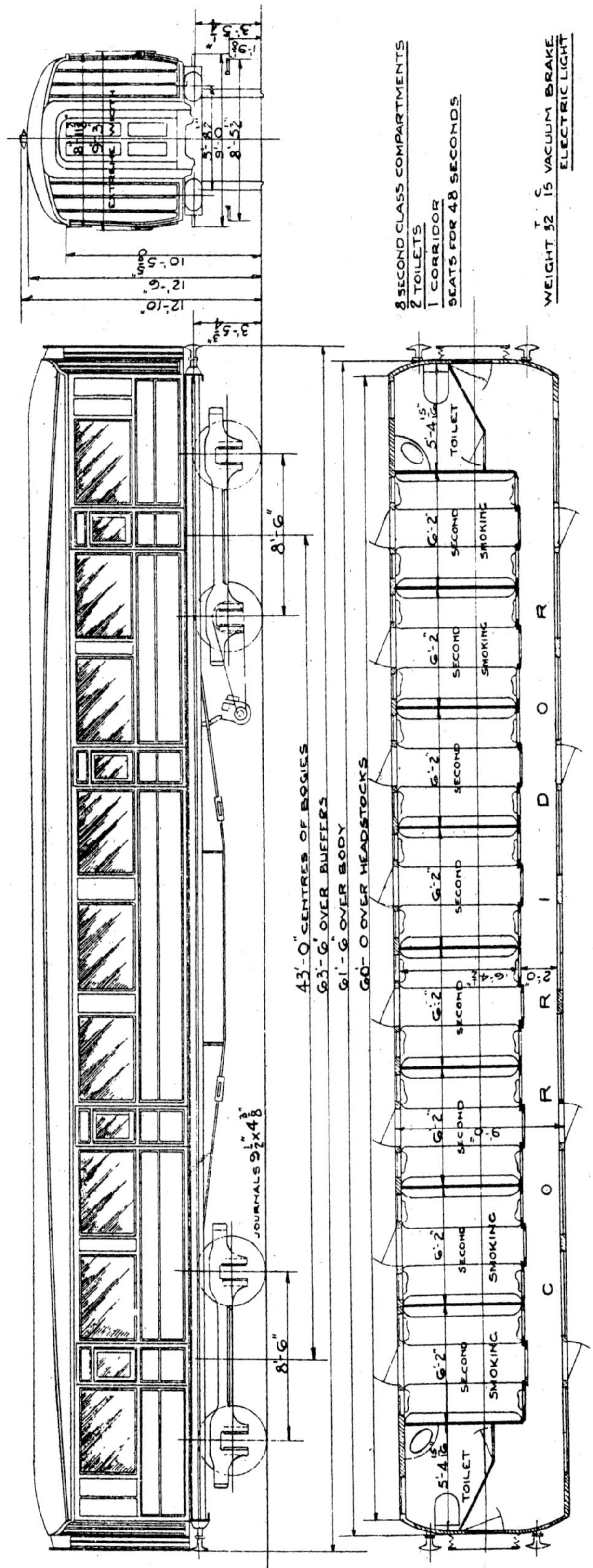

**Diagram 21**

*8 SECOND CLASS COMPARTMENTS · 2 TOILETS · 1 CORRIDOR · SEATS FOR 48 SECONDS*

*WEIGHT 32 T C · 15 VACUUM BRAKE · ELECTRIC LIGHT*

43'-0" CENTRES OF BOGIES · 63'-6" OVER BUFFER · 61'-6" OVER BODY · 60'-0" OVER HEADSTOCKS · JOURNALS 9½" × 4½"

# Open third: (TOV)

### DIAGRAM 27

Drawing 12030D, and of 9ft width, chosen in preference to an earlier discarded type which was similar to Diagram 22 and lacked lavatories. As with the contemporary restaurant cars, Diagram 27 vehicles were fitted with glass-louvred saloon windows, and had one lavatory and luggage shelves.

These dual-purpose coaches were intended to provide dining accommodation and, as such, sat 2 + 1 when meals were being served, otherwise they were expected to seat 3 + 1. Not all were branded as Restaurant Cars, despite being used for this purpose. A 2 + 2 version was produced in the all-steel Diagram 28 stock.

In the 1924/5 CBP, the NEA vehicle was built for inclusion in the Newcastle-Swansea set, to run with a restaurant first, and the SSA example was intended for the Glasgow-Southampton through carriage working.

### DIAGRAM 27A

The 9ft 3in version – strangely, the LNER did not otherwise indicate these greater width designs by a suffix to the original standard type but, instead, gave them new Diagram numbers.

Two other changes from Diagram 27 to be noted are that there were two saloons only, and that metal-framed sliding ventilators were fitted. Some coaches had intermediate armrests to indicate 3 + 1 seating.

The GE section and East Coast allocations were lettered Restaurant Car but the markings were later removed. Two were built in 1930 for Liverpool St-Cromer sets. The GE section embarked on the renumbering of its TOVs, bringing them into the number series for its restaurant cars. During the 1930s (and later), the GC section used the combination of a TOV and restaurant first for its principal Marylebone-Manchester/Bradford expresses.

The NEA coaches under the 1929/30 programme were built for excursion traffic. No 22314 was converted to a buffet car on Dia 185 in 1934, to work on the 12noon Newcastle-York and 6.15pm return.

No 21308 was the first LNER coach with a welded underframe.

In BR days these vehicles tended to be used as ordinary open thirds.

### DIAGRAM 27C

Minor differences in the internal layout to Diagram 27A, and fitted with the deeper pattern of sliding ventilator.

Some were built for the East Coast fleet, their construction made possible by government finance to the LNER for development works, but were built contrary to the wishes of the Hotels Department who wanted pantry thirds; three were soon transferred to the Areas. The 1936/7 construction included some allocated to special party use, organisers of long-distance excursions preferring these coaches to the TTOs – the open thirds with bucket seats.

### DIAGRAM 150

Very similar to Diagram 27, but with 2 + 2 seating. Ordered, along with other vehicles, under the 1930/1 CBP in order to provide a new set for the 5.45pm Kings Cross-Leeds/Bradford. On this working, a Dia 150 car was used for dining service, working next to a restaurant/kitchen third.

### DIAGRAM 225

Two Diagram 22 vehicles (see second opens) transferred from the GE section to the NEA and converted to near Diagram 27 form.

### DIAGRAM CLC 82

New coaches to LNER-style designs were supplied to the Cheshire Lines Committee after 1923. This vehicle, CLC No 700, was a one-off design with 2 + 2 seating, and resembled none of the existing standard LNER open third designs, having two lavatories, luggage shelves and seating similar to the Diagram 27.

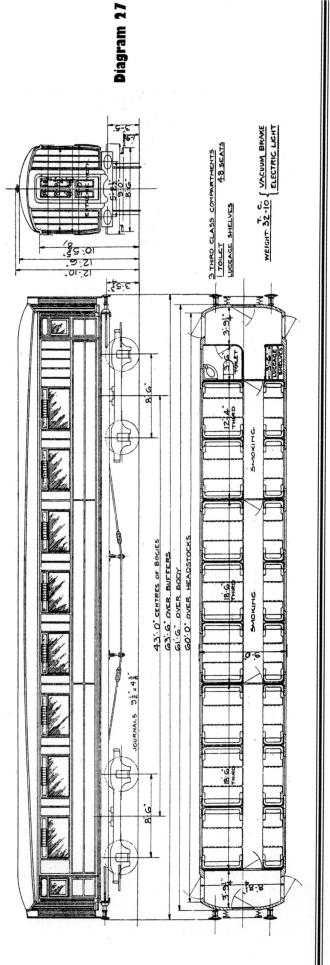

**Diagram 27**

43'·0" CENTRES OF BOGIES
63'·6" OVER BUFFERS
61'·6" OVER BODY
60'·0" OVER HEADSTOCKS

JOURNALS 9½" × 4¾"

3 THIRD CLASS COMPARTMENTS
1 TOILET
LUGGAGE SHELVES          48 SEATS

T. C.
WEIGHT 32-10      } VACUUM BRAKE
                    ELECTRIC LIGHT

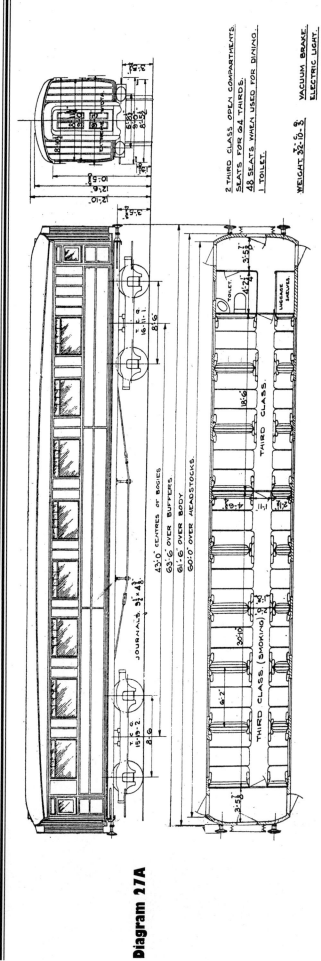

**Diagram 27A**

43'·0" CENTRES OF BOGIES
63'·6" OVER BUFFERS
61'·6" OVER BODY
60'·0" OVER HEADSTOCKS

JOURNALS 9½" × 4¾"

2 THIRD CLASS OPEN COMPARTMENTS
SEATS FOR 64 THIRDS.
48 SEATS WHEN USED FOR DINING.
1 TOILET.

WEIGHT 32-10-3      VACUUM BRAKE.
                    ELECTRIC LIGHT.

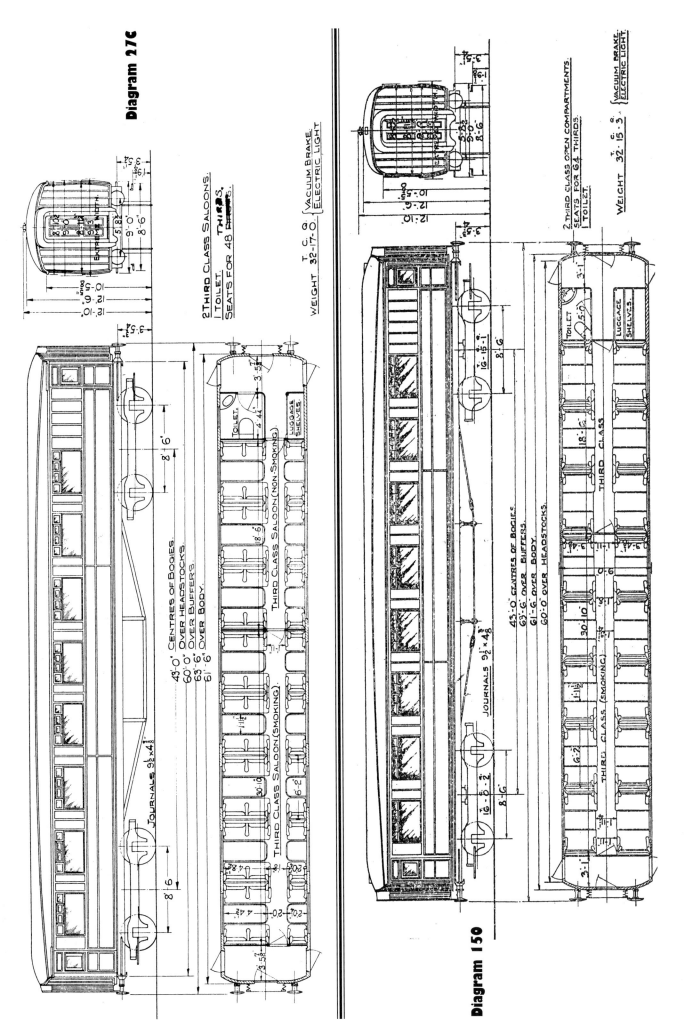

**Diagram 276**

2 THIRD CLASS SALOONS.
1 TOILET.
SEATS FOR 48 THIRDS.

WEIGHT 32-17-0. T.C.Q. {VACUUM BRAKE
ELECTRIC LIGHT.

43'-0" CENTRES OF BOGIES.
60'-0" OVER HEADSTOCKS.
63'-6" OVER BUFFERS.
61'-6" OVER BODY.

JOURNALS 9½ × 4¼"

THIRD CLASS SALOON (NON-SMOKING).

THIRD CLASS SALOON (SMOKING).

**Diagram 150**

2 THIRD CLASS OPEN COMPARTMENTS.
SEATS FOR 64 THIRDS.
1 TOILET.

WEIGHT 32-15-3. T.C.Q. {VACUUM BRAKE.
ELECTRIC LIGHT.

43'-0" CENTRES OF BOGIES.
63'-6" OVER BUFFERS.
61'-6" OVER BODY.
60'-0" OVER HEADSTOCKS.

JOURNALS 9½ × 4¾

THIRD CLASS.

THIRD CLASS (SMOKING).

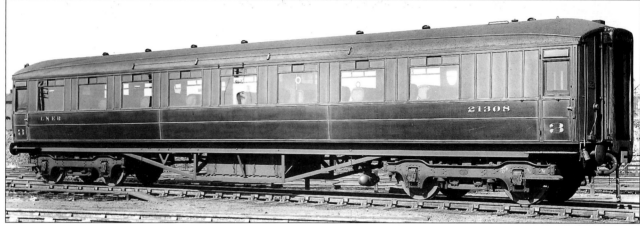

Top: **Diagram 27A open third No 61711 (built Doncaster 1931) which was lettered as a Restaurant Car as built. It was later renumbered 6118 by the GE section, and became 12190 under the 1943 renumbering, by which time the RC lettering had been removed.**

Above: **Diagram 27A open third No 21308 (built York 1934, and 12145 under the 1943 renumbering). This was the first standard coach to be built with a welded underframe. This photograph is of interest in depicting a vehicle after it had been in traffic for a while with grime already lodging in the areas around the panel beading.**

Below: **A Scarborough-Leeds express enters Seamer on 4 June 1947 behind 'C7' Atlantic No 2975. The leading vehicle is a Diagram 27A open third, built in 1935, which features the deeper window ventilators typical of later Gresley stock.**

Bottom: **Diagram 150 open third No 4175 (built Doncaster 1931, and 12927 under the 1943 renumbering). Despite their 2 + 2 seating, the pair of vehicles to this Diagram were used for dining service.**

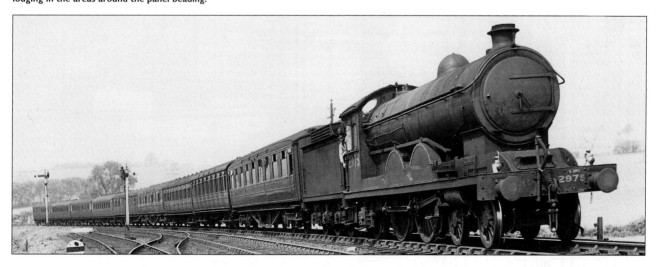

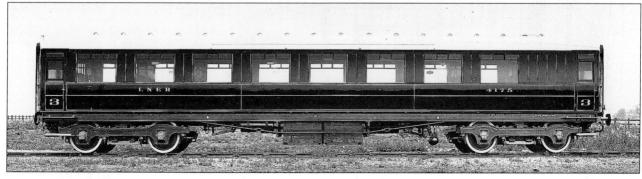

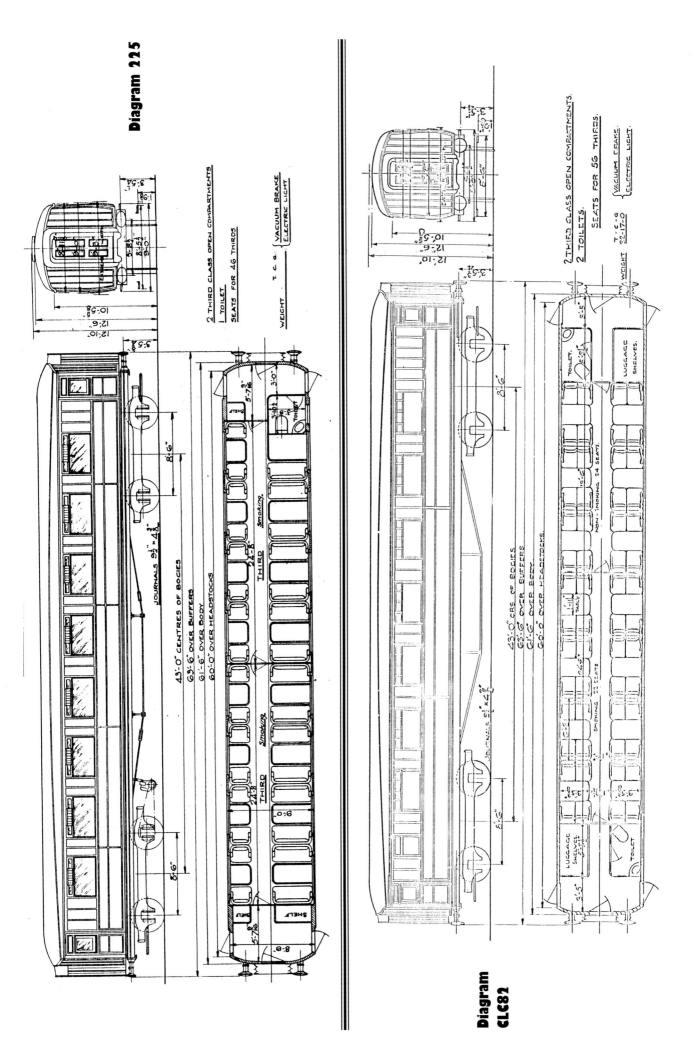

**Diagram 225**

2 THIRD CLASS OPEN COMPARTMENTS.
1 TOILET
SEATS FOR 46 THIRDS

WEIGHT    T. C. Q.    VACUUM BRAKE
ELECTRIC LIGHT

JOURNALS 9½" × 4½"

43'-0" CENTRES OF BOGIES
63'-6" OVER BUFFERS
61'-6" OVER BODY
60'-0" OVER HEADSTOCKS

THIRD   Smoking
THIRD   Smoking

**Diagram GLG82**

2 THIRD CLASS OPEN COMPARTMENTS.
2 TOILETS.

SEATS FOR 56 THIRDS.

WEIGHT    T. C. Q.
22-17-0

VACUUM BRAKE.
ELECTRIC LIGHT.

43'-0" CRS OF BOGIES
63'-6" OVER BUFFERS
61'-6" OVER BODY
60'-0" OVER HEADSTOCKS

JOURNALS 8'-1" × 4'-5"

LUGGAGE
SHELVES.
TOILET.

NON-SMOKING 24 SEATS.
SMOKING 32 SEATS

LUGGAGE
SHELVES.
TOILET.

35

## LIST OF OPEN THIRDS (TOVs):

| Diag No | CBP | Order No | Compts/ seats | Built | Original number/changes | 1943 number |
|---|---|---|---|---|---|---|
| **Built 1925** | | | | | | |
| 27* | 1924/5 | 75 | 2† 48 | DK | 2389, 3315, 21772, 22170, 10113Y (22315) | 12127/31/28-30 |
| **Built 1926** | | | | | | |
| 27* | 1925/6 | 110 | 3† 48 | DK | 5524/5/7/8 | 12132-5 |
| **Built 1929** | | | | | | |
| 27A* | 1928/9 | 246 | 2† 64 | DR | 4152 | 12176 |
| | | | | | 5541-6 | 12177-82 |
| | - | | | MET | 61705/6 | – /12185 |
| | | | | | (6100/1) | Cromer sets 6100 DEA 1940 |
| **Built 1930** | | | | | | |
| 27A* | 1929/30 | 311 | 2† 48 | YK | 21084, 21212, 21508, 21954, 22238/73, 22314/71, 22410/71 | 12136/7/46-9, – /12150-2 22314 converted to buffet car on Dia 185, 1934 |
| | | | | | 315/37/45/57 | 12163/6/7/70 |
| | | | | | 61707-10 (6102-5) | 12186-9 |
| 27A* | 1930/1 | 382 | 2† 48 | | 22660 | 12153 Leeds-Glasgow set |
| **Built 1931** | | | | | | |
| 27A* | 1930/1 | 382 | 2† 48 | DR | 5554/5 | 12183/4 |
| | | | | | 61711 (6118) | 12190 |
| | | 401 | | | 321/53 | 12164/9 |
| 150 | 1930/1 | 383 | 2† 64 | DR | 4175/6 | 12927/8 |
| **Built 1932** | | | | | | |
| 27A* | 1930/1 | 382 | 2† 48 | DR | 61712/3 (6119/20) | – /12192 |
| | | | | | 3888/9 | 12174/5 |
| **Built 1933** | | | | | | |
| 27A* | 1933 | 503 | 2† 64 | DR | 21301-4 | 12138-41 |
| | | | 2† 48 | | 175 (744) | - |
| | | | | | PV, 1934 for 8am Newcastle-Kings Cross and 5.30pm return | DEA, Wood Green 1945 u/f reused |
| **Built 1934** | | | | | | |
| 27A* | 1933 | 503 | 2† 64 | YK | 21305-8 | 12142-5 21308 welded u/f |
| | | | 2† 48 | | 327/46/88/96/8 | 12165/8/71/2/– 398 DEA |
| | | | | | 61850-5 (6121-4, 6125[24137], 6126) | 12193-6/62/97 |
| | 1934 | 534 | 2† 48 | | 1140/1 (61995/6) | 12198/9 Trans 1938 |
| **Built 1935** | | | | | | |
| 27A* | 1935/6 | 621 | 2† 48 | YK | 23803-10 | 12154-61 |
| **Built 1936** | | | | | | |
| 27C* | 1935/6 | - | 2† 48 | CR | #41029/30 | 12215/6 |
| | | | | | #22250, | 12204-9 |
| | | | | | #24130-4 | |
| | | | | | #1655-7 | 12217-9 |
| | | | | | (41059/60, 6125) | Trans 1938 |
| | | | | | #1658-60 | 1658-60 |
| **Built 1937** | | | | | | |
| 27C* | 1936 | - # | 2† 48 | CR | #24135/6/8-40 | 12210-4 |
| CLC 82 | - | - | 2† 56 | CR | CLC 700 | M999M |

The following vehicles were allocated to Scottish Region stock after 1949, and the number prefixed by SC: 12127-31, 12142-5, 12154/5, 12177, 12185-8, 12209-11, 12927/8.

# Tourist open third: (TTO)

## DIAGRAM 186

Although the green and cream painted Tourist stock had been introduced in the 1933 CBP, for the following year's programme teak-bodied open thirds and brake open thirds were built for the GN section, and the type was ordered in quantity over the next few years, eventually numbering 407. All were fitted with the individual bucket-type seats also used in the green and cream painted Tourist stock. There was no hard and fast rule as which type of stock was to be ordered for excursion duties except that the cream and green stock was 'unclassed', and the teak bodied vehicles, third-class. In due course, the Diagram 186 vehicles were also allocated to general service train sets and were widely used during wartime on regular long-distance trains.

Peppercorn wrote to the various LNER works managers in 1946 on the subject of the bucket seats: '(they) have never been popular with the travelling public ... whilst I cannot undertake the replacement of bucket seats in all open thirds ... I am prepared to fit (standard seats) where the (bucket) seats have to be renewed.' The majority of, if not all, Diagram 186 coaches were re-seated in time.

Otherwise, there were few variations as between individual Diagram 186 coaches, except that the exterior panelling was to shorter lengths in some examples while some vehicles had riveted rather than welded underframes.

At least eight of the Dia 186 coaches were used in ambulance trains during World War 2 but afterwards reverted to their original form.

No 13369 was the prototype cafeteria car to be authorised by the Railway Executive and was converted at Eastleigh Works, being out-shopped in February 1952. For its new role, principally for use on excursion trains, the interior was rebuilt with tip-up seating for 48 passengers, with fixed tables and a bar/counter with display cabinets. The layout was arranged for self-service. Somewhat surprisingly, this vehicle retained its old number rather than being renumbered in the LNER catering vehicle series.

Another interesting use for these vehicles came with the introduction of the Scottish Region's Television Train, operated from 1956. A brake vehicle was rigged up as a soundproofed studio, and programmes were transmitted by closed circuit tv to monitors mounted above the internal door at each end of the open seconds. Sound broadcasting was also possible from individual vehicles to the train as a whole. The Diagram 186 coaches adapted for use in the train were: 13233/62/74, 13429/64, 13510/21, these running with Dia 196 brake open second 16642, Dia 40A vestibuled brake second 16197 (the cinema car), with a BR Mark 1 bogie van as the generator coach. The train usually ran with a Tourist buffet car, Nos 9140 or 9142. Not long after being used for an excursion from Glasgow-Blackpool and back, the open seconds and brake seconds went for scrap in the autumn of 1964.

The numbers of these vehicles in service dwindled fast during the 1962-4 period, such that all had been condemned by 1967, except one –

Diagram 186 open third, by now second-class, No E13416E (built York 1935, and formerly 43663). Seen at Cambridge in September 1956, and in BR carmine and cream livery. Note the typical wooden and canvas vestibule shield, and also the body side panelling with the panelling in five sections.

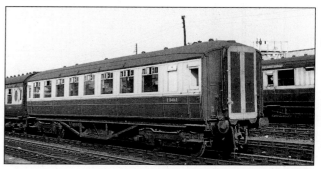

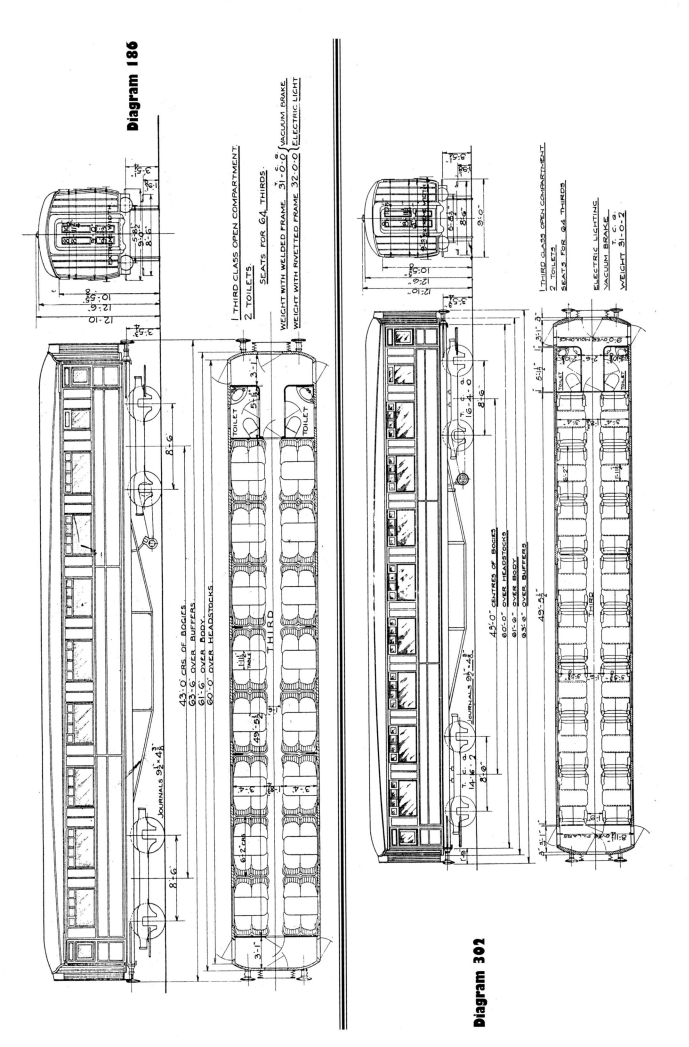

**Diagram 186**

1 THIRD CLASS OPEN COMPARTMENT.
2 TOILETS.
SEATS FOR 64 THIRDS.
WEIGHT WITH WELDED FRAME 31-0-0 } T.C.a.
WEIGHT WITH RIVETTED FRAME 32-0-0 } VACUUM BRAKE
ELECTRIC LIGHT

43'-0" CRS. OF BOGIES.
63'-6" OVER BUFFERS.
61'-6" OVER BODY.
60'-0" OVER HEADSTOCKS.

THIRD

JOURNALS 9½"×4¾"

**Diagram 302**

1 THIRD CLASS OPEN COMPARTMENT.
2 TOILETS.
SEATS FOR 64 THIRDS.
ELECTRIC LIGHTING
VACUUM BRAKE } T.C.a.
WEIGHT 31-0-2

43'-0" CENTRES OF BOGIES.
60'-0" OVER HEADSTOCKS.
61'-6" OVER BODY.
63'-6" OVER BUFFERS.

THIRD

JOURNALS 9½"×4¾"

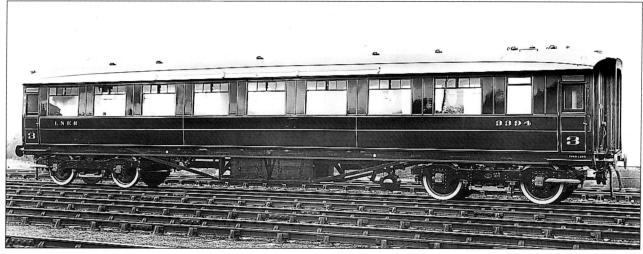

Diagram 186 open third No 3394 (built York 1934, and 13352 under the 1943 renumbering).

13586 – which had somehow escaped the net following its listing for scrapping in 1965. The underframes of Nos 13321/48 and 13532/60 were used by BR for Carflat wagons, employed in carrying new cars and other road vehicles.

## DIAGRAM 302

Fitted with high-backed 'standard seats' from new (as were the matching Dia 303 brake open thirds), but otherwise identical to Dia 186.

### LIST OF OPEN THIRDS (TTOs):

| Diag No | CBP | Order No | Compts/ seats | Built | Original number/changes | 1943 number |
|---------|-----|----------|---------------|-------|--------------------------|-------------|
| **Built 1934** | | | | | | |
| 186* | 1934 | 559 | 1† 64 | YK | 43600-19/64 | 13354-73, Welded u/fs |
| | | 560 | | | | 13417 |
| | | | | | 3390/3/4 | 13350-2 |
| | | | | | 21309 | 13218 |
| | | | | | 13369 converted to a cafeteria car by BR | |
| **Built 1935** | | | | | | |
| 186* | 1934 | 559 | 1† 64 | YK | 43620-63 | 13374-81/ –, 13382-13416 43628 W/O Goole 1941, u/f reused. 43610/6/20/38/9, 43650/1 used as sitting cars in ambulance trains during WW2, and returned to service as open thirds |
| | | 1935/6 594 | | | 22501-16 | 13219-25/ –, 13226-33 |
| | | | | | 22508 W/O Westborough 1941 | |
| | | 622 | | | 52243-56 | 13535-48 |
| | | | | | 52257-9 | 13549-51 |
| | | | | | 23814-25 | 13234-45 |
| | | | | | 3142/55 | 13344/6 |
| | | | | | 7405/6 | 13619/20 |
| **Built 1936** | | | | | | |
| 186* | 1935/6 | - | 1† 64 | BHM M-C | 23973-97 #24083-90, 24108-24 | 13271-95 – /13296-13302/19-35 |
| | | | | | 24083 W/O Westborough 1941 | |
| | | - | | | 52269-75 | 13552-8 |
| | | | | | 3972 | 13353 |
| | | - | BHM | | #23948-64, #24125-9 | 13246-62, 13336-40 |
| | | | | | #310/80 | 13341/2 |
| | | - | M-C | | #24091-24106 | 13303-18 |
| | | - | BHM | | #23965-72 | 13263-70 |

| Diag No | CBP | Order No | Compts/ seats | Built | Original number/changes | 1943 number |
|---------|-----|----------|---------------|-------|--------------------------|-------------|
| **Built 1937** | | | | | | |
| 186* | 1937 | - | 1† 64 | M-C | 43665-43730 | 13418-68/ –, 13470-5/ – /6-82 43673/83/92/3, 43703/5/18/24 used as sitting cars in ambulance trains during WW2, and returned to service as open thirds |
| | | | | | 52285-96 | 13559-70 |
| | | | | | 394, 3145 | 13343/5 |
| **Built 1938** | | | | | | |
| 186* | 1938 | - | 1† 64 | M-C | 3328/45/51 | 13347-9 |
| | | - | | | 43731-82 | 13483-13534 |
| | | - | | | 56850-95 | 13571-13616 |
| | | - | | | 761/2 | 13617/8 |
| **Built 1939** | | | | | | |
| 302 | 1939 | 959 | 1† 64 | DR | 3342/55/76, 3802/11/5/6/8 | 13774-81 |

The following vehicles were allocated to Scottish Region stock after 1949, and the number prefixed by SC: 13224-6/8-62, 13264-71/4/5/7-81, 13417-25/9/30/60-5, 13495-512/9-21, 13610

---

# Vestibuled third: (TK)

## DIAGRAM 23

A 1923 standard design, to 9ft width and built with three-a-side seating for East Coast use, and with four-a-side seating for the Areas. Intermediate armrests were fitted to some existing vehicles from 1934 onwards.

Some 100 of this type featured in the 1924 CBP, over half of the total being for East Coast service, in particular to be included in the 'Flying Scotsman' sets, while those for the NEA were intended for excursion traffic, and those for the GC section, for Hull-Liverpool workings.

From 1930, new stock allocated to the East Coast displaced Dia 23 vehicles for transfer to the Areas. By 1935, Dia 23 coaches were no longer regularly allocated to the principal East Coast sets, and the last in East Coast stock was transferred away in 1937.

Nos 1007/12 of this Diagram were converted in 1928 to serve as the 'Toilet thirds' used in the 'Flying Scotsman' sets, each being equipped with a hairdressing saloon and ladies' retiring room. Transferred to Diagram 23A and described in this book under Special Stock.

In BR days fifteen Dia 23 vehicles supplied underframes for Carflats and two – 12014/9 – became camping coaches. Taken as a whole they were more than usually accident-prone, and five were lost in accidents involving passenger trains: 1014 at Welwyn in 1935, 12084 and 12098 at Tollerton and Witham (Essex), both in 1950, and 12010 at York in 1958. Two were victims of enemy action during World War 2.

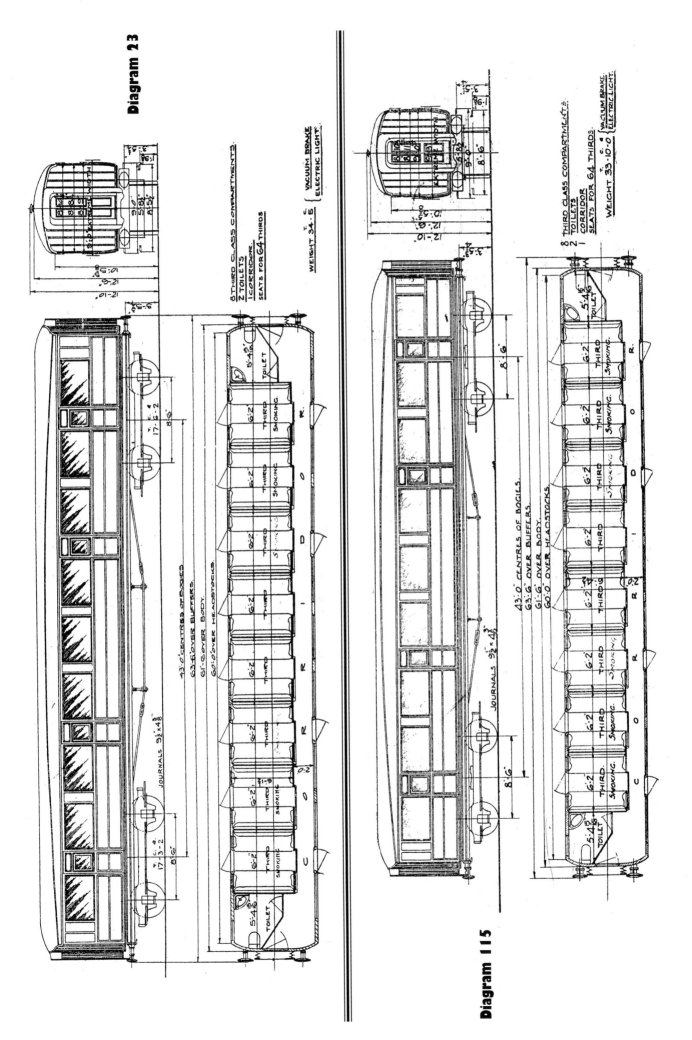

**Diagram 23**

8 THIRD CLASS COMPARTMENTS
2 TOILETS
1 CORRIDOR
SEATS FOR 64 THIRDS

WEIGHT 34·5 { VACUUM BRAKE
ELECTRIC LIGHT

**Diagram 115**

8 THIRD CLASS COMPARTMENTS
2 TOILETS
1 CORRIDOR
SEATS FOR 64 THIRDS

WEIGHT 33·10·0 { VACUUM BRAKE
ELECTRIC LIGHT

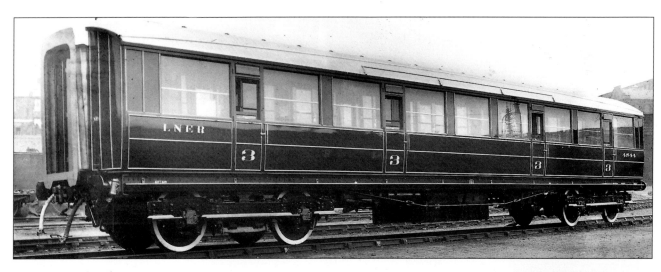

Top: **The photographer at Dukinfield and Gorton Works was a bit more adventurous than his counterparts at Doncaster and York. Diagram 23 vestibule third No 4844 was built at York in 1927, and became 12056 under the 1943 renumbering.**

Above: **Diagrams and official photographs tended to favour the corridor side of vestibuled coaches, but here is a latter-day picture of a Diagram 23 vehicle. By now E12088E, it was built at York in 1926 as No 5519. When photographed on Southern territory at Appledore in June 1958, it had just a year's life ahead of it.**

## DIAGRAM 115

Numbering over 500, this was the 9ft 3in width version of Diagram 23 and so was almost identical to Diagram 21 which had been built to the wider dimension for the Continental boat trains. The layout of Diagram 115 was identical to Diagrams 21 and 23. Originally built with four-a-side seating.

Later vehicles were fitted with intermediate armrests from new, and were built on welded underframes. With the entry into service of the end-door vestibuled thirds from the mid-1930s, the Diagram 115 vehicles effectively declined in status and thereafter were built mainly for less important cross-country duties, often to replace non-vestibuled stock.

Nos 24594-24601 were turned out with British Standard gangways for use on through workings to the LMS, such as Newcastle-Liverpool, and Harrogate-Southport. Although complete sets working on to the LMS had Pullman gangways, the LNER continued to build a limited number of coaches for the NEA and SSA with BS gangways where they were to be formed in trains with LMS vehicles.

The underframes of Nos 12304/34/51/86/99, 12436, 12577/8, 12603/22, 12702 were used by BR for Carflat wagons, employed in carrying new cars and other road vehicles.

## LIST OF VESTIBULED THIRDS (TKs):

| Diag No CBP | Order No | Compts/ seats | Built | Original number/changes | 1943 number |
|---|---|---|---|---|---|
| **Built 1924** | | | | | |
| 23* | 1924/5 47 | 8:48 | YK | 10019-32J (1000-13) | 12039-41/92-7, 12019, 12098/9 ¶1007/12 − see Dia 23A. |
| | | | | [4462-4, 52041-3, 52083/¶/4/5, 3922, 52152/¶/3] | Transfers 1930-7 12098 W/0 1950 |
| **Built 1925** | | | | | |
| 23* | 1924/5 57 | 8:48 | YK | 10033-68J, 1050/1 (1014-51) [ − /42517-25, 31156-61/3-72/4/6/7, 52182, 4465-8/71/2/4/6] | − /12060-8, 12020-38, 12100, 12042-9 1014 W/0 Welwyn 12100 DEA 1944 Transfers 1930-8 |
| | | | | 7485-8 (3683-6) | 12015-8 Transferred CBP 1928/9 |
| | | | | 10075/6Y (21127, 22347) 21001/15, 21501, 22102/56, 22169/88/92, 22285/355/90, 5500-9 | 12004/12 12002/3/5-11/3-14 all built as≠ 12071-3/− /5-80 5503 DEA, High Meads 1944 |

Above: It would be difficult to identify the extra width of a Diagram 115 coach, but there is no problem in identifying the angle-iron trussing of 1938-built E12651E, painted in BR maroon livery and photographed at speed when formed in a Saturdays only Hull-Kings Cross train in July 1964. It had been built as No 56007, one of a batch of Birmingham RCW-built vestibule thirds. Apart from being intended as general replacements of older stock, construction of the 40 thirds in this batch was also justified on the grounds of their use as strengthening vehicles for Saturdays only Doncaster/Sheffield to East Coast trains, in place of non-vestibuled, non-lavatory stock.

Also of interest is the vehicle to 12651's rear, a Diagram 298 end-door vestibule second, E13758E, (built in 1939 as No 1815) showing the compartment side without doors to the compartments; in 12651's case, all compartments had exterior doors. The standard end door designs do not feature in this book. The photograph captures well the essential characteristics of the Gresley teak panelled vehicles.

**Built 1926**

| | | | | | |
|---|---|---|---|---|---|
| 23* | 1924/5 57 | 8: 64 | YK | 5517-20 | 12087/— /8/9 5518 DEA, Middlesbrough 1942 |
| | 1925/6 111 | | DK | 61626-33 4819/25/8/35/6 1194/5 (42532/3) | 12101-8 ≠ 12050-4 12069/70 Trans 1935/6 |
| | | | | 5510-5 | 12081-6 12084 W/O 1950 |

**Built 1927**

| | | | | | |
|---|---|---|---|---|---|
| 23* | 1925/6 111 | 8: 64 | YK | 4840/4/9/55/8, 5521/2 | 12055-9/90/1 |

**Built 1928**

| | | | | | |
|---|---|---|---|---|---|
| 115* | 1928/9 277 | 8: 64 | YK | 3953-62 5395, 5602/5/6/8/14/6, 5618/20/3/4/35/7 | 12494-12503 12612-12624 |

**Built 1929**

| | | | | | |
|---|---|---|---|---|---|
| 115* | 1928/9 277 | 8: 64 | YK | 21183, 21478, 22136/78, 22208/36/66, 22352/62, 22461 | 12250/60/4/ — /5-7, 12274-6 |

**Built 1930**

| | | | | | |
|---|---|---|---|---|---|
| 115* | 1929/30 310 | 8: 64 | YK | 358/64/77/82/6, 392/5/7, 3102, 3114/43/67/70 | 12451/2/4/6/8, — /61-3/5/8/9, 12471 392 DEA |
| | 1930/1 358 | | YK | 1114-9 (42526-31) | 12599-12604 Transferred 1937 |
| | 1930/1 - | | M-C | 22333-5 | 12268-70 |

**Built 1931**

| | | | | | |
|---|---|---|---|---|---|
| 115* | 1930/1 381 | 8: 64 | YK | 21187, 21208, 21229/55/96, 21319/68, 21401/37, 21699, 21724/95, 22491/2/9, 22500/25, 22565, 22942, 23567 4173/4 334/73/84/7 1320-3 (52183-6) | 12251-9/61-3, 12277-84  12504/5 12450/3/7/9 12625-8 Trans 1938 |
| | - | | M-C | 22336-8, 3112/32/40/68, 3171/90, 3214, 3236/48/50/61, 3267/84/91/4, 3307/17/9-21, 3324/49/56/74, 3378/95 | 12271-3 12464/6/7/70, 12472-93 |

**Built 1933**

| | | | | | |
|---|---|---|---|---|---|
| 115* | 1933 504 | 8: 64 | YK | 167 (42516), 168 | 12598, 12716 167 Trans 1936 168 PV, 1934 for 8am Newcastle-Kings Cross and 5.30pm return |

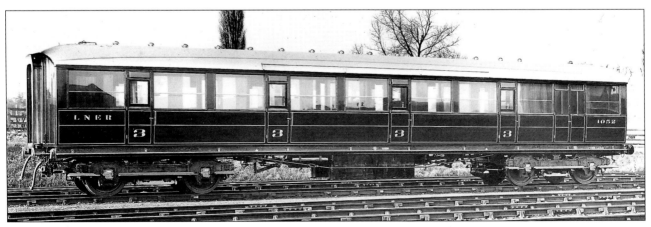

The locker thirds had a luggage compartment for the use of passengers, the double, corridor-side doors of which are at the right-hand of the body in this picture of No 1052. This was one of the three TGs to Diagram 24, and was built at York in 1926. Transferred to the NSA as 750, the post-1943 running number was 12111.

| | | | | | | |
|---|---|---|---|---|---|---|
| 115* | 1934 | 508 | 8: 64 | YK | 1435-40 (2926-31) | 12245-8/ — /9 Trans 1938/9 2930 W/O |
| | | | | | 1441-72 | 12717-48 |

**Built 1935**

| | | | | | | |
|---|---|---|---|---|---|---|
| 115* | •1935/6 | 619 | 8: 64 | YK | 1474-82 4971-91 | 12749-57 12506-26 |
| | | - | | BHM | 41031-48 52260-8 | 12528-45 12629-30/ — /1-6 52262 W/O 1941 |
| | | | | | 23853-98 | 12285-12330 |

**Built 1936**

| | | | | | | |
|---|---|---|---|---|---|---|
| 115* | •1935/6 | 659 | 8: 48 | YK | 1523 4992 | 12758 12527 |
| | 1935/6 | - | | BHM | 23899-23917 7407-10/31-4 #41049-58 #711, 791 | 12331-49 12708-15 12546-55 12706/7 |

**Built 1937**

| | | | | | | |
|---|---|---|---|---|---|---|
| 115* | 1937 | - | 8: 48 | BHM | 52278-84 24390-24438 | 12637-43 12350-61/ — /2-97 24402 DEA 1942 |

**Built 1938**

| | | | | | | |
|---|---|---|---|---|---|---|
| 115* | 1937 | - | 8: 48 | BHM | 24439-79 | 12398-12423/ — /4-37 |
| | 1938 | - | | | 41151-92 56000-39 | 12556-97 12644-66/ — /7-72, - /12673-81 56023/30 W/O |
| | | - | | | 60654-63 60664 | 12688-97 12698 |
| | special | - | | | | |

**Built 1939**

| | | | | | | |
|---|---|---|---|---|---|---|
| 115* | 1939 | 947 | 8: 48 | YK | 24590-24601 | 12438-49 24594-601 with BS gangways |
| | | | | | 43783-9 56040-3 60774-9 | 12605-11 12682-5 12699-12704 |

The following vehicles were allocated to Scottish Region stock after 1949, and the number prefixed by SC: 12002-12, 12040/1, 12051-5, 12069, 12245/6/8/9-54/6-9, 12268-70, 12286-91/4/8/9/301-4/9, 12334-9, 12350-2/5/6/8/9, 12398/9/402-4/6-12/5-8/24, 12438-41, 12494-7, 12504/5, 12573-8, 12598-601, 12639/41-3, 12716-9/21/2/5

# Locker third: (TG)

## DIAGRAM 24

The East Coast Joint Stock featured locker third and composite coaches, intended to provide passengers undertaking long journeys with accommodation for their luggage in the same vehicle. On each side of the coach body there were double hinged doors for access, and the luggage compartment had its own double doors opening into the corridor.

Diagram 24 was effectively the design for Diagram 23 with the locker compartment taking the place of one passenger compartment and the adjacent lavatory. It was an updated version of the ECJS Diagram 18, built in 1906.

Two of the vehicles were diagrammed in the sets working the 8.25pm Kings Cross-Edinburgh, and its return working. Considerably more use was made of the locker composites in East Coast workings. The three coaches were transferred from East Coast stock under the 1938 CBP which included new locker composites – for the 'Flying Scotsman' and other principal trains – rather than replacement locker thirds.

## LIST OF LOCKER THIRDS (TGs):

| Diag No | CBP | Order No | Compts/ seats | Built | Original number/ changes | 1943 number |
|---|---|---|---|---|---|---|
| **Built 1926** | | | | | | |
| 24 | 1924/5 | 51 | 7: 56 | YK | 1052-4 (750/1/3) | 12111-3 Trans 1939 |

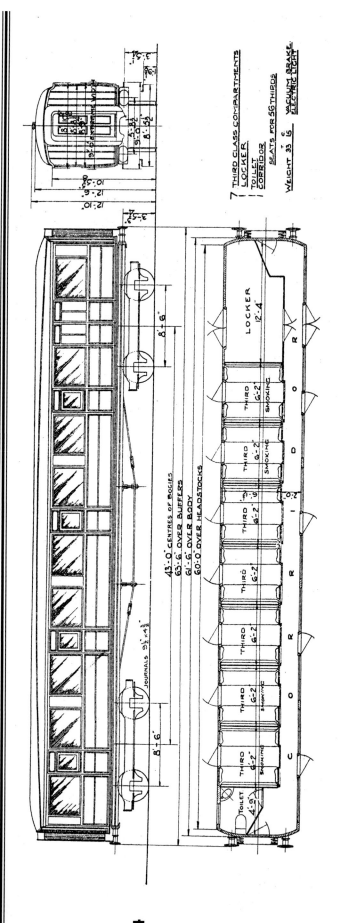

Diagram 24

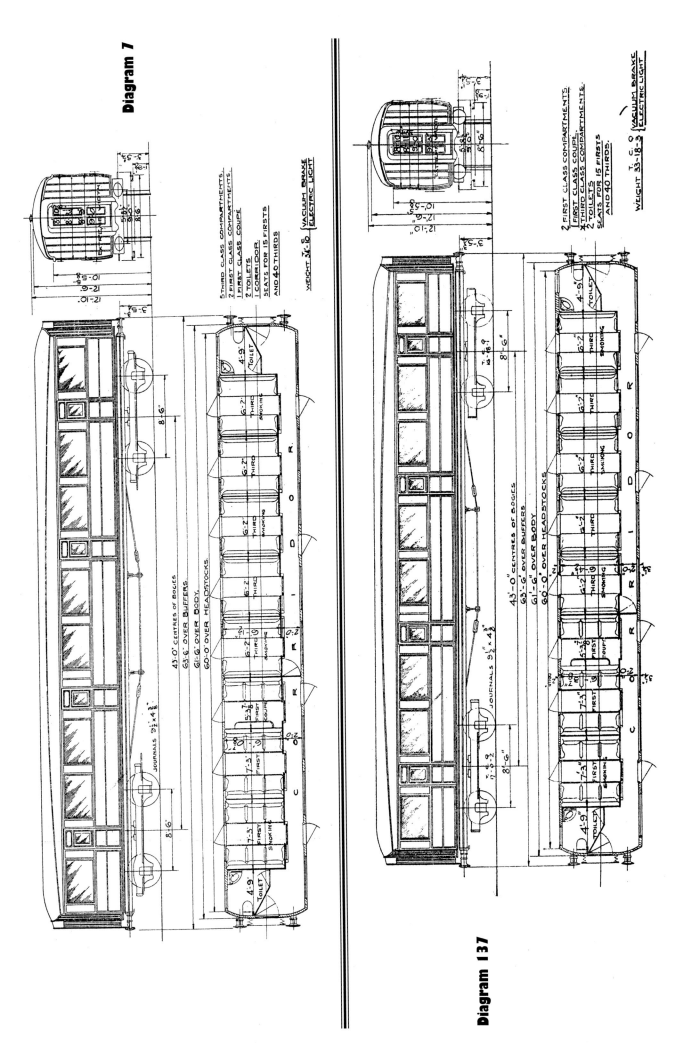

# Vestibuled composites: (CKL) (2½ – 5)

## DIAGRAM 7

One of the 1923 standard 9ft width diagrams, drawing 11999D. There were three types of vestibule composite, some 2½ first + 5 third-class compartments, some 3½ first + four third-class compartments, and some locker composites for East Coast service.

The half – or coupé – compartment – was a consequence of adhering to the standard dimensions of 7ft 3in and 6ft 2in between partitions for first and third-class compartments respectively within a standard body length. The space 'left over' was used for the lavatories, and a coupé compartment. The latter had a shelf fixed to the compartment partition opposite the seats.

The 1924 East Coast vehicles – for the 'Flying Scotsman' and afternoon Scotsmen – had three-a-side seating in the third-class. Later vehicles had four-a-side seating but intermediate armrests were fitted to many of these coaches in the mid-1930s. The East Coast allocation remained in the EC fleet until early in World War 2 and were employed on overnight trains rather than being transferred away, as had been the case with the contemporary thirds.

Nos 7878/9 were built with Pullman gangways and vacuum braking for the Northern Scottish Area, to be used on the Aberdeen-Inverness services, along with thirds to Dia 23. Operating problems seem to have arisen when they were coupled to the BS-gangwayed LMS stock formed in these trains. The Diagram 7 composites, as well as the vestibule thirds, were transferred to the Southern Scottish Area, in exchange for BS gangwayed stock.

No 1063 was experimentally fitted during the mid-1920s with electric heaters in the compartments and an electric water boiler in each lavatory, as part of Gresley's attempts to find new approaches to train heating. The development led to the adoption of pressure ventilation and heating.

## DIAGRAM 137

The 9ft 3in width version of Diagram 7, constructed from 1928 and until 1940. Later vehicles had welded underframes, as well as intermediate armrests, and earlier examples were similarly modified with intermediate armrests, with a resultant reduction in seating capacity. A limited number of composites built from 1934-6 with chrome-plated fittings in the first-class also had chrome-plated corridor fittings in the third-class.

The underframes of Nos 18327/9/39/58 were used by BR for Carflat wagons, employed in carrying new cars and other road vehicles.

# (CKL) (3½ – 4)

## DIAGRAM 6

The alternative type of vestibule composite for general service, also on drawing 11999D.

A batch was built in 1926 for GE section main line use and these coaches were dual fitted at first.

Some of this type were built as late as 1929, after the general introduction of 9ft 3in width stock, for use in the GC section's Marylebone-Manchester and Marylebone-Bradford expresses, along with matching 9ft 3in width brake thirds, thirds, open thirds and restaurant cars.

## DIAGRAM 6A

Diagram 6, but first and second-class. One vehicle – 63798 – was originally shown on the diagram and was built for GE section Continental boat trains, and dual-fitted to work with ex-GER vehicles. No 63799 is also shown on some records as Diagram 6A, and certainly the 1943 renumbering book shows Nos 63798/9 appearing in the list *after* the other GE section vehicles in this batch.

## DIAGRAM 130

The 9ft width version of Diagram 6. These were the usual accompaniment for brake thirds in made-up sets such as those built under the 1929/1930 CBP and later. A number of these coaches were contractor-built.

As with all the standard vestibuled stock, later vehicles featured an extensive use of Rexine for internal finishes. Those built by BRCW and other contractors in 1935 were described as having grey Rexine for the side wall panelling in the first-class, and ivory Rexine on the ceiling, and brown and cream respectively in the third-class. The upholstery was velvet moquette in the first-class, and brown moquette in the third-class.

Later examples also had intermediate armrests and welded underframes.

The underframes of Nos 18178/80/3, 18211/39/45/78 were used by BR for Carflat wagons, employed in carrying new cars and other road vehicles.

## LIST OF VESTIBULE COMPOSITES (CKLs):

| Diag No CBP | Order No | Compts/ seats | Built | Original number/changes | 1943 number |
|---|---|---|---|---|---|
| **Built 1924** | | | | | |
| 7* | 1924/5 45 | 2½/5 :15/30 | YK | 10151-6J (1061-6) [64132-4, 7766/81,1066] | 18027-9/32/3/6 Transfers 1939/40 |
| **Built 1926** | | | | | |
| 6* | 1925/6 65 115 | 3½/4 : 21/32 | YK | 63792-7, 63800 51869/70 | 18008-14  ≠ 18000/1 |
| 6A* | 1925/6 65 | 3½/4 : 21/32 | YK | 63798/9¶ | 18015/6  ≠ |
| ¶ 63799 possibly built on Dia 6 and altered to first/second composite later | | | | | |
| 7* | 1925/6 65 115 | 2½/5 : 15/40 | YK | 7878/9 (32376/7) 51871 151/4/5/6/7/8, 162/3/83 (789, 52046/7, 790, 58100-3, 64131) 7880/1 | 18017/8 18019 18030/20/1/31/22-6  Transfers 1930-9 18034/5 |

Diagram 130 vestibuled composite No 32378 (built York 1930, and 18269 under the 1943 renumbering). In masking the photograph for printing, the works' photographer has excised the roof-mounted ventilators.

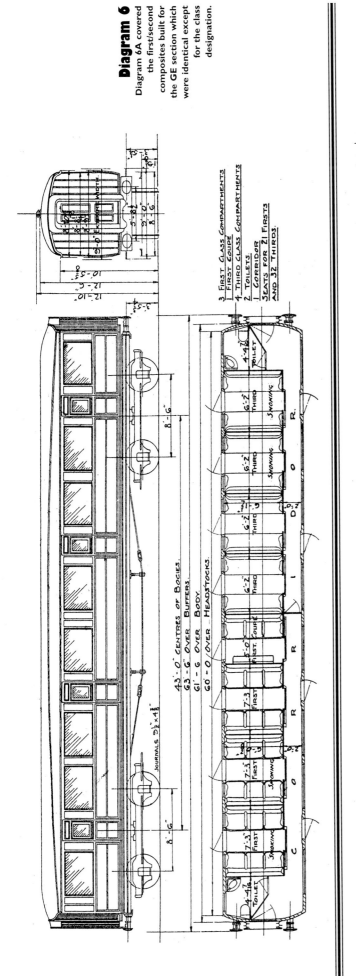

**Diagram 6**

Diagram 6A covered the first/second composites built for the GE section which were identical except for the class designation.

JOURNALS 9½ × 4¾

43'-0" CENTRES OF BOGIES.
63'-6" OVER BUFFERS.
61'-6" OVER BODY.
60'-0" OVER HEADSTOCKS.

3 FIRST CLASS COMPARTMENTS
1 FIRST COUPÉ
4 THIRD CLASS COMPARTMENTS
2 TOILETS
1 CORRIDOR
SEATS FOR 21 FIRSTS
AND 32 THIRDS.

TOILET  SMOKING  THIRD 6'-2"  SMOKING  THIRD 6'-2"  THIRD 6'-2"  THIRD 6'-2"  FIRST COUPÉ 5'-0"  SMOKING  FIRST 7'-3"  SMOKING  FIRST 7'-3"  SMOKING  FIRST 7'-3"  TOILET

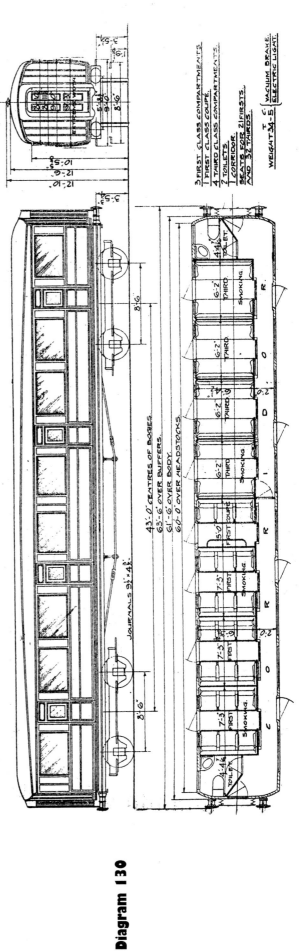

**Diagram 130**

JOURNALS 9½ × 4¾

43'-0" CENTRES OF BOGIES.
63'-6" OVER BUFFERS.
61'-6" OVER BODY.
60'-0" OVER HEADSTOCKS.

3 FIRST CLASS COMPARTMENTS
1 FIRST CLASS COUPÉ
4 THIRD CLASS COMPARTMENTS
7 TOILETS
1 CORRIDOR
SEATS FOR 21 FIRSTS
AND 32 THIRDS.

T.C. { VACUUM BRAKE.
       ELECTRIC LIGHT.
WEIGHT 34-5.

45

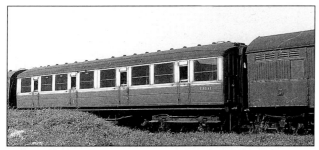

Diagram 6A vestibule composite No E18016E (built York 1926, as 63799). This was a first/second-class composite. Photographed at Stratford in August 1958, it was condemned a couple of months later.

| Diag No CBP | Order No | Compts/ seats | Built | Original number/changes | 1943 number |
|---|---|---|---|---|---|
| **Built 1929** | | | | | |
| 6* | 1928/9 | 254 | YK | 51872-7 | 18002-7 |
| | | 3½/4 : 21/32 | | | |
| **Built 1930** | | | | | |
| 130* | 1929/30 | 317 | YK | 32378/81/90/1, 32429 | 18269/70/2/3/5 |
| | | 3½/4 : 21/32 | | | |
| | 1930/1 | - | CR | 22428-31 | 18166-9 |
| 137* | 1930/1 | 364 | DR | 1259/60 | 18360/1 |
| | | 2½/5 : 15/40 | | | |
| **Built 1931** | | | | | |
| 130* | 1930/1 | - | CR | 32441/2 | 18276/7 |
| | | 3½/4 : 21/32 | | | |
| **Built 1934** | | | | | |
| 130* | 1933 | 492 | YK | 63861-4 32385, 32401/53, 32559-61 | 18302-5 18271/4/8-81 |
| | | 3½/4 : 21/32 | | | |
| **Built 1935** | | | | | |
| 130* | 1934 | 567 | YK | 32275/86, 32306 | 18267/8/– 32306 W/O Castlecary 1937 |
| | | 3½/4 : 21/24 | | | |
| | 1935/6 | - | M-C | 23918-47 | 18170-99 |
| | 1935/6 | - | BHM | 51878-94 | 18282-98 |
| | | | | 7761/70/1 | 18313-5 |
| **Built 1937** | | | | | |
| 130* | 1937 | 773 | YK | 24337-66 | 18200-19/ – /20-8 24357 DEA 1942 |
| | | 3½/4 : 21/24 | | | |
| 137* | 1935/6 | 699 | YK | 42757/8 | 18316/7 |
| | | 2½/5 : 15/30 | | | |
| **Built 1938** | | | | | |
| 130* | 1937 | 773 | YK | 24367-86 | 18229-42/ – /4-8 |
| | | 3½/4 : 21/24 | | | |
| | 1938 | 863 | YK | 64101/2 | 18306/7 |
| 137* | 1937 | 772 | YK | 51896-8 | 18320-2 |
| | | 2½/5 : 15/30 | | | |
| | 1938 | 862 | YK | 64103-18 | 18324-39 |
| **Built 1939** | | | | | |
| 130* | 1938 | 863 | YK | 24510-7 | 18249-56 |
| | | 3½/4 : 21/24 | | | |
| | 1939 | 948 | DR | 24602-11 | 18257-66 |

| | | | | | |
|---|---|---|---|---|---|
| **Built 1940** | | | | | |
| 130* | 1939 | 975 | YK | 58104-6 | 18299-18301 |
| | | 3½/4 : 21/24 | | | |
| | | | YK | 64135-9 | 18308-12 |
| 137* | 1939 | 964 | DR | 42793/4 | 18318/9 |
| | | 2½/5 : 15/30 | DR | 58117/8 | – /18323 58117 DEA 1943 |
| | | | DR | 64140-59 | 18340-4/ – , 18346-59 64145 DEA, u/f reused |

The following vehicles were allocated to Scottish Region stock after 1949, and the number prefixed by SC: 18000, 18002-4, 18017/8/37/46, 18163/7, 18178-80/2/3/93, 18209-12, 18239/41/4/7, 18276/8-80,18316/7, 18324-7, 18355-9

# Locker composites:(CG)

### DIAGRAM 8

The standard 9ft width 1923 design for the East Coast stock, on drawing 11998D, featuring 2½ first-class, 4 third-class compartments and a locker – or luggage – compartment with hinged doors.

These vehicles went into traffic on the 'Flying Scotsman' where they were usually employed as the Kings Cross-Glasgow Queen Street through coach during the winter timetable, and for the relief 'Flying Scotsman' in summer.

Further examples were built in 1926.

With the arrival in 1928 of Nos 1292-4 to Diagram 116, the Diagram 8 vehicles were held as spares for the principal East Coast sets, or used on overnight trains, such as for the Aberdeen portion of the 'Night Scotsman', and the Edinburgh portion of the 10.35pm from Kings Cross.

Some were refurbished in the 1930s and, apart from being retrimmed, received intermediate armrests. Transfers to Areas began in 1938, to the NSA, NEA and GN and GC sections.

### DIAGRAM 116

The 9ft 3in width version of Diagram 8, and similarly built for the East Coast stock only.

When included in East Coast sets Nos 5/6 which were used on the afternoon Scotsmen, Nos 121 and 1294 were wired and were available for at-seat wireless reception from the summer of 1932 until the end of 1935.

Transfers to Areas began in 1938 with the delivery of end-door locker composites to the East Coast fleet.

### LIST OF LOCKER COMPOSITES (CGs):

| Diag No CBP | Order No | Compts/ seats | Built | Original number/changes | 1943 number |
|---|---|---|---|---|---|
| **Built 1924** | | | | | |
| 8* | 1924/5 | 46 | YK | 10168-76] (1067-75) [22253-5, 42800-5] | 18037-45 Transfers 1938 18045 W/O after acc Bounds Green, 1947 |
| | | 2½/4 : 15/24 | | | |

**Diagram 8 locker composite No 186 (built Doncaster 1926, transferred in August 1938 to the NSA as 7763, and 18047 under the 1943 renumbering). Once again, the double doors to the luggage compartment are prominent.**

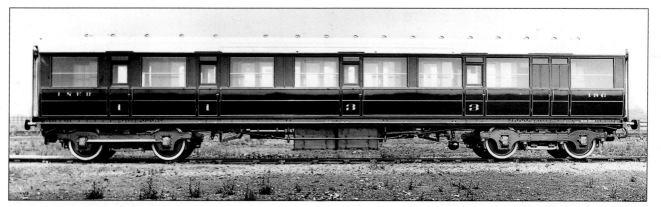

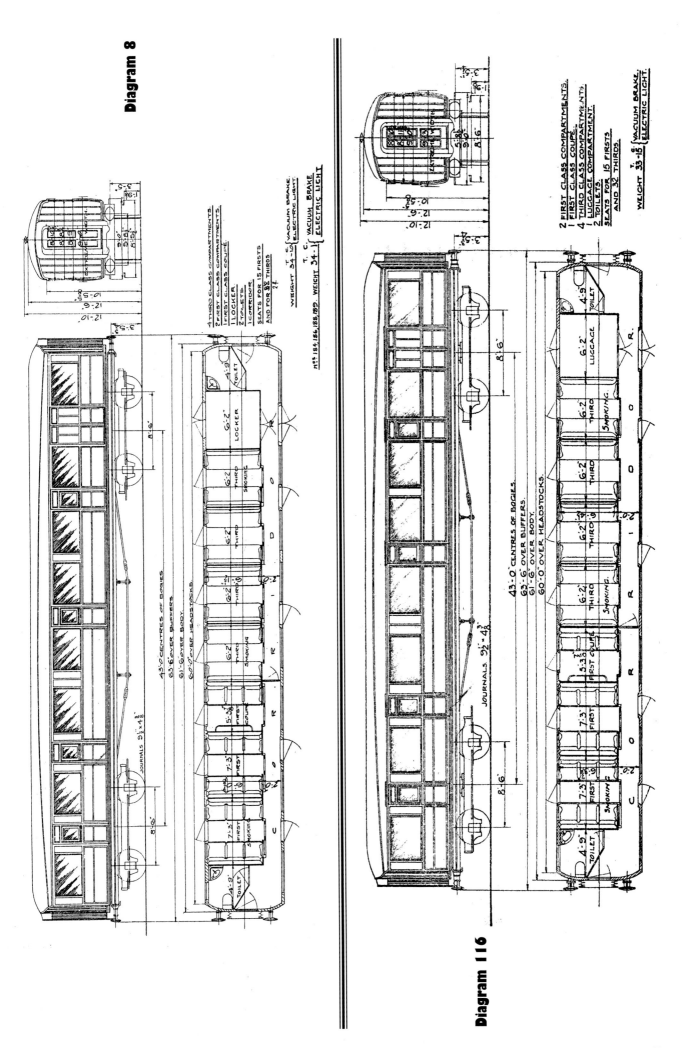

**Diagram 8**

4 THIRD CLASS COMPARTMENTS
2 FIRST CLASS COMPARTMENTS
1 FIRST CLASS COUPÉ.
1 LOCKER
2 TOILETS.
1 CORRIDOR.
SEATS FOR 15 FIRSTS
AND FOR 32 THIRDS
24

nºˢ 184,186,188,189

T.C. {VACUUM BRAKE
ELECTRIC LIGHT.
WEIGHT 34 · 10

T.C. {VACUUM BRAKE
ELECTRIC LIGHT.
WEIGHT 34 · 1

43'- 0" CENTRES OF BOGIES.
63'- 6" OVER BUFFERS.
61'- 6" OVER BODY.
60'- 0" OVER HEADSTOCKS.

JOURNALS 9½" × 4⅞"

**Diagram 116**

2 FIRST CLASS COMPARTMENTS.
1 FIRST CLASS COUPÉ.
4 THIRD CLASS COMPARTMENTS.
1 LUGGAGE COMPARTMENT.
2 TOILETS.
SEATS FOR 15 FIRSTS
AND 32 THIRDS

T.C. {VACUUM BRAKE.
ELECTRIC LIGHT.
WEIGHT 33 · 15

43'- 0" CENTRES OF BOGIES.
63'- 6" OVER BUFFERS.
61'- 6" OVER BODY.
60'- 0" OVER HEADSTOCKS.

JOURNALS 9½" × 4⅞"

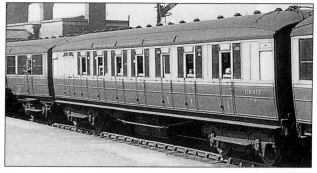

Diagram 116 locker composite No E18165E (built York 1928, and originally No 1294). In BR carmine and cream livery when photographed from the compartment side at Gloucester in August 1956, and marshalled in a cross-country holiday train. The coupé compartment is third from the end, and the double doors are to be seen on the left-hand end in the photograph.

| Diag No CBP | Order No | Compts/ seats | Built | Original number/changes | 1943 number |
|---|---|---|---|---|---|
| **Built 1926** | | | | | |
| 8* | 1925/6 116 | 2½/4 :15/32 | DR | 184/6/8/9 (7762-5) | 18046-9 Transfers 1938/9 |
| **Built 1928** | | | | | |
| 116* | 1927/8 195 | 2½/4 : 15/32 | YK | 1292 (7780), 1293/4 | 18163-5 Transfer 1938 |
| **Built 1929** | | | | | |
| 116* | 1928/9 255 | 2½/4 : 15/32 | YK | 121 (7768) | 18162 Transfer 1939 |

The following vehicles were allocated to Scottish Region stock after 1949, and the number prefixed by SC: 18037/46, 18163

# Vestibuled brake firsts: (BFKL)

One might ask how the LNER managed to require six diagrams of vestibule brake firsts when no more than a score of vehicles was built from 1923. The answer is that the type was specified for particular services and existed in no less than four versions: with two, three, four and five-compartments. New vehicles were specified – the official term was 'justified' – over the years for particular trains, thereby displacing the earlier examples for the special traffic requirements which increased markedly during the late 1930s.

### DIAGRAM 30

The 9ft width, three-compartment right-handed design, ie with the brake compartment to the right when looking at the plan of the coach. This was one of the 1923 standard types, to Drawing 12009D.

One only was built, for the Newcastle-Swansea set ordered under the 1924 CBP.

### DIAGRAM 29

The 9ft 3in width, five-compartment left-handed design, to a drawing produced by Doncaster.

Three were planned for the 1926 CBP but, according to the Traffic Committee meeting of 1 July 1926, 'in view of present circumstances (ie the General Strike) ... were assigned to the 1927 Building Programme ... '

Trains making use of these vehicles were the 1.40pm and 5.45pm Kings Cross-York/Harrogate and West Riding. Nos 4203/4/6 were among the first new standard stock to the have 'improved atmospheric pressure heaters', adopted following complaints of inadequate heating with the previous type. Nos 4204/6 were used on the 'Northern Belle' luxury cruise train during the mid/late 1930s.

### DIAGRAM 136

The 9ft 3in width version of Diagram 30 and, surprisingly for 1928, also bereft of a guard's ducket.

Headrests and lift-up type armrests fitted to both vehicles in the mid-1930s.

### DIAGRAM 142

A two-compartment design built in 1930 for the new train set for the 9am Leeds-Glasgow and 4pm return expresses. This diagram had a guard's ducket.

The 1938-built vehicle was also built for the Leeds-Glasgow and return working.

### DIAGRAM 149

A four-compartment vehicle, first built for use in the Harrogate portion of the 5.45pm Kings Cross-West Riding.

The 1937-built GN section vehicles were for the Kings Cross-Scarborough through coaches, and the 1938 coaches for the Leeds Flyer.

The three NEA examples dating from 1939 were for use on through workings from Newcastle/Hull-Liverpool and return, and so had BS gangways with Pullman adaptors fitted.

### DIAGRAM 300

A updated form of Diagram 136 with very minor changes, notably the provision of a guard's ducket, and oak flooring extending the width of the vehicle at the double-door openings.

These four 1939-built vehicles were for use in the Harrogate portions of the 1.40pm and 5.50pm from Kings Cross, and the Hull section of the 7.15pm from Kings Cross.

Diagram 149 vestibuled brake first No 24489 (built York 1939, and 11068 under the 1943 renumbering). York photograph dated May 1939. This was one of several vehicles to Order Nos 858/860 to be built with BS vestibules (with adaptors) for use on cross-country workings to/from the LMS, principally Hull and Newcastle-Liverpool expresses.

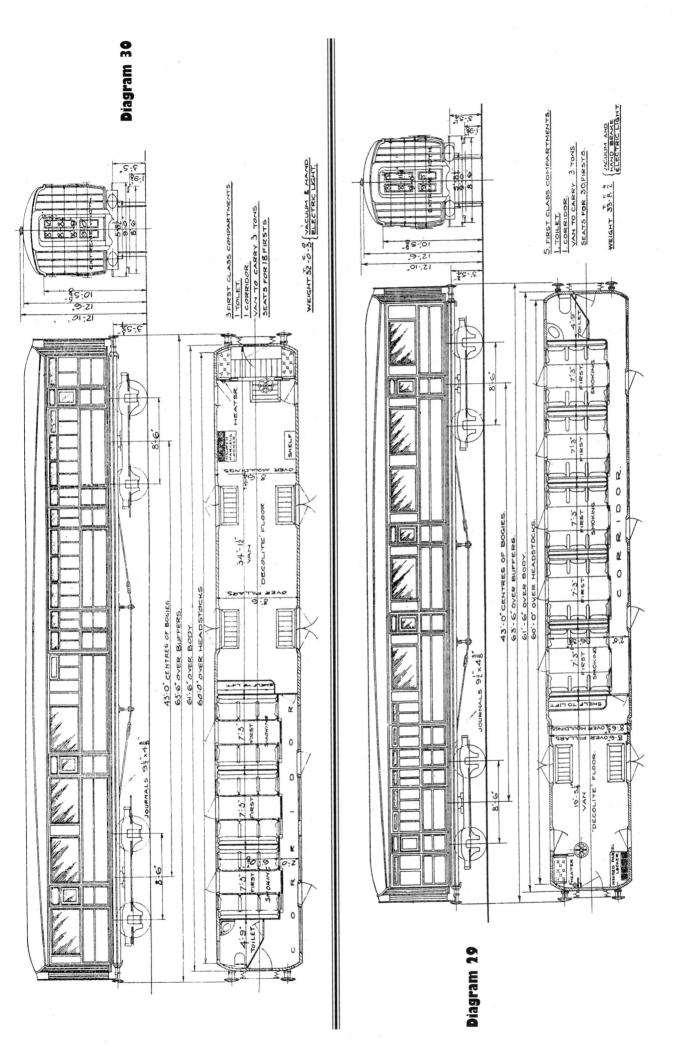

**Diagram 30**

3 FIRST CLASS COMPARTMENTS,
1 TOILET,
1 CORRIDOR,
VAN TO CARRY 3 TONS.
SEATS FOR 18 FIRSTS.

WEIGHT 32·0·3 $\left\{ \begin{array}{l} \text{VACUUM & HAND} \\ \text{ELECTRIC LIGHT.} \end{array} \right.$

43'·0" CENTRES OF BOGIES.
63'·6" OVER BUFFERS.
61'·6" OVER BODY.
60'·0" OVER HEADSTOCKS.

JOURNALS 9½" × 4⅝"

**Diagram 29**

5 FIRST CLASS COMPARTMENTS,
1 TOILET,
1 CORRIDOR,
VAN TO CARRY 3 TONS.
SEATS FOR 30 FIRSTS.

WEIGHT 33·8·2 $\left\{ \begin{array}{l} \text{VACUUM AND} \\ \text{HAND BRAKE} \\ \text{ELECTRIC LIGHT.} \end{array} \right.$

43'·0" CENTRES OF BOGIES.
63'·6" OVER BUFFERS.
61'·6" OVER BODY.
60'·0" OVER HEADSTOCKS.

JOURNALS 9½" × 4⅜"

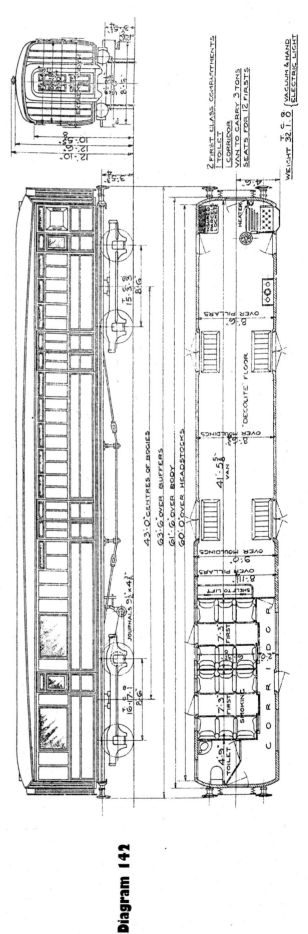

**Diagram 136**

3 FIRST CLASS COMPARTMENTS.
TOILET
CORRIDOR.
VAN TO CARRY 3 TONS
SEATS FOR 18 FIRSTS.

WEIGHT 32.7.3 { T.C.G. VACUUM & HAND.
ELECTRIC LIGHT.

43'.0" CENTRES OF BOGIES.
63'.6" OVER BUFFERS.
61'.6" OVER BODY.
60'.0" OVER HEADSTOCKS.

JOURNALS 9½"×4⅜"

34'.½" VAN.

DECOLITE FLOOR.

OVER MOULDINGS.

8'.6" OVER PILLARS.

7'.3" FIRST SMOKING
7'.3" FIRST SMOKING
7'.3" FIRST SMOKING

CORRIDOR

4'.9" TOILET

SHELF TO LIFT

**Diagram 142**

2 FIRST CLASS COMPARTMENTS.
TOILET
CORRIDOR
VAN TO CARRY 3 TONS
SEATS FOR 12 FIRSTS

WEIGHT 32.1.0 { T.C.G. VACUUM & HAND
ELECTRIC LIGHT

43'.0" CENTRES OF BOGIES.
63'.6" OVER BUFFERS.
61'.6" OVER BODY.
60'.0" OVER HEADSTOCKS.

JOURNALS 9½"×4⅜"

41'.5⅝" VAN.

OVER "DECOLITE" FLOOR

8'.6" OVER PILLARS

OVER MOULDINGS

9'.0" OVER MOULDINGS
8'.11" OVER PILLARS

SHELF TO LIFT

7'.3" FIRST
7'.3" FIRST
7'.3" FIRST SMOKING

CORRIDOR

4'.9" TOILET

50

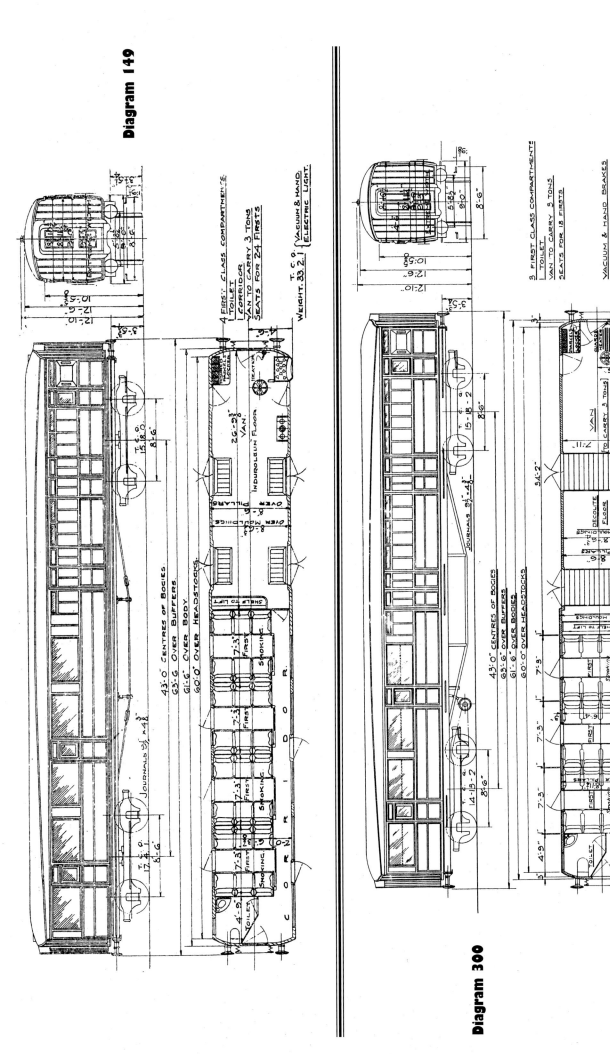

**Diagram 149**

43'·0" CENTRES OF BOGIES.
63'·6" OVER BUFFERS.
61'·6" OVER BODY.
60'·0" OVER HEADSTOCKS.

4 FIRST CLASS COMPARTMENTS
1 TOILET
1 CORRIDOR
VAN TO CARRY 3 TONS
SEATS FOR 24 FIRSTS

WEIGHT. 33.2.1 {VACUUM & HAND.
(ELECTRIC LIGHT.

**Diagram 300**

43'·0" CENTRES OF BOGIES.
63'·6" OVER BUFFERS.
61'·6" OVER BODIES.
60'·0" OVER HEADSTOCKS.

3 FIRST CLASS COMPARTMENTS
1 TOILET
VAN TO CARRY 3 TONS
SEATS FOR 18 FIRSTS

VACUUM & HAND BRAKES
ELECTRIC LIGHT
WEIGHT 30·12·0

A down at heel brake first on Diagram 29, by now BR's E11042E. This had been No 4203, built at Doncaster in 1927. This shows all too well the scabrous effect of worn BR carmine and cream livery on a Gresley coach. Photographed at Stratford in May 1956.

## LIST OF BRAKE FIRSTS (BFKLs):

| Diag No | CBP | Order No | Compts/ seats | Built | Original number/ changes | 1943 number | |
|---------|-----|----------|---------------|-------|------------------------|-------------|---|
| **Built 1925** | | | | | | | |
| 30 | 1924/5 | 69 | 3: 18 | DR | 10010Y (21130) | 11045 | |
| **Built 1927** | | | | | | | |
| 29* | 1926/7 | 152 | 5: 30 | DR | 4203/4/6 | 11042-4 | |
| **Built 1928** | | | | | | | |
| 136 | 1927/8 | 191 | 3: 18 | YK | 4162/3 | 11046/7 | |
| **Built 1930** | | | | | | | |
| 142* | 1930/1 | 379 | 4: 24 | DR | 22611 | 11062 | Leeds-Glasgow set |
| **Built 1931** | | | | | | | |
| 149* | 1930/1 | 378 | 4: 24 | DR | 4110 | 11069 | |
| **Built 1937** | | | | | | | |
| 149* | 1936 | 712# | 4: 24 | YK | #4164/5 | 11070/1 | |

To ambulance trains WW2, returned to service as brake firsts.

| Diag No | CBP | Order No | Compts/ seats | Built | Original number/ changes | 1943 number | |
|---------|-----|----------|---------------|-------|------------------------|-------------|---|
| **Built 1938** | | | | | | | |
| 142* | 1937 | 768 | 2: 12 | YK | 24290 | 11063 | |
| 149* | 1937 | 769 | 4: 24 | YK | 4166/7 | 11072/3 | |
| **Built 1939** | | | | | | | |
| 149* | 1938 | 858 | 4: 24 | YK | 24487-9 | 11066-8 | BS gangways |
| 300 | 1939 | 958 | 3: 18 | DR | 4168-71 55230 | 11137-40 11141 | |

4167 (above) and 24487 converted for use in SHAEF 'Rapier' train, WW2 and returned to service as brake firsts.

# Vestibuled brake seconds:(BSKL)

## DIAGRAM 35

One only, built in 1925 for the Hook of Holland Continental boat train. Apart from being second-class, it was identical to the four-compartment brake third design on Diagram 38.

| Diag No | CBP | Order No | Compts/ seats | Built | Original number/ changes | 1943 number |
|---------|-----|----------|---------------|-------|------------------------|-------------|
| 35 | 1924/5 | 60 | 4: 24 | SF | 10018E (62514) | - |

# Brake open third: (BTO)

Built for excursion train use.

## DIAGRAM 135

One saloon, with seats for 32 passengers, 24 when dining.

Just two examples, built in 1930 for the NEA and to be formed in a set with Diagram 27A open thirds, having the similar shallow, metal-framed window ventilators, and also the conventional high-backed seats.

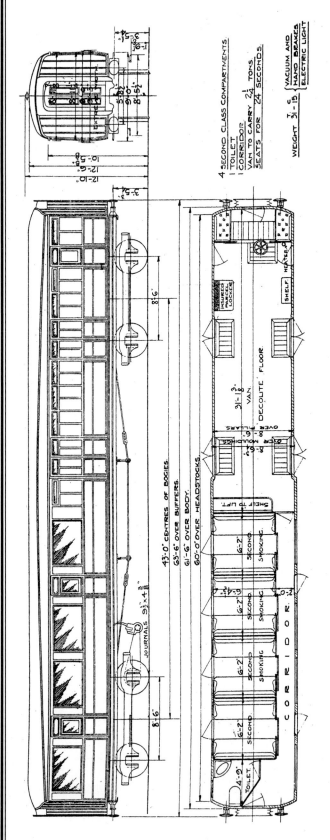

**Diagram 35**

4 SECOND CLASS COMPARTMENTS
1 TOILET
1 CORRIDOR
VAN TO CARRY 2¼ TONS
SEATS FOR 24 SECONDS
WEIGHT 31-15 { VACUUM AND HAND BRAKES ELECTRIC LIGHT

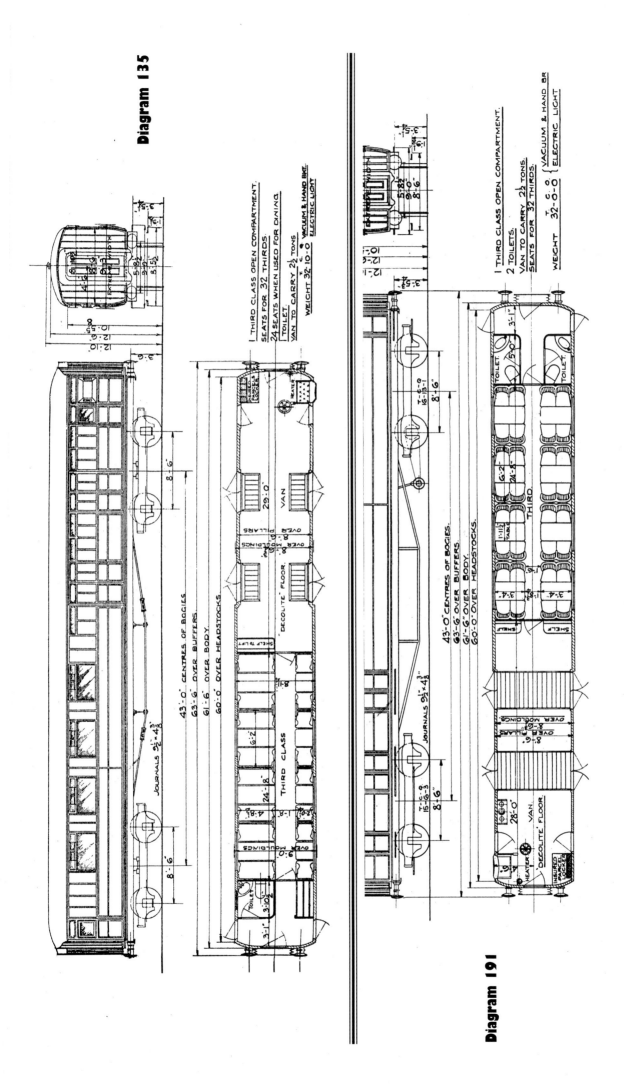

**Diagram 135**

1 THIRD CLASS OPEN COMPARTMENT.
SEATS FOR 32 THIRDS.
24 SEATS WHEN USED FOR DINING.
TOILET.
VAN TO CARRY 2½ TONS.
WEIGHT 32·10·0 { VACUUM & HAND BRE.
ELECTRIC LIGHT

43'·0" CENTRES OF BOGIES.
63'·6" OVER BUFFERS.
61'·6" OVER BODY.
60'·0" OVER HEADSTOCKS.

JOURNALS 9½"×4¾"

29'·0" VAN

THIRD CLASS

24'·8"

DECOLITE FLOOR.

**Diagram 191**

1 THIRD CLASS OPEN COMPARTMENT.
2 TOILETS.
VAN TO CARRY 2½ TONS.
SEATS FOR 32 THIRDS.
WEIGHT 32·0·0 { VACUUM & HAND BR
ELECTRIC LIGHT

43'·0" CENTRES OF BOGIES.
63'·6" OVER BUFFERS.
61'·6" OVER BODY.
60'·0" OVER HEADSTOCKS.

JOURNALS 9½"×4¾"

THIRD.

28'·0" VAN.

DECOLITE' FLOOR

53

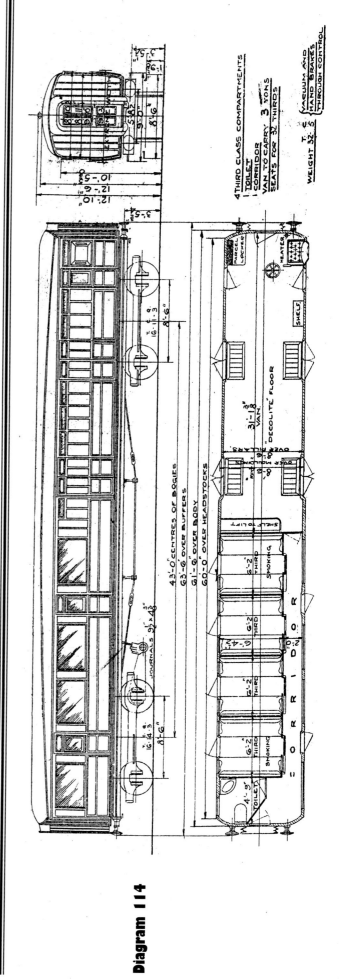

**Diagram 39**

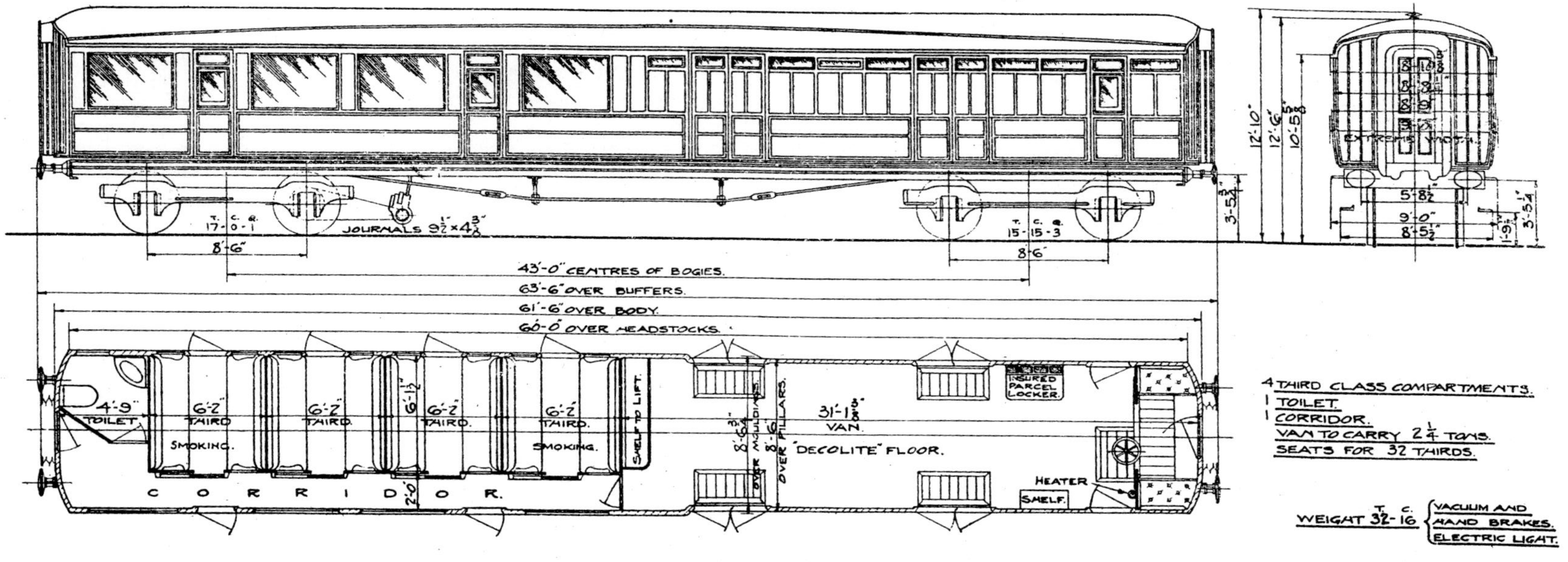

4 THIRD CLASS COMPARTMENTS.
1 TOILET
1 CORRIDOR
VAN TO CARRY 2½ TONS
SEATS FOR 32 THIRDS

T.C. VACUUM AND
HAND BRAKES
WEIGHT 32·16 ELECTRIC LIGHT.

43'-0" CENTRES OF BOGIES.
63'-6" OVER BUFFERS
61'-6" OVER BODY
60'-0" OVER HEADSTOCKS

31'-1⅝" VAN.
OVER PILLARS.

DECOLITE FLOOR.

CORRIDOR

THIRD SMOKING.

**Diagram 114**

4 THIRD CLASS COMPARTMENTS
1 TOILET
1 CORRIDOR
VAN TO CARRY 3 TONS
SEATS FOR 32 THIRDS

T.C. VACUUM AND
HAND BRAKES
WEIGHT 32·5 THROUGH CONTROL

43'-0" CENTRES OF BOGIES
63'-6" OVER BUFFERS
61'-6" OVER BODY
60'-0" OVER HEADSTOCKS

31'-1⅝" VAN.
DECOLITE FLOOR.

CORRIDOR

THIRD SMOKING.

**Diagram 324**

**Diagram 37**

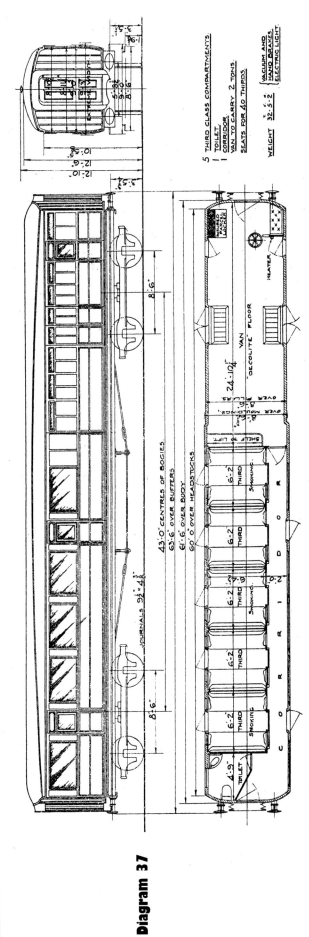

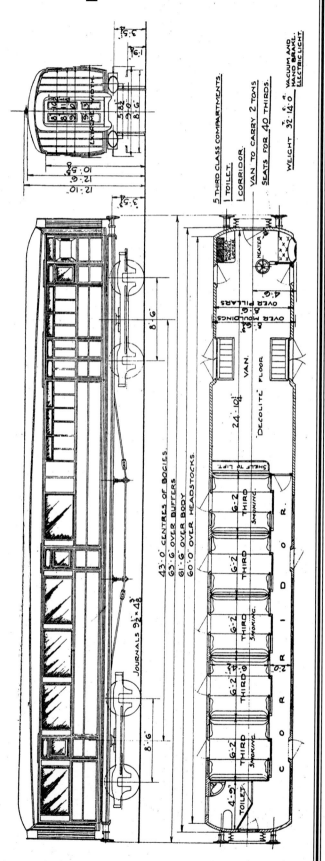

Diagram 37A

## (BTKL) (5)

### DIAGRAM 37

A 9ft 3in width design, and without guard's ducket. Some were later fitted with intermediate armrests.

### DIAGRAM 37A

The standard 9ft 3in width version, but with the brake/luggage compartment tapering to a 8ft 6in width onwards from the luggage compartment double doors, instead of for the full length of the brake/luggage compartment as was the case with Diagram 37.

Later vehicles with welded underframes and intermediate armrests.

A number were converted for use in ambulance trains during World War 2.

## (BTKL) (6)

### DIAGRAM 36

Favoured by the GC section and NSA only, and of 9ft width.

No 5762 was badly damaged in the Canfield Tunnel (London) collision of 1933, and was replaced by a new vehicle with the same number on Diagram 36.

### DIAGRAM 178

The 9ft 3in width counterpart of Diagram 36, and largely built – in two batches – for the GC section.

The underframes of Nos 16013/8/24/6/64/82/6, 16126/48/94, 16273/85/90, 16348/57, 16495, 16507 were used by BR for Carflat wagons, employed in carrying new cars and other road vehicles.

### LIST OF BRAKE THIRDS (BTKLs):

| Diag No CBP | Order No | Compts/ seats | Built | Original number/ changes | 1943 number | |
|---|---|---|---|---|---|---|
| **Built 1924** | | | | | | |
| 40* | 1924/5 | 44 | 3: 18 | YK | 10118 – 23J (1055-60) | 16166-71 |
| | | | | | [52094-9] | Transfers 1935/6 |
| **Built 1925** | | | | | | |
| 40* | 1924/5 | 70 | 3: 24 | DR | 10132-4C (5763-5) | 16160-2 | RH |
| | | | | | 5243 | 16159 | |
| | | | | | 10136Y (1112) [4935] | 16157 | ≠ |
| | | | | | 2223/4, 2243 [1113], then [4939] | 16137/8/58 ≠ | |
| | | | | | 62537-40 62539 W/O Sleaford N Jct, 1937 | 16173/4/– /5 ≠ | |
| | | | | | 10124-31N (4740/53/4/7, 4758/64/79/82) | 16148-55 | |
| 38 | 1924/5 | 59 | 4: 32 | SF | 62515 (4930) | 16122 | Continental boat set |
| | | 74 | 4: 24 | SF | 10149J (2243) | 16120 | |
| | | | | | 10150J (1113) [22058] | 16121 | |

The transfers of Dia 40 10136Y and 2243 to East Coast stock took place in 1926, as exchanges for Dia 38 10149 and 1113.

| Diag No CBP | Order No | Compts/ seats | Built | Original number/ changes | 1943 number | |
|---|---|---|---|---|---|---|
| **Built 1926** | | | | | | |
| 36* | 1925/6 | 114 | 6: 48 | DR | 5750-2/62, 7631/2 | 16000-2/ – /4/5 5762 W/O 1933 |
| 39 | 1925/6 | 112 | 4: 32 | YK | 4788/90/3/5, 4800/13/5 5741-9 | 16123-9 16130/– /1-4/– /5/6 |
| 40* | 1924/5 | 70 | 3: 24 | DR | 62541/2 22154, 22202 | 16176/7 ≠ 16139/40 |
| | 1925/6 | 112 | | YK | 112-5/38-40, 142/3/5-8/50 | 16163/4/78/9 16172/41/65/42-7, 16156 |
| | | | | | (52044/5, 755/63, 52100, 3934, 52091, 3938/95, 31003, 31198/9, 31201, 4934) | |

Diagram 37A five-compartment brake GE16099E (No 62789, built Doncaster 1938) saw wartime service in an ambulance train. Photographed at Cambridge in May 1964. The 'GE' regional prefix was applied in the early 1960s to stock coming under the Line Manager, Great Eastern of the Eastern Region.

## Built 1927

| 37* | 1926/7 | 153 | 5: 40 | DR | 4706-8/19 | 16006-8/— |
4719 DEA Channelsea 1943

## Built 1928

| 40A* | 1927/8 | 193 | 3: 24 | DR | 1262-4 | 16194/7/8 |
(4940, 767/8) Transferred 1937, 1939/39

## Built 1929

| 37A* | 1929/30 | 313 | 5: 40 | DR | 41346-50 | 16064-8 |
| 40A* | 1928/9 | 251 | 3: 24 | YK | 3986/7/9-91 | 16189-93 |
120 (31197) — W/O Aberdeen 1938

| 114* | 1928/9 | 249 | 4: 32 | YK | 41351-4 | 16363-6 |
41351-4 to ambulance trains WW2 and returned to service as brake thirds

52201-12  16371-82
16373 to bullion van on Dia 362, 1949

52201-4/6-11 to ambulance trains WW2 and returned to service as brake thirds

## Built 1930

| 114* | 1930/1 | 314 | 4: 32 | YK | 21059 | 16244 |
3293, 3310/25, 16314-21/ — /3
3337/50/4/7/64,
3370/2  3370 W/O Carlisle 1931

| | | 359 | | YK | 1107/9 | 16370/46 |
(52093, 3993) Trans 1935

| | | 384 | | | 4941-7 | 16351-7 |
4941-3 to ambulance trains WW2 and returned to service as brake thirds

21863, 22226, 16245-7
22383

| | | - | | BHM | 22384, 22654 | 16248/9 |
3485/9, 3607/8, 16326-31/ — /3,
3615/8/60/2/6/9, 16334-7
3673/82

| 40A* | 1929/30 | 315 | 3: 24 | YK | 3379/80 | 16187/8 |
| | 1930/1 | - | | BHM | 22364-8 | 16182-6 |
| | | | | | 5773/4 | 16195/6 |

## Built 1931

| 114* | 1930/1 | 384 | 4: 32 | YK | 4948-52 | 16358-62 |
| | | | | | 3406/35 | 16324/5 |
| | | | | | 1108/60/1 | 16396-8 |
| | | 424 | | | 3370 | 16322 Accident replacement |

## Built 1932

| 114* | 1931/2 | 440 | 4: 32 | DK | 4936/8 | 16349/50 |
| | | | | | 3930/3 | 16338/9 |

## Built 1933

| 36* | - | 517 | 6: 36 | DK | 5762 | 16003 Accident replacement |
| 114* | 1933 | 491 | 4: 32 | DK | 3940/63/5-8 | 16340-5 |
| 174* | 1933 | 490 | 3: 24 | DR | 3969/88 | 16478/9 |
| | | | | | 62651-4 | 16480/1/ — /3 |
| | | | | | 1265 (62847) | 16493 Transferred 1941 |

## Built 1934

| 37A* | 1933 | 512 | 5: 30 | YK | 52213-8 | 16089-94 |
| 40A* | 1933 | 490 | 3: 18 | DR | 22180/1 | 16180/1 BS gangways |
| 114* | 1933 | 510 | 4: 24 | DR | 52233-42 | 16383-92 |
| | 1934 | 564 | | YK | 1228-30/2/6 | 16399-16403 |
| | | | | | 1231 (24675) | 16313 Trans 1941 |
| 174* | 1934 | 562 | 3: 18 | YK | 1000-5/44 | 16496-9/4/5, |
(7556-9, 764/6, 16500
7560)  Trans 1938/9

| 178* | 1933 | 511 | 6: 36 | DK | 52219-32 | 16505-18 |

## Built 1935

| 174* | 1934 | 562 | 3: 18 | YK | 1045-9 | 16501/2, |
(7561, 1046, 16491/ — /2 Trans 1940/1
62844-6)  62845 DEA Norwich, 1942

## Built 1936

| 37A* | 1935/6 | 663 | 5: 30 | YK | 24022-66 | 16009-34/ — /5-52 |
| | | | | | 41355-8 | 16069-72 |
| 114* | 1935/6 | 650 | 4: 24 | YK | 62750 (62516) | 16726 |

Converted on Dia 292 as brake second for 'Hook Continental' set, 1938 and renumbered.

| | | 694 | | YK | 41359/60 | 16367/8 |
| | | | | | 7584/5 | 16394/5 |
16394 W/O Doncaster 1947

| 178* | •1935/6 | 658 | 6: 36 | YK | 1539 | 16527 |
| | 1935/6 | 658 | | | 41361/2 | 16503/4 |

## Built 1937

| 37A* | 1937 | 770 | 5: 30 | YK | 41062-7 | 16058-63 |
| 114* | 1937 | 771 | 4: 24 | YK | 24291-24336 | 16250/1/ — /2-94 |
24293 DEA Middlesbrough
1942 — u/f reused on 16854

| | | | | | 31214/5 | 16347/8 |

## Built 1938

| 37A* | 1938 | 837 | 5: 30 | DR | 41381-7 | 16073-9 |
16073 DEA Wood Green 1945,
u/f re-used on 70635

| | | | | | 62785-98 | 16095-16108 |

62786/9/91/2/3/8 to ambulance trains WW2, returned to service as brake thirds.

## Built 1939

| 37A* | 1938 | 837 | 5: 30 | DR | 24480-4 | 16053-7 |
| | | | | | 41388-90 | 16080-2 |
| | 1939 | 952 | | YK | 41391-6 | 16083-8 |
16087 W/O Tollerton, 1954

| | | | | | 62831-6 | 16109-14 |
| 114* | 1938 | 860 | 4: 24 | YK | 24490-24509 | 16295/ — /6-16309, |
— /16310-2
24495/9 BS gangways
24491, 24506 DEA

| | 1939 | 954 | | YK | 43151 | 16369 |
| | | | | | 57458/9 | 16393/ — |
| 174* | 1939 | 960 | 3: 18 | DR | 24662 | 16477 |
| | | | | | 62837-62843 | 16484-16490 |

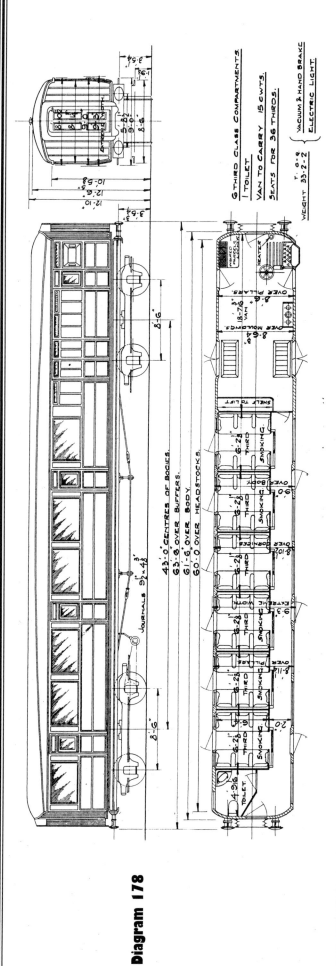

## Diagram 36

6 THIRD CLASS COMPARTMENTS.
1 TOILET.
VAN TO CARRY 15 CWTS.
SEATS FOR 48 THIRDS.

WEIGHT T. 5. 2. 2. {VACUUM & HAND BRAKES
ELECTRIC LIGHT.

43'-0" CENTRES OF BOGIES.
63'-6" OVER BUFFERS.
61'-6" OVER BODY.
60'-0" OVER HEADSTOCKS.

JOURNALS 9½" × 4⅞"

## Diagram 178

6 THIRD CLASS COMPARTMENTS.
1 TOILET.
VAN TO CARRY 15 CWTS.
SEATS FOR 36 THIRDS.

WEIGHT 33. 2. 2. {T. 0. 9.
VACUUM & HAND BRAKE
ELECTRIC LIGHT.

43'-0" CENTRES OF BOGIES.
63'-6" OVER BUFFERS.
61'-6" OVER BODY.
60'-0" OVER HEADSTOCKS.

JOURNALS 9½" × 4⅞"

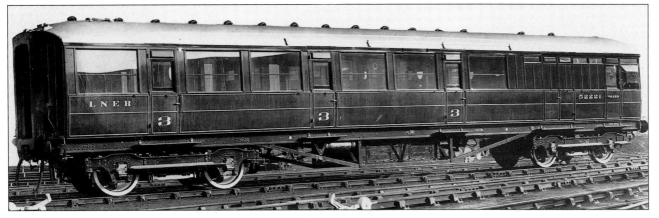

| Diag No | CBP | Order No | Compts/ seats | Built | Original number/ changes | 1943 number |
|---------|-----|----------|---------------|-------|--------------------------|-------------|
| **Built 1940** | | | | | | |
| 178* | 1939 | 953 | 6: 36 | YK | 57450-7 | 16519-21/ − /3-6 |
| **Built 1941** | | | | | | |
| 37A* | 1940 | 1008 | 5: 40 | YK | 62848-62852 | 16115-9 |

The following vehicles were allocated to Scottish Region stock after 1949, and the number prefixed by SC: 16000/6/7, 16009/11/3/6-20/4/6/31/3/4/8, 16058/9, 16064/6, 16093/5/7/8/100/1/4-6, 16109-13/8, 16120-6, 16139-43, 16148-52, 16170/1, 16186-92/4/7/8, 16254/5/7/60/2/70/2/3/5/7/8/90, 16306/11/4/6/7/20/1, 16329-31, 16336, 16340/4/5, 16356-8/61/2/9, 16382/3/7, 16393/7, 16476/7/80/6/9, 16491-3/5-7, 16501/6-9, 16519

# Vestibuled brake composites:(BCKL)

These were generally built for through coach workings to destinations not served by direct trains. The Southern Scottish Area, for instance, had a variety of internal workings such as Glasgow-Mallaig, as well as inter-Area services such as Glasgow-York/Scarborough, and the through portion from Aberdeen/Edinburgh-St Pancras which was conveyed from Carlisle on an LMS express.

Another use was referred to in the LNER general instructions relating to the distribution, equipment and cleaning of rolling stock: 'Brake composites for the use of officers in charge of troops must have throughout corridors.'

Various combinations of first and third-class compartments accounted for the number of Diagrams that were produced. Each design had two lavatories, one for the first-class, the other for third-class.

*Right: **This from 'on high' three-quarters photograph shows the compartment side of a Diagram 175 brake composite, BR E10110E. This coach had been built by York as 42886 in 1939, and had not long been outshopped in maroon livery when seen at Thorne North in June 1957.***

*Below: **Diagram 134 vestibuled brake composite No 495 (built Dukinfield 1932, and 10049 under the 1943 renumbering).***

The Gorton/Dukinfield cameraman gives us a good study of No 52221, a Diagram 178 six-compartment brake third built at Dukinfield in 1934, and numbered 16507 under the 1943 scheme.

# (BCKL) (2 − 4)

### DIAGRAM 31
The 9ft width type, without guard's ducket.
Built for the GC section.

### DIAGRAM 134
The 9ft 3in width type, with guard's ducket.
The NEA vehicles dating from 1930 were built to provide the through Sheffield-Glasgow coach which was conveyed on the Leeds-Glasgow train. This type was also built for the GE section for through workings to other Areas, such as Harwich Town-Glasgow.

### DIAGRAM 175
A 9ft 3in width type, very similar to Diagram 134 but with angle-iron trussing and slight changes in compartment partition-to-partition measurements. The most numerous type of brake composite.

Those delivered immediately before and just after the outbreak of World War 2 included vehicles for Leeds-Whitby; Newcastle-Sheffield/Southampton/Bournemouth workings (NEA); and Bridlington/Harrogate/Hull/Scarborough through coaches from Kings Cross, (GN section).

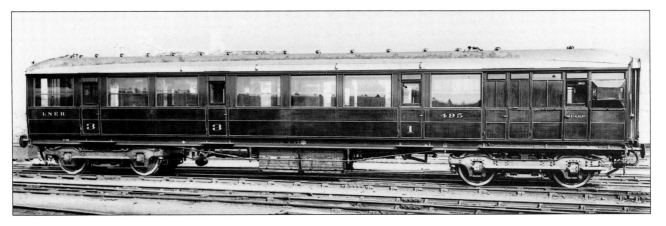

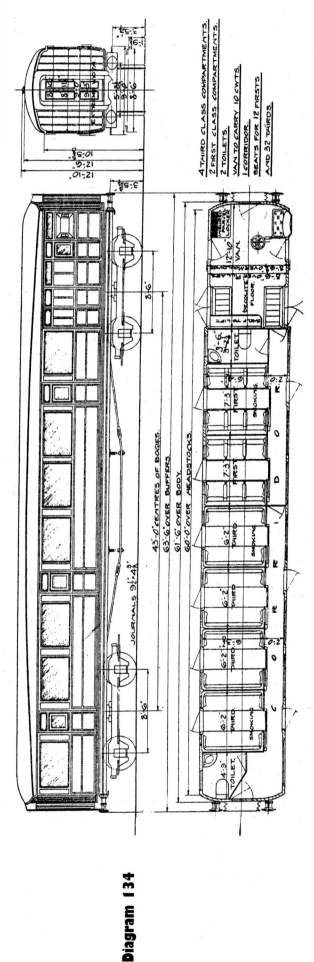

**Diagram 31**

4 THIRD CLASS COMPARTMENTS.
2 FIRST CLASS COMPARTMENTS
2 TOILETS.
VAN TO CARRY 10 CWTS.
1 CORRIDOR.
SEATS FOR 12 FIRSTS
AND 32 THIRDS.

**Diagram 134**

4 THIRD CLASS COMPARTMENTS.
2 FIRST CLASS COMPARTMENTS.
2 TOILETS.
VAN TO CARRY 10 CWTS.
1 CORRIDOR.
SEATS FOR 12 FIRSTS
AND 32 THIRDS.

## Diagram 175

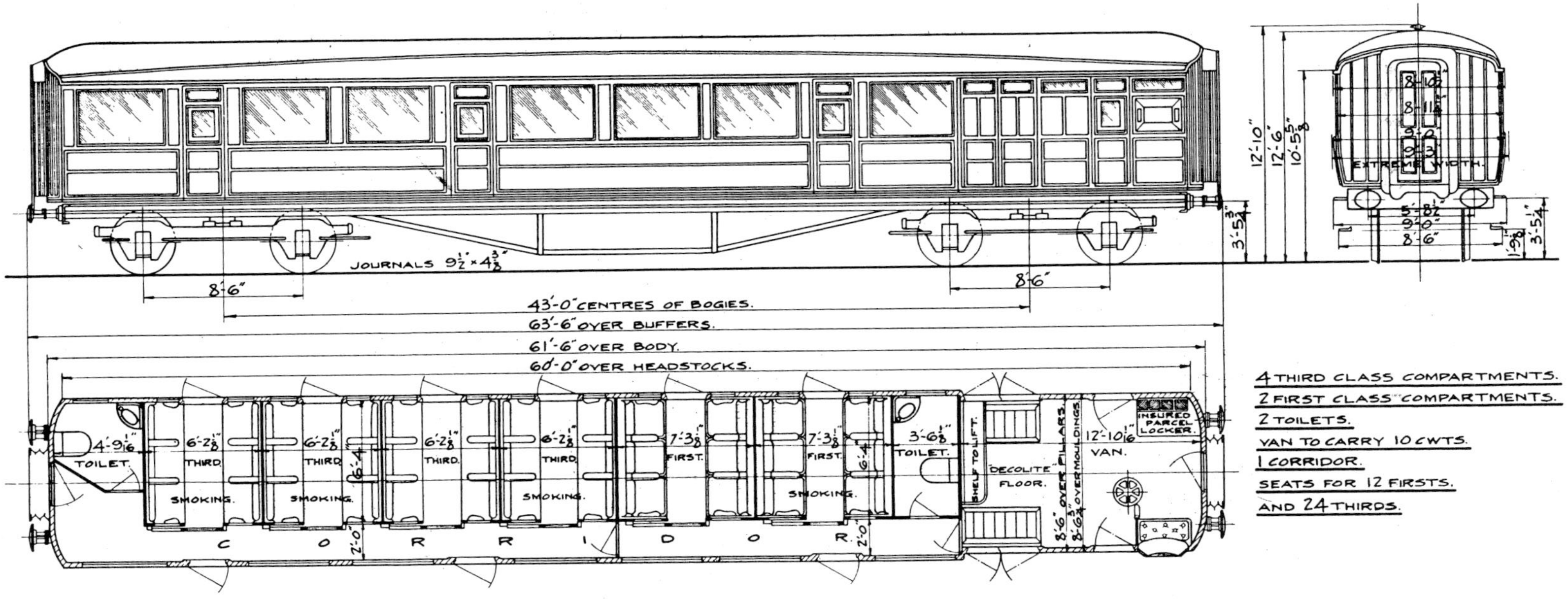
JOURNALS 9½" × 4⅜"
8'6"
8'6"
43'-0" CENTRES OF BOGIES.
63'-6" OVER BUFFERS.
61'-6" OVER BODY.
60'-0" OVER HEADSTOCKS.
12'-10"
12'-6"
10'-5⅝"
3'-5¾"
3'-5¼"
EXTREME WIDTH.
5'-8½"
9'-0"
8'-6"
TOILET.
THIRD
SMOKING.
FIRST.
VAN.
INSURED PARCEL LOCKER.
DECOLITE FLOOR.
SHELF TO LIFT.
8'-6" OVER PILLARS.
8'-6¾" OVER MOULDINGS.
C O R R I D O R
4 THIRD CLASS COMPARTMENTS.
2 FIRST CLASS COMPARTMENTS.
2 TOILETS.
VAN TO CARRY 10 CWTS.
1 CORRIDOR.
SEATS FOR 12 FIRSTS.
AND 24 THIRDS.

## Diagram 32

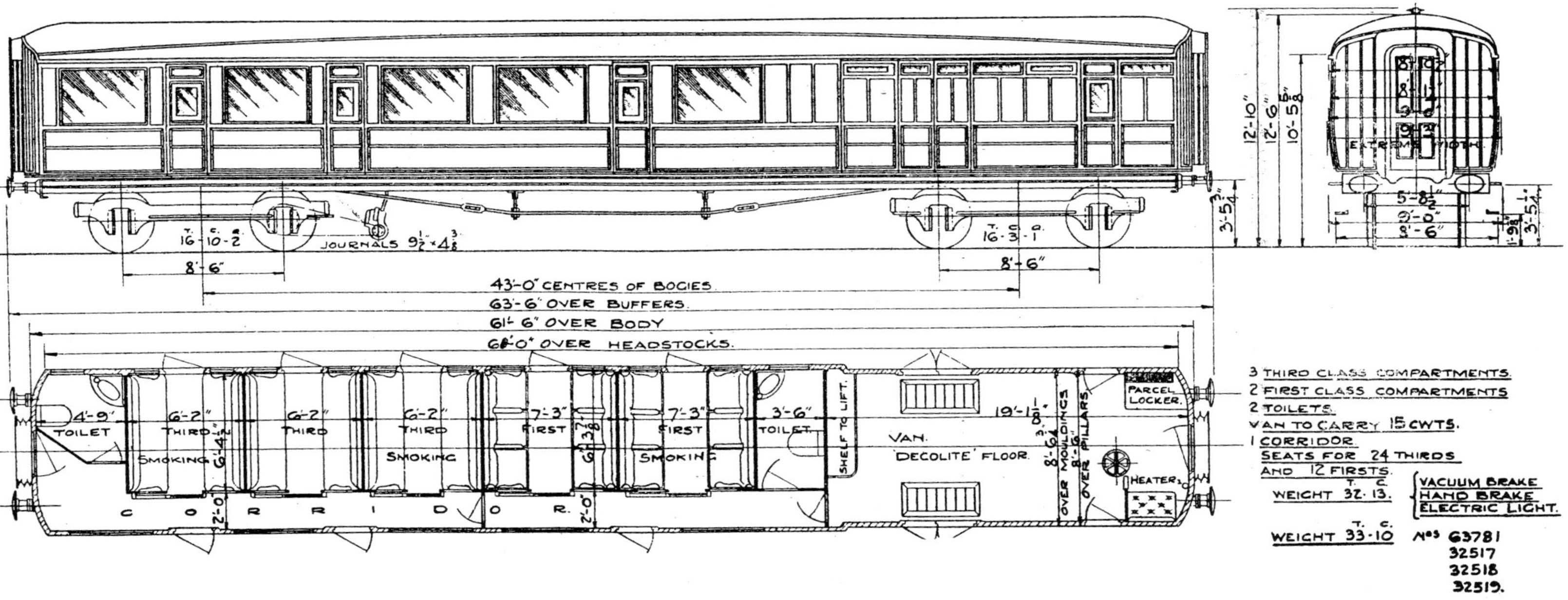
JOURNALS 9½" × 4⅜"
T. C. Q. 16-10-2
T. C. Q. 16-3-1
8'-6"
8'-6"
43'-0" CENTRES OF BOGIES.
63'-6" OVER BUFFERS.
61'-6" OVER BODY.
60'-0" OVER HEADSTOCKS.
12'-10"
12'-6"
10'-5⅝"
3'-5¾"
3'-5¼"
EXTREME WIDTH.
5'-8½"
9'-0"
8'-6"
TOILET
THIRD
SMOKING
FIRST
VAN.
DECOLITE FLOOR.
SHELF TO LIFT.
PARCEL LOCKER.
HEATER.
OVER MOULDINGS
OVER PILLARS.
C O R R I D O R.
3 THIRD CLASS COMPARTMENTS.
2 FIRST CLASS COMPARTMENTS
2 TOILETS.
VAN TO CARRY 15 CWTS.
1 CORRIDOR.
SEATS FOR 24 THIRDS
AND 12 FIRSTS.
WEIGHT 32.13. T. C.
VACUUM BRAKE
HAND BRAKE
ELECTRIC LIGHT.
WEIGHT 33-10 T. C.
Nos 63781
32517
32518
32519.

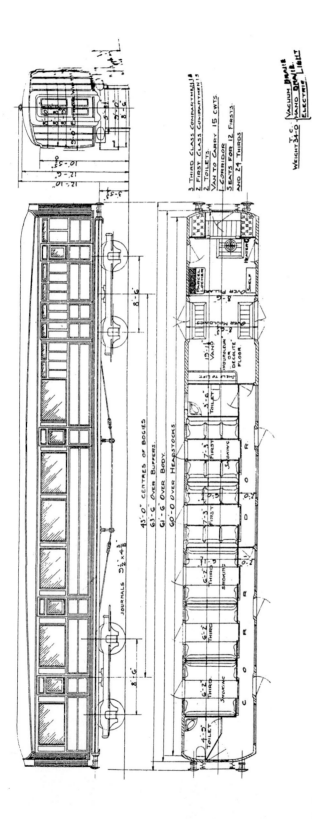

**Diagram 33**

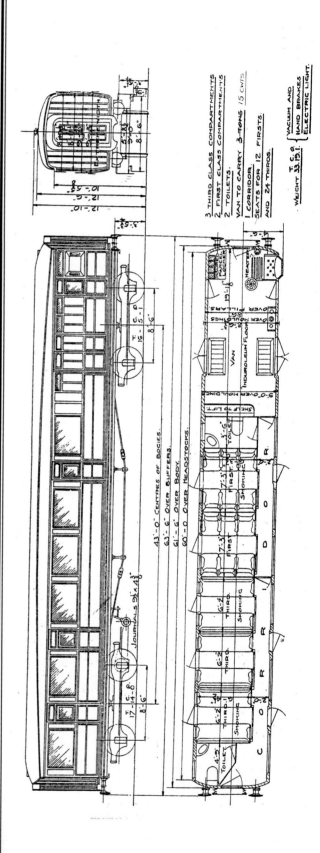

**Diagram 143**

The leading coach in this Cambridge-Kings Cross express is a **Diagram 143 brake composite, the least numerous Diagram of this type. Close examina-**
tion reveals the coach to be **No 4236 (later 10065), and the engine is 'D15/2' 4-4-0 No 8890, looking spick and span near Hatfield in July 1937.**

# (BCKL) (2 – 3)

### DIAGRAM 32

The 9ft 3in width type, without guard's ducket.
Some later fitted with intermediate armrests in the third-class.

### DIAGRAM 33

The 9ft 3in width type, without guard's ducket.

### DIAGRAM 143

The 9ft 3in width type, with guard's ducket.
Later examples to be built had intermediate armrests in the third-class. Nos 24665-7 were built with BS gangways for use on the Harrogate-Southport/Newcastle-Liverpool workings. Nos 1589/90 in East Coast stock were used for turns such as the Kings Cross-Tyne Commission Quay coach which on specified days was conveyed on the 1.20pm from Kings Cross, to return on the 8.15am from Newcastle the following day.

# (BCKL) (2 – 2)

### DIAGRAM 34

A 9ft 3in width type, without guard's ducket. Included in the first 1923 standard types and to drawing 12006D.
At its February 1923 meeting, the Traffic Committee noted that 'there was a general shortage of this type of vehicle (brake composite) on the LNER.' Accordingly, the 1924 CBP featured 12 to Diagram 34 for East Coast services. Some of these were held as strengthening vehicles for use on the 'Flying Scotsman' and afternoon Scotsmen.
Refurbishing of the East Coast vehicles took place from 1934 when intermediate armrests were fitted in the third-class and the compartments retrimmed. Although displaced from the day trains, the Diagram 34 coaches continued in use on Anglo-Scottish overnight trains such as the through portions to/from Inverness via Forres, and to/from Fort William, on the 'Highlandman', and for the Glasgow section of the 'Night Scotsman'. In the summer 1937 timetable, an East Coast vehicle was dia-

**A number of the Diagram 34 brake composites were converted to third-class only during World War 2, but not No 1105, the subject of this photograph, built at Doncaster in 1926. This remained in East Coast stock until being renumbered 10028.**

grammed to cover an Immingham-Glasgow through coach working which was run in connection with steamship cruises then operating out of Immingham. On the northbound journey, the coach was conveyed on the relief 'Flying Scotsman'.
Transfers took place from late 1930s, and some of those passing to the Areas were later designated as brake thirds on Diagram 324.

### DIAGRAM 127

A 9ft 3in width type, with guard's ducket.
Ten were built for the East Coast in 1937 to replace earlier vehicles passing to the Areas.

### DIAGRAM 316

The 9ft 3in width type, with guard's ducket. Vehicles deferred from the 1939 CBP.
The underframes of Nos 10059, 10110 were used by BR for Carflat wagons, employed in carrying new cars and other road vehicles.

## LIST OF BRAKE COMPOSITES (BCKLs):

| Diag No | CBP | Order No | Compts/ seats | Built | Original number/ changes | 1943 number |
|---|---|---|---|---|---|---|
| **Built 1924** | | | | | | |
| 34* | 1924/5 | 48 | 2/2 :12/12 | YK | 10177/8J (1076/7) [52180/1] | 10020/1 <br><br> Transfers 1936/7 |
| **Built 1926** | | | | | | |
| 31 | 1925/6 | 66 | 2/4 : 12/32 | YK DR | 5547-9 5550-2 | 10000-2 10003- 5 10004 W/O Hinksey, 1944 |
| 33 | 1924/5 | 66 | 2/3 : 12/24 | YK | 22287, 32279 | 10014/5 |
| 34* | 1924/5 | 66 | 2/2 : 12/12 | YK | 1078-87 (42881/2, 2328, 1081¶/2¶, 24680¶, 42883, 24681¶, 1086¶, 24683¶) | 10017/8/6, 16852¶, 16853¶/47¶, 10019, 16848¶/9¶,16850¶ <br> ¶ Converted to third brake from 1942. |
| | | 117 | | DR | 1098¶/9, 1105/10/25/6 | 16851¶, 10027-31 |
| **Built 1927** | | | | | | |
| 32* | 1926/7 | 178 | 2/3 : 12/24 | DR | 480/1 | 10011/2 |

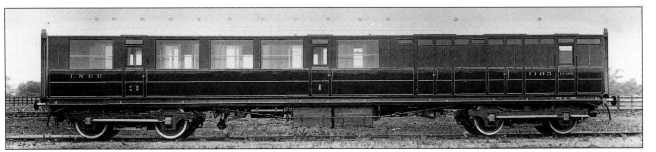

An unidentified Diagram 34 brake composite is next to 'J69/1' 0-6-0T No 68576 observed in the midst of shunting at Stratford on 25 March 1956.

### Built 1929

| | | | | | | |
|---|---|---|---|---|---|---|
| 32* | 1928/9 | 256 | 2/3<br>: 12/24 | DR | 32517-9<br>63781 | 10006-8<br>10013 |
| 127* | 1928/9 | 257 | 2/2<br>: 12/16 | YK | 122 | 10036 |

### Built 1930

| | | | | | | |
|---|---|---|---|---|---|---|
| 32* | 1929/30 | 319 | 2/3<br>: 12/24 | YK | 32524-6 | 10009/ – /10<br>32525 W/O Carlisle 1931 |
| 127* | 1930/1 | - | 2/2<br>: 12/16 | BHM | 32531/2 | 10034/5 |
| 134* | 1929/30 | 318 | 2/4<br>: 12/32 | YK | 21643, 22248 | 10046/7 |
| 143* | 1930/1 | 387 | 2/3<br>: 12/24 | DR | 22652 | 10058 Leeds-Glasgow set |

### Built 1931

| | | | | | | |
|---|---|---|---|---|---|---|
| 143* | 1930/1 | 387 | 2/3<br>: 12/24 | DR | 4236/7 | 10065/6 |

### Built 1932

| | | | | | | |
|---|---|---|---|---|---|---|
| 134* | 1930/1<br>1931/2 | 388<br>446 | 2/4<br>: 12/32 | YK<br>DK | 63853-60<br>494/5 | 10050-7<br>10048/9 |
| 143* | - | 424 | 2/3<br>: 12/24 | YK | 32525 | 10064 Accident replacement<br>for 32525 built 1930 |

### Built 1933

| | | | | | | |
|---|---|---|---|---|---|---|
| 127* | 1933 | 493 | 2/2<br>: 12/16 | DK | 21671/87 | 10032/3 |
| 175* | 1933 | 494 | 2/4<br>: 12/32 | DK | 32556-8 | 10097-9 |

### Built 1934

| | | | | | | |
|---|---|---|---|---|---|---|
| 143* | 1934 | 568 | 2/3<br>: 12/18 | DK | 1127 | 10074 |

### Built 1936

| | | | | | | |
|---|---|---|---|---|---|---|
| 175* | 1935/6 | 629 | 2/4<br>: 12/24 | YK | 42872-6<br>42873 W/O Woodhead 1944<br>42874 W/O fire Stukeley, 1938<br>1532-8 | 10104/ – / – /6/7<br><br><br>10134-40 |

### Built 1937

| | | | | | | |
|---|---|---|---|---|---|---|
| 127* | 1936 | 715# | 2/2<br>: 12/12 | YK | #1689-97 | 10037-45 |
| 143* | 1935/6 | 701 | 2/3<br>: 12/18 | YK | 42877-80<br>51895<br>1589/90 | 10067-70<br>10073<br>10075/6 |
| 175* | 1935/6<br>1937 | 700<br>776 | 2/4<br>: 12/24 | YK<br>YK | 24067-78<br>7913<br>24387-9<br>42777-80<br>51866-8 | 10077-88<br>10133<br>10089-91<br>10100-3<br>10112-4 |

### Built 1939

| | | | | | | |
|---|---|---|---|---|---|---|
| 175* | 1938 | 864 | 2/4<br>: 12/24 | YK | 42884-6<br>58700-2<br>64124-30<br>1826-30 | 10108-10<br>10115-7<br>10118-24<br>10141-5 |

### Built 1940

| | | | | | | |
|---|---|---|---|---|---|---|
| 143* | 1939 | 965 | 2/3<br>: 12/18 | DR | 24663-7<br>42887/8 | 10059-63<br>10071/2 |
| 175* | 1939 | 961 | 2/4<br>: 12/24 | YK | 24612-6<br>64160-7 | 10092-6<br>10125-32 |
| | | 974 | | YK | 42892 | 10111 Accident replacement |
| 316 | 1939 | 966 | 3/3<br>: 18/18 | DR | 42889-91 | 10156-8 |

The following vehicles were allocated to Scottish Region stock after 1949, and the number prefixed by SC: 10075/6, 16851/2

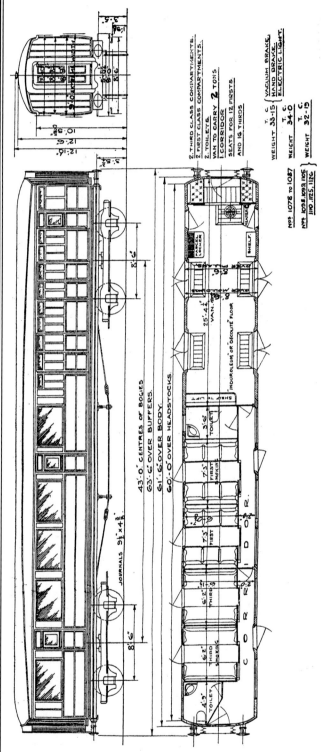

## Diagram 34

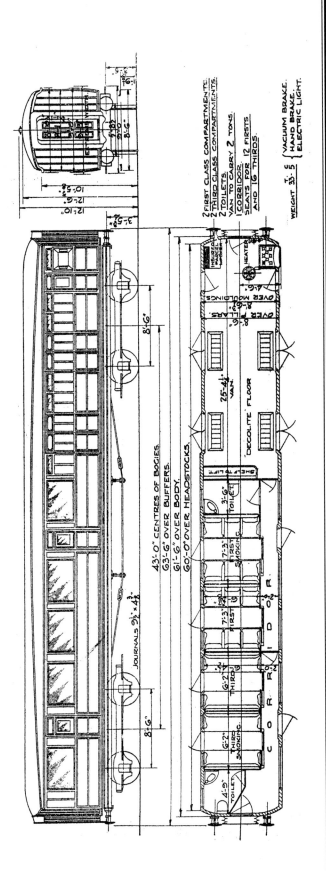

**Diagram 127**

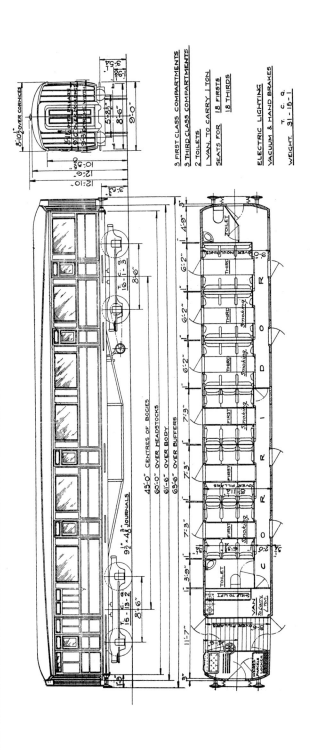

**Diagram 316**

# 52ft 6in GENERAL SERVICE COACHES
## Vestibuled/open stock

In June 1923, Gresley informed Stamer at Darlington that the standard coaches should be designed with bodies for 51ft and 60ft underframes. Later that year, Gresley again wrote to Stamer to say that it had been decided at the 30 November meeting of the Superintendents and Passenger Managers that all corridor stock should be 60ft and all non-corridor stock, 51ft, except in the case of the GE section, 'on account of the length of Liverpool Street platforms.'

This referred to the problems imposed by the layout and facilities at Liverpool Street where there was a restriction on train lengths at those platforms available to main line services on the Colchester and Cambridge routes. In the early days of Grouping, there were a number of through carriages in the various GE section expresses and, if all of these were to be made up with, say, 61ft 6in vehicles, then the length of the trains would have exceeded the length of the platforms, and consequently would have interfered with the working of the station. The GER's vestibuled stock was generally to a 54ft – or 50ft – length, and indeed the London suburban lines' working was planned around vehicles not exceeding 54ft in length.

So far so good, but the reader may well comment that the Continental boat trains of 1925 were composed of 61ft 6in vehicles, so how could this be explained? The answer would appear to be that set trains of a specified number of vehicles, and arriving/departing at a specified time, *could* be accommodated, but not vestibuled stock for general service. Yet there is another discrepancy because, as we shall see, 61ft 6in open thirds and accompanying restaurant cars to the same lengths were built for the GE section workings! Also, the longer length stock was specified by the GE section management for principal cross-country services originating outside London such as Harwich-Liverpool/York/Glasgow.

Somewhat curiously, the 1924/5 CBP included eight vestibuled 61ft 6in thirds to Diagram 23, two brake thirds to Diagram 40, and nine composites to Diagram 6, part of an order described by the Superintendents as '43 vehicles for the GE section to be built to the new 60ft length', and including the two Continental boat train sets with their distinguishing second-class, vacuum-fitted only coaches. The others were dual-fitted and included third-class stock obviously not intended to work on boat trains.

These 61ft 6in vehicles for GE main line services, built in 1926, are something of an anomaly, given the decision taken in 1923 to specify the shorter vestibuled vehicles for general service. The body length over bow ends of the latter was 52ft 6in, on the 51ft underframe.

Seemingly, the drawings for the shorter vehicles were not ready as soon after Grouping as those for the 60ft underframe stock. In the meantime, the LNER was keen to re-equip principal GE section expresses. The 1923 Building Programme comprised new stock whose construction was planned by the constituent companies, and those recommended by the new management. For the GE section, no less than 69 new vestibuled coaches were in the programme and the justification for their construction was given as 'for main line services to obviate overcrowding ... and to replace six-wheeled stock'. In addition, 14 former ambulance coaches of GE design were restored for normal use and taken into stock. These entered service as open firsts and open thirds, two, curiously, being completed as open thirds for the North Eastern Area, and later designated LNER Diagram No 26.

As a temporary expedient, the LNER's CME's department no doubt looked at the available designs for vestibuled stock that had been inherited from constituent companies and which would provide vehicle types conforming to the GE section's required length. Having apparently discarded the option of using GER designs, the authorities opted for types designed at Darlington for the North Eastern Railway's own use, and modified for the GE section. The 57 vehicles actually built to the NER-style designs were mounted on the Gresley compound bolster bogies and were dual-brake fitted. For the time being, it had been decided that new GE section main line stock, other than in complete trains, would be equipped with both air and vacuum braking. By 1927, most new stock for the GE section, other than for the inner and outer suburban services, was built with vacuum braking only.

The 1925/6 Building Programme included the first 52ft 6in length vestibuled stock, to drawings produced at Darlington, the thirds and brake thirds involved being built at the former GE's Stratford Works. For all the shorter length standard stock, there was usually one compartment fewer, as compared with the equivalent 61ft 6in design, and all were to 9ft 3in width, except for Diagrams 25 and 42, these being to 9ft width. Limited construction of these 52ft 6in vehicles continued until 1928, the construction of some having been deferred 'in view of the present financial situation and the falling-off of receipts'. Investment available for the GE

One of the coaches to North Eastern design built for the GE section in 1924/5: this is 53ft 6in vestibuled brake third No 1055E in a painted finish, and with BS gangways, screw couplings, dual braking and compound bolster bogies. To NE Diagram 209, and GE Diagram 14600-555E. Under the 1925 renumbering it became 62508.

An express leaves Cromer behind 'D15/2' 4-4-0 No 8825. The first two coaches, a brake third and a composite, are of the GE section 52ft 6in stock, followed by an ex-GER restaurant car.

section rolling stock was concentrated on the renewal of suburban sets.

At the meeting of the Joint Locomotive and Traffic Committee on 5 January 1928, a memo was submitted by Wedgwood detailing the condition of the rolling stock on the GE section. One immediate consequence was that an increase in the numbers of cleaning staff was recommended, and subsequently approved. A full report from Wedgwood followed at the committee's meeting next month and this revealed that of the GE section's stock of 2,600 main line passenger caches, 1,482 were six-wheeled. Wedgwood noted that 'Every available coach was continually in use in summer and suburban stock was used for long-distance ordinary and excursion trains. In view of the intensive road competition for long-distance traffic, it was more than ever necessary to make main line services more attractive.'

Wedgwood proposed that 30 new vacuum-only vestibuled coaches (for Liverpool St-Cromer expresses) should be built in advance of stock on the normal building programme, and that the restaurant cars would have electric cooking equipment, to be employed for the first time on the GE section. The Joint Locomotive and Traffic Committee recommended to the Board that the chief general manger's proposals should be adopted and it was decided to put the order to outside contractors. Of the 30 new coaches, all were to standard 52ft 6in designs, apart from the open thirds and restaurant kitchen firsts, these being to the 61ft 6in length. Metropolitan Carriage Wagon & Finance was the successful bidder, and the new sets entered service in July 1929. Their interiors conformed to the standard specification of the time, and their features are described in the Introduction, in the section dealing with these matters. No designs were produced for 52ft 6in catering vehicles.

The effect of the two new sets for the Cromer service was to show up the age of the vehicles used in other trains on this service, with the result that the 1930/1 CBP included new stock for the 3.10pm Liverpool St-Cromer and its return working; these were of 52ft 6in stock, except for the open thirds. Although the LNER's suspension of new coach construction in 1932 affected the fulfilment of orders for new GE section stock, the 1934 CBP programme included 20 coaches for Cromer and Clacton services, then came the 1935 programme, with the delivery of four-coach sets (made up of two CKLVs and two BTKLVs) for use on the Liverpool St-Hunstanton, and Norwich via Ely services. A number of vestibuled thirds were built for strengthening main line sets. The 1935/6 CBP included for the first time a 52ft 6in open third type, and this was built for use on guaranteed excursions and private charter trains.

The mid/late 1930s saw the completion of a number of 52ft 6in vestibuled coaches, those under the 1937 programme being ordered to replace six-wheeled stock still in use on important main line and cross-country trains, while those in the 1938 programme were intended to displace the remaining pre-Grouping coaches in the Norwich/Cromer sets. However, a change in the GE section's operating management seems to have coincided with a realisation that 61ft 6in stock was, after all, acceptable for general service and so the last 52ft 6in vehicles entered traffic in 1938.

From the mid-1930s, the 52ft 6in vestibuled coaches had welded underframes, intermediate armrests, and shoulder-lights in third-class compartments.

With the 1943 renumbering of LNER coaching stock, the 52ft 6in vehicles were at first allocated blocks of numbers within the main 1xxxx series for vestibuled stock but, in the event, retained their existing GE section 6xxx and 6xxxx numbers, later with 'E' prefixes and suffixes. However, it seemed interesting to include the intended numbers in the new 1xxxx series!

## Open firsts: (FO)

### DIAGRAM 197

Two vehicles only, with two saloons – smoking and non-smoking – and one lavatory, this design effectively being the equivalent of the longer length Diagram 4.

### LIST OF OPEN FIRSTS (FOs):

| Diag No | CBP | Order No | Compts/ seats | Built | Original/1943 number |
|---------|-----|----------|---------------|-------|----------------------|
| **Built 1935** | | | | | |
| 197 | 1934 | 577 | 2† 33 | YK | 6463/4 |

Intended 1943 Nos: 11105/6

**Diagram 197**

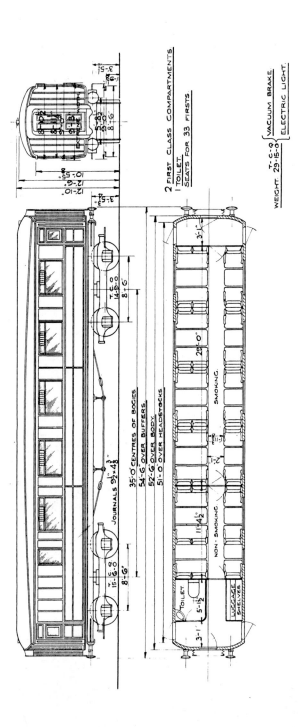

35'-0" CENTRES OF BOGIES.
54'-6" OVER BUFFERS.
52'-6" OVER BODY.
51'-0" OVER HEADSTOCKS.

2 FIRST CLASS COMPARTMENTS
1 TOILET
SEATS FOR 33 FIRSTS

WEIGHT. 29-15-0 T·C·Q { VACUUM BRAKE.
ELECTRIC LIGHT.

NON-SMOKING.          SMOKING.

TOILET          LUGGAGE SHELVES

**Diagram 140**

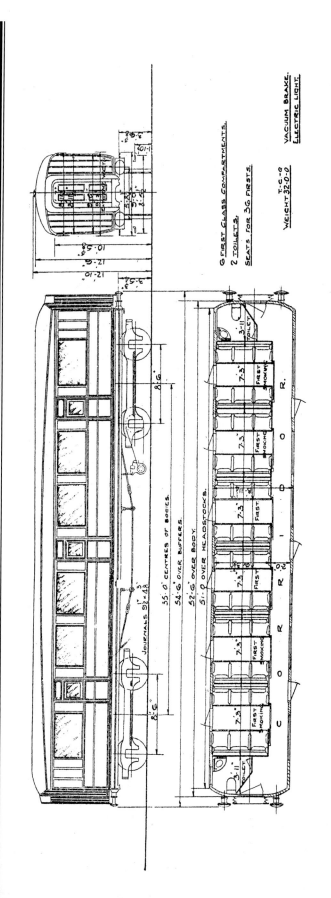

35'-0" CENTRES OF BOGIES.
54'-6" OVER BUFFERS.
52'-6" OVER BODY.
51'-0" OVER HEADSTOCKS.

6 FIRST CLASS COMPARTMENTS.
2 TOILETS.
SEATS FOR 36 FIRSTS.

WEIGHT 32-0-0 T·C·Q { VACUUM BRAKE.
ELECTRIC LIGHT.

FIRST SMOKING    FIRST SMOKING    FIRST    FIRST    FIRST SMOKING    FIRST SMOKING
TOILET                                                                    TOILET
C O R R I D O R

# Vestibuled first (FKL)

### DIAGRAM 140

This type was first ordered for the two 1929 Cromer sets.

Of those built in 1930, all were for main line expresses, including one in the 1930/1 CBP next only in priority to re-equipment of the 'Flying Scotsman' sets. This was a single vestibuled first for the Esbjerg boat train.

### LIST OF VESTIBULE FIRSTS (FKLs):

| Diag No | CBP | Order No | Compts/ seats | Built | Original/1943 number | |
|---|---|---|---|---|---|---|
| **Built 1929** | | | | | | |
| 140* | 1928/9 | - | 6: 36 | MET | 6452/3 | Cromer sets |
| **Built 1930** | | | | | | |
| 140* | 1930/1 | 376 | 6: 36 | YK | 6454-9 | 6457 W/O fire Knebworth, 1943 |
| **Built 1934** | | | | | | |
| 140* | 1933 | 507 | 6: 36 | DR | 6461/2 | |
| **Built 1935** | | | | | | |
| 140* | 1934 | 556 | 6: 36 | YK | 6465 | |
| **Built 1936** | | | | | | |
| 140* | •1935/6 | 556 | 6: 36 | YK | 6466 | DEA 1940 |
| **Built 1938** | | | | | | |
| 140* | 1937 | 802 | 6: 36 | YK | 6484 | |

Intended 1943 Nos: 11050-61

---

# Vestibuled seconds: (SKL)

### DIAGRAM 141A

Identical to Diagram 141 but second-class, for use on Continental boat trains.

### LIST OF VESTIBULED SECONDS (SKLs):

| Diag No | CBP | Order No | Compts/ seats | Built | Original/1943 number | |
|---|---|---|---|---|---|---|
| **Built 1930** | | | | | | |
| 141A* | 1929/30 | 309 | 7: 56 | YK | 6990/1 | Reclassified thirds to Dia 141 in 1942 |

Intended 1943 Nos: 12759/60

Right: **Diagram 140 vestibuled first No E6459E (built York, 1930). Seen at Shirebrook North in September 1955, it still retains a teak finish.**

Below: **Diagram 140 vestibuled first No 6452 (built Metropolitan CWF). This was one of the coaches forming the two Cromer sets which entered service in 1929.**

# Open thirds: (TOV and TTO)

### DIAGRAM 182 (TOV)

Two saloons – smoking and non-smoking – and one lavatory. Usual saloon seating, as in Diagram 27 stock, and arranged 2 + 1 with armrests, but in 6½ bays.

Four only, dating from 1934 and intended to make up an excursion set.

### DIAGRAM 216 (TTO)

With 6½ bays, as Diagram 182, but with 2 + 2 seating layout, in bucket seats, and with two lavatories.

These were intended for guaranteed excursions and private charters. For some reason, only two brake open thirds were built, despite the original request from the SPMs that there should be six. The GE section had no cream and green painted Tourist stock, and possessed 69 open thirds for excursion work, including those to Diagrams 182 and 216, and some of GER design.

### LIST OF OPEN THIRDS (TOVs AND TTOs):

| Diag No | CBP | Order No | Compts/ seats | Built | Original/1943 number | |
|---|---|---|---|---|---|---|
| **Built 1934** | | | | | | |
| 182* | 1934 | 576 | 2† 39 | YK | 61882/3 | TOVs |
| **Built 1935** | | | | | | |
| 182* | 1934 | 561 | 2† 39 | YK | 61884/5 | TOVs |
| **Built 1936** | | | | | | |
| 216 | 1935/6 | 639 | 1† 52 | YK | 60500-18 | TTOs |
| | | 661 | | | 60519-52 | |

Intended 1943 Nos: 61882-5, to be 13214-7; Nos 60500-52, to be 13621-72.

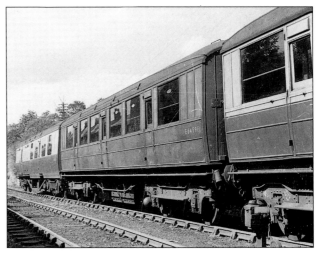

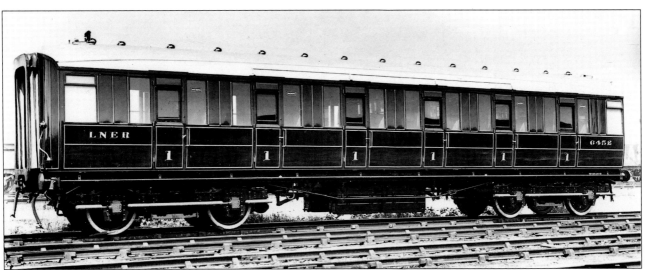

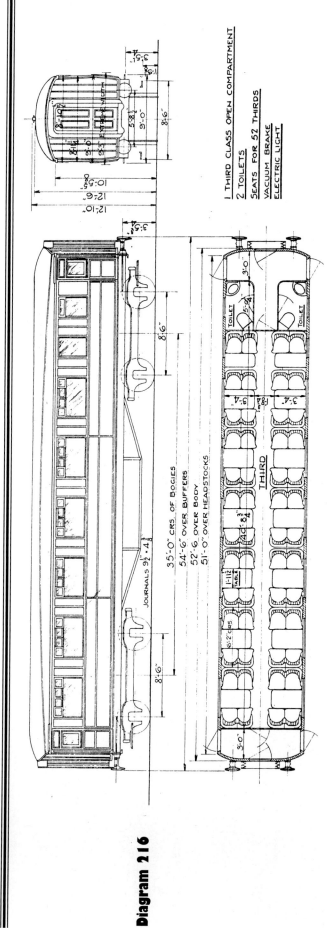

**Diagram 182**

2 THIRD CLASS COMPARTMENTS.
TOILET
SEATS FOR 39 THIRDS.

T·C·&} VACUUM BRAKE.
WEIGHT 30·5·0 } ELECTRIC LIGHT.

35'-0" CENTRES OF BOGIES.
54'-6" OVER BUFFERS.
52'-6" OVER BODY.
51'-0" OVER HEADSTOCKS.

JOURNALS 9½" × 4¾".

NON-SMOKING.

SMOKING.

**Diagram 216**

1 THIRD CLASS OPEN COMPARTMENT
2 TOILETS
SEATS FOR 52 THIRDS
VACUUM BRAKE
ELECTRIC LIGHT

35'-0" CRS OF BOGIES.
54'-6" OVER BUFFERS
52'-6" OVER BODY
51'-0" OVER HEADSTOCKS

JOURNALS 9½" × 4¾"

THIRD

Diagram 216 open third No 60525 (built York, 1936). It was photographed at Bromley South on 21 June 1936 formed in a cross-country holiday train probably bound for the Kent Coast - illustrating that even purpose-built excursion stock was borrowed at peak times.

# Vestibuled thirds: (TKL)

### DIAGRAM 25

A 9ft width seven-compartment vehicle, with 8 in x 4 in journals on the bogies.

Limited to a single batch, built at Stratford Works in 1926.

### DIAGRAM 141

As compared with Diagram 25, the differences comprised compartments 6ft 2in between partitions, in common with the 61ft 6in thirds, with the result that the lavatories were slightly smaller than those in Diagram 25 which had 6ft 1in compartments. The lavatories were noticeably more cramped than were those in 61ft 6in stock. The bogies had 9in x 4in journals.

### LIST OF VESTIBULED THIRDS (TKLs):

| Diag No | CBP | Order No | Compts/ seats | Built | Original/1943 number | |
|---|---|---|---|---|---|---|
| **Built 1926** | | | | | | |
| 25 | 1925/6 | 107 | 7: 56 | SF | 61634-46 | ≠ |
| **Built 1929** | | | | | | |
| 141* | 1928/9 | - | 7: 56 | MET | 61697-61704 | Cromer sets |

**Right: A Diagram 141 coach, by now E61966E (built York 1937). With angle-iron trussing. It was photographed at Colwyn Bay in August 1964, three months before withdrawal.**

**Below: Diagram 141 vestibuled third No 61793 (built York 1934), from the compartment side. Note that there is just one panel depth between the compartments of a third-class coach such as this, compared with two panels' depth of the firsts such as No 6452 illustrated earlier.**

| Diag No | CBP | Order No | Compts/ seats | Built | Original/1943 number | |
|---|---|---|---|---|---|---|
| **Built 1930** | | | | | | |
| 141* | 1929/30 | 309 | 7: 56 | YK | 61714-21 | |
| **Built 1931** | | | | | | |
| 141* | 1930/1 | 380 | 7: 56 | YK | 61722-31 | |
| **Built 1932** | | | | | | |
| 141* | 1930/1 | 380 | 7: 56 | YK | 61732-6 | 61736 W/O 1937 Sleaford N Jct |
| **Built 1933** | | | | | | |
| 141* | 1933 | 505 | 7: 56 | YK | 61737-61 | 61753 DEA |
| | - | 464 | | | 61762 | Replacement for GER vehicle lost in fire |
| **Built 1934** | | | | | | |
| 141* | 1933 | 508 | 7: 56 | YK | 61763-93 | |
| | 1934 | 533 | | | 61866-73 | 61866 W/O |
| | | 558 | | | 61874-81 | 61874 DEA |
| **Built 1935** | | | | | | |
| 141* | 1935/6 | 623 | 7: 56 | DK | 61957-9 | |
| **Built 1937** | | | | | | |
| 141* | 1935/6 | 718 | 7: 56 | YK | 61960-74 | |
| **Built 1938** | | | | | | |
| 141* | 1937 | 803 | 7: 42 | YK | 60554-60603 | 60599 W/O Knebworth 1943 |

Intended 1943 Nos: Diag 25, 12114-25, Diag 141, 12761-12926

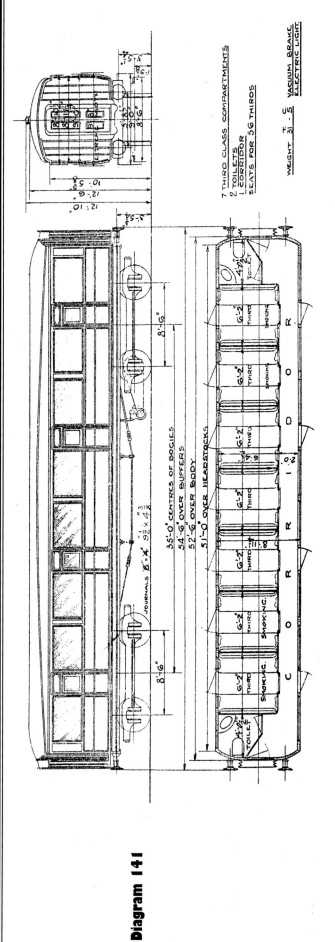

**Diagram 25**

JOURNALS 8" x 4"

35'-0" CENTRES OF BOGIES
54'-6" OVER BUFFERS
52'-6" OVER BODY
51'-0" OVER HEADSTOCKS

4'-4" TOILET

6'-1" THIRD SMOKING  6'-1" THIRD SMOKING  6'-1" 7-9 THIRD SMOKING  6'-1" THIRD SMOKING  6'-1" THIRD SMOKING  6'-1" THIRD

C   O   R   R   I   D   O   R

4'-4" TOILET

7 THIRD CLASS COMPARTMENTS
2 TOILETS
1 CORRIDOR
SEATS FOR 56 THIRDS.

WEIGHT 31 6

VACUUM BRAKE
ELECTRIC LIGHT

8'-6"   8'-6"

10'-5"
12'-6"
12'-10"
3'-5½"
1'-6¾"

---

**Diagram 141**

JOURNALS 8" x 4"

35'-0" CENTRES OF BOGIES
54'-6" OVER BUFFERS
52'-6" OVER BODY
51'-0" OVER HEADSTOCKS

4'-4½" TOILET

6'-2" THIRD SMOKING  6'-2" THIRD SMOKING  6'-2" 7-9 THIRD  6'-2" 7-11.8 THIRD  6'-2" THIRD SMOKING  6'-2" THIRD SMOKING.

C   O   R   R   I   D   O   R

4'-4½" TOILET

7 THIRD CLASS COMPARTMENTS
2 TOILETS
1 CORRIDOR
SEATS FOR 56 THIRDS

WEIGHT 31 6

VACUUM BRAKE
ELECTRIC LIGHT

8'-6"   8'-6"

10'-5"
12'-6"
12'-10"
3'-5½"
1'-6¾"

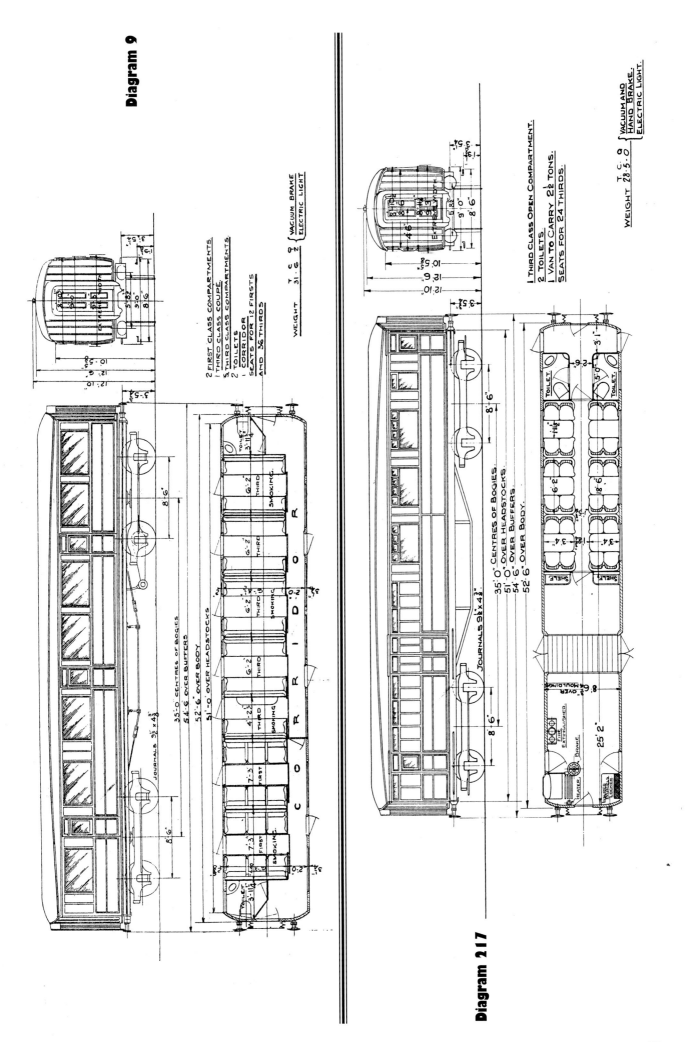

**Diagram 9**

2 FIRST CLASS COMPARTMENTS.
1 THIRD CLASS COUPÉ.
5 THIRD CLASS COMPARTMENTS.
2 TOILETS.
1 CORRIDOR.
SEATS FOR 12 FIRSTS
AND 36 THIRDS.

WEIGHT 31.6.2 T. C. G. { VACUUM BRAKE. ELECTRIC LIGHT.

**Diagram 217**

1 THIRD CLASS OPEN COMPARTMENT.
2 TOILETS.
1 VAN TO CARRY 2½ TONS.
SEATS FOR 24 THIRDS.

WEIGHT 28.5.0 T. C. G. { VACUUM AND HAND BRAKE. ELECTRIC LIGHT.

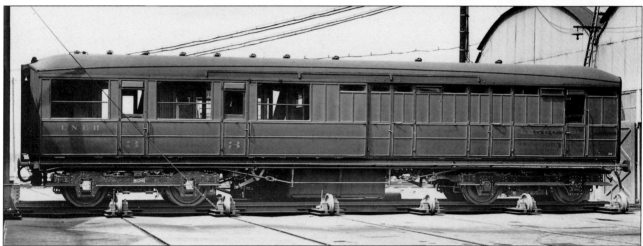

# Vestibuled composites: (CKL) (2 – 4½)

## DIAGRAM 9

The only design of vestibuled composite to the 52ft 6in length.

Top: **An earlier Diagram 9 vestibuled composite (with bar trussing) is behind 'C14' 4-4-2T No 6128 working an unidentified Class 'B' train near Ipswich in 1938. The whole rake of coaches would appear to be on the 51ft underframes.**

Above: **A Stratford Works photograph of Diagram 41 vestibuled brake third No 62560 (built York 1927). Works attention seems to have been given to the bogies while the bodywork exhibits the work-stained appearance of the teak bodied stock after some time in traffic.**

## LIST OF VESTIBULED COMPOSITES (CKLs):

| Diag No | CBP | Order No | Compts/ seats | Built | Original/1943 number | |
|---|---|---|---|---|---|---|
| **Built 1926** | | | | | | |
| 9* | 1926/7 | 174 | 2/4¹/² : 12/36 | DR | 63801/2 | 63802 withdrawn by 1943 |
| **Built 1928** | | | | | | |
| 9* | 1927/8 | 194 | 2/4¹/² : 12/36 | YK | 63810-22 | |
| **Built 1929** | | | | | | |
| 9* | 1928/9 | - | 2/4¹/² : 12/36 | MET | 63823-30 | Cromer sets |
| **Built 1931** | | | | | | |
| 9* | 1930/1 | 386 | 2/4¹/² : 12/36 | YK | 63837-46 | |
| **Built 1932** | | | | | | |
| 9* | 1930/1 | 386 | 2/4¹/² : 12/36 | YK | 63847-52 | |
| **Built 1933** | | | | | | |
| 9* | - | 463 | 2/4¹/² : 12/36 | YK | 63865/6 | Replacements for GER vehicles lost in fire |
| **Built 1934** | | | | | | |
| 9* | 1933 | 513 | 2/4¹/² : 12/27 | YK | 63871-4 | |
| | 1934 | 536 | | | 63875-8 | |
| **Built 1935** | | | | | | |
| 9* | 1934 | 566 | 2/4¹/² : 12/27 | YK | 63879-86 | |
| | 1935/6 | 628 | | YK | 63967-82 | 63979 W/O 1940 |
| **Built 1937** | | | | | | |
| 9* | 1935/6 | 698 | 2/4¹/² : 12/27 | YK | 63983-94 | |
| | 1937 | 805 | | | 63291-4 | |
| **Built 1938** | | | | | | |
| 9* | 1937 | 805 | 2/4¹/² : 12/27 | YK | 63295-63319 | |

Intended 1943 Nos: 18050-18161

# Open brake thirds: (BTO)

### DIAGRAM 217
The matching brakes for the excursion sets made up of Diagram 216 open thirds.

### LIST OF OPEN BRAKE THIRDS (BTOs):

| Diag No | CBP | Order No | Compts/ seats | Built | Original/1943 number |
|---|---|---|---|---|---|
| **Built 1935** | | | | | |
| 217 | 1935/6 | 626 | 1† 24 | DK | 62748/9 |

Intended 1943 Nos: 16717/8

# Vestibuled brake thirds: (BTKLV)

### DIAGRAM 41
The 9ft 3in width version, and with vacuum braking only. No guard's ducket.

### DIAGRAM 42
The 9ft width version, dual-fitted as built, and contemporary with the Diagram 25 thirds.

### DIAGRAM 146
The most numerous type, of 9ft 3in width and almost identical to Diagram 41, but with a guard's ducket.

### LIST OF VESTIBULED BRAKE THIRDS (BTKLs):

| Diag No | CBP | Order No | Compts/ seats | Built | Original/1943 number | |
|---|---|---|---|---|---|---|
| **Built 1926** | | | | | | |
| 42 | 1925/6 | 108 | 3: 24 | SF | 62549/50 | ≠ |
| **Built 1927** | | | | | | |
| 41* | 1926/7 | 146 | 3: 24 | YK | 62556-70 | 62569 W/O Hilgay, 1939 |
| | | 173 | | DR | 62551-5 | |
| **Built 1928** | | | | | | |
| 41* | 1927/8 | 192 | 3: 24 | DR | 62598-62607 | |
| **Built 1929** | | | | | | |
| 41* | 1928/9 | 250 | 3: 24 | YK | 62610-5 | |
| | | - | | MET | 62616-23 | Cromer sets |
| **Built 1930** | | | | | | |
| 146* | 1929/30 | 312 | 3: 24 | DR | 62630-9 | |
| | 1930/1 | 385 | | DR | 62640-3 | |
| **Built 1932** | | | | | | |
| 146* | 1930/1 | 385 | 3: 24 | DR | 62644-9 | |
| **Built 1934** | | | | | | |
| 146* | 1933 | 509 | 3: 18 | DR | 62655-8 | 62658 W/O |
| | 1934 | 535 | | YK | 62659-62 | |
| **Built 1935** | | | | | | |
| 146* | 1934 | 563 | 3: 18 | YK | 62663-5 | |
| **Built 1936** | | | | | | |
| 146* | 1935/6 | 607 | 3: 18 | YK | 62751-60 | |
| | | 667 | | | 62761-6 | |
| **Built 1938** | | | | | | |
| 146* | 1937 | 804 | 3: 18 | YK | 62769-84 | 62779 DEA, u/f used again |

Intended 1943 Nos: 62549/50, to be 16242/3; Nos 62551-62623, to be 16199-16241; 62630-65/62751-62766/9-84, to be 16406-66.

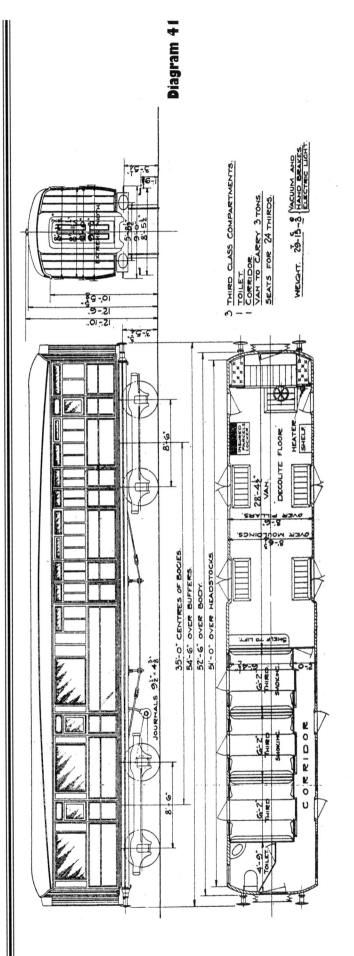

Diagram 41

3 THIRD CLASS COMPARTMENTS.
TOILET.
CORRIDOR.
VAN TO CARRY 3 TONS.
SEATS FOR 24 THIRDS.
WEIGHT. 29-15-3 { VACUUM AND HAND BRAKES. ELECTRIC LIGHT.

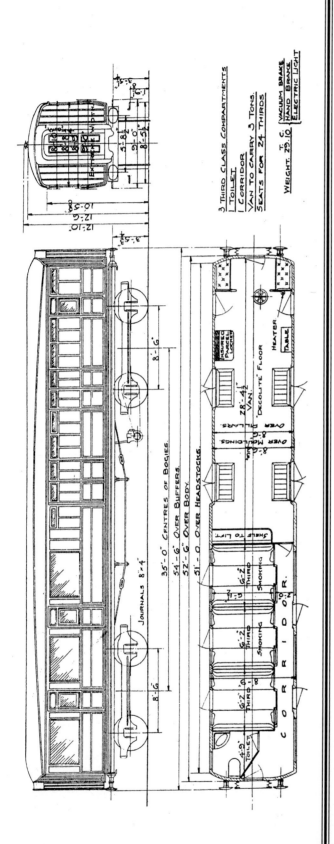

**Diagram 42**

3 THIRD CLASS COMPARTMENTS
1 TOILET
1 CORRIDOR
VAN TO CARRY 3 TONS.
SEATS FOR 24 THIRDS

T.C.
WEIGHT 29.10

VACUUM BRAKE
HAND BRAKE
ELECTRIC LIGHT

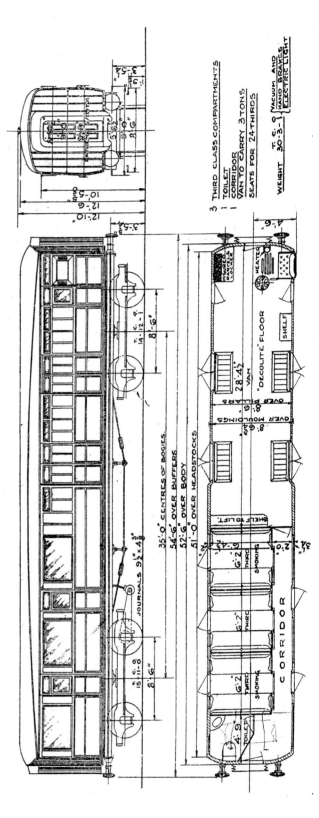

**Diagram 146**

3 THIRD CLASS COMPARTMENTS
1 TOILET
1 CORRIDOR
VAN TO CARRY 3 TONS.
SEATS FOR 24 THIRDS

T.C.Q
WEIGHT 30·3·1

VACUUM AND
HAND BRAKES
ELECTRIC LIGHT

# NON-VESTIBULED COACHES
## teak-bodied and non-articulated

As we have seen, the designs for non-vestibuled coaches were produced at the same time as those for the vestibuled stock, and were ready for the production of coaches under the 1924 CBP. The general features were noted in the Introduction, including the fact that the non-vestibuled stock made use of the 51ft underframe, with screw couplings.

The bodies of the non-vestibuled coaches were flat-ended, and with beading the overall length over the body was 51ft 1½in. Where possible, the distance between the compartment partitions was standardised at 7ft 3in for the first-class, and at 6ft 2in for the third-class. Generally speaking, the specifications adopted in 1923 were maintained until the last teak-bodied non-articulated coach was constructed in 1938. Thereafter, non-articulated coaches were steel-panelled, using the basic designs of the teak-panelled stock.

For the 1924 CBP, the priorities for new construction were listed as vestibuled stock for premier services, but non-vestibuled stock showed up strongly and there were no less than 186 of these vehicles on order. In general, the justification for their construction was to allow the displacement of four and six-wheeled stock, and in particular those without heating. That year's building programme included some stock to pre-Grouping design, such as a 56ft first and a couple of similar length thirds for the GC section, as well as firsts, thirds and brake thirds for the same section which had Gresley outline, teak bodies on 56 or 60ft GCR design underframes recovered from ambulance trains.

The 51ft standards in the 1924 programme included firsts; lavatory composites, with all compartments having access to a lavatory, by means of internal side-corridors, and a five-compartment brake third. As for the last-named, the operating superintendents soon made known their requirements for brake thirds with fewer compartments, such that in time there were designs with three, four, five and six compartments. These were no doubt appropriate to services' needs for handling parcels, mails and fish traffic in the van compartments which were of varying capacity, in terms of the maximum weight of traffic that could be carried.

Despite the number of non-articulated, non-vestibuled coaches built by the LNER in the mid and late 1920s, principally for the NEA and SSA, the major task at that time was that of building block sets of articulated trains for the London suburban services operated by the GN and GE sections. Many of the non-articulated, non-vestibuled coaches were built by contrac-

tors, and the designs themselves varied little except that stock for the NEA and the GE section was dual-fitted, up to and including those built in 1928.

Vestibuled stock was ordered for the NEA in the early 1930s, to replace recently built standard non-vestibule coaches on some of the longer workings within the Area, the North Eastern Railway having been content to roster non-vestibuled stock where other railways would have used vestibuled coaches. The main recipient of the transferred stock, from the 1930/1 CBP onwards, was the SSA, and here the transfers either went to make up complete sets for services such as Helensburgh-Glasgow, or Glasgow or Edinburgh-Dundee. Transfers to the GE section were to enable inroads to be made into that section's legion of non-bogie vehicles. The transfers were used either on main line stopping trains or, for example, on the Felixstowe branch where air-braked stock was displaced.

The GE section had standardised much of its London suburban operations on sets of 54ft coaches, particularly on the Liverpool Street-Ilford/Shenfield service. As explained in the Introduction, the initiative for new coaches came either from the need to replace life-expired stock scheduled for condemnation, or to provide trains to serve new traffic. Under the 1935 programme, it was intended to break-up four-wheeled GER coaches used on the North Woolwich line, and to replace them with GER bogie stock from the Ilford service. In turn, these were to be replaced by new coaches. So that these would conform with the existing 54ft GER stock, some dating from 1922/3, the new stock was to be of the same length, and mounted on similar single-bolster bogies with inside solebars. Their bodies were similar to the Gresley non-vestibuled stock, except that the compartment partition to partition dimensions were similarly economical with space as those of the quint-art suburban trains. Eight, eight-coach trains of this Ilford stock were built by contractors under the 1935/6 CBP.

The Great Northern and Great Central Railways had been members of the Cheshire Lines Committee, and supplied stock for its operations. This contribution continued after 1923, and teak-bodied coaches to the Gresley outline was built for the CLC (but on 56ft, or 58ft underframes), or else sold to the Committee from LNER stock, these being 51ft coaches.

**A Glasgow Queen St-Blanefield train near Cadder in August 1932 headed by 'C16' 4-4-2T No 9441. Its train comprises a four-coach set of teak bodied, non-vestibuled stock - brake third; third; composite; brake third.**

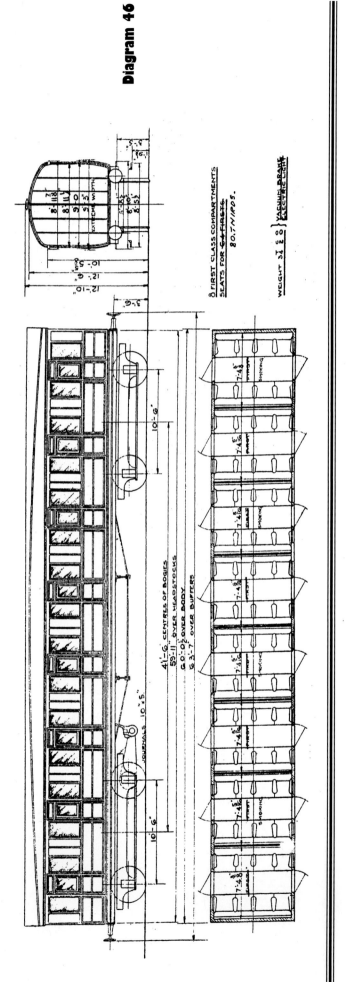

**Diagram 46**

8 FIRST CLASS COMPARTMENTS
SEATS FOR 64 FIRSTS
80.7 W/H P05.

WEIGHT 31₂₆₈ } VACUUM BRAKE
ELECTRIC LIGHT

EXTREME WIDTH

41'-6" CENTRES OF BOGIES
59'-11½" OVER HEADSTOCKS
60'-0½" OVER BODY
63'-7" OVER BUFFERS

JOURNALS 10"x5"

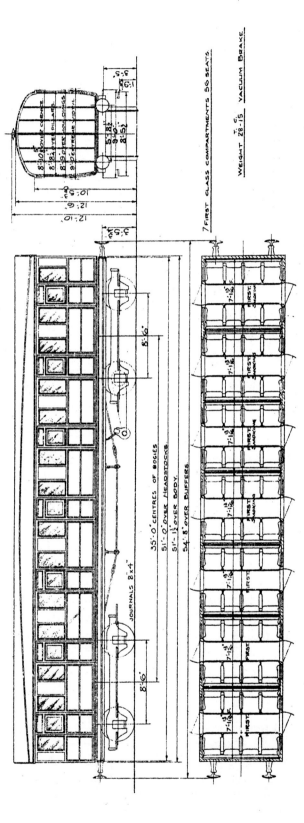

**Diagram 47**

7 FIRST CLASS COMPARTMENTS 56 SEATS

WEIGHT T.C. 28-15 VACUUM BRAKE

35'-0" CENTRES OF BOGIES
51'-0" OVER HEADSTOCKS
51'-1½" OVER BODY
54'-8" OVER BUFFERS

JOURNALS 8"x4"

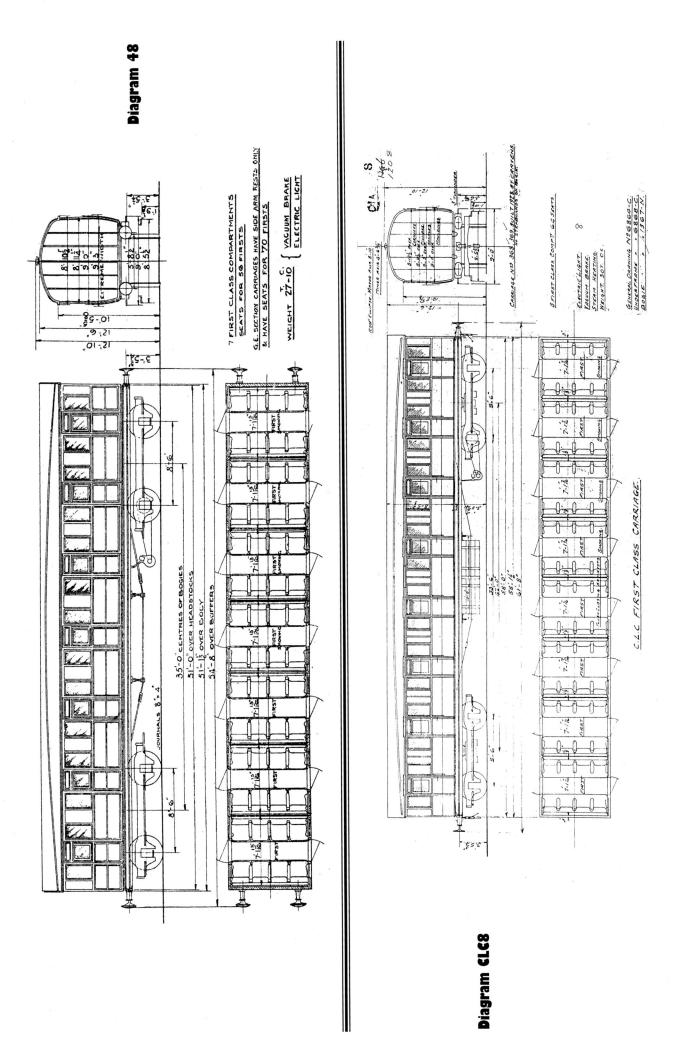

**Diagram 48**

7 FIRST CLASS COMPARTMENTS
SEATS FOR 56 FIRSTS
G.E. SECTION CARRIAGES HAVE SIDE ARM RESTS ONLY
& HAVE SEATS FOR 70 FIRSTS

T.C. { VACUUM BRAKE
      { ELECTRIC LIGHT
WEIGHT 27-10

35'-0 CENTRES OF BOGIES
51'-0" OVER HEADSTOCKS
51'-1½ OVER BODY
54'-8 OVER BUFFERS

JOURNALS 8"x 4"

**Diagram CLC8**

CARRIAGE Nºs 368, 369 BUILT 1921 BY CRAVENS.
WITH STANDARD 8ft. BOGIE

8 FIRST CLASS COMP¹ 64 SEATS

ELECTRIC LIGHT.
VACUUM BRAKE.
STEAM HEATING.
WEIGHT. 30T. 0c.

GENERAL DRAWING Nº 6868a-C.
UNDERFRAME " 6868-C.
BOGIE " 1367-N.

C.L.C. FIRST CLASS CARRIAGE.

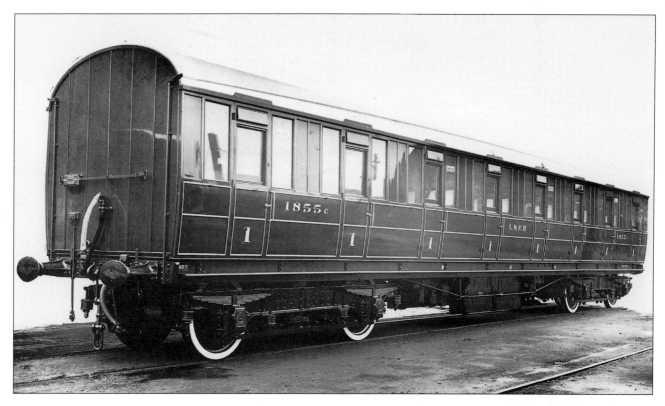

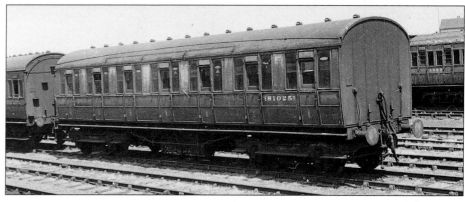

Above: **Gorton/Dukinfield photograph of Diagram 46 first No 1855C (later 51855), built in 1924 on the 60ft underframe of a Great Central-built ambulance vehicle, and retaining GCR pattern oval-headed buffers. This vehicle was converted to a composite on Diagram 283 and was eventually renumbered 88283.**

Right: **Diagram 48 first E81025E, built York 1927 as 31875, and seen at Peterborough in 1955 when it still carried the worn remains of LNER livery.**

# Firsts: (F)

## DIAGRAM 46

A 1924 design, employing underframes of GCR design, recovered from ambulance train vehicles.

While one of the batch became all-third, the others were altered as composites and designated Diagram 283.

## DIAGRAM 47

A 51ft 1½in by 9ft standard design, featuring in the 1924 CBP.

Some were altered as composites and appear in this guise under Diagrams 188/189.

## DIAGRAM 48

The 9ft 3in width version of Diagram 47, and hence the more numerous type.

First-class accommodation in coaches allocated to the GE section had armrests at each ends of the seating only, and consequent greater capacity. The GE section stock was used on main line stopping trains, such as to Ipswich, and for Liverpool St-Royal Albert Docks boat trains. Some were reclassified as thirds from 1942.

## DIAGRAM CLC 8

A 58ft underframe vehicle for the CLC, without an LNER equivalent as it had eight compartments. Similarly with four-a-side seating, as with most of Diagram 47. The CLC coaches had no stepboards on the bogies.

## LIST OF FIRSTS (Fs):

| Diag No | CBP | Order No | Compts/ seats | Built | Original number/ changes | 1943 number |
|---|---|---|---|---|---|---|
| **Built 1924** | | | | | | |
| 46 | 1924/5 | 38 | 8: 64 | DK | 51855/6, 51857(4288), 51858 | 88283, 82000, 88282/4 |
| 51855/7/8 to compos on Dia 283; 51856 to all-third on Dia 46 | | | | | | |
| **Built 1925** | | | | | | |
| 47* | 1924/5 | 42 | 7: 56 | SF | 10248-62B (31881/3/4/6-9 31893-5/7-9, 31902/3) | 81000-12/— /3 |
| 31902 altered to composite on Dia 189 in 1935 and renumbered 32546 (88141) | | | | | | |
| **Built 1926** | | | | | | |
| 47* | 1925/6 | - | 7: 56 | MID | 31904/7-10, 31915/7/8/20 | 81014-22 |
| **Built 1927** | | | | | | |
| 48* | 1926/7 | 148 | 7: 56 | YK | 31875-8/, 31901/11/62, 31985, 32024/30/1/63, 32076/78/82/93, 32113, 32128/9/32/9/49/51 6446-51 | 81025-8/36-40/—, 81041-3/— /4/— /— 81045/— /— /6 81048-53 |
| 32063/93, 32128/9/39/49 converted to composites on Dia 189 in 1935 and renumbered 32547-52 (88142-7) | | | | | | |

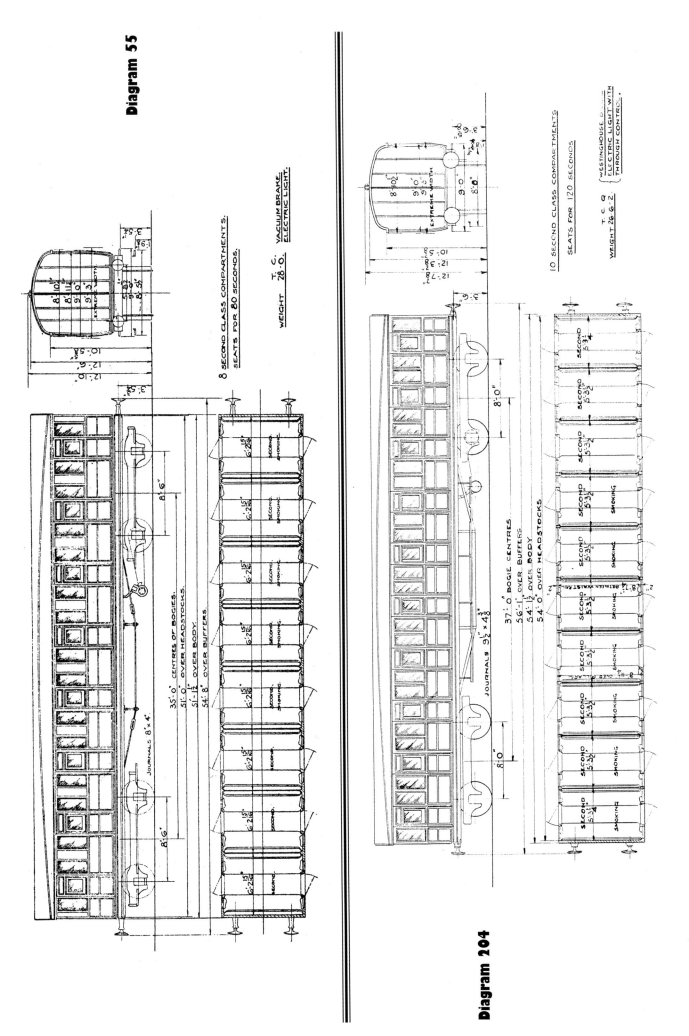

**Diagram 55**

8 SECOND CLASS COMPARTMENTS.
SEATS FOR 80 SECONDS.

T.C.
WEIGHT 28.O.
VACUUM BRAKE.
ELECTRIC LIGHT.

35'.O" CENTRES OF BOGIES.
51'.O" OVER HEADSTOCKS.
51'.1½" OVER BODY.
54'.8" OVER BUFFERS.

JOURNALS 8' × 4".

**Diagram 204**

10 SECOND CLASS COMPARTMENTS
SEATS FOR 120 SECONDS.

T.C.G
WEIGHT 26.6.2.
WESTINGHOUSE &
ELECTRIC LIGHT WITH
THROUGH CONTROL.

37'.O BOGIE CENTRES.
56'.1" OVER BUFFERS.
54'.1½" OVER BODY.
54'.O" OVER HEADSTOCKS.

JOURNALS 9½" × 4¾"

### Built 1928

| 48* | 1927/8 | 206 | 7: 56 | DK | 31872/3, 31912/4 | 81023/4/9/30 |
|---|---|---|---|---|---|---|
| CLC 8 | - | - | 8: 64 | CR | CLC 368/369 | 10624/5§ |

### Built 1929

| 48* | 1929/30 | 322 | 7: 56 | DK | 51655/6 | 88316, 81047 |
|---|---|---|---|---|---|---|

51655 altered in 1938 to a composite on Dia 306

### Built 1931

| 48* | 1930/1 | 396 | 7: 56 | DK | 31919/27/8, 31930/2 | 81031-5 |
|---|---|---|---|---|---|---|

### Built 1934

| 48* | 1933 | 497 | 7: 70 | DK | 6460 | 81054 |
|---|---|---|---|---|---|---|

### Built 1936

| 48* | 1935/6 | 693 | 7: 70 | YK | 6469-82 | 81055-68 |
|---|---|---|---|---|---|---|

The following vehicles were allocated to Scottish Region stock after 1949, and the number prefixed by SC: 81008-18/23, 81031-3, 81036-44, 81056-61, 82000

§ Numbers allocated after 1950 by the London Midland Region. Became M10624M etc, but not probably renumbered until 1953/4 having run until then as M368 etc.

# Seconds: (S)

### DIAGRAM 55

Identical to Diagram 57 thirds, and transferred to that Diagram with the withdrawal of second-class facilities on the GE section's London area services.

### DIAGRAM 204

Ilford stock. The interior finish and features were generally as for the first-class of the composites in these sets. The metal fittings of the second-class were teak-painted, rather than polished brass as in the first-class, a way no doubt of defining second-class where the compartments were in any case no more spacious than third-class!

Transferred to Diagram 203 on the withdrawal of second-class facilities on the GE section London area services.

Following electrification between Liverpool St and Shenfield in 1949, redundant Ilford stock remained out of use for some time but, in due course, many vehicles were used to provide underframes for non-gangwayed stock built for the London Tilbury & Southend section, and for covered carriage trucks (CCTs) principally intended for Anglo-Scottish car-carrying services introduced from 1956. The conversion of 100 such CCTs was approved by the Eastern Area Board in June 1956 of which 35 were former Ilford stock vehicles.

**A Diagram 56/57 third is first vehicle in this unidentified train entering Darlington behind 'D3' 4-4-0 No 4348 in May 1932.**

## LIST OF SECONDS (Ss):

| Diag No CBP | Order No | Compts/ seats | Built | Original number/ changes | 1943 number |
|---|---|---|---|---|---|
| **Built 1927** | | | | | |
| 55 | 1926/7 | - | 8: 80 | GLO | 6988/9 | 82360/1 |
| | | | | | Later thirds to Dia 57 |
| **Built 1935** | | | | | |
| 204 | 1935/6 | - | 10: 120 | CR | 6575-99 | 82403- 27 |
| | | | | | Ilford stock Air braked |

The underframes, running gear and body framing of 82412/7/8/20/1/5 were used for non-gangwayed third-class open lavatory vehicles built at Doncaster Works in 1953 to Diagram 375.

The underframes, running gear and body framing of 82408-11/5/9/23 were used for CCT vehicles built at Stratford Works in 1956/7 to Diagram 10.

# Thirds: (T)

### DIAGRAM 56

To the 9ft width and, combined with Diagram 57, comprising the most numerous single type of non-vestibuled coach, many being built by contractors.

The majority of those built for the NEA were transferred to the SSA and other Areas, as from the 1930/1 CBP and in subsequent programmes. The NEA had originally specified that its coaches should not have through lighting control which *was* fitted when the Diagram 56/57 vehicles were transferred. By this time, the original air brake fittings had been removed from those delivered new with dual-braking. The earlier GE section coaches were also dual-braked.

### DIAGRAM 57

The 9ft 3in width third.

### DIAGRAM 58

A 1924 design, employing underframes of GCR design, recovered from ambulance train vehicles.

### DIAGRAM 204

Ilford stock. As with the seconds, many vehicles were used to provide underframes for non-gangwayed stock built for the London Tilbury & Southend section, and for covered carriage trucks (CCTs) principally intended for Anglo-Scottish car-carrying services introduced from 1956.

### DIAGRAM CLC 20

Effectively identical to LNER Diagram 58, but lacking stepboards on the bogies.

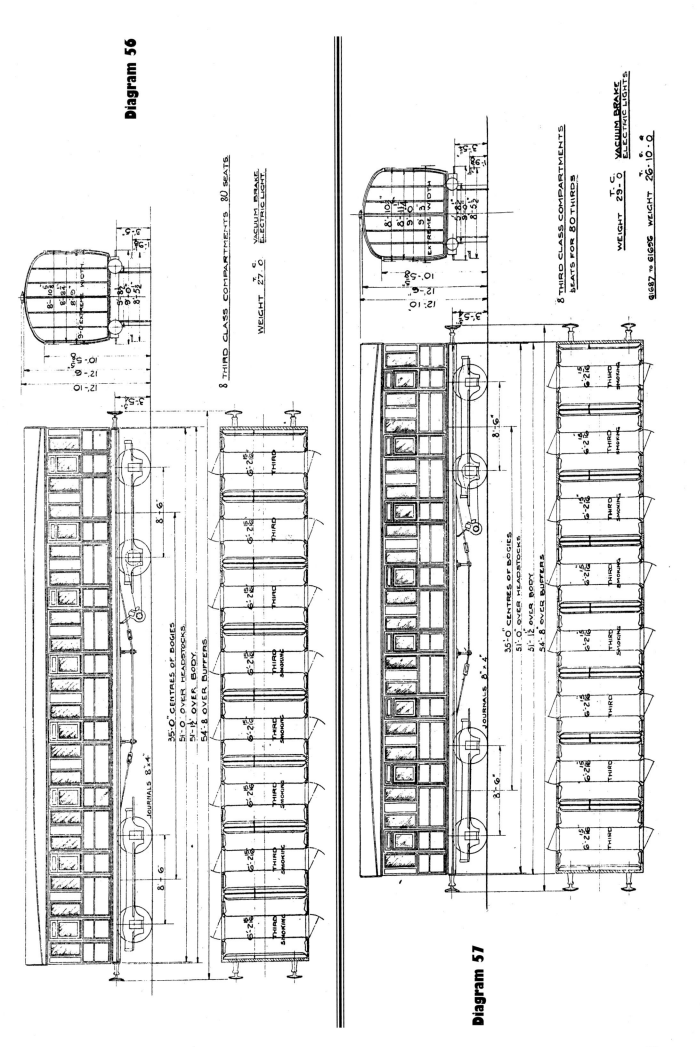

**Diagram 56**

8 THIRD CLASS COMPARTMENTS 80 SEATS.

WEIGHT 27·0  T.C.  VACUUM BRAKE
ELECTRIC LIGHT

35'-0" CENTRES OF BOGIES
51'-0" OVER HEADSTOCKS.
51'-12" OVER BODY.
54'-8" OVER BUFFERS.

JOURNALS 8"×4"

**Diagram 57**

8 THIRD CLASS COMPARTMENTS
SEATS FOR 80 THIRDS.

WEIGHT 29·0  T.C.  VACUUM BRAKE
ELECTRIC LIGHTS

91687 TO 61926  WEIGHT 26·10·0  T.C.

35'-0" CENTRES OF BOGIES
51'-0" OVER HEADSTOCKS
51'-12" OVER BODY
54'-8" OVER BUFFERS

JOURNALS 8"×4"

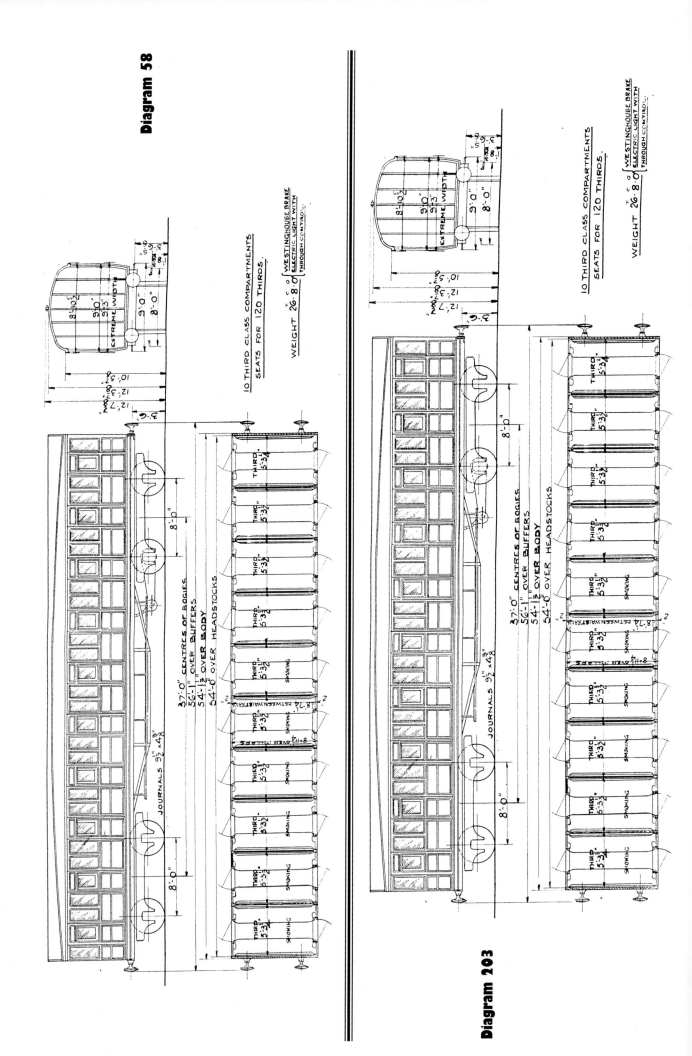

**Diagram 58**

EXTREME WIDTH

10 THIRD CLASS COMPARTMENTS
SEATS FOR 120 THIRDS.

WEIGHT 26·8·0 { WESTINGHOUSE BRAKE
ELECTRIC LIGHT WITH
THROUGH CONTROL.

JOURNALS 9½" × 4¾"

37'-0" CENTRES OF BOGIES.
56'-1" OVER BUFFERS
54'-1½" OVER BODY
54'-0" OVER HEADSTOCKS

8'-0"

8'-0"

8'+11¾" OVER PILLARS
8'-7¾" BETWEEN WAIST RAILS

| THIRD 5'-3½" | THIRD 5'-3½" | THIRD 5'-3½" | THIRD 5'-3½" | THIRD 5'-3½" | THIRD 5'-3½" | THIRD 5'-3½" | THIRD 5'-3½" | THIRD 5'-3½" | THIRD 5'-3½" |
|---|---|---|---|---|---|---|---|---|---|
| SMOKING | SMOKING | SMOKING | SMOKING | SMOKING | | | | | |

**Diagram 203**

EXTREME WIDTH

10 THIRD CLASS COMPARTMENTS
SEATS FOR 120 THIRDS.

WEIGHT 26·8·0 { WESTINGHOUSE BRAKE
ELECTRIC LIGHT WITH
THROUGH CONTROL.

JOURNALS 9½" × 4¾"

37'-0" CENTRES OF BOGIES.
56'-1" OVER BUFFERS
54'-1½" OVER BODY
54'-0" OVER HEADSTOCKS

8'-0"

8'-0"

8'+11¾" OVER PILLARS
8'-7¾" BETWEEN WAIST RAILS

| THIRD 5'-3½" | THIRD 5'-3½" | THIRD 5'-3½" | THIRD 5'-3½" | THIRD 5'-3½" | THIRD 5'-3½" | THIRD 5'-3½" | THIRD 5'-3½" | THIRD 5'-3½" | THIRD 5'-3½" |
|---|---|---|---|---|---|---|---|---|---|
| SMOKING | SMOKING | SMOKING | SMOKING | SMOKING | | | | | |

# LIST OF THIRDS (Ts):

| Diag No | CBP | Order No | Compts/ seats | Built | Original number/ changes | 1943 number |
|---|---|---|---|---|---|---|

**Built 1924**

| 58 | 1924/5 | 39 | 9: 108 | DK | 51722-5, 51851(41126), 51852-4 | 82363-6/2/7-9 |

**Built 1925**

| 56* | 1924/5 | 49 | 8: 80 | YK | 10263-82B (3671/2/5-9/81, 3688/90-3/5-8, 3723-5) | 82064-83, |
| | | | | | 320/35/50, 355/66/7, 3109/25/6/51/80, 3194/7, 3219/55/7/68, 3271/6/88 | 82023-42 |
| | | | | | 10303-23Y ≠ (22358, 21234[61891], 22323, 21169, 22199, 21603, 22353[61892], 22193[776], 21088/11, 22048, 22476, 22291[787], 21713, 21656, 22419[794], 22207[796], 22281, 21873, 21218, 22183) above became: 82019/141/018/04/16/09/142/7, 82003/1/14/21, 82148, 82012/11, 82149/50, 82017/13, 82005/15 | |
| | | - | | CL | 22046/9/55, 22065/96 (60617-21) | 82110-2/– /3 ≠ |
| | | - | | CR | 22135/47, 22200/19, 22242/79/92, 22348/59, 22396/450/551, 22940/1/3, (31028/2/30/4/42/40/15, 61889, 22359§, 31035, 60622/3, 61890, 22941§, 775) | 82099/8, 82100/1/4/3, 82097, 82139, 82020, 82102/14/5, 82140, 82022, 82146 all ≠ |
| | | | | | § ie, not transferred from NEA | |
| | | - | | RYP | 3470/1/3-5 | 82059-63 |

**Built 1926**

| 56* | 1924/5 | - | 8: 80 | BHM | 61616-25 | 82116-25  ≠ |
| | | | | GLO | 3353/9/63/71, 3385/8/91, 3392, 3400/53 | 82049-58 |
| | | | | HN | 3327/40/3/6/7 | 82044-8 |
| | | | | MET | 3326 | 82043 |
| | | | | MET | 21086, 21476/96, 21512, 21621 | 82002/6/7/8/10 |
| | | | | | 21010/2, 21163, 21477/92, 22104/9/14, 22132/58/9/74, 22210 (3839/60, 3771, 3803/21/52, 3777, 3805/66/27/54/79/3781) | 82091/4/84/7/9/92/85 82088/95/90/3/6/86 |
| | | | | ≠ | 21475, 21597, 22152, 22256/72 (4496/9, 4500-2) | 82105-9 |
| | | | | | 21009, 21136/67, 21469, 21718, 22124/55/71, 22220/49/52/89/95 (61856/64/86/61/57/62/3/58/87/8, 61859/65/60) | 82126/34/6/1/27/32, 82133/28/37/8/29, 82135/30 |
| | | | | | 21175, 22264/99 (765/73/4) | 82143-5 |

**Built 1927**

| 57* | 1926/7 | - | 8: 80 | CL | 3819/20/4/9/30, 3832/3/5-7 | 82268-77 |

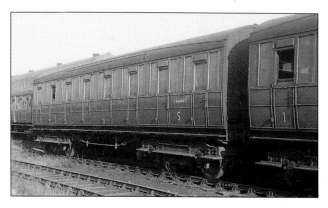

Top: **Diagram 56 non-vestibuled second No E82110E (built Clayton 1925 as 22046, later 60617).** Push-pull fitted for the Epping-Ongar service, and seen condemned at Stratford in February 1959.

Above: **Diagram 57 non-vestibuled second No SC82172E (built York 1928, as 338),** seen at Cairneyhill in June 1960, and a late survivor not being withdrawn until December 1962.

| | | | | CR | 61647-86 | 82310-49 |
| | | | | | 311/28/31/89, 3169/79/86, 3195/6, 3217 | 82168/70/1/9, 82286, 82287, 82191/5/6, 82203 |
| | | | | GLO | 21047, 21143, 21178, 21622, | 82303, 82153, 82264, 82155/7, 82305, 82285, 82304 |
| | | | | | 21872, 22052, 22318/85 (3749, 21143§, 3806, 21622§, 21872§, 3831, 3858, 3791) | |
| | | | | | § ie, not transferred from NEA | |
| | | | | HN | 21103/15, 21867, 22145/87, 22221/32/88, 22331/43 (52027, 21115§, 52028, CLC 573, CLC 572, 52029, CLC 571, 52030, CLC 570, 22343§) | 82306, 82152, 82307, M14961E, M14960E, 82308/ – / 82309, M14958E, 82162 |
| | | | | | § ie, not transferred from NEA | |
| | | | | MET | 3235/51, 3338/58/68/9, 3642, 3655/9/80, 3722/53/8-60/2-6/8/70/2-6, 3778-80/2-90/2-4/6-8, 3801/4/12-4 | 82205/8/17-29 82230-4/6-57/9-63/5-7 |
| | | | | RYP | 21118/25, 22101 (3767/95, 3808) | 82235/58, 82302 |
| | | | | | 3840-5/7 | 82278-84 |
| | 1927/8 | 205 | | YK | 21022, 21206, 21714, 22127/68, 22290, 22325/60/87 | 82151/4/6/8-61/3/4 ≠ |

**Built 1928**

| 57* | 1927/8 | 205 | 8: 80 | YK | 21177, 22370/61, 325/38/49, 359/61/8/9, 376, 3101/31, 3146/9/53, 3154/60/2/74/92, 3201/5/8/12/5/21/49/59, 3260/4 | 82165-7  ≠ 82169/72-8, 82180-8/94, 82197/9-202, 82204/7/11-3 |
| CLC 20 | - | - | 9:108 | CR | CLC 360-363 | M14999M, M15000-2M§ |

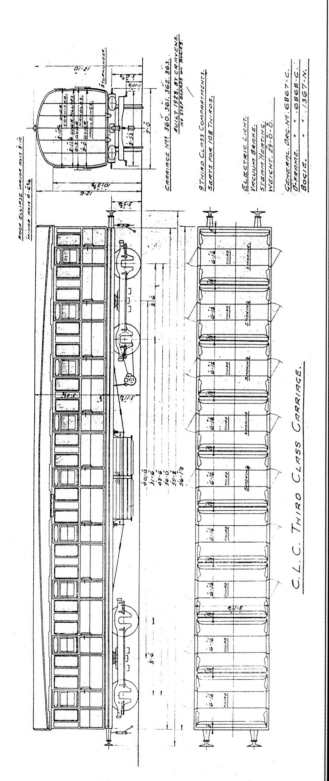

Diagram CL620

C.L.C. THIRD CLASS CARRIAGE.

9 THIRD CLASS COMPARTMENTS.
SEATS FOR 108 THIRDS.

ELECTRIC LIGHT.
VACUUM BRAKE.
STEAM HEATING.
WEIGHT. 29.0.0.

GENERAL DRG. N°. 6867.C.
O-FRAME. " " 6868.C.
BOGIE. " " 1367.N.

CARRIAGE N°S 360, 361, 362, 363.
BUILT 1928, BY CRAVENS.
NO STEP BOARDS OR BRAKES.

---

**Built 1929**

| | | | | | | |
|---|---|---|---|---|---|---|
| 57* | 1928/9 | 248 | 8: 80 | DK | 3970/1/4-85 61687-96 | 82288-82301 82350-9 |

**Built 1930**

| | | | | | | |
|---|---|---|---|---|---|---|
| 57* | 1929/30 | 323 | 8: 80 | DK | 3176/82/7/9, 3202/45/52/6, 3274/85/6 | 82189/90, 82192/3/8, 82206/9/10/4-6 |

**Built 1935**

| | | | | | | |
|---|---|---|---|---|---|---|
| 203 | 1935/6 | - | 10: 120 | RYP | 60074-60100 | 82376-82402 |
| | | | | | Ilford stock Air braked | |

The following vehicles were allocated to Scottish Region stock after 1949, and the number prefixed by SC: 82001/5/7/9/13/5-60/2/4-72/4-7/9-84/6-95/9, 82100-9, 82115, 82127-30/2/7/8, 82140/2/3/8-75/7-9, 82181-6/8-99, 82200-2/4-6/8-10/4-8, 82220/2, 82228-87, 82290-3/5/7/9-306/8/9/11-6/8/22/7/30/9/44-6/9, 82351/6-8/62/3/8.

§ Numbers allocated after 1950 by the London Midland Region. Became M14999M or E etc, but not probably renumbered until 1953/4, having run until then as M360 etc.

The underframes, running gear and body framing of 82378/85/90/1/4/8 were used for non-gangwayed third-class vehicles built at York Works in 1953 to Diagram 372.

The underframes, running gear and body framing of 82379/80/93/402 were used for CCT vehicles built at Stratford Works in 1956/7 to Diagram 10.

# Composites: (C)
## (C) (4 – 3)

### DIAGRAM 51

The main type of non-lavatory composite, but less numerous than Diagrams 49/50 – see below.

The GE examples had armrests at the ends of the first-class seats only and a higher seating capacity.

### DIAGRAM 110

The GE section's first/second-class composite, later altered to first/third-class and transferred to Diagram 51.

### DIAGRAM 188

A former Diagram 47 first, converted to a composite and renumbered in 1935. Although the diagram shows that the armrests were retained, note that five-a-side seating was indicated.

### DIAGRAM 189

Former Diagram 48 firsts, converted to composites and renumbered in 1935. Although the diagram shows that the armrests were retained, note that five-a-side seating was indicated.

## (C) (4 – 5)

### DIAGRAM 205

Ilford stock. Later altered to first/third-class. As with the seconds and thirds, several vehicles were used to provide underframes for non-gangwayed stock built for the London Tilbury & Southend section, and for covered carriage trucks (CCTs) principally intended for Anglo-Scottish car-carrying services introduced from 1956.

## (C) (miscell)

### DIAGRAM 215

A one-off for the GE section, with two first-class, and five third-class compartments.

### DIAGRAM 283

Former Diagram 46 firsts, converted to composites and renumbered in 1938 when the armrests were removed, giving six-a-side seating in the third-class.

**Diagram 51**

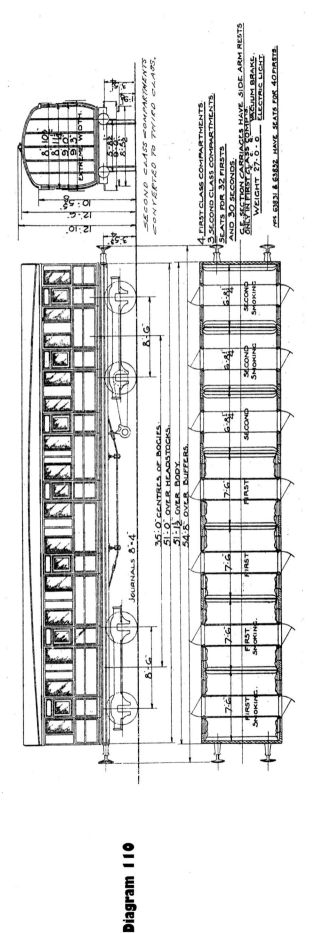

JOURNALS 8″×4″

35′-0″ CENTRES OF BOGIES
51′-0″ OVER HEADSTOCKS
51′-1½″ OVER BODY
54′-8″ OVER BUFFERS

4 FIRST CLASS COMPARTMENTS
3 THIRD CLASS COMPARTMENTS
SEATS FOR 32 FIRSTS
AND 30 THIRDS

WEIGHT T. C. O. VACUUM FITTED
27 · 10 · 8 ELECTRIC LIGHT

G.E.SECTION VEHICLES HAVE SIDE ARM RESTS
ONLY & HAVE SEATS FOR 40 FIRSTS.

THIRD SMOKING · THIRD SMOKING · THIRD · FIRST · FIRST · FIRST SMOKING · FIRST SMOKING

**Diagram 110**

JOURNALS 8″×4″

35′·0″ CENTRES OF BOGIES.
51′·0″ OVER HEADSTOCKS.
51′·1½″ OVER BODY.
54′·8″ OVER BUFFERS.

SECOND CLASS COMPARTMENTS
CONVERTED TO THIRD CLASS.

4 FIRST CLASS COMPARTMENTS.
3 SECOND CLASS COMPARTMENTS.
SEATS FOR 32 FIRSTS
AND 30 SECONDS.

G.E. SECTION CARRIAGES HAVE SIDE ARM RESTS
ONLY IN FIRST CLASS COMPTS.
WEIGHT 27·0·0 VACUUM BRAKE.
ELECTRIC LIGHT.

N°S 62831 & 62852 HAVE SEATS FOR 40 FIRSTS.

SECOND SMOKING · SECOND SMOKING · SECOND · FIRST · FIRST · FIRST SMOKING · FIRST SMOKING

**Diagram 188**

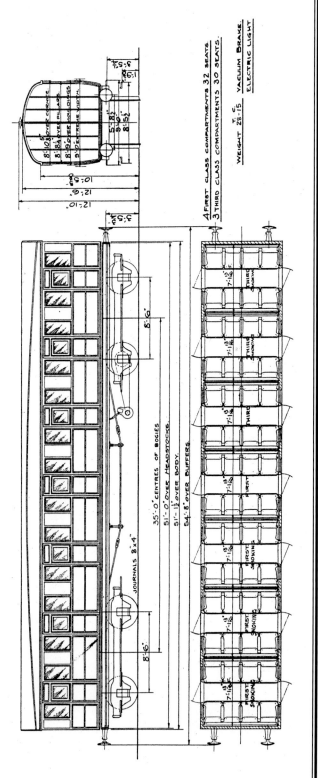

8'-10½" OVER CENTRE
8'-8¼" OVER PILLARS
8'-9" OVER MOULDINGS
9'-2" EXTREME WIDTH

10'-5½"
12'-6"
12'-10"

5'-8½"
9'-0"
8'-5½"

A FIRST CLASS COMPARTMENTS 32 SEATS.
3 THIRD CLASS COMPARTMENTS 30 SEATS.

T. C.
WEIGHT 28·15    VACUUM BRAKE.
ELECTRIC LIGHT

35'-0" CENTRES OF BOGIES.
51'-0" OVER HEADSTOCKS.
51'-1½" OVER BODY.
54'-8" OVER BUFFERS.

8'-6"
8'-6"

JOURNALS 8 x 4"

THIRD
SMOKING    7'-1⅛"
THIRD
SMOKING    7'-1⅛"
THIRD    7'-0"
FIRST
SMOKING    7'-1⅛"
FIRST
SMOKING    7'-1⅛"
FIRST
SMOKING    7'-1⅛"

---

**Diagram 205**

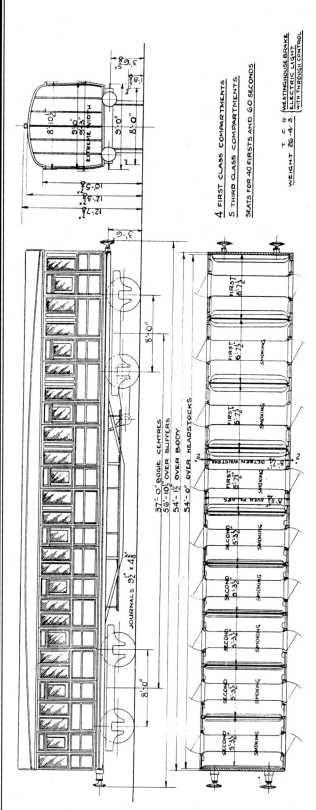

8'-10½"
9'-0"
9'-0"
8'-0"
EXTREME WIDTH

10'-5½"
12'-3½"
12'-7½"

3'-0"
3'-3"

4 FIRST CLASS COMPARTMENTS
5 THIRD CLASS COMPARTMENTS
SEATS FOR 40 FIRSTS AND 60 SECONDS

T. C. Q.    WESTINGHOUSE BRAKE
WEIGHT 26·4·3.   ELECTRIC LIGHT
WITH THROUGH CONTROL

37'-0" BOGIE CENTRES
56'-10½" OVER BUFFERS
54'-1⅛" OVER BODY
54'-0" OVER HEADSTOCKS

8'-0"
8'-0"

JOURNALS 9½ x 4⅛"

FIRST 6'-7½"
FIRST 6'-7½"   SMOKING
FIRST 6'-7½"   SMOKING
FIRST 6'-7½"   SMOKING
FIRST 6'-7½"   SMOKING
8'-7¼" BETWEEN WAISTRAIL
8'-11¼" OVER PILLARS
SECOND 5'-3¾"   SMOKING
SECOND 5'-3¾"   SMOKING
SECOND 5'-3¾"   SMOKING
SECOND 5'-3¾"   SMOKING
SECOND 5'-3¾"   SMOKING

## DIAGRAM 306

Former Diagram 48 first, converted to a composites and renumbered in 1938 when the armrests were removed, giving six-a-side seating in the lone third-class compartment.

## DIAGRAM CLC 52

On a 56ft underframe and with no equivalent LNER Diagram.

## LIST OF COMPOSITES (Cs):

| Diag No CBP | Order No | Compts/ seats | Built | Original number/ changes | 1943 number | |
|---|---|---|---|---|---|---|
| **Built 1927** | | | | | | |
| 51* | 1926/7 176 | 4/3 : 32/30 | SF | 32459-67 | 88104-12 | |
| **Built 1928** | | | | | | |
| 51* | 1927/8 211 | 4/3 : 32/30 | DK | 32277, 32310/1 | 88101-3 | |
| | 1928/9 258 | | | 32513-6 | 88113-6 | |
| | | | | 63261-5 | 88117-21 | |
| | | | | 40 first-class seats | 63265 push-pull | |
| CLC 52 | - - | 4/4 : 32/48 | CR | CLC 436, 448-450 | 16893-6§ | |
| **Built 1929** | | | | | | |
| 51* | 1929/30 329 | 4/3 : 40/30 | DK | 63833-6 | 88124-7 | |
| 110* | 1929/30 328 | 4/3 : 40/30 | DK | 63831/2 | 88122/3 | |
| | | First/second compos, later on Dia 51 | | | | |
| **Built 1935** | | | | | | |
| 205 | 1935/6 - | 4/5 : 40/60 | GLO | 64058-81 | 82428-51 | Ilford stock |
| | | First/second compos, later first/third | | | | Air braked |
| **Built 1936** | | | | | | |
| 215 | 1935/6 637 | 2/6 : 20/60 | DK | 63891 | 88148 | |
| | | First/ second compo, later first/third | | | | |
| **Built 1937** | | | | | | |
| 51* | 1935/6 668 | 4/3 : 40/30 | DK | 63944-7 | 88128-31 | |
| 110* | 1935/6 669 | 4/3 : 32/30 | DK | 63948/9 | 88132/3 | |
| | | First/second compos, later on Dia 51 | | | | |
| **Built 1943** | | | | | | |
| 205 | special 1028 | 4/5 : 40/60 | YK | 64075 | 82445 | |
| | | New body, original DEA. | | | | |

§ Numbers allocated after 1950 by the London Midland Region. Became M16893M or E etc, but not probably renumbered until 1953/4 having run until then as M436 etc.

The underframes, running gear and body framing of 82430/1/7/40/2/3 were used for non-gangwayed composite vehicles built at Doncaster Works in 1953 to Diagram 374.

The underframes, running gear and body framing of 82434/6/9/51 were used for CCT vehicles built at Stratford Works in 1956/7 to Diagram 10.

The underframe of 88111 was used for CCT E96203 built at Doncaster Works in 1960 under BR Lot 30674.

# Lavatory composites: (CL)

The LNER standard semi-corridor lavatory composite was intended for longer workings, and had internal corridors for access to the lavatory in each class, the first-class corridor on one side and the third-class, on the opposite side of the body. There were long windows along each corridor side, except in the case of Diagram 244.

The layout was a success and was perpetuated for the prewar steel-panelled designs, the postwar LNER designs, and by BR for the non-vestibuled standard stock.

Ilford stock Diagram 205 non-vestibuled second No E82432E (built Gloucester 1935 as first/second composite No 64062). Probably disused since Shenfield electrification but seen at Stratford in August 1957. Note the GER-pattern bogies.

## DIAGRAM 49

The 9ft width version.

## DIAGRAM 50

The 9ft 3in width version.

## DIAGRAM 244

An unusual variant, with reduced first-class accommodation as compared with Diagrams 49/50, and without the long windows to the corridor alongside the first-class.

All were built for the GE section. They constituted part of a major – and much needed – re-equipment in the mid/late 1930s of the section's outer suburban and branch line stock, in a drive to eliminate pre-Grouping six-wheeled coaches. Three were dual-fitted as built.

## LIST OF LAVATORY COMPOSITES (CLs):

| Diag No CBP | Order No | Compts/ seats | Built | Original number/ changes | 1943 number | |
|---|---|---|---|---|---|---|
| **Built 1925** | | | | | | |
| 49* | 1924/5 63 | 3/4 : 19/33 | SF | 32284/96, 32304/28 | 88000-3 | |
| **Built 1926** | | | | | | |
| 49* | 1925/6 - | 3/4 : 19/33 | MID | 32331/6/62/3 | 88004-7 | |
| | | | | 63782-91 | 88008-16/– | ≠ |
| **Built 1927** | | | | | | |
| 50* | 1926/7 150 | 3/4 : 19/33 | YK | 63266-75 | 88069-76/–/7 | |
| | | | | 32344/73, | 88019/22/3/5/7/9 | |
| | | | | 32436/54/6/8 | | |
| | 175 | | DR | 63276-90 | 88078-92 | |
| **Built 1928** | | | | | | |
| 50* | 1927/8 210 | 3/4 : 19/33 | DK | 32323/34/46/51, | 88017/8/20/1, | |
| | | | | 32480-93 | 88030-43 | |
| **Built 1929** | | | | | | |
| 50* | 1928/9 259 | 3/4 : 19/33 | DK | 32494-32512 | 88044-62 | |
| **Built 1930** | | | | | | |
| 50* | 1929/30 327 | 3/4 : 19/33 | DK | 32443/55/7 | 88024/6/8 | |
| | 1930/1 398 | | DK | 32520-3 | 88063-6 | |
| **Built 1931** | | | | | | |
| 50* | 1930/1 398 | 3/4 : 19/33 | DK | 32529/30 | 88067/8 | |
| **Built 1934** | | | | | | |
| 50* | 1933 498 | 3/4 : 19/33 | DK | 63867-70 | 88093-6 | |

## Diagram 215

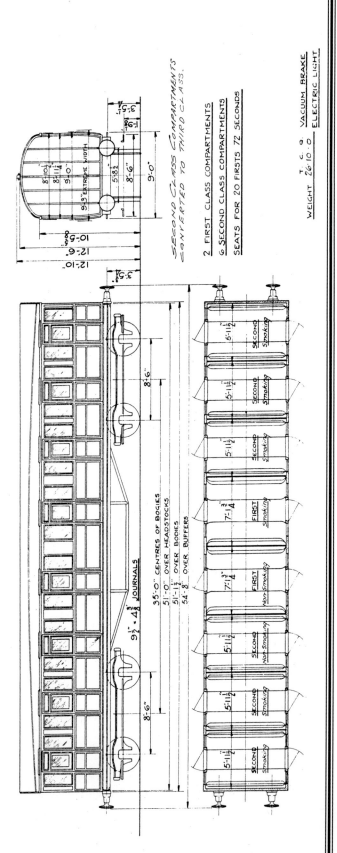

SECOND CLASS COMPARTMENTS
CONVERTED TO THIRD CLASS.

2 FIRST CLASS COMPARTMENTS
6 SECOND CLASS COMPARTMENTS

SEATS FOR 20 FIRSTS 72 SECONDS

T. C. G.  VACUUM BRAKE
WEIGHT  26·10·0  ELECTRIC LIGHT

## Diagram 283

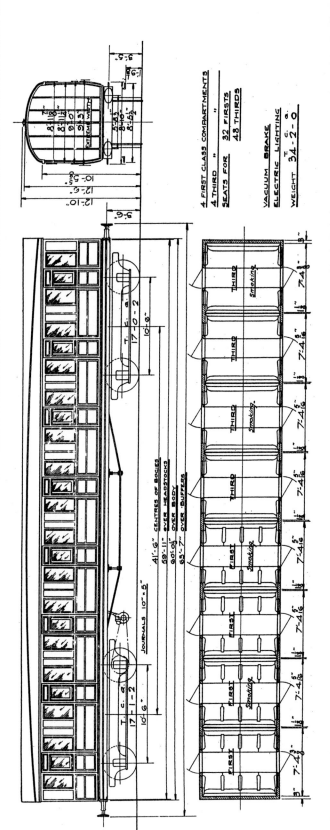

4 FIRST CLASS COMPARTMENTS
4 THIRD   "        "

SEATS FOR   32 FIRSTS
            48 THIRDS

VACUUM BRAKE
ELECTRIC LIGHTING
WEIGHT  T. C. G.  34·2·0

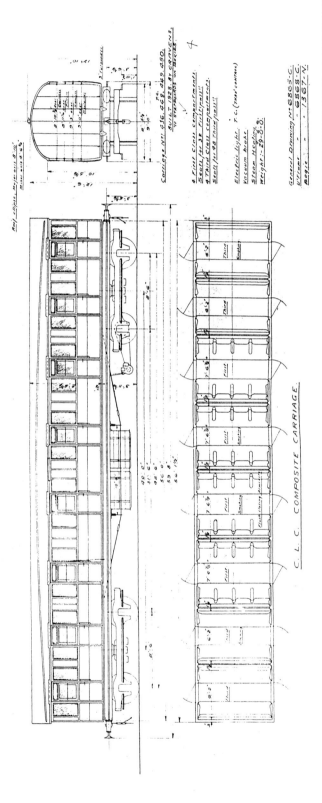

**Diagram CLC52**

C.L.C. COMPOSITE CARRIAGE

*(drawing annotations, partly legible:)*
Carriage Nos 436, 468, 449, 450.
BUILT 1928 BY CRAVENS w STEPBOARDS on BOGIES.

4 First Class compartments
Seats for 32 First Class
4 Third Class compartments
Seats for 48 Third Class

Electric light    T.C. (TRAIN CONTROL)
Vacuum brake
Steam Heating
Weight :- 29-0-0

General Drawing Nº 6865-C.
Vitreal :- 6868-C.
Bogie :- 1367-N.

| | | | | | | | |
|---|---|---|---|---|---|---|---|
| 50* | 1934 | 569 | 3/4 : 19/33 | YK | 63887-90 | 88097-88100 | |

**Built 1936**

| | | | | | | | |
|---|---|---|---|---|---|---|---|
| 244 | 1935/6 | - | 2/5 : 13/41 | CR RYP | 63892-63917 63918-43 63898-900 ≠ 63940 DEA Stratford 1940 | 88201-26 88227-48/ — /9-51 | |

The following vehicles were allocated to Scottish Region stock after 1949, and the number prefixed by SC: 88024/53.

The underframes of 88007/30/44 were used for CCTs E96200/2/1 built at Doncaster Works in 1960 under BR Lot 30674.

# Brake thirds: (BT)
## (BT) (3)

### DIAGRAM 66
The 9ft width version, without guard's ducket and with two sets of double doors to the guard's brake/luggage compartment. Van labelled to carry three tons.

### DIAGRAM 119
The 9ft 3in width version, with guard's ducket.

### LIST OF BRAKE THIRDS (BTs):

| Diag No CBP | Order No | Compts/ seats | Built | Original number/ changes | 1943 number |
|---|---|---|---|---|---|
| **Built 1926** | | | | | |
| 66 | 1925/6 - | 3: 30 | BHM | 3645/7/51/3, 3654/6-8, 3661/3/5/7/8/70 | 86158-71 |
| **Built 1928** | | | | | |
| 119* | 1927/8 208 | 3: 30 | DK | 3490/5, 3606/9, 3611/46/9/64 | 86768-70/ — /2/4-6 |
| 119* | 1928/9 253 | | YK | 31018/9/20, 31031/3/6/7, 31043/6/56/8/9/62 | 86777-89 |
| **Built 1930** | | | | | |
| 119* | 1928/9 331 | 3: 30 | YK | 3610/2 | 86771/3 |

The following vehicles were allocated to Scottish Region stock after 1949, and the number prefixed by SC: 86163-7, 86768/9/72/4-6.

## (BT) (4)

### DIAGRAM 64
The 9ft width version, without guard's ducket and with two sets of double doors to the guard's brake/luggage compartment. Van labelled to carry two and a half tons.

### DIAGRAM 65
The 9ft 3in width version of Diagram 64.

### DIAGRAM 128
As Diagram 65, but with guard's ducket.
One transferred to the CLC in 1932.

### LIST OF BRAKE THIRDS (BTs):

| Diag No CBP | Order No | Compts/ seats | Built | Original number/ changes | 1943 number |
|---|---|---|---|---|---|
| **Built 1926** | | | | | |
| 64 | 1925/6 - | 4: 40 | CL | 3631/2/4, 3635/7/8/41/3 | 86050-7 |

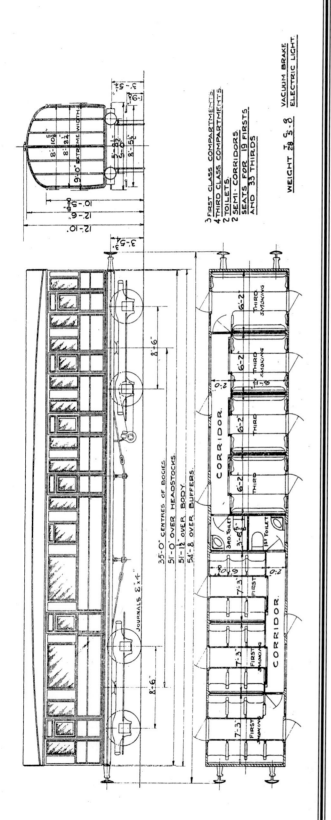

**Diagram 49**

3 FIRST CLASS COMPARTMENTS
4 THIRD CLASS COMPARTMENTS
2 TOILETS
2 SEMI-CORRIDORS
SEATS FOR 19 FIRSTS
AND 33 THIRDS

VACUUM BRAKE
ELECTRIC LIGHT

WEIGHT 28.5.8 T.C.

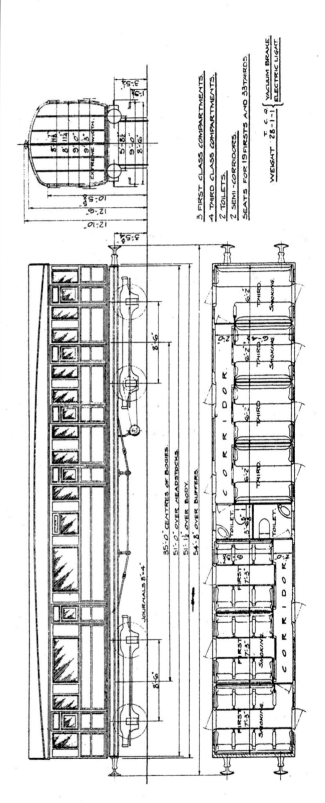

**Diagram 50**

3 FIRST CLASS COMPARTMENTS
4 THIRD CLASS COMPARTMENTS
2 TOILETS
2 SEMI-CORRIDORS
SEATS FOR 19 FIRSTS AND 33 THIRDS

VACUUM BRAKE
ELECTRIC LIGHT

WEIGHT 28-1-1 T.C.2

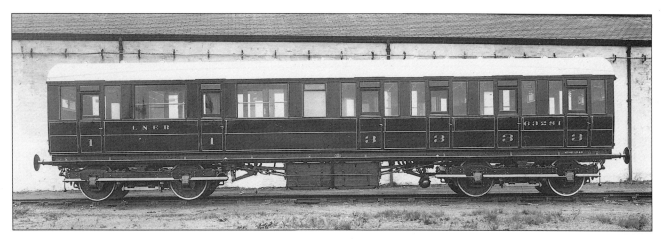

Above: **Diagram 50 non-vestibuled composite No 63281 (built Doncaster 1927).Later 88083.**

Left: **Diagram 50 non-vestibuled composite No E88052E (built Dukinfield 1929 as 32502), photographed condemned at Stratford in February 1959.**

**Build 1926 (cond)**

| | | | | | |
|---|---|---|---|---|---|
| | | | | | 21002/3/5/6/8 86058-61, ¶86997 (62668-71, 7571¶)<br>¶ Converted to Dia 320,1942 and reno 7571 |
| 65* | 1925/6 | 149 | 4: 40 | YK | 317/29/42/3/52, 86063-75/—/6-9/86983¶/<br>362/79/85/99, 86084/5<br>3107/20/72/7/84/5/98,<br>3216/31/3¶,<br>3287, 3331<br>¶ 3233 to Dia 317, 1940 |

**Built 1927**

| | | | | | |
|---|---|---|---|---|---|
| 65* | 1926/7 | 149 | 4: 40 | YK | 21633, 21790 86984¶, 86156<br>(7572¶/3)<br>Transfers 1935 ¶ converted to Dia 317 in 1940<br>3644, 86116-26<br>3731-4/6/7/8, 86134-53<br>3741-3<br>62571-90§<br>§Detail differences from the rest on this Dia |
| | 1927/8 | 207 | | YK | 22313, 86062, 86157<br>22369 (7574) Transferred 1935<br>3275/7/9/83, 86080-3/6-94,<br>3332/3/6, 86096-8, 86100/6-8/10<br>3341/4/60/2/5/73/7,<br>3383/4/7, 3408/29/48,<br>3454 |

**Built 1928**

| | | | | | |
|---|---|---|---|---|---|
| 65* | 1927/8<br>1928/9 | 207<br>252 | 4: 40 | YK | 3375, 3992/4, 86095,<br>31002/10/2/6/7 86127-33<br>62608/9 86154/5 |
| 128* | 1927/8 | 207 | 4: 40 | YK | 22312 Trans 1932<br>(CLC 590) M22532M after c 1950 |

**Built 1930**

| | | | | | |
|---|---|---|---|---|---|
| 65* | 1929/30 | 324 | 4: 40 | YK | 3386/9, 3396/7, 86099, 86101-5<br>3401/4,<br>3452/8/88/96/9, 86109/11-5<br>3609 |
| 128* | 1929/30<br>1930/1 | 324<br>397 | 4: 40 | YK | 62624-9 86806-9/ — /11<br>3687/9 86798/9 |

**Built 1931**

| | | | | | |
|---|---|---|---|---|---|
| 128* | 1930/1 | 397 | 4: 40 | DK | 3694/9, 86800-5<br>3735/9/44/7 |

The following vehicles were allocated to Scottish Region stock after 1949, and the number prefixed by SC: 86050-3, 86063-9/80/2/6-93/6-8, 86100/6-8, 86111-5, 86127-31, 86798/9, 86800-5

# (BT) (5)

### DIAGRAM 61
The 9ft 3in width version, without guard's ducket, and with one set of double doors. Van labelled to carry two tons.

### DIAGRAM 62
The 9ft width version of Diagram 61. Guard's door next the passenger compartments, instead of towards the vehicle's brake end. Without the customary end windows.

### DIAGRAM 63
The 9ft width version of Diagram 61, but with the more customary layout as compared to Diagram 62, and with van end windows.

### DIAGRAM 117
Generally as Diagram 63, but with guard's ducket.

### LIST OF BRAKE THIRDS (BTs):

| Diag No CBP | Order No | Compts/ seats | Built | Original number/ changes | 1943 number |
|---|---|---|---|---|---|
| **Built 1925** | | | | | |
| 62 | 1924/5 | 62 | 5: 50 | YK | 10324-47B 86018-41<br>(3477/9/80/3/4,<br>3486/7/91/2/4/7,<br>3501/52/70/92/4,<br>3597-9, 3601/2/4,<br>3605/14) |
| 62 | 1924/5 | - | 5: 50 | CR | 3616/9/22/7-9 86042-7 |
| **Built 1926** | | | | | |
| 63 | 1925/6 | - | 5: 50 | CR | 62543-8 ≠<br>62543-6 altered to Dia 254,<br>1938 became 86878-81<br>62547/8 as Dia 63 became 86048/9 |
| **Built 1927** | | | | | |
| 61* | 1926/7 | 161 | 5: 50 | DK | 3745/6/8, 86008-16<br>3750-2/4-6 |
| **Built 1928** | | | | | |
| 61* | 1926/7 | 161 | 5: 50 | DK | 3757 86017 |
| **Built 1930** | | | | | |
| 117 | 1929/30 | 330 | 5: 50 | DK | 5771/2 86766/7 |

The following vehicles were allocated to Scottish Region stock after 1949, and the number prefixed by SC: 86034-47.

# Diagram 244

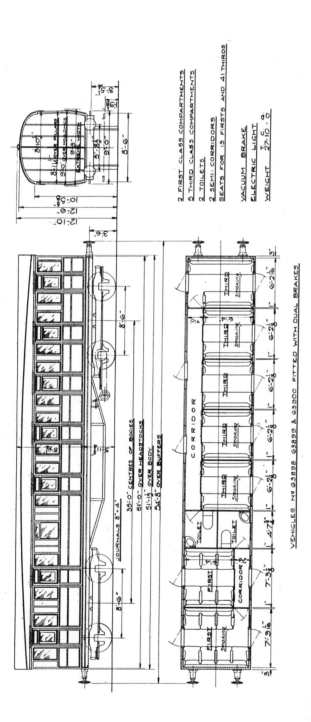

2 FIRST CLASS COMPARTMENTS
5 THIRD CLASS COMPARTMENTS
2 TOILETS
2 SEMI-CORRIDORS
SEATS FOR 13 FIRSTS AND 41 THIRDS

VACUUM BRAKE
ELECTRIC LIGHT
WEIGHT    27-10-0

VEHICLES Nº G3898, G3899 & G3900 FITTED WITH DUAL BRAKES

# Diagram 66

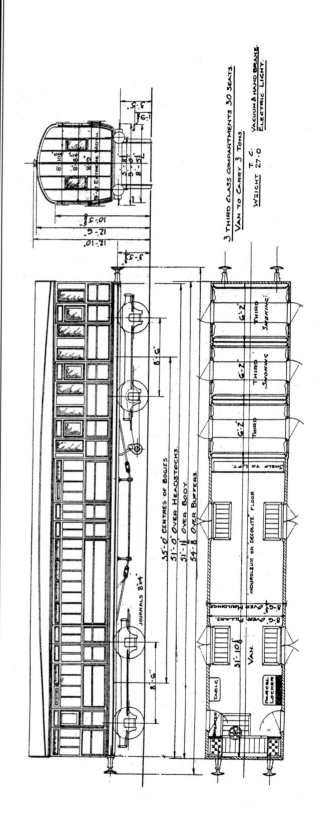

3 THIRD CLASS COMPARTMENTS  30 SEATS
VAN TO CARRY 3 TONS.

T. C.   VACUUM & HAND BRAKE.
WEIGHT 27-0     ELECTRIC LIGHT.

Above: **A Diagram 66 non-vestibuled brake third is behind 'J83' 0-6-0T No 9826 shunting at Edinburgh Waverley in 1929. The picture illustrates the length of van of this type of brake third.**

Right: **Another view of one of the three-compartment brake thirds. This is Diagram 119 No E86773E (the former No 3612, built York 1930).**

Below right: **Diagram 65 non-vestibuled brake second No E86138E (built York 1927, as 62575). Converted to push-pull, and seen with push-pull fitted second No E82134E to Diagram 56. Built by Metro in 1926 as 21136 and, later, the GE section's 61864.**

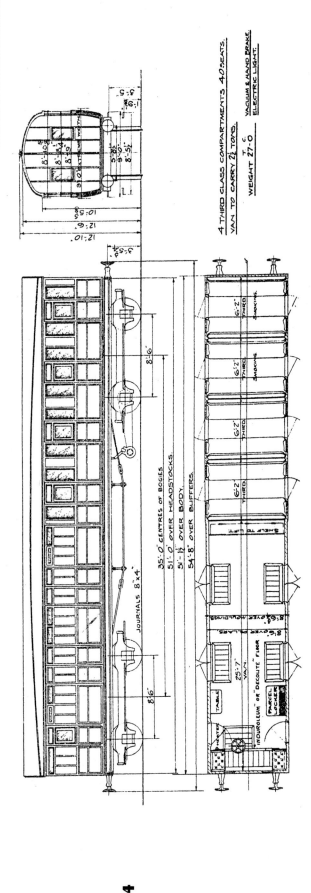

## Diagram 119

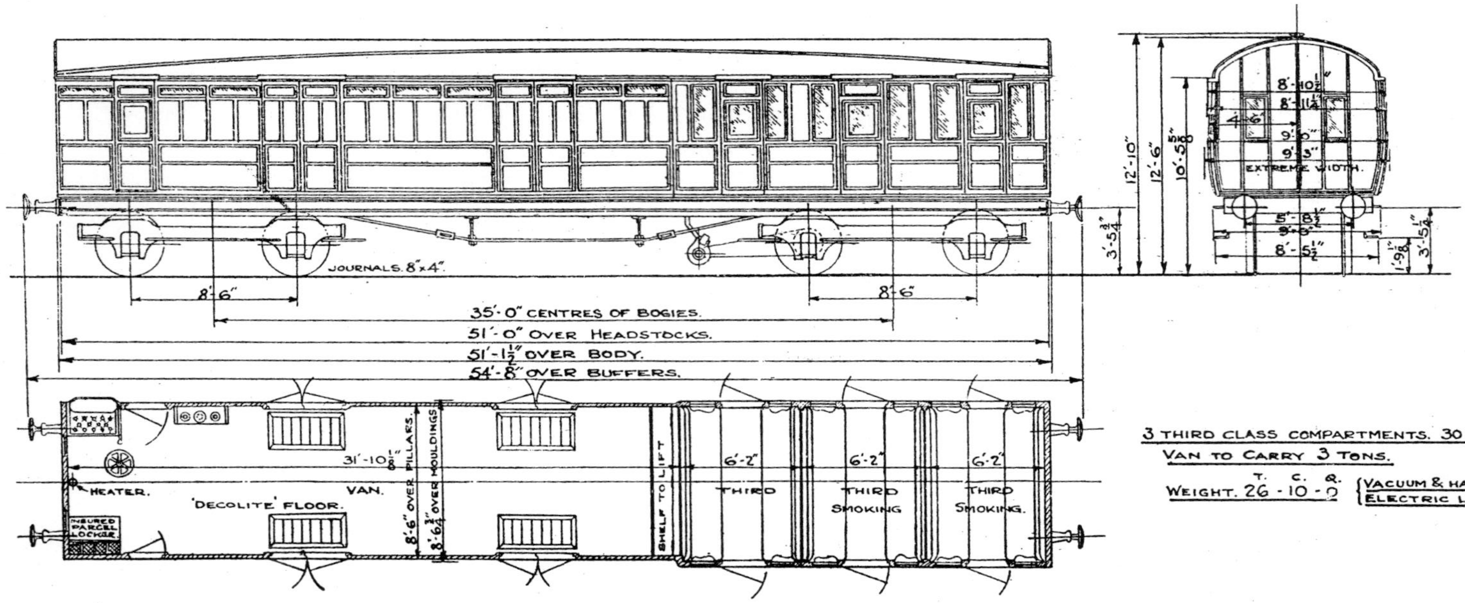

3 THIRD CLASS COMPARTMENTS. 30 SEATS
VAN TO CARRY 3 TONS.
T. C. & {VACUUM & HAND BRAKE
WEIGHT 26-10-2 {ELECTRIC LIGHT.

## Diagram 64

4 THIRD CLASS COMPARTMENTS 40 SEATS.
VAN TO CARRY 2½ TONS.
T. C. {VACUUM & HAND BRAKE
WEIGHT 27-0 {ELECTRIC LIGHT.

**Diagram 65**

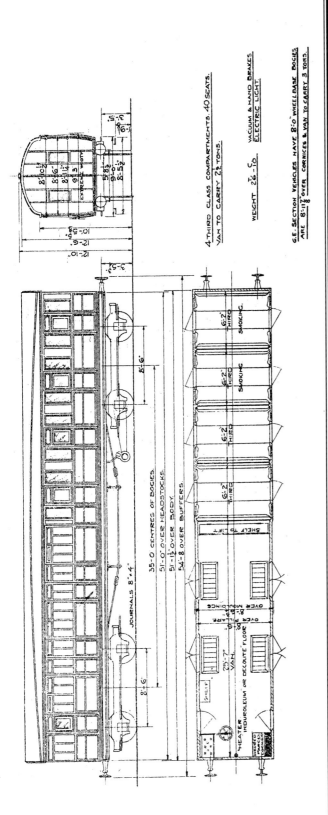

35'-0" CENTRES OF BOGIES.
51'-0" OVER HEADSTOCKS.
51'-1½" OVER BODY.
54'-8" OVER BUFFERS.

JOURNALS 8"×4".

4 THIRD CLASS COMPARTMENTS. 40 SEATS.
VAN TO CARRY 2½ TONS.

WEIGHT 26-10.  VACUUM & HAND BRAKES
ELECTRIC LIGHT.

G.E. SECTION VEHICLES HAVE 8'-0" WHEELBASE BOGIES
ARE 8'-11⅞" OVER CORNICES & VAN TO CARRY 3 TONS.

**Diagram 128**

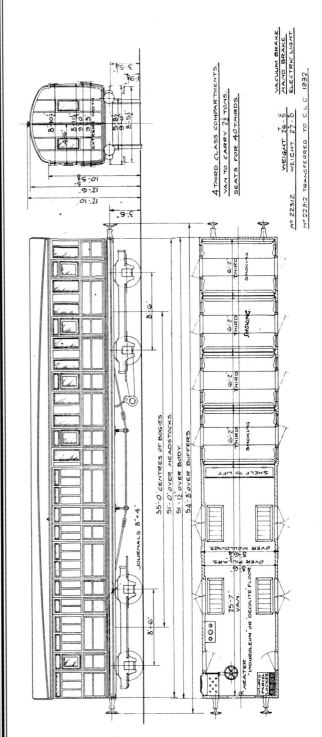

35'-0" CENTRES OF BOGIES.
51'-0" OVER HEADSTOCKS.
51'-1½" OVER BODY.
54'-8" OVER BUFFERS.

JOURNALS 8"×4".

4 THIRD CLASS COMPARTMENTS.
VAN TO CARRY 2½ TONS.
SEATS FOR 40 THIRDS.

Nº 22312.

WEIGHT 26-5.  VACUUM BRAKE
WEIGHT 27-0.  HAND BRAKE
ELECTRIC LIGHT.

Nº 22312 TRANSFERRED TO C.L.C. 1932.

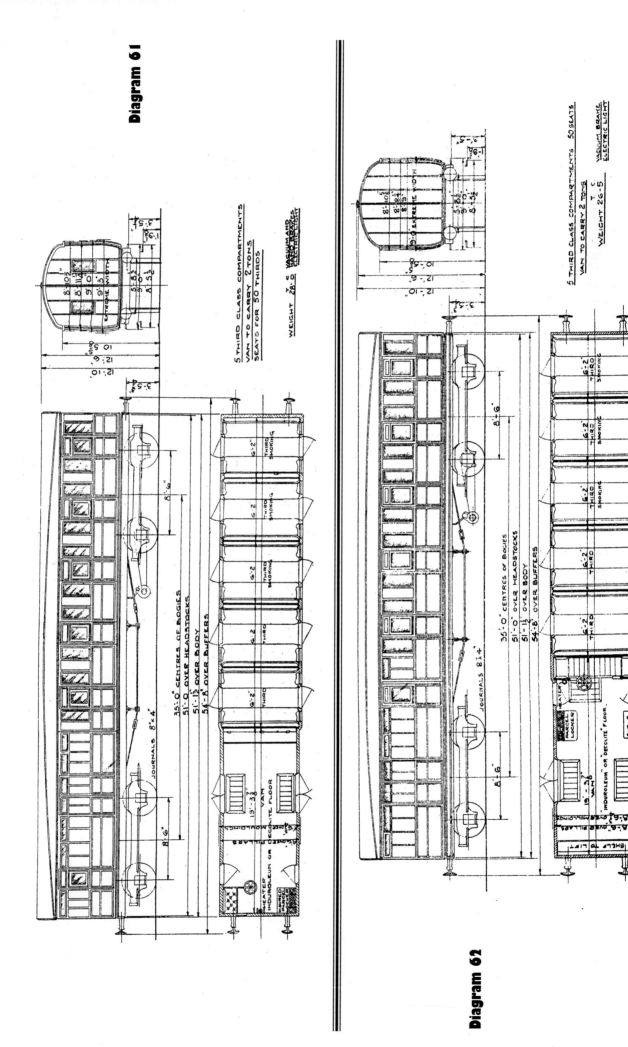

Diagram 61

5 THIRD CLASS COMPARTMENTS
VAN TO CARRY 2 TONS
SEATS FOR 50 THIRDS

VACUUM AND
HAND BRAKES
ELECTRIC LIGHT

WEIGHT T.C.
28·0

Diagram 62

5 THIRD CLASS COMPARTMENTS   50 SEATS
VAN TO CARRY 2 TONS
WEIGHT T.C.
26·5

VACUUM BRAKE
ELECTRIC LIGHT

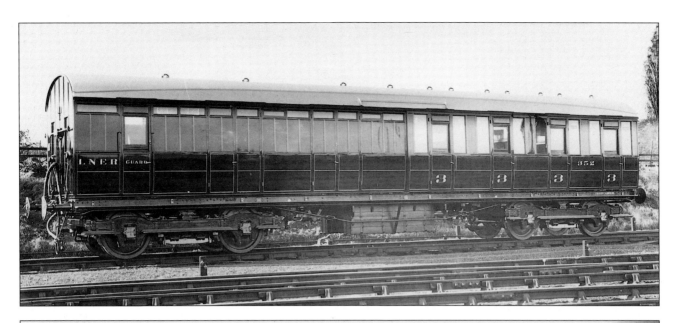

# (BT) (6)

### DIAGRAM 59

The GCR design 56ft ex-ambulance coach underframe used for a Gresley outline design. One set of double doors each side, and with the van labelled to carry two tons. No end windows, and with handrails to access steps.

### DIAGRAM 60

To 9ft 3in width, with a single pair of doors to each side of the guard's/luggage compartment, one of each pair opening inwards, the other outwards. Van labelled to carry one and a half tons.

### DIAGRAM 133

As Diagram 60, but with guard's ducket.

### DIAGRAM 246

Very similar to Diagram 133, but with angle-iron trussing, and with minor differences to the guard's/luggage van, including a droplight in one of the double doors.

Built for Marylebone suburban services where they ran with teak-bodied articulated and non-vestibuled twins.

Top: **Diagram 65 non-vestibuled brake third No 352 (built York 1926, and later 86067 in the 1943 renumbering).**

Above: **Diagram 62 non-vestibuled brake second No SC86043E (built Cravens 1925 as 3619). Seen at Cairneyhill in June 1960, and condemned in October 1960.**

### DIAGRAM CLC 37

On a (new) 56ft underframe, and similar to LNER Diagram 59.

### LIST OF BRAKE THIRDS (BTs):

| Diag No | CBP | Order No | Compts/ seats | Built | Original number/ changes | 1943 number |
|---|---|---|---|---|---|---|
| *Built 1924* | | | | | | |
| 59 | 1924/5 | 40 | 6: 72 | DK | 5978, 51715-21 | 86000-7 |
| *Built 1928* | | | | | | |
| 60* | 1926/7 | 162 | 6: 60 | DK | 21113, 22167/277 | M22536/7/5M after 1950 ≠ |
| | Transferred to CLC as 575, 586, 574 1930, 1932,1930 | | | | | |
| 133 | 1926/7 | 209 | 6: 60 | YK | 21750, 22060/92 | – /M22538/9M after 1950 |
| | Transferred to CLC as 588/7/9 1932 588 DEA | | | | | |
| CLC 37* | - | - | 6: 72 | CR | CLC 300, 301 | 22630/1§ |

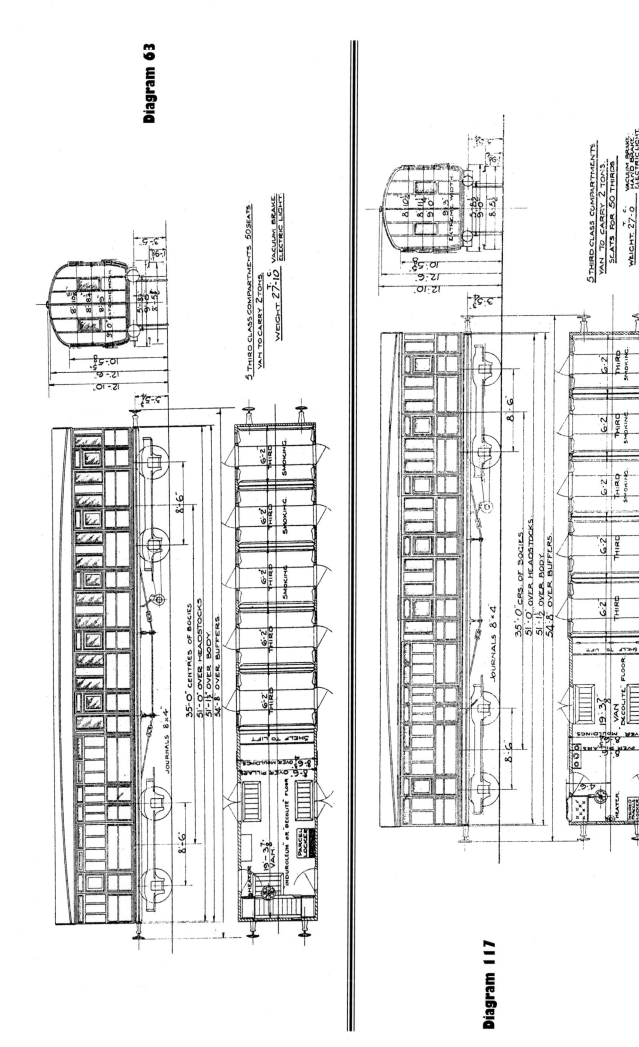

**Diagram 63**

5 THIRD CLASS COMPARTMENTS, 50 SEATS
VAN TO CARRY 2 TONS
T.C. VACUUM BRAKE    ELECTRIC LIGHT
WEIGHT 27·10

**Diagram 117**

5 THIRD CLASS COMPARTMENTS
VAN TO CARRY 2 TONS
SEATS FOR 50 THIRDS
T.C.    VACUUM BRAKE
HAND BRAKE
WEIGHT 27·0    ELECTRIC LIGHT

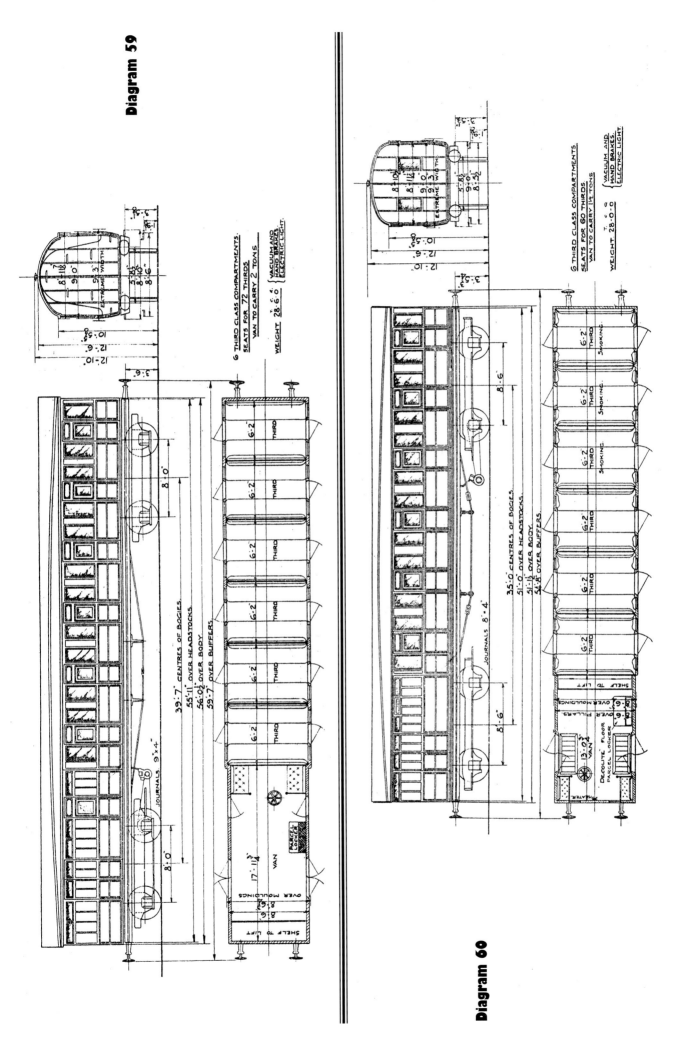

**Diagram 59**

6 THIRD CLASS COMPARTMENTS.
SEATS FOR 72 THIRDS
VAN TO CARRY 2 TONS
WEIGHT 28·6·0 { VACUUM AND HAND BRAKE ELECTRIC LIGHT.

**Diagram 60**

6 THIRD CLASS COMPARTMENTS.
SEATS FOR 60 THIRDS
VAN TO CARRY 1½ TONS
WEIGHT 28·0·0 { VACUUM AND HAND BRAKES ELECTRIC LIGHT.

**Diagram 133**

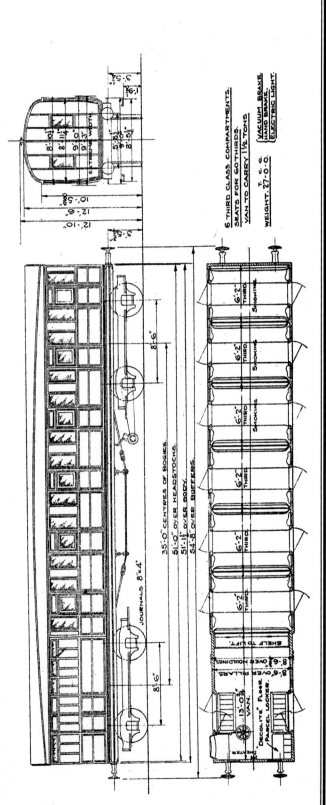

6 THIRD CLASS COMPARTMENTS.
SEATS FOR 60 THIRDS.
VAN TO CARRY 1½ TONS.

T. C. Q.
WEIGHT. 27·0·0.

VACUUM BRAKE.
HAND BRAKE.
ELECTRIC LIGHT.

**Diagram 246**

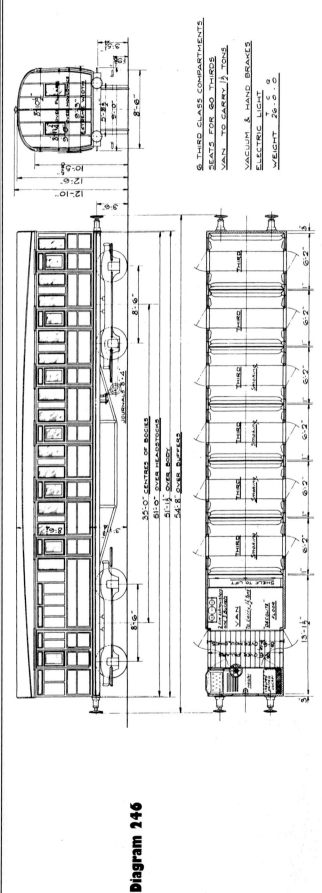

6 THIRD CLASS COMPARTMENTS
SEATS FOR 60 THIRDS
VAN TO CARRY 1½ TONS

VACUUM & HAND BRAKES
ELECTRIC LIGHT

T. C. Q.
WEIGHT 26·0·0

**Diagram CLC37**

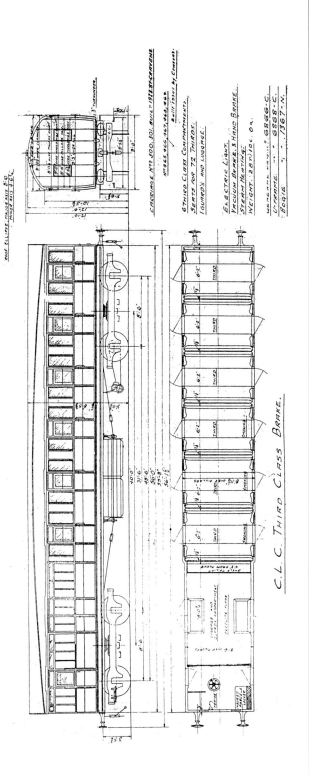

CARRIAGE N°S 300, 301. BUILT 1928 BY CRAVENS

Built 1980 by Craven?

6 THIRD CLASS COMPARTMENTS.
SEATS FOR 72 THIRDS.
1 GUARD'S AND LUGGAGE.

ELECTRIC LIGHT.
VACUUM BRAKE, & HAND BRAKE.
STEAM HEATING.
WEIGHT : 28 T 10 C. 0 Q.

| WORKING WIDTH : | 6' 8 6/8 C. |
| U-FRAME | " | 6' 3 6/8 C. |
| BOGIE | " | 1' 3 6/7 N. |

C.L.C. THIRD CLASS BRAKE.

---

**Diagram 202**

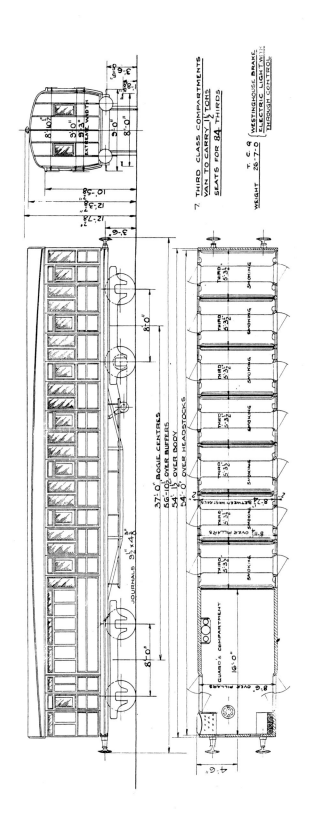

7. THIRD CLASS COMPARTMENTS
VAN TO CARRY 1½ TONS
SEATS FOR 84 THIRDS

T. C. Q
WESTINGHOUSE BRAKE.
ELECTRIC LIGHT WITH
THROUGH CONTROL.

WEIGHT 26-7-0

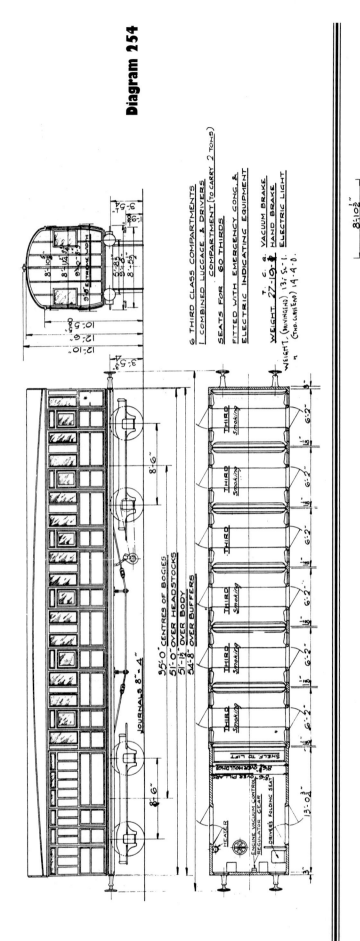

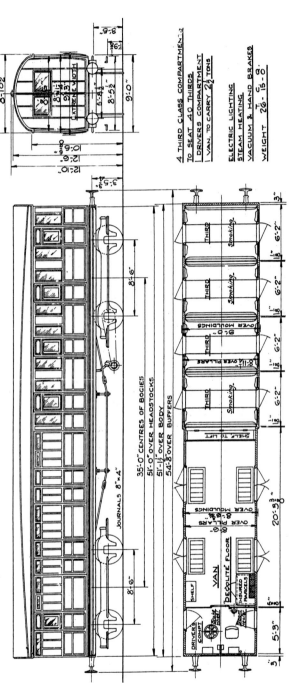

**Diagram 254**

6 THIRD CLASS COMPARTMENTS
1 COMBINED LUGGAGE & DRIVERS
COMPARTMENT (TO CARRY 2 TONS)

SEATS FOR 60 THIRDS

FITTED WITH EMERGENCY GONG &
ELECTRIC INDICATING EQUIPMENT

T. C. & VACUUM BRAKE
HAND BRAKE
ELECTRIC LIGHT

WEIGHT 27-19-0

WEIGHT (HAVING END) 13-15-1.
" (THD.CLASS END) 14-4-0.

35'-0" CENTRES OF BOGIES
51'-0" OVER HEADSTOCKS
51'-1½" OVER BODY
54'-8" OVER BUFFERS

JOURNALS 8" × 4"

8'-6"

THIRD Smoking

ENGINE VACUUM CONTROL
REGULATOR GEAR

DRIVERS FOLDING SEAT

HEATER

SHELF TO LIFT

**Diagram 317**

4 THIRD CLASS COMPARTMENTS
TO SEAT 40 THIRDS
1 DRIVERS COMPARTMENT
1 VAN. TO CARRY 2½ TONS

ELECTRIC LIGHTING
STEAM HEATING
VACUUM & HAND BRAKES
WEIGHT 26 - 15 - 0.

35'-0" CENTRES OF BOGIES
51'-0" OVER HEADSTOCKS
51'-1½" OVER BODY
54'-8" OVER BUFFERS

JOURNALS 8" × 4"

8'-6"

THIRD Smoking

VAN

DRIVERS COMPT

SHELF TO LIFT

INSURED
PARCELS

**Built 1930/1**

| | | | | | | |
|---|---|---|---|---|---|---|
| CLC 37* | - | - | 6: 72 | CR | CLC 465-469 | 22632-6§ |

**Built 1938**

| | | | | | | |
|---|---|---|---|---|---|---|
| 246 | 1937 | 794 | 6: 60 | DK | 52303-18 | 86838-53 |
| | 1938 | 849 | | DK | 57300-3 | 86854-7 |

§ Numbers allocated after 1950 by the London Midland Region. Became M22630M or E etc, but not probably renumbered until 1953/4 having run until then as M465 etc.

# (BT) (7)

## DIAGRAM 202

Ilford stock. With a single pair of doors each side of the guard's compartment, one of each pair opening inwards, the other outwards. Van labelled to carry one and a half tons.

### LIST OF BRAKE THIRDS (BTs):

| Diag No | CBP | Order No | Compts/ seats | Built | Original number/ changes | 1943 number | |
|---|---|---|---|---|---|---|---|
| **Built 1935** | | | | | | | |
| 202 | 1935/6 | - | 7: 84 | CR | 62074-86 | 86812-24 | Ilford stock |
| | | | | RYP | 62087-99 | 86824-37 | Air braked |

The underframes, running gear and body framing of 86814/5/7/20/3/33 were used for non-gangwayed brake third vehicles built at York Works in 1953 to Diagram 373.

The underframes, running gear and body framing of 86812/37 were used for CCT vehicles built at Stratford Works in 1956/7 to Diagram 10.

# Ordinary brake third – driving carriage: (BT)

## DIAGRAM 254

Diagram 63 brake thirds converted in 1936 for auto-train working in the Norwich area of the GE section, in replacement of Clayton steam rail-cars. Ran with ex-GER coaches to form a two-coach set. 62543 (86878) with ex-GER 61570; 62544 (86879) with ex-GER 61569; 62545 (86880) with ex-GER 61573; 62546 (86881) with ex-GER 61572.

## DIAGRAM 317

Diagram 65 brake thirds converted in 1940 for auto-train working in the SSA and NSA.

## DIAGRAM 320

One Diagram 64 brake thirds converted in 1942 for auto-train working in the NSA.

Details under appropriate brake third diagrams.

Diagram 202 non-vestibuled brake third No E86829E (built Pickering 1935 as 62091). Seen at Peterborough in June 1955, probably having been disused since the Shenfield electrification in 1949 but not officially withdrawn until February 1958.

# Brake composites: (BC)

Four designs of non-vestibuled brake composite were built, only for the Southern Scottish Area.

## DIAGRAM 52

To 9ft 3in width, with two first-class and three third-class compartments. One set of double doors to each side of the luggage/guard's van which was labelled to carry two tons.

## DIAGRAM 53

To 9ft 3in width, with two first-class and two third-class compartments. One set of double doors to each side of the luggage/guard's van which was labelled to carry two and a half tons.

## DIAGRAM 54

To 9ft width, with two first-class and two third-class compartments. One set of double doors to each side of the luggage/guard's van which was labelled to carry two and a half tons.

## DIAGRAM 118

To 9ft 3in width, with two first-class and four third-class compartments. One set of double doors to each side of the luggage/guard's van which was labelled to carry 10 cwt.

## DIAGRAM 318

Diagram 118 brake thirds converted in 1940 for auto-train working.

### LIST OF BRAKE COMPOSITES (BCs):

| Diag No | CBP | Order No | Compts/ seats | Built | Original number/ changes | 1943 number |
|---|---|---|---|---|---|---|
| **Built 1926** | | | | | | |
| 54 | 1925/6 | - | 2/2 : 16/20 | CL | 32364/7 | 80012/3 |
| **Built 1927** | | | | | | |
| 52 | 1926/7 | 165 | 2/3 : 16/30 | DK | 32468-75 | 80000-7 |
| 53 | 1926/7 | 177 | 2/2 : 16/20 | SF | 32476-9 | 80008-11 |
| **Built 1930** | | | | | | |
| 118 | 1929/30 | 326 | 2/4 : 16/40 | DK | 32527/8 | 80082/3 |
| | 1930/1 | 399 | | DK | 32533/4 | 80326/7 |

Converted for push-pull working on Dia 318 1940

**Diagram 320**

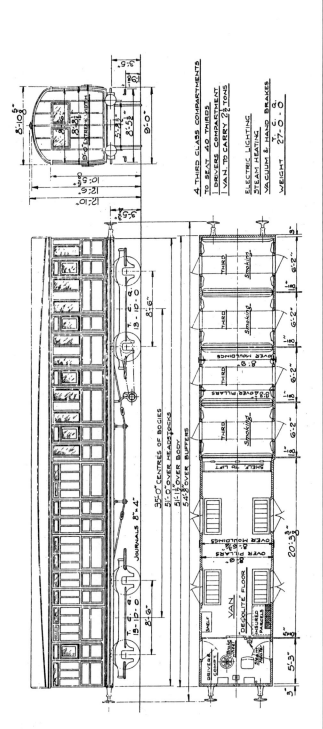

4 THIRD CLASS COMPARTMENTS
TO SEAT 40 THIRDS
1 DRIVERS COMPARTMENT
1 VAN. TO CARRY 2½ TONS

ELECTRIC LIGHTING
STEAM HEATING
VACUUM & HAND BRAKES
T. C. Q.
WEIGHT 27-0-0

**Diagram 52**

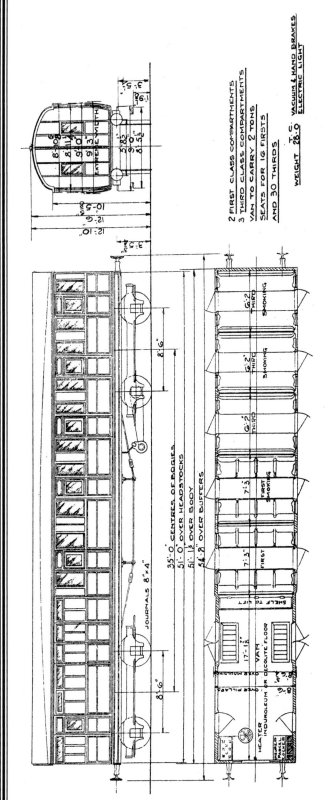

2 FIRST CLASS COMPARTMENTS
3 THIRD CLASS COMPARTMENTS
VAN TO CARRY 2 TONS
SEATS FOR 16 FIRSTS
AND 30 THIRDS

T. C.
WEIGHT 28·0
VACUUM & HAND BRAKES
ELECTRIC LIGHT

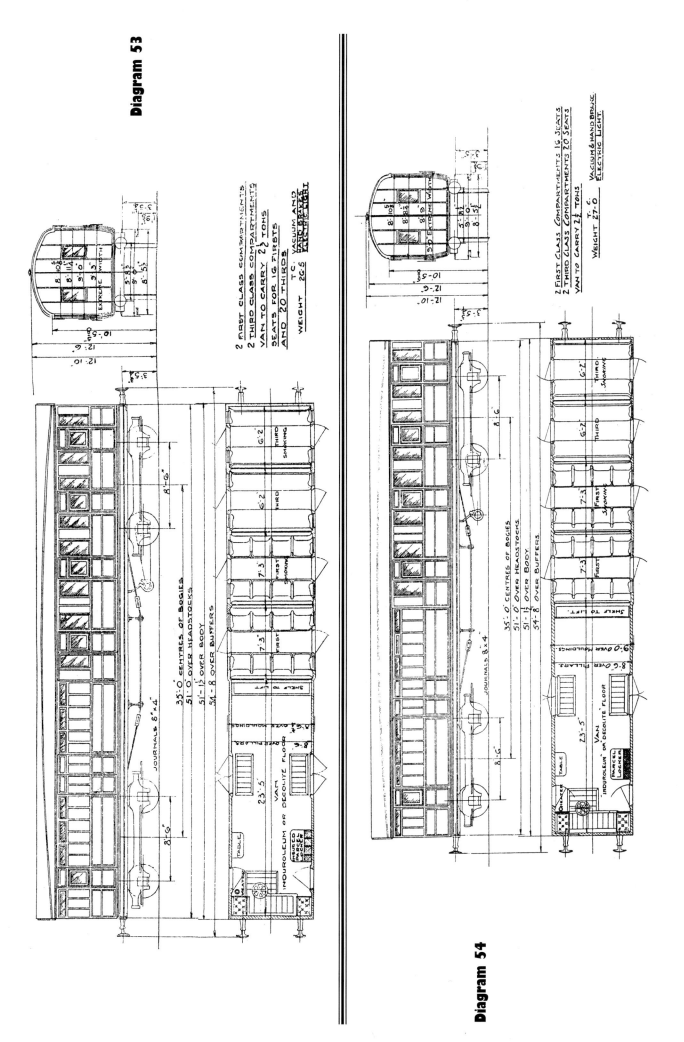

**Diagram 53**

2 FIRST CLASS COMPARTMENTS
2 THIRD CLASS COMPARTMENTS
VAN TO CARRY 2½ TONS
SEATS FOR 16 FIRSTS
AND 20 THIRDS

T.C. VACUUM AND
HAND BRAKE
ELECTRIC LIGHT

WEIGHT 26.5

**Diagram 54**

2 FIRST CLASS COMPARTMENTS 16 SEATS
2 THIRD CLASS COMPARTMENTS 20 SEATS
VAN TO CARRY 2½ TONS

T.C. VACUUM & HAND BRAKE
ELECTRIC LIGHT

WEIGHT 27.0

# Diagram 118

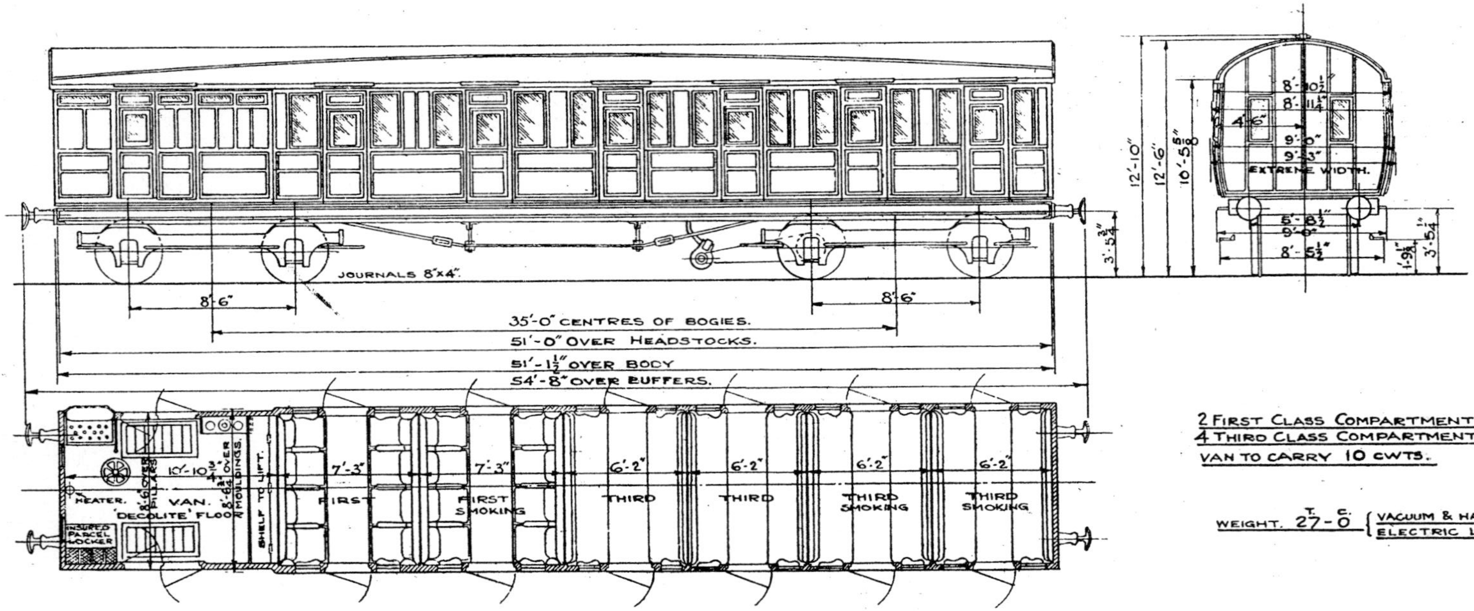

2 FIRST CLASS COMPARTMENTS 16 SEATS.
4 THIRD CLASS COMPARTMENTS 40 SEATS.
VAN TO CARRY 10 CWTS.

WEIGHT. 27-0. { VACUUM & HAND BRAKE
ELECTRIC LIGHT.

35'-0" CENTRES OF BOGIES.
51'-0" OVER HEADSTOCKS.
51'-1½" OVER BODY.
54'-8" OVER BUFFERS.
JOURNALS 8"×4".

THIRD SMOKING
THIRD SMOKING
THIRD
THIRD
FIRST SMOKING
FIRST

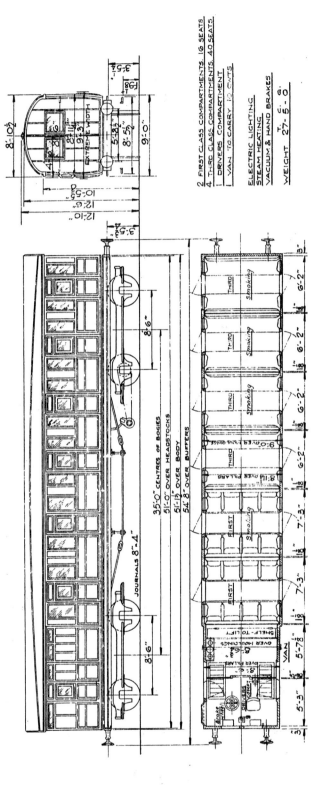

# Diagram 318

2 FIRST CLASS COMPARTMENTS. 16 SEATS.
4 THIRD CLASS COMPARTMENTS. 40 SEATS.
1 DRIVERS COMPARTMENT
1 VAN TO CARRY 10 CWTS.

ELECTRIC LIGHTING
STEAM HEATING
VACUUM & HAND BRAKES
WEIGHT 27-5-0

35'-0" CENTRES OF BOGIES.
51'-0" OVER HEADSTOCKS.
51'-1½" OVER BODY.
54'-8" OVER BUFFERS.
JOURNALS 8"×4".

THIRD Smoking
THIRD Smoking
THIRD Smoking
THIRD
FIRST Smoking
FIRST
VAN

# ARTICULATED TWINS/
# QUADRUPLETS/QUINTUPLETS

Gresley was *the* proponent of articulation in Britain, and although the LMS and GWR each made some use of the principle, it was with no great enthusiasm. The introduction of articulated vehicles was an expedient on Gresley's part to try to cure the poor riding of six-wheeled East Coast Joint Stock vehicles which were paired, articulated and mounted on three bogies. This experiment dated from 1907, and its success meant that Gresley used articulation for new London suburban stock introduced by the Great Northern Railway from 1910. These were twins, and from the early days of World War I some twin articulated stock was built for GNR main line services. Next came the quintuplet dining car set for the Leeds service, and this entered traffic in 1921. In the first year of Grouping, ten non-vestibuled twins were built to an order placed by the GNR during the previous year, and these were for semi-fast services to/from Kings Cross.

As the LNER planned the introduction of new stock, Gresley's keenness for articulation soon became evident. The production of quad art sets for the London suburban services of the GN section had begun before Grouping, and, apart from new coaches, this included the reformation of the 1910 articulated twins in quad arts, in some cases involving the construction of new coaches to make up the four-coach units. The re-equipment of the rolling stock used on the GE section London suburban services was urgent, and this provided another opportunity for the use of articulation. The priority was to replace stock used on the Enfield and Chingford services, and first thoughts were to build 15 suburban trains,

**A down train formed of two quad arts on Holloway bank in 1937 behind 'N2' 0-6-2T No 4757. Leading is a quad of Diagrams 72-75. Alongside the 'N2' in a siding is a Diagram 40 vestibule brake third.**

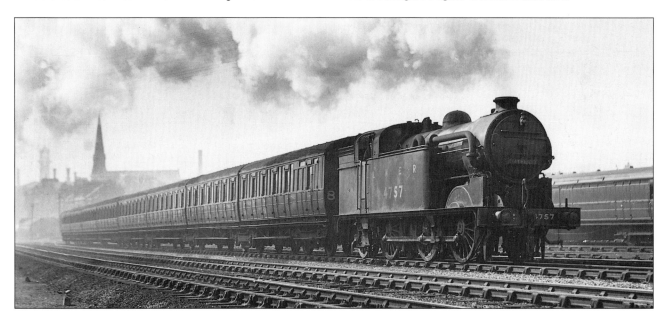

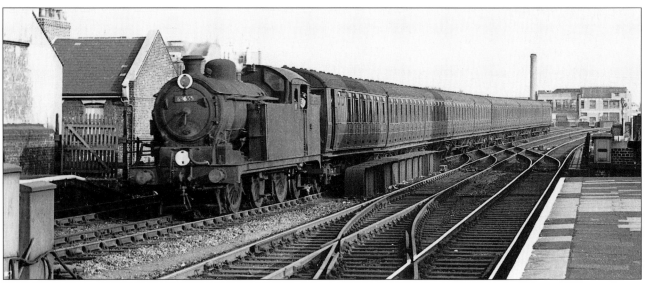

Two quint arts in use on a Liverpool St-Chingford train approaching Hackney Downs on 12 August 1955 behind 'N7' 0-6-2T No 69655.

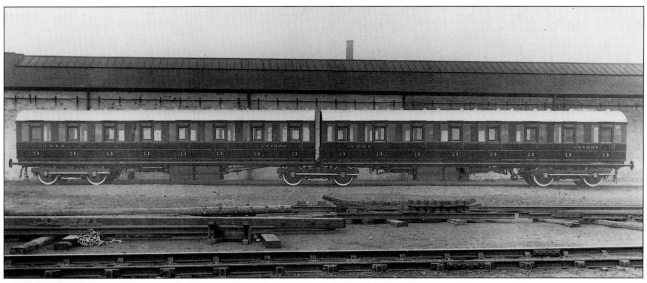

Twin brake third formed of a Diagram 105 vehicle (left-hand coach No 44322) and 106 (right-hand coach No 44321). Built at Doncaster, 1930, and withdrawn in 1939 as a result of the Hatfield accident.

each made up of two sets of four 54ft coaches. At a meeting of the SPMs in December 1923 instead it was decided to build quintuplet sets with 43ft 6in bodies, formed into ten-coach trains.

Meanwhile, as explained in the section dealing with restaurant cars, the use of articulation spread to catering vehicles.

Not until the late 1920s was there an opportunity to build articulated twins similar to those GNR examples which had entered service in the early months of Grouping. The newcomers were again for the GN section, to be used on the Kings Cross-Welwyn Garden City/Letchworth service, and they were built in 1929/30. Similar designs of vehicles, this time made up into quad arts, were specified to work the GE section's Liverpool St-Hertford East service. Whereas the GNR vehicles had 55ft 5¼in underframes (over the headstocks), the 1929/30 twins had 51ft underframes – not quite standard as they measured an extra ⅛in over the headstocks! The 55ft 5¼in underframe reappeared from the mid-1930s, in twins built for the GN and GC sections. Having appeared after agreement for general use of 9ft 3in wide coaches, none of the twins was built to the 9ft width twins, and the brake vehicles all featured a guard's ducket.

More non-vestibuled twins were built from 1935, to re-equip the Marylebone suburban services, and for the GN section main line stopping trains, and local services in Lincolnshire and the Nottingham area. Gresley's enthusiasm for articulation extended to stock supplied to the Cheshire Lines Committee, for which 24 twins were built by Cravens in 1937 and these were generally similar to the LNER designs.

During 1937/8, more teak-bodied twins were constructed, for the GC section, and the Southern Scottish Area. One proposal for articulated twins and triplets did not materialise. The original plans for new GE section stock in the 1935 CBP included one train formed of twin arts, and another of triple arts for Ipswich-Liverpool St and return workings. In the event, non-articulated coaches were specified in the augmented 1935/6 CBP.

Usual practice with the twins was that these were used to make up set trains of, say, four, six or eight coaches, often with additional non-articulated coaches. For instance, a typical Marylebone outer suburban set comprised twin brake third; twin third; and a non-articulated third and a brake third. GN outer suburban trains might be formed: twin brake composite; twin composite; twin composite or twin third; twin brake composite.

Gresley himself claimed that, apart from a lower first cost, articulation brought a saving in train weight, improved riding, greater resistance to collision impact, and less chance of telescoping. Norman Newsome, an authoritative and first-hand observer of LNER coaching stock practice, commented to the author: 'I always felt that Gresley overdid articulation. It would have been better just restricted to twins. HNG always said that there was a saving, either in weight or cost. That was debatable.'

# Twin-arts

## Twin thirds: Third + third

### DIAGRAMS 105, 106

Twins for GN section outer suburban services. Diagram 105 used also in combination with brake third Dia 125 for twins, and in GE section Hertford quads.

### LIST OF ARTICULATED TWIN THIRDS:

| Diag No | CBP | Order No | Compts/ seats | Built | Original number/ changes | 1943 number |
|---|---|---|---|---|---|---|
| **Built 1929** | | | | | | |
| 105* | 1929/30 | 332 | 8: 80 | DR | 44302 | 82373 |
| 106* | | | 8: 80 | DR | 44301 | 82372 |
| **Built 1930** | | | | | | |
| 105* | 1929/30 | 332 | 8: 80 | DR | 44312/22 | 82375/ - 44321/2 |
| 106* | | | 8: 80 | DR | 44311/21 | 82374/ - W/O Hatfield 1939 |
| **Built 1940** | | | | | | |
| 105* | special | 982 | 8: 80 | DR | 44152 | 82371 Accident replacement |
| 106* | | | 8: 80 | DR | 44151 | 82370 for 44321/2 |

## Twin brake thirds:

### Third + brake third

### DIAGRAMS 105, 125

Twins for GN section outer suburban services, and for the GC section.

### Brake third + third

### DIAGRAM 273

For Glasgow and Edinburgh suburban services, to make up train sets.

### Brake third + third

### DIAGRAM 278

For Glasgow and Edinburgh suburban services, to make up train sets.

### CLC DIA 83

Very similar to LNER Diagram 278.

**Diagram 105**

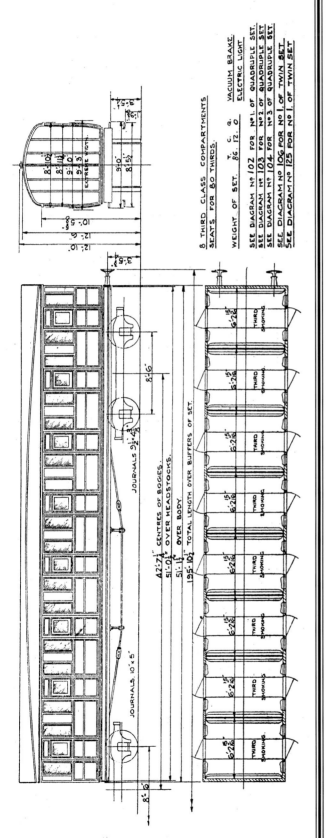

8 THIRD CLASS COMPARTMENTS
SEATS FOR 80 THIRDS.

WEIGHT OF SET. T.C.Q. 86. 12. 0   VACUUM BRAKE.
                                  ELECTRIC LIGHT

SEE DIAGRAM Nº 102 FOR Nº 1. OF QUADRUPLE SET.
SEE DIAGRAM Nº 103 FOR Nº 2. OF QUADRUPLE SET
SEE DIAGRAM Nº 104 FOR Nº 3. OF QUADRUPLE SET
SEE DIAGRAM Nº 106 FOR Nº 1. OF TWIN SET
SEE DIAGRAM Nº 125 FOR Nº 1. OF TWIN SET

42'-7½" CENTRES OF BOGIES.
51'-0½" OVER HEADSTOCKS.
51'-1½" OVER BODY
195'-10½" TOTAL LENGTH OVER BUFFERS OF SET.

JOURNALS. 10" × 5"

**Diagram 106**

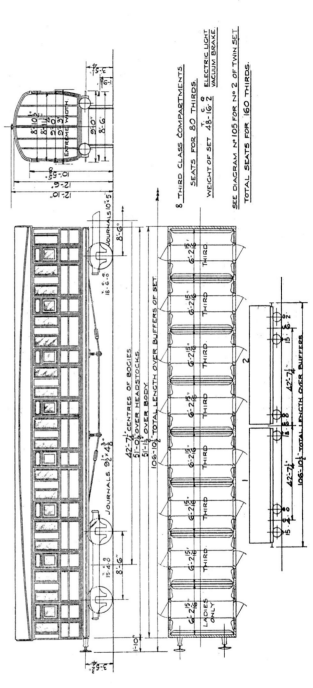

8 THIRD CLASS COMPARTMENTS
SEATS FOR 80 THIRDS.

WEIGHT OF SET 48. 16. 2   ELECTRIC LIGHT
                          VACUUM BRAKE

SEE DIAGRAM Nº 105 FOR Nº 2 OF TWIN SET
TOTAL SEATS FOR 160 THIRDS.

42'-7½" CENTRES OF BOGIES.
51'-0" OVER HEADSTOCKS.
51'-1½" OVER BODY
106'-10½" TOTAL LENGTH OVER BUFFERS OF SET.

JOURNALS 9½" × 4¾"

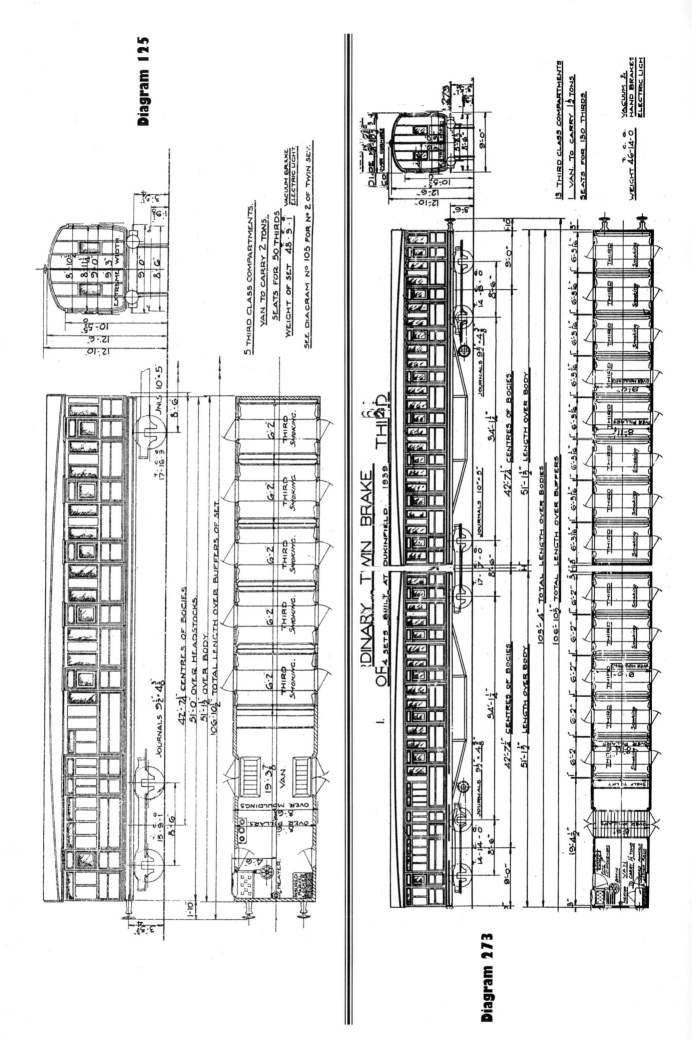

**Diagram 125**

5 THIRD CLASS COMPARTMENTS.
VAN TO CARRY 2 TONS.
SEATS FOR 50 THIRDS.
WEIGHT OF SET 48·9·1
VACUUM BRAKE
ELECTRIC LIGHT
SEE DIAGRAM Nº 105 FOR Nº 2 OF TWIN SET.

ORDINARY TWIN BRAKE THIRD
OF 4 SETS BUILT AT DUKINFIELD. 1939.

13 THIRD CLASS COMPARTMENTS
1 VAN. TO CARRY 1½ TONS
SEATS FOR 130 THIRDS

T. C. Ø.
WEIGHT 46·14·0
VACUUM &
HAND BRAKE.
ELECTRIC LIGHT

**Diagram 273**

## Diagram 278

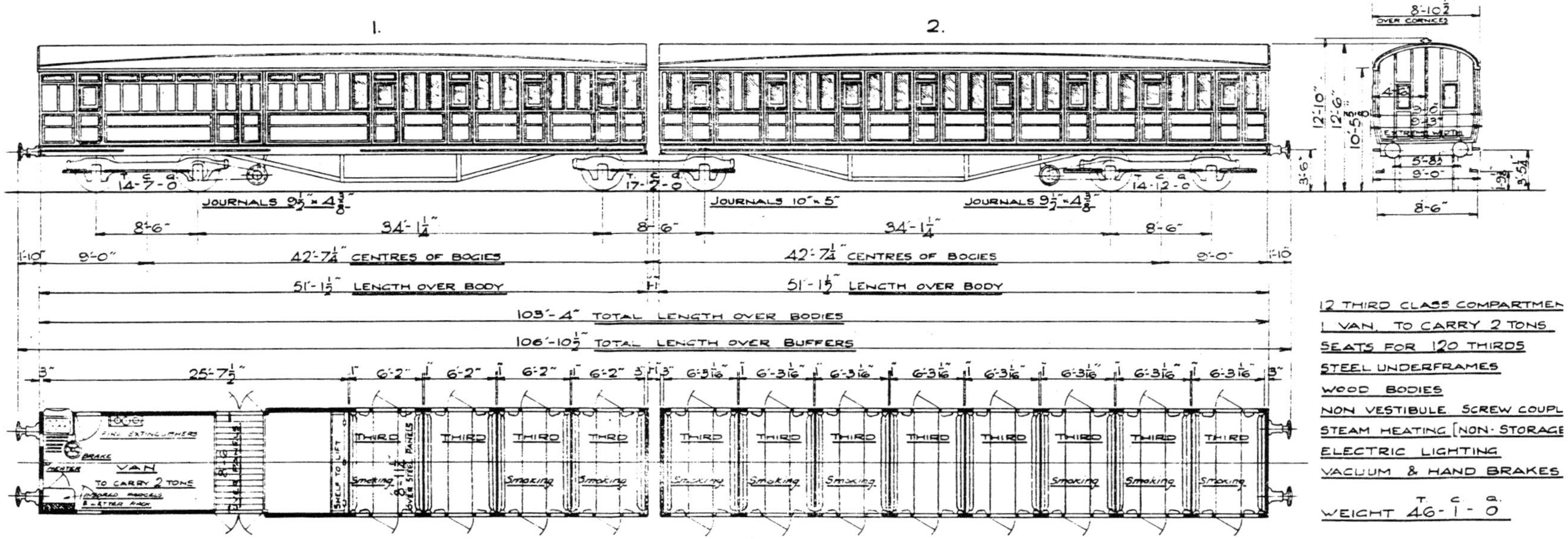
12 THIRD CLASS COMPARTMEN
1 VAN, TO CARRY 2 TONS
SEATS FOR 120 THIRDS
STEEL UNDERFRAMES
WOOD BODIES
NON VESTIBULE SCREW COUPL
STEAM HEATING [NON-STORAGE
ELECTRIC LIGHTING
VACUUM & HAND BRAKES
WEIGHT T. C. Q. 46 - 1 - 0
JOURNALS 9½" x 4¾"
JOURNALS 10" x 5"
42'-7¼" CENTRES OF BOGIES
51'-1½" LENGTH OVER BODY
103'-4" TOTAL LENGTH OVER BODIES
106'-10½" TOTAL LENGTH OVER BUFFERS
THIRD
Smoking
VAN
TO CARRY 2 TONS
BRAKE
FIRE EXTINGUISHERS
SHELF TO LIFT
8'-10½" OVER CORNICES

## Diagram CLC83

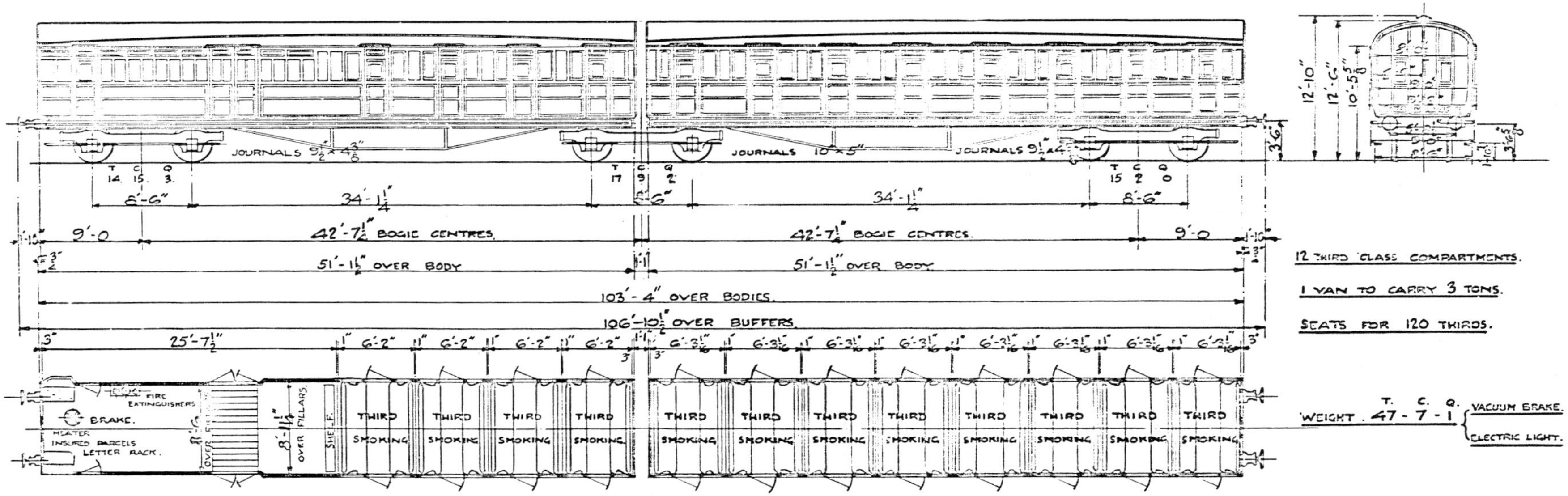
12 THIRD CLASS COMPARTMENTS.
1 VAN TO CARRY 3 TONS.
SEATS FOR 120 THIRDS.
WEIGHT. T. C. Q. 47 - 7 - 1 VACUUM BRAKE. ELECTRIC LIGHT.
JOURNALS 9½" x 4¾"
JOURNALS 10" x 5"
42'-7¼" BOGIE CENTRES.
51'-1½" OVER BODY
103'-4" OVER BODIES.
106'-10½" OVER BUFFERS.
THIRD
SMOKING
BRAKE.
FIRE EXTINGUISHERS
HEATER
INSURED PARCELS
LETTER RACK.
OVER PILLARS.
SHELF.

## LIST OF TWIN BRAKE THIRDS:

| Diag No CBP | Order No | Compts/seats | Built | Original number/changes | 1943 number |
|---|---|---|---|---|---|
| *Built 1929* | | | | | |
| 105* (Third) | 1928/9 263 | 8: 80 | DR | 44172/44202 | 86791/3 |
| 125* (Brake third) | | 5: 50 | DR | 44171/44201 | 86790/2 |
| *Built 1930* | | | | | |
| 105* (Third) | 1929/30 333 | 8: 80 | DR | 52502/12 | 86795/7 |
| 125* (Brake third) | | 5: 50 | DR | 52501/11 | 86794/6 |
| *Built 1937* | | | | | |
| CLC 83 (Brake third) | - | 4: 40 | CR | CLC 701/7/9, CLC 715/7/23 | 60101/7/9/15/7/23§ |
| (Third) | - | 8: 80 | CR | CLC 702/8, CLC 710/6/8/24 | 60102/8/10/6/8/24§ |
| *Built 1938* | | | | | |
| 278 (Brake third) | 1938 873 | 4: 40 | DK | 32736/8/40/2 | 86926/8/30/2 |
| (Third) | | 8: 80 | DK | 32737/9/41/3 | 86927/9/31/3 |
| *Built 1939* | | | | | |
| 273 (Brake third) | 1938 875 | 5: 50 | DK | 32752/4/6/8 | 86918/20/2/4 |
| (Third) | | 8: 80 | DK | 32753/5/7/9 | 86919/21/3/5 |

§ Numbers allocated after 1950 by London Midland Region. Became M60101M or E etc.

The following vehicles were allocated to Scottish Region stock after 1949, and the number prefixed by SC: 86918-21/4/5, 86926-33.

# Twin brake composites:
## Brake third + lavatory composite

### DIAGRAMS 107, 108
Built for the GN section outer suburban services.

Twin Nos 44261/2 and twin third Nos 44321/2 were the rear vehicles of the 8.25am Cambridge-Kings Cross, and were wrecked (and withdrawn as a result) when the train was run into near Hatfield by the 7.15am Peterborough-Kings Cross on 26 January 1939.

### DIAGRAM 210
Articulated twins for the Marylebone suburban services, and GN outer suburban and main line stopping trains, also used for local workings on the GN section, such as Boston-Peterborough/ Lincoln.

### DIAGRAM 213
For Marylebone suburban services.

### DIAGRAM 214
For Marylebone suburban services.

## Brake third + first

### DIAGRAM 272
For Glasgow/Edinburgh suburban services.

### LIST OF TWIN BRAKE COMPOSITES:

| Diag No CBP | Order No | Compts/seats | Built | Original number/changes | 1943 number |
|---|---|---|---|---|---|
| *Built 1929* | | | | | |
| 107* (Brake third) | 1929/30 332 | 4: 40 | DR | 44211/21 | 80070/2 |
| 108* (Lavatory composite) | | 3/4 : 23/39 | DR | 44212/22 | 80071/3 |
| *Built 1930* | | | | | |
| 107* (Brake third) | 1929/30 332 | 4: 40 | DR | 44231/41/51/61 | 80074/6/8/ — |
| 108* (Lavatory composite) | | 3/4 : 23/39 | DR | 44232/42/52/62 44261/2 W/O Hatfield 1939 | 80075/7/9/ — |
| *Built 1935* | | | | | |
| 210* (Brake third) | 1935/6 640 | 6: 60 | DR | 52541/51/61 | 80178/80/2 |
| (Lavatory composite) | | 2/5 : 14/48 | DR | 52542/52/62 | 80179/81/3 |
| *Built 1936* | | | | | |
| 210* (Brake third) | 1935/6 640 | 6: 60 | DK | 45201/11/21/31, 45241/51/61/71, 45281/91, 45301/11, 45321/31/41/51/61 | 80100/2/4/6/8, 80110/2/4/6/8, 80120/2/4/6/8, 80130/2 |
| | 675 | | | 45561/71/81/91, 45601, 45611/21/31/41, 45651, 45661/71/81/91, 45701/11/21/31/41 | 80134/6/8/40/2, 80144/6/8/50/2, 80154/6/8/60/2, 80164/6/8/70 |
| | 640 | | | 52571/81 | 80184/6 |
| (Lavatory composite) | 640 | 2/5 : 14/48 | DK | 45202/12/22/32, 45242/52/62/72, 45282/92, 45302/12, 45322/32/42/52/62 | 80101/3/5/7/9, 80111/3/5/7/9, 80121/3/5/7/9, 80131/3 |
| | 675 | | | 45562/72/82/92, 45602, 45612/22/32/42/52, 45662/72/82/92, 45702, 45712/22/32/42 | 80135/7/9/41/3, 80145/7/9/51/3, 80155/7/9/61/3, 80165/7/9/71 |
| | 640 | | | 52572/82 | 80185/7 |
| 213* (Brake third) | 1935/6 641 | 5: 50 3/4 | DK | 52591, 52601/11 | 80188/90/2 |
| (Lavatory composite) | | : 22/38 | DK | 52592, 52602/12 | 80189/91/3 |
| 214* (Brake third) | 1935/6 642 | 6: 60 4/3 | DK | 52621/31/41 | 80200/2/4 |
| (Lavatory composite) | | : 30/28 | DK | 52622/32/42 | 80201/3/5 |
| *Built 1937* | | | | | |
| 210* (Brake third) | 1935/6 675 | 6: 60 | DK | 45751/61/71 | 80172/4/6 |
| (Lavatory composite) | | 2/5 : 14/48 | DK | 45752/62/72 | 80173/5/7 |
| 213* (Brake third) | 1935/6 676 | 5: 50 3/4 | DK | 52651/61/71 | 80194/6/8 |
| (Lavatory composite) | | : 22/38 | DK | 52652/62/72 | 80195/7/9 |
| 214* (Brake third) | 1935/6 677 | 6: 60 4/3 | DK | 52681/91, 52701 | 80206/8/10 |
| (Lavatory composite) | | : 30/28 | DK | 52682/92, 52702 | 80207/9/11 |
| *Built 1938* | | | | | |
| 214* (Brake third) | 1937 796 | 6: 60 | DK | 52543 | 80212 |
| (Lavatory composite) | | 4/3 : 30/28 | DK | 52544 | 80213 |
| 214* (Brake third) | 1938 850 | 6: 60 | DK | 53700/2/4/6 | 80215/7/9/21 |
| (Lavatory composite) | | 4/3 : 30/28 | DK | 53701/3/5/7 | 80214/6/8/20 |
| *Built 1939* | | | | | |
| 272 (Brake third) | 1938 874 | 5: 50 | DK | 32744/6/8/50 | 80290/2/4/6 |
| (First) | | 7: 56 | DK | 32745/7/9/51 | 80291/3/5/7 |
| *Built 1941* | | | | | |
| 107* (Brake third) | special 981 | 4: 40 | DR | 44131 | 80080 |
| 108* (Lavatory composite) | | 3/4 : 23/39 | DR | 44132 | 80081 Accident replacement |

The following vehicles were allocated to Scottish Region stock after 1949, and the number prefixed by SC: 80290-7.

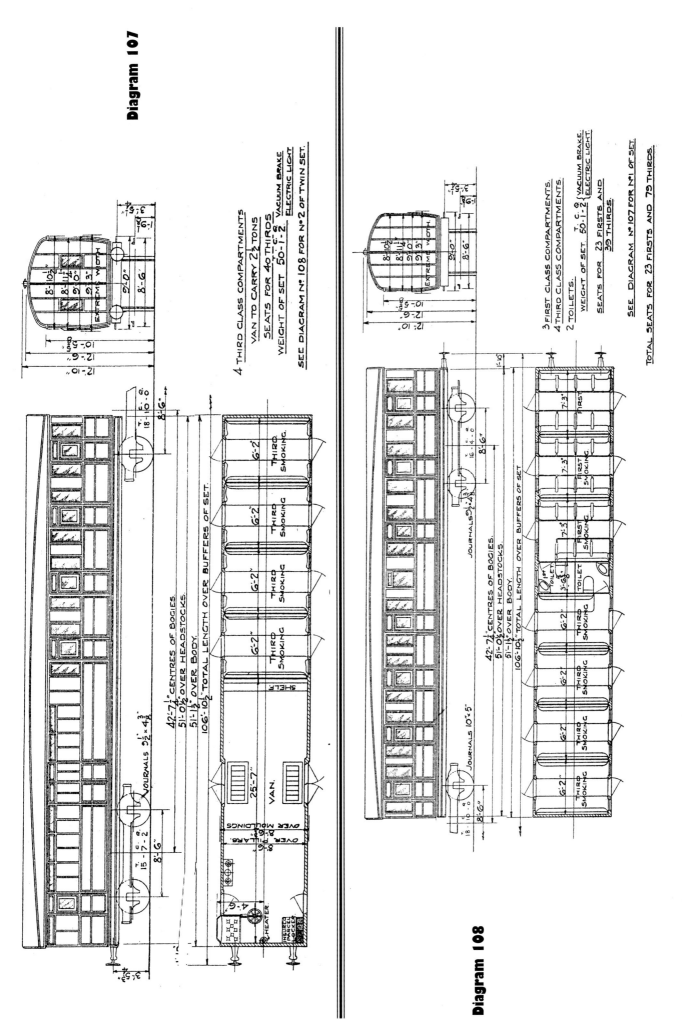

**Diagram 107**

EXTREME WIDTH

4 THIRD CLASS COMPARTMENTS.
VAN TO CARRY 2½ TONS.
SEATS FOR 40 THIRDS.
WEIGHT OF SET. 50-1-2. { VACUUM BRAKE.
ELECTRIC LIGHT.

SEE DIAGRAM Nº 108 FOR Nº 2 OF TWIN SET.

JOURNALS 5½ × 4¾

42'-7¼" CENTRES OF BOGIES.
51'-0½" OVER HEADSTOCKS.
51'-1½" OVER BODY.
106'-10½" TOTAL LENGTH OVER BUFFERS OF SET.

6'-2" THIRD SMOKING.
6'-2" THIRD SMOKING.
6'-2" THIRD SMOKING.
6'-2" THIRD SMOKING.

SHELF

25'-7"

VAN.

OVER MOULDINGS
OVER PILLARS

HEATER

INSURED PARCELS PACKED

**Diagram 108**

3 FIRST CLASS COMPARTMENTS.
4 THIRD CLASS COMPARTMENTS.
2 TOILETS.
WEIGHT OF SET. 50-1-2. { T. C. Q. VACUUM BRAKE.
ELECTRIC LIGHT.

SEATS FOR 23 FIRSTS AND 39 THIRDS.

SEE DIAGRAM Nº 107 FOR Nº 1 OF SET.

TOTAL SEATS FOR 23 FIRSTS AND 79 THIRDS.

JOURNALS 10"×5"

42'-7¼" CENTRES OF BOGIES.
51'-0½" OVER HEADSTOCKS.
51'-1½" OVER BODY.
106'-10½" TOTAL LENGTH OVER BUFFERS OF SET

6'-2" THIRD SMOKING.
6'-2" THIRD SMOKING.
6'-2" THIRD SMOKING.
TOILET
FIRST SMOKING 7'-3"
FIRST 7'-3"
FIRST 7'-3"

121

A Diagram 210 twin, with the lavatory composite leading, is next to 'C1' Atlantic No 3286 passing New Southgate with a down semi-fast in 1936.

## Twin composites:

### Lavatory composite + third

#### DIAGRAMS 123, 124

Built for the GN section outer suburban services.

#### DIAGRAM CLC 84

A unique type, with the lavatory composite not dissimilar in layout and external appearance to a non-articulated lavatory composite of Diagram 50, with long windows on the corridor sides. A curiosity of the design was that the end compartments of the lavatory composite, first and third-class alike, had no access to the internal corridor leading to the lavatory, a potential trap for the unwary!

#### LIST OF TWIN COMPOSITES:

| Diag No CBP | Order No | Compts/ seats | Built | Original number/ changes | 1943 number |
|---|---|---|---|---|---|
| **Built 1929** | | | | | |
| 123* 1929/30 332 (Lav compo) | | 3/4 : 23/39 | DR | 44272 | 88135 |
| 124* (Third) | | 8: 80 | DR | 44271 | 88134 |

| | | | | | |
|---|---|---|---|---|---|
| **Built 1930** | | | | | |
| 123* 1929/30 332 (Lav compo) | | 3/4 : 23/39 | DR | 44282/92 | 88137/9 |
| 124* (Third) | | 8: 80 | DR | 44281/91 | 88136/8 |
| **Built 1937** | | | | | |
| (Composite) - | | 3/4 : 20/34 | CR | CLC 704/6, CLC 712/4/20/2 | 60104/6/12/4/20/2§ |
| CLC 84 - (Third) | - | 8: 80 | CR | CLC 703/5, CLC 711/3/9/21 | 60103/5/11/3/9/21§ |

§ Numbers allocated after 1950 by London Midland Region. Became M60103M or E etc.

## Twin composites:

### Third + first

#### DIAGRAMS 124, 126

Built for the GN section outer suburban services and for the GC section. For some reason, when Diagram 242 was introduced the vehicles on Diagrams 124 and 126 were transferred to the new diagram.

#### DIAGRAM 242

Virtually – but not quite! – identical to Diagrams 124 and 126, later LNER practice being to show both/all the articulated vehicles on one diagram sheet. Built for the Marylebone suburban services.

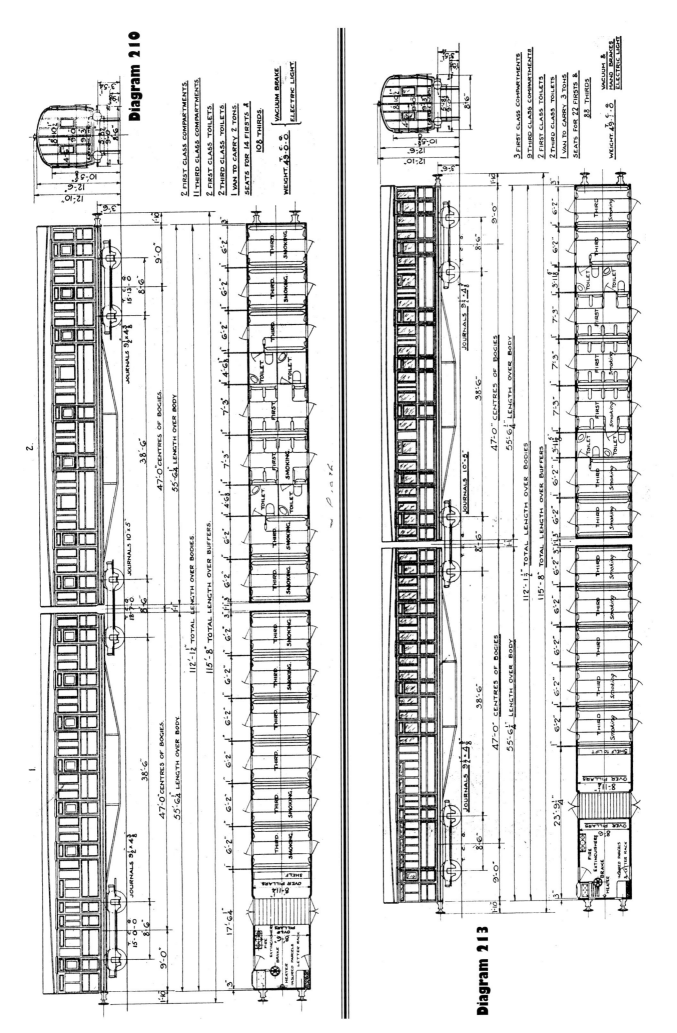

**Diagram 210**

2 FIRST CLASS COMPARTMENTS
11 THIRD CLASS COMPARTMENTS
2 FIRST CLASS TOILETS
2 THIRD CLASS TOILETS
1 VAN TO CARRY 2 TONS
SEATS FOR 14 FIRSTS &
108 THIRDS.

VACUUM BRAKE
ELECTRIC LIGHT

WEIGHT 49·0·0

**Diagram 213**

3 FIRST CLASS COMPARTMENTS
9 THIRD CLASS COMPARTMENTS
2 FIRST CLASS TOILETS
2 THIRD CLASS TOILETS
1 VAN TO CARRY 3 TONS
SEATS FOR 22 FIRSTS &
88 THIRDS.

VACUUM &
HAND BRAKES
ELECTRIC LIGHT

WEIGHT 49·1·0

Twin brake composite E80212E/E80213E, the latter nearest the camera. To Diagram 214. (Built Dukinfield 1938, as 52543/4). Photographed at Manchester Victoria in October 1959, and withdrawn in December 1961.

## DIAGRAM 274

For Glasgow/Edinburgh suburban services.

## LIST OF TWIN COMPOSITES:

| Diag No CBP | Order No | Compts/ seats | Built | Original number/ changes | 1943 number |
|---|---|---|---|---|---|
| **Built 1929** | | | | | |
| 124* (Third) | 1928/9 | 263 | 8: 80 | DR | 44181/91 | 88153/5 |
| 126* (First) | | 7: 56 | DR | 44182/92 | 88154/6 Later on Dia 242 |
| **Built 1930** | | | | | |
| 124* (Third) | 1929/30 | 333 | 8: 80 | DR | 52522/32 | 88198, 88200 |
| 126* (First) | | 7: 56 | DR | 52521/31 | 88197/9 Later on Dia 242 |
| **Built 1937** | | | | | |
| 242* (First) | 1937 | 795 | 7: 56 | DK | 52752/4/6/8/ 60/2/4, | 88157/9/61/3/5/7, |
| | | | | 52766/8/70/2/4/6 | 88169/71/3/5/7/9/81 |
| (Third) | | | 8: 80 | DK | 52751/3/5/7/9/61/3, 52765/7/9/71/3/5 | 88158/60/2/4/6/8, 88170/2/4/6/8/80/2 |
| **Built 1938** | | | | | |
| 242* (First) | 1937 | 795 | 7: 56 | DK | 52778/80/2 | 88183/5/7 |
| | 1938 | 851 | | DK | 52800/2/4/6 | 88189/91/3/5 |
| | | 872 | | DK | 32733/5 | 88150/2 |
| (Third) | 1937 | 795 | 8: 80 | DK | 52777/9/81 | 88184/6/8 |
| | 1938 | 851 | | DK | 52801/3/5/7 | 88190/2/4/6 |
| | | 872 | | DK | 32732/4 | 88149/51 |

Dia 242 to form articulated twins for Marylebone suburban services — order Nos 795/851; Glasgow and Edinburgh — order No 872.

| | | | | | |
|---|---|---|---|---|---|
| **Built 1939** | | | | | |
| 274 (First) | 1938 | 876 | 7: 56 | DK | 32760 | 88280 |
| (Composite) | 1938 | | 4/3 :32/30 | DK | 32761 | 88281 |

The following vehicles were allocated to Scottish Region stock after 1949, and the number prefixed by SC: 88149-52.

# Quadruplets

## GN section London suburban quad arts

The quad art sets of the GN section London suburban services are so well-known that it is easy to forget that there were some other Gresley quad arts, namely those built for the Liverpool St-Hertford East services. These had more in common with the twin arts just described than with the GN suburban quads.

The GN trains were derived from the twins introduced on the GNR from 1910, and rebuilt as quad arts after World War I. Completely new quad art sets featured in the GNR's 1922 building programme, and they entered traffic during the first year of Grouping. These were of two types and were used together to form a train, with accommodation for all three classes. The styling of the coaches followed GNR Gresley practice, with fanlights above the door droplights, and GNR-style guard's duckets. During 1923, further sets were built, this time following LNER practice with windows full height to the cant-rail, hit and miss ventilators to the doors, but retaining the guard's duckets. So far, the 8ft wheelbase bogie had been used for these quad arts but the 8ft 6in heavy type was now introduced, experience having shown that the earlier choice was not man enough for the job. An increase in weight was another consequence of using the heavy bogie.

Eight trains composed of the two types of quad art were included in the 1923 building programme, but were not completed until the following year. At the time, there were hopes that electrification of the GN inner suburban services would be sanctioned shortly by the LNER Board, with the result that the underframes of some of the quad arts were designed so that they could accommodate powered bogies. Again, the 8ft 6in bogies were used but, from 1925, the 8ft heavy type was adopted although the types were later interchanged between some sets. The 'B' diagram series sets had recessed guard's compartment doors, and an extreme body width of 9ft 3in. The other sets had an extreme width of 9ft 3¾in.

The quad arts were hardly luxurious and they, and the quint arts constructed for the GE section, were termed 'suburban trains'. Neither were the partition to partition dimensions of the compartments generous, but the stock was not intended to woo the passenger by reason of comfort – more important was their role as people-movers, in which they excelled for some 30-40 years. The external finish of the suburban trains, and some features of their interiors were accordingly utilitarian. Details are given in the Introduction.

The prospect of electrification resulted in deferment of further quad art sets in the 1924 programme, but more were included in the 1925 CBP, and during the course of its fulfilment the LNER Board

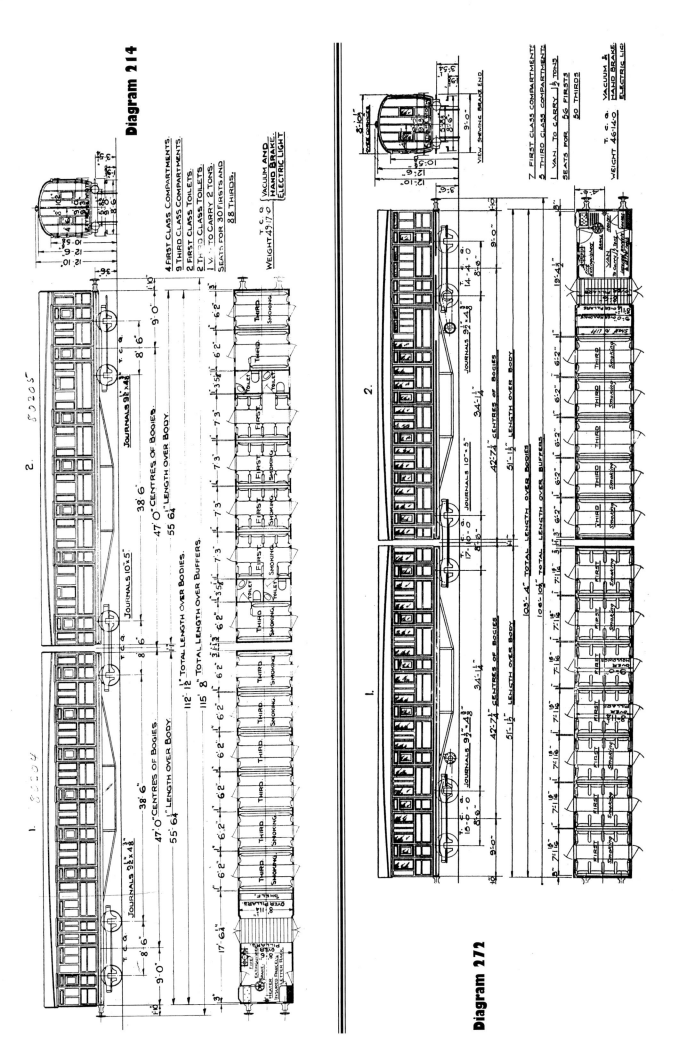

**Diagram 214**

4 FIRST CLASS COMPARTMENTS.
9 THIRD CLASS COMPARTMENTS.
2 FIRST CLASS TOILETS.
2 THIRD CLASS TOILETS.
VAN. TO CARRY 2 TONS.
SEATS FOR 30 FIRSTS AND
88 THIRDS.

T. C. Q. VACUUM AND
HAND BRAKE.
WEIGHT 49·17·0 ELECTRIC LIGHT.

**Diagram 272**

7 FIRST CLASS COMPARTMENTS
5 THIRD CLASS COMPARTMENTS
1 VAN. TO CARRY 1½ TONS.
SEATS FOR 56 FIRSTS
50 THIRDS

T. C. Q. VACUUM &
HAND BRAKE.
WEIGHT 46·14·0 ELECTRIC LIGHT

VIEW SHEWING BRAKE END.

**Diagram 123**

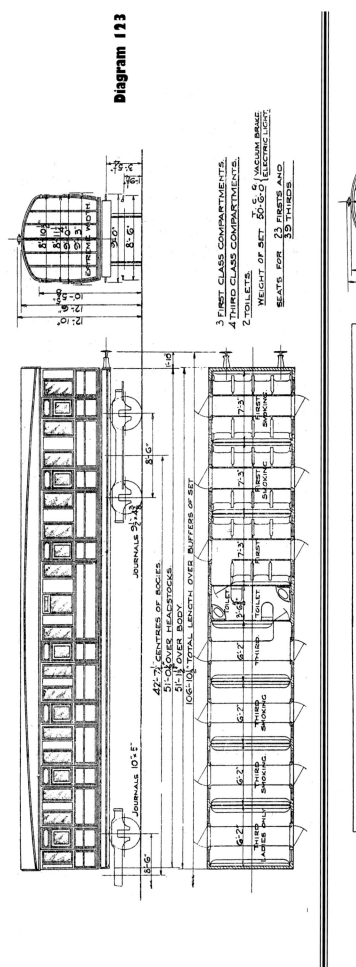

3 FIRST CLASS COMPARTMENTS.
4 THIRD CLASS COMPARTMENTS.
2 TOILETS.

WEIGHT OF SET 50-6-0 { T.C.Q. VACUUM BRAKE
ELECTRIC LIGHT.

SEATS FOR 23 FIRSTS AND 39 THIRDS.

**Diagram 124**

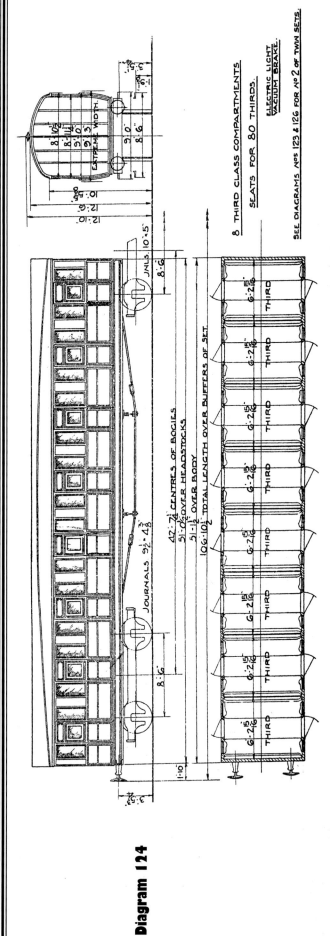

8 THIRD CLASS COMPARTMENTS.

SEATS FOR 80 THIRDS.

ELECTRIC LIGHT.
VACUUM BRAKE.

SEE DIAGRAMS Nos 123 & 126 FOR Nº 2 OF TWIN SETS.

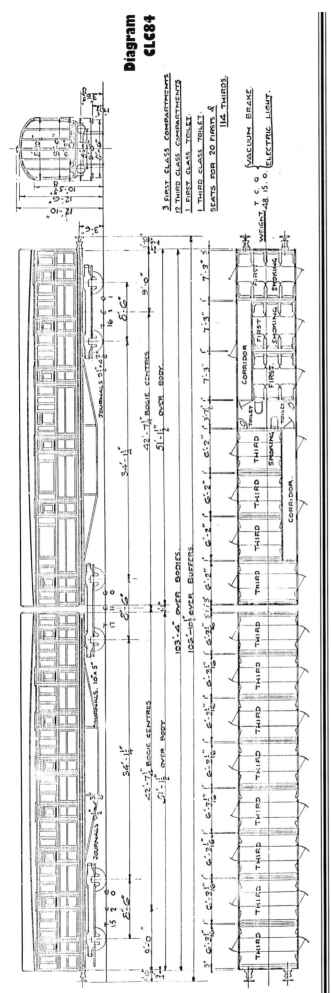

Diagram GL084

3 FIRST CLASS COMPARTMENTS
12 THIRD CLASS COMPARTMENTS
1 FIRST CLASS TOILET
1 THIRD CLASS TOILET
SEATS FOR 20 FIRSTS &
114 THIRDS.

VACUUM BRAKE
ELECTRIC LIGHT.

WEIGHT 48.15.0.

decided not to proceed with electrification. More delays followed as a result of the adverse financial climate arising from the General Strike, but the construction of further quad arts soon recommenced in earnest, to continue until 1929. The building of yet more was contemplated but the onset of the Depression was reason enough to stop construction for good.

The last-built sets had one distinction, that of illuminated destination boxes at the brake ends, with roller blinds featuring the destinations. Some of the earlier sets were later fitted with these boxes, with the result that 40 out of 48 sets were so equipped. From 1929, the GN section London suburban services were worked entirely by Gresley quad arts, of GNR or LNER origins, and 20 of GN origin were gas-lit.

## Brake second

### DIAGRAMS 68, 68A, 68B

Diagram 68 with 8ft bogies as built; some later received the 8ft 6in variety. No guard's ducket.

Diagram 68A. With 8ft 6in bogies as built, at least one vehicle later with the 8ft type. Detail variations as compared to Diagram 68, mainly to do with the underframe and buffing gear. No guard's ducket.

Diagram 68B. With 8ft bogies as built; some later received the 8ft 6in variety. Guard's ducket.

There were variations to the style of the exterior panelling of the guard's/van compartment of the three varieties of Diagram 68.

## Second

### DIAGRAMS 69, 69A

Diagram 69A with 8ft 6in bogies as built, at least one vehicle later with the 8ft type. Detail variations as compared to Diagram 69, mainly to do with the underframe and buffing gear.

## First/third composite

### DIAGRAMS 70, 70A

Diagram 70A with 8ft 6in bogies as built, at least one vehicle later with the 8ft type. Detail variations as compared to Diagram 70, mainly to do with the underframe and buffing gear.

## First/third composite

### DIAGRAMS 71, 71A

Diagram 71A with 8ft 6in bogies as built, at least one vehicle later with the 8ft type. Detail variations as compared to Diagram 71, mainly to do with the underframe and buffing gear.

## Brake third

### DIAGRAMS 72, 72A, 72B

Diagram 72 with 8ft bogies as built; some later received the 8ft 6in variety. No guard's ducket.

Diagram 72A. With 8ft 6in bogies as built, at least one vehicle later with the 8ft type. Detail variations as compared to Diagram 72, mainly to do with the underframe and buffing gear. No guard's ducket.

Diagram 72B. With 8ft bogies as built; some later received the 8ft 6in variety. Guard's ducket.

There were variations to the style of the exterior panelling of the guard's/van compartment of the three varieties of Diagram 72.

## Third

### DIAGRAMS 73, 73A

Diagram 73A with 8ft 6in bogies as built, at least one vehicle later with the 8ft type. Detail variations as compared to Diagram 73, mainly to do with the underframe and buffing gear.

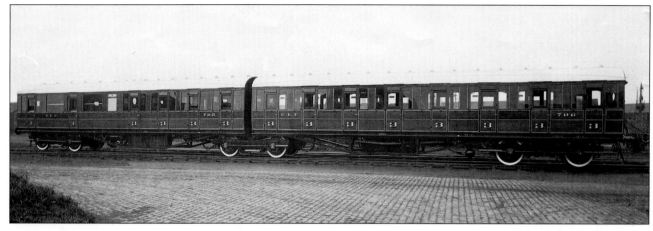

Doncaster photograph of a Cheshire Lines Committee twin composite to Diagram 84. Nos 705 (left-hand, is the lavatory composite) and 706 (right-hand, the third). Built by Cravens in 1937, these became M60105/60106M after 1950.

# Third

## DIAGRAMS 74, 74A

Diagram 74A with 8ft 6in bogies as built, at least one vehicle later with the 8ft type. Detail variations as compared to Diagram 74, mainly to do with the underframe and buffing gear.

# Third

## DIAGRAMS 75, 75A

Diagram 75A with 8ft 6in bogies as built, at least one vehicle later with the 8ft type. Detail variations as compared to Diagram 75, mainly to do with the underframe and buffing gear.

NB: The 'B' diagram series sets had recessed guard's compartment doors and an extreme width of 9ft 3in. The other sets had an extreme width of 9ft 3¾ in.

Each suburban train was formed: BS + S + C + C +T + T + T+ BT

## LIST OF GN LONDON SUBURBAN QUAD ART VEHICLES:

| Diag No CBP | Order No | Compts/ seats | Built | Original number/ changes | 1943 numbers |
|---|---|---|---|---|---|
| **Built 1924** | | | | | |
| 72B* Brake third | 1923 - | 5: 60 | DR | 8131, 8811/21/ 31/41/51/61/71 | 86360-3, 86364-7, 86368-71, |
| 73* Third | | 7: 84 | DR | 8132, 8812/22/ 32/42/52/62/72 | 86372-5, 86376-9, 86380-3, |
| 74* Third | | 8: 96 | DR | 8133, 8813/23/ 33/43/53/63/73 | 86384-7, |
| 75* Third | | 8: 96 | DR | 8134, 8814/24/ 34/44/54/64/74 | 86388-91 |

Dias 72B, 73-75 also referred to as GN Dia 467B

Later 48131- 4, 48811-4 etc

| | | | | | |
|---|---|---|---|---|---|
| 71* Composite (1st/3rd) | 1923 - | 3 3rd/ 4 1st :36/40 | DR | 8894/904/14/ 24/34/44/54/64 | 86255-2, 86259-56, 86263-60, |
| 70* Composite (1st/3rd) | | 4 1st/ 3 3rd :40/36 | DR | 8893/903/13/ 23/33/43/53/63 | 86267-4, 86271-68, 86275-2, 86279-6, 86283-80 |
| | | | DR | | |
| 69* Second | | 7: 84 | DR | 8892/902/12/ 22/32/42/52/62 | |
| 68B* Brake second | | 5: 60 | DR | 8891/901/11/ 21/31/41/51/61 | |

Later 48894- 1, 48904-1 etc

Dias 68B-71 also referred to as GN Dia 478

| Diag No CBP | Order No | Compts/ seats | Built | Original number/ changes | 1943 numbers |
|---|---|---|---|---|---|
| **Built 1925** | | | | | |
| 72* Brake third | 1925/6 - | 5: 60 | CL/ ¶MID | 48321/31/41/51 | 86316/20/4/8 |
| 73* Third | | 7: 84 | | 48322/32/42/52 | 86317/21/5/9 |
| 74* Third | | 8: 96 | | 48323/33/43/53 | 86318/22/6/30 |
| 75* Third | | 8: 96 | | 48324/34/44/54 | 86319/23/7/31 |

¶Two trains CL, two trains built by MID

| | | | | | |
|---|---|---|---|---|---|
| 71* Composite (1st/3rd) | 1925/6 - | 3 3rd/ 4 1st :36/40 | CL/ ¶MID | 48384/94/404/974 | 86207/11/5/9 |
| 70* Composite (1st/3rd) | | 4 1st/ 3 3rd :40/36 | | 48383/93/403/973 | 86206/10/4/8 |
| 69* Second | | 7: 84 | | 48382/92/402/972 | 86205/9/13/7 |
| 68* Brake second | | 5: 60 | | 48381/91/401/971 | 86204/8/12/6 |

| **Built 1926** | | | | | |
|---|---|---|---|---|---|
| 72* Brake third | 1925/6 - | 5: 60 | MET /MID¶ | 48361/71 | 86332/6 |
| 73* Third | | 7: 84 | | 48362/72 | 86333/7 |
| 74* Third | | 8: 96 | | 48363/73 | 86334/8 |
| 75* Third | | 8: 96 | | 48364/74 | 86335/9 |

¶ One set MET one set MID

| | | | | | |
|---|---|---|---|---|---|
| 71* Composite (1st/3rd) | 1925/6 - | 3 3rd/ 4 1st :36/40 | MET /MID¶ | 48984/94 | 86223/7 |
| 70* Composite (1st/3rd) | | 4 1st/ 3 3rd :40/36 | | 48983/93 | 86222/6 |
| 69* Composite | | 7: 84 | | 48982/92 | 86221/5 |
| 68* Brake second | | 5: 60 | | 48981/91 | 86220/4 |

¶ One set MET, one set MID

| **Built 1927** | | | | | |
|---|---|---|---|---|---|
| 72* Brake third | 1927/8 - | 5: 60 | MID | 47921/31/41/51 | 86300/4/8/12 |
| 73* Third | | 7: 84 | | 47922/32/42/52 | 86301/5/9/13 |
| 74* Third | | 8: 96 | | 47923/33/43/53 | 86302/6/10/4 |
| 75* Third | | 8: 96 | | 47924/34/44/54 | 86303/7/11/5 |

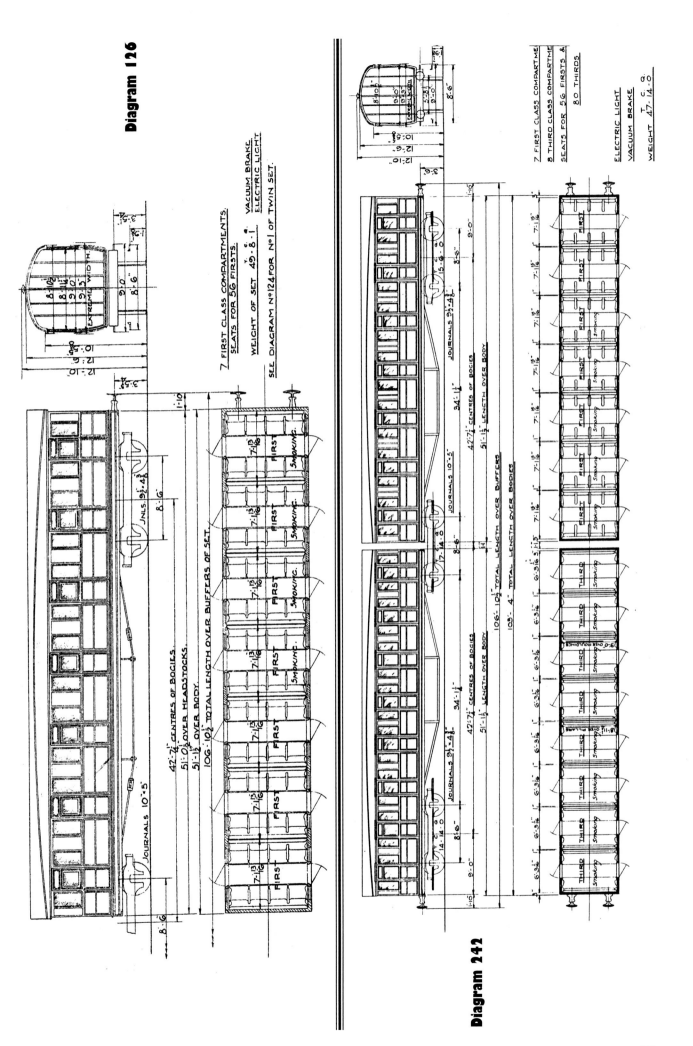

**Diagram 126**

EXTREME WIDTH

7 FIRST CLASS COMPARTMENTS.
SEATS FOR 56 FIRSTS.
WEIGHT OF SET 49·8·1.
SEE DIAGRAM N°124 FOR N°1 OF TWIN SET.

VACUUM BRAKE.
ELECTRIC LIGHT.

JOURNALS 10"×5"
JNLS 9½"×4⅛"

42'·7½" CENTRES OF BOGIES.
51'·0" OVER HEADSTOCKS.
51'·1½" OVER BODY.
106'·10½" TOTAL LENGTH OVER BUFFERS OF SET.

FIRST · FIRST · FIRST · FIRST SMOKING · FIRST SMOKING · FIRST SMOKING · FIRST SMOKING

**Diagram 242**

EXTREME WIDTH

7 FIRST CLASS COMPARTME...
8 THIRD CLASS COMPARTME...
SEATS FOR 56 FIRSTS &
80 THIRDS.

ELECTRIC LIGHT.
VACUUM BRAKE.
WEIGHT 47·14·0.
T C a

JOURNALS 9½"×4⅛"
JOURNALS 10"×5"
JOURNALS 9½"×4⅛"

42'·7½" CENTRES OF BOGIES.
51'·1½" LENGTH OVER BODY.
42'·7½" CENTRES OF BOGIES.
51'·1½" LENGTH OVER BODY.
106'·10½" TOTAL LENGTH OVER BUFFERS.
105'·4" TOTAL LENGTH OVER BODIES.

FIRST · FIRST · FIRST · FIRST SMOKING · FIRST SMOKING · FIRST SMOKING · FIRST SMOKING
THIRD · THIRD · THIRD SMOKING · THIRD SMOKING · THIRD SMOKING · THIRD SMOKING · THIRD SMOKING

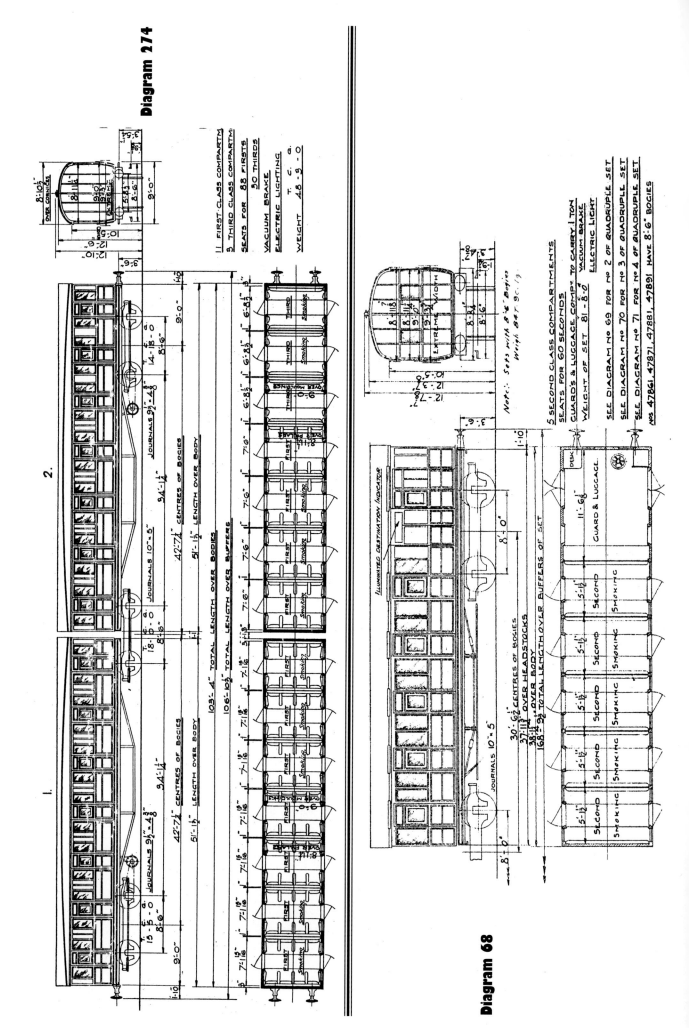

**Diagram 274**

11 FIRST-CLASS COMPARTM.
5 THIRD CLASS COMPARTM(H)
SEATS FOR 88 FIRSTS
30 THIRDS
VACUUM BRAKE
ELECTRIC LIGHTING
T. C. a.
WEIGHT 48.3.0

Note:- Sets with 8'6" Bogies
Weigh 84T 9C 19

5 SECOND CLASS COMPARTMENTS
SEATS FOR 60 SECONDS
GUARDS & LUGGAGE COMPT. TO CARRY 1 TON
VACUUM BRAKE
WEIGHT OF SET 81.8.0
ELECTRIC LIGHT

SEE DIAGRAM No 69 FOR No 2 OF QUADRUPLE SET
SEE DIAGRAM No 70 FOR No 3 OF QUADRUPLE SET
SEE DIAGRAM No 71 FOR No 4 OF QUADRUPLE SET
Nos 47861, 47871, 47881, 47891 HAVE 8'6" BOGIES

**Diagram 68**

130

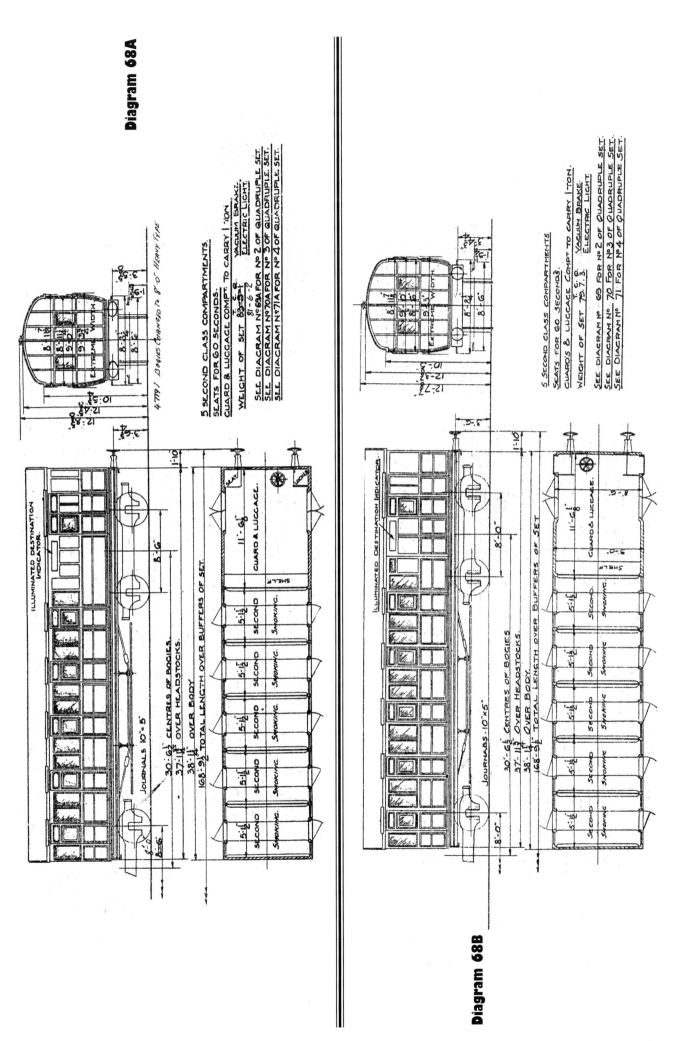

## Diagram 68A

ILLUMINATED DESTINATION INDICATOR.

EXTREME WIDTH

4·7·9·/ BOGIES CHANGED TO 8'·0" HEAVY TYPE

JOURNALS 10"×5"

30'·6½" CENTRES OF BOGIES.
37'·1½" OVER HEADSTOCKS.
38'·1¼" OVER BODY.
168'·9½" TOTAL LENGTH OVER BUFFERS OF SET.

| SECOND | SECOND | SECOND | SECOND | SECOND |
|--------|--------|--------|--------|--------|
| SMOKING | SMOKING | SMOKING | SMOKING | SMOKING |
| 5·1½ | 5·1½ | 5·1½ | 5·1½ | 5·1½ |

GUARD & LUGGAGE.

SHELL

SEAT

LOCKER

11'·6½"

5 SECOND CLASS COMPARTMENTS.
SEATS FOR 60 SECONDS.
GUARD & LUGGAGE COMPT. TO CARRY 1 TON.
WEIGHT OF SET   T. C. R.
                83·3·1
                8'·6·2

SEE DIAGRAM Nº 69A FOR Nº 2 OF QUADRUPLE SET.
SEE DIAGRAM Nº 70A FOR Nº 3 OF QUADRUPLE SET.
SEE DIAGRAM Nº 71A FOR Nº 4 OF QUADRUPLE SET.

## Diagram 68B

ILLUMINATED DESTINATION INDICATOR.

EXTREME WIDTH

JOURNALS 10"×5"

30'·6½" CENTRES OF BOGIES.
37'·11½" OVER HEADSTOCKS.
38'·1¼" OVER BODY.
168'·9½" TOTAL LENGTH OVER BUFFERS OF SET.

| SECOND | SECOND | SECOND | SECOND | SECOND |
|--------|--------|--------|--------|--------|
| SMOKING | SMOKING | SMOKING | SMOKING | SMOKING |
| 5·1½ | 5·1½ | 5·1½ | 5·1½ | 5·1½ |

GUARD & LUGGAGE.

SHELF

11'·6½"

5 SECOND CLASS COMPARTMENTS.
SEATS FOR 60 SECONDS.
GUARDS & LUGGAGE COMPT TO CARRY 1 TON.
WEIGHT OF SET   T. C. R.
                79·7·3.

SEE DIAGRAM Nº 69 FOR Nº 2 OF QUADRUPLE SET.
SEE DIAGRAM Nº 70 FOR Nº 3 OF QUADRUPLE SET.
SEE DIAGRAM Nº 71 FOR Nº 4 OF QUADRUPLE SET.

131

**Diagram 69**

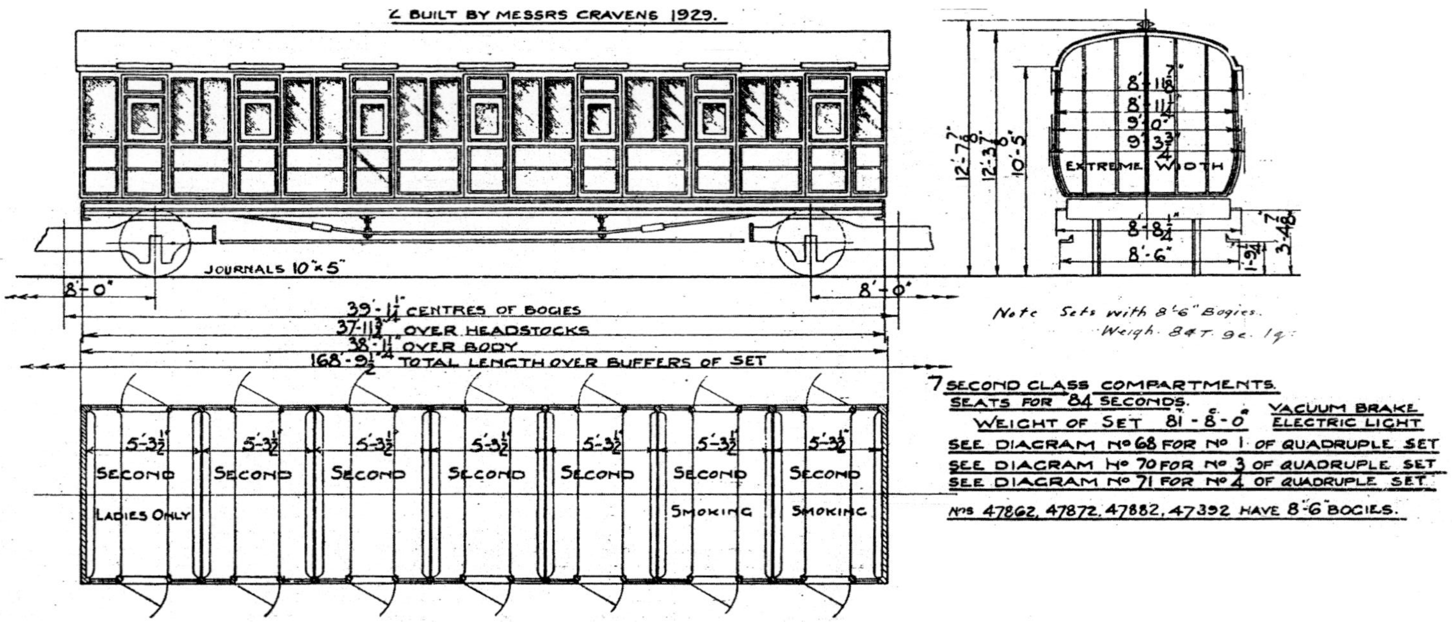

2 BUILT BY MESSRS CRAVENS 1929.

JOURNALS 10"×5"

EXTREME WIDTH

Note: Sets with 8'6" Bogies.
Weigh 84T 9c 1¼.

39'-11" CENTRES OF BOGIES.
37'-11" OVER HEADSTOCKS.
38'-11" OVER BODY.
168'-2¼" TOTAL LENGTH OVER BUFFERS OF SET.

| 5'-3½" | 5'-3½" | 5'-3½" | 5'-3½" | 5'-3½" | 5'-3½" | 5'-3½" | 5'-3½" |
| SECOND | SECOND | SECOND | SECOND | SECOND | SECOND | SECOND | SECOND |
| LADIES ONLY | | | | SMOKING | SMOKING | SMOKING | |

7 SECOND CLASS COMPARTMENTS.
SEATS FOR 84 SECONDS.
WEIGHT OF SET 81-8-0.

VACUUM BRAKE
ELECTRIC LIGHT

SEE DIAGRAM No 68 FOR No 1 OF QUADRUPLE SET
SEE DIAGRAM No 70 FOR No 3 OF QUADRUPLE SET
SEE DIAGRAM No 71 FOR No 4 OF QUADRUPLE SET

Nos 47862, 47872, 47882, 47892 HAVE 8'6 BOGIES.

**Diagram 70A**

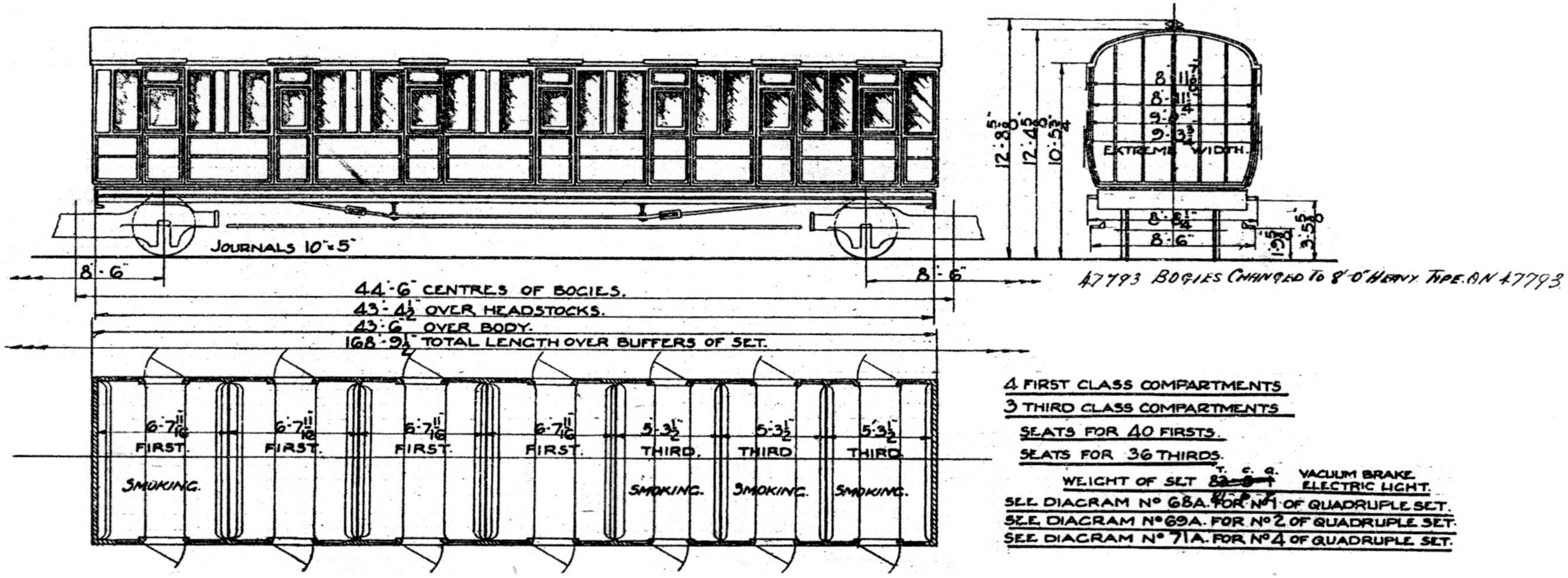

JOURNALS 10"×5"

EXTREME WIDTH

47793 BOGIES CHANGED TO 8'-0" HEAVY TYPE ON 47793

44'-6" CENTRES OF BOGIES.
43'-4½" OVER HEADSTOCKS.
43'-6" OVER BODY.
168'-2¼" TOTAL LENGTH OVER BUFFERS OF SET.

| 6'-7½" | 6'-7½" | 6'-7½" | 6'-7½" | 5'-3½" | 5'-3½" | 5'-3½" | 5'-3½" |
| FIRST. | FIRST. | FIRST. | FIRST. | THIRD. | THIRD. | THIRD. | THIRD. |
| SMOKING. | | | FIRST. | SMOKING. | SMOKING. | SMOKING. | |

4 FIRST CLASS COMPARTMENTS.
3 THIRD CLASS COMPARTMENTS.
SEATS FOR 40 FIRSTS.
SEATS FOR 36 THIRDS.

WEIGHT OF SET

VACUUM BRAKE
ELECTRIC LIGHT

SEE DIAGRAM No 68A. FOR No 1 OF QUADRUPLE SET.
SEE DIAGRAM No 69A. FOR No 2 OF QUADRUPLE SET.
SEE DIAGRAM No 71A. FOR No 4 OF QUADRUPLE SET.

**Diagram 71**

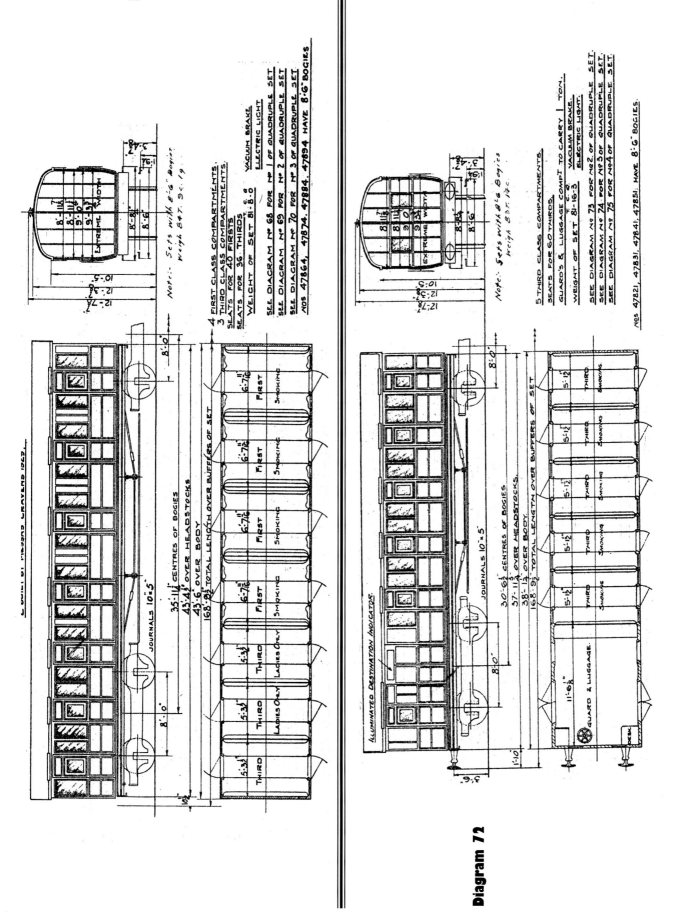

BUILT BY METRO CRAVENS 1927.

JOURNALS 10"×5"

8'·0"

35'·11½" CENTRES OF BOGIES
43'·4½" OVER HEADSTOCKS
43'·6" OVER BODY
168'·9½" TOTAL LENGTH OVER BUFFERS OF SET

EXTREME WIDTH

Note:- Sets with 8'·6" Bogies weigh 84T. 9c. 1q.

4 FIRST CLASS COMPARTMENTS.
3 THIRD CLASS COMPARTMENTS.
SEATS FOR 36 THIRDS.
SEATS FOR 40 FIRSTS.
WEIGHT OF SET 81·8·0.
VACUUM BRAKE.
ELECTRIC LIGHT.

SEE DIAGRAM Nº 68 FOR Nº 1 OF QUADRUPLE SET.
SEE DIAGRAM Nº 69 FOR Nº 2 OF QUADRUPLE SET.
SEE DIAGRAM Nº 70 FOR Nº 3 OF QUADRUPLE SET.
Nos 47864, 47874, 47884, 47894 HAVE 8'·6" BOGIES.

| THIRD | THIRD | THIRD | THIRD | FIRST | FIRST | FIRST | FIRST |
|-------|-------|-------|-------|-------|-------|-------|-------|
| | LADIES ONLY | LADIES ONLY | | SMOKING | SMOKING | SMOKING | SMOKING |

5'·3⅜" 5'·3⅜" 6'·7⅞" 6'·7⅞" 6'·7⅞" 6'·7⅞"

---

**Diagram 72**

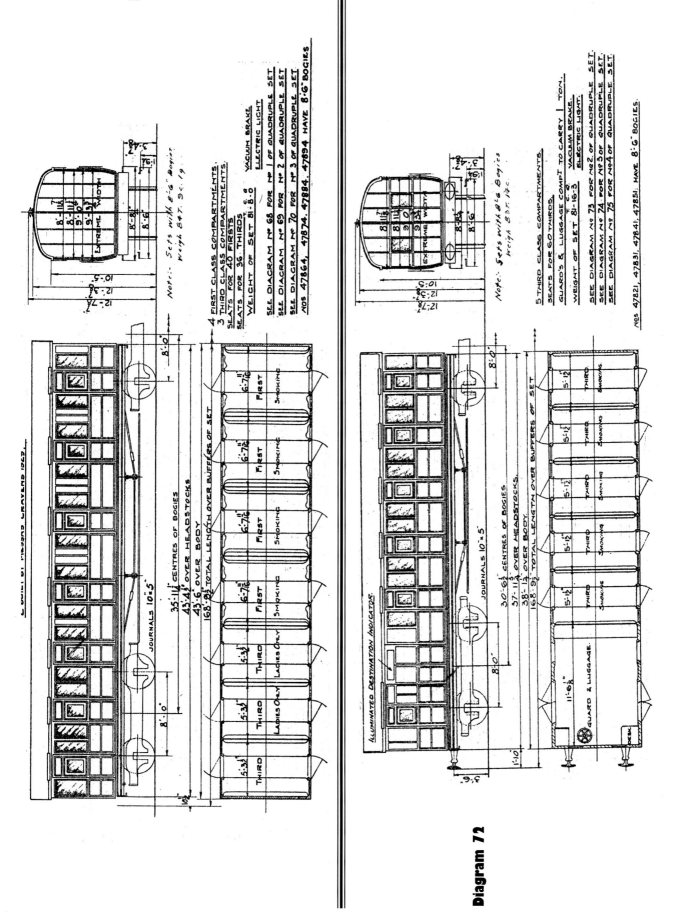

ILLUMINATED DESTINATION INDICATOR.

JOURNALS 10"×5"

8'·0"

30'·6½" CENTRES OF BOGIES
37'·11½" OVER HEADSTOCKS
38'·1½" OVER BODY
168'·9½" TOTAL LENGTH OVER BUFFERS OF SET

EXTREME WIDTH

Note:- Sets with 8'·6" Bogies weigh 83T. 13c.

5 THIRD CLASS COMPARTMENTS.
SEATS FOR 60 THIRDS.
GUARD'S & LUGGAGE COMP'T TO CARRY 1 TON.
WEIGHT OF SET 81·16·3.
VACUUM BRAKE.
ELECTRIC LIGHT.

SEE DIAGRAM Nº 73 FOR Nº 2 OF QUADRUPLE SET.
SEE DIAGRAM Nº 74 FOR Nº 3 OF QUADRUPLE SET.
SEE DIAGRAM Nº 75 FOR Nº 4 OF QUADRUPLE SET.

Nos 47821, 47831, 47841, 47851 HAVE 8'·6" BOGIES.

| GUARD & LUGGAGE. | THIRD | THIRD | THIRD | THIRD | THIRD |
|------------------|-------|-------|-------|-------|-------|
| | SMOKING | SMOKING | SMOKING | SMOKING | SMOKING |

11'·6⅛" 5'·1½" 5'·1½" 5'·1½" 5'·1½" 5'·1½"

Below: **Diagram 71 quad art third E86211E (built Clayton 1925, as 48394). Part of set No 78 and photographed at Moorgate, 1956.**

Bottom: **Diagram 72B quad art brake third E86380E (built Doncaster 1924, as 48851). Part of set No 73 and photographed at Moorgate, 1956. Note the GNR-pattern fanlights and guard's ducket.**

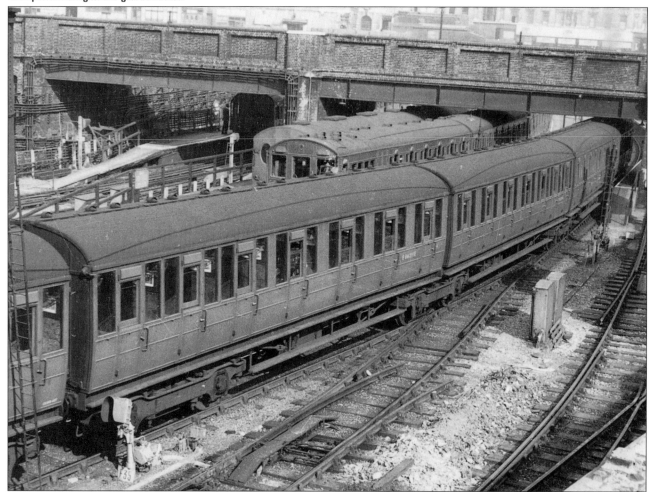

EXTREME WIDTH.

8.11⅞
9.6
8.6
9.3
8.8¼
8.6
10.5
12.3½
12.7½

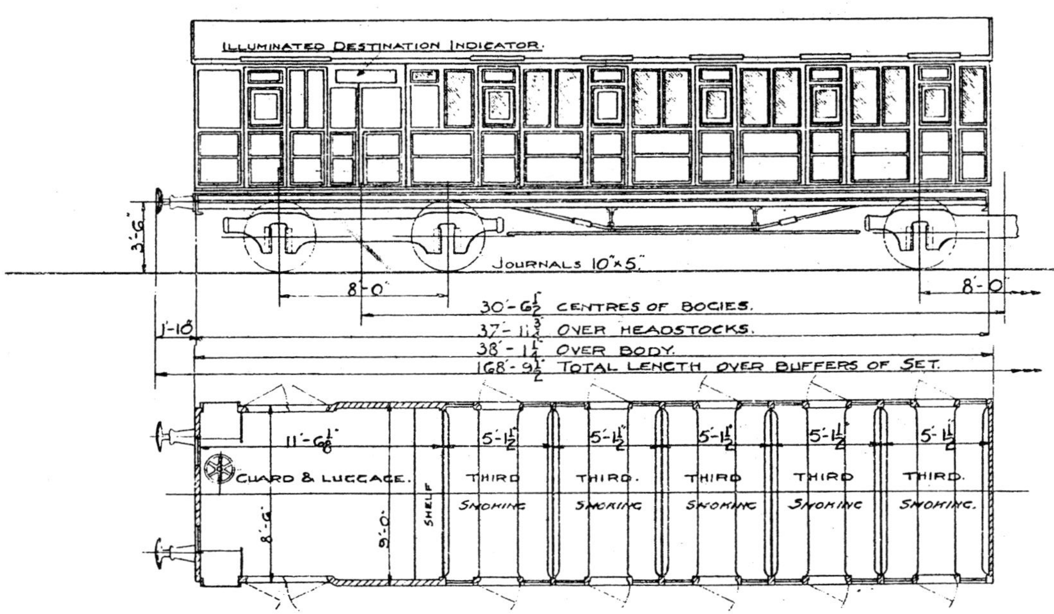

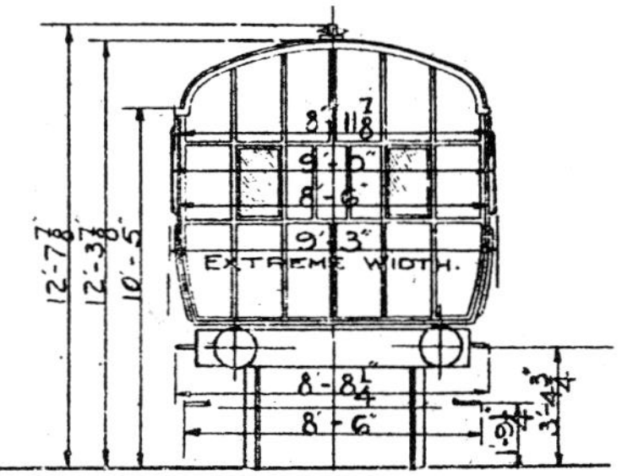

5 THIRD CLASS COMPARTMENTS.

SEATS FOR 60 THIRDS.

GUARD'S & LUGGAGE COMPT TO CARRY 1 TON.

WEIGHT OF SET 79.8.0  T.C.G.  VACUUM BRAKE  ELECTRIC LIGHT

SEE DIAGRAM No 73 FOR No 2 OF QUADRUPLE SET.
SEE DIAGRAM No 74 FOR No 3 OF QUADRUPLE SET.
SEE DIAGRAM No 75 FOR No 4 OF QUADRUPLE SET.

ILLUMINATED DESTINATION INDICATOR.

JOURNALS 10"× 5".

30.6½ CENTRES OF BOGIES.
37.11¼ OVER HEADSTOCKS.
38.1¼ OVER BODY.
168.9½ TOTAL LENGTH OVER BUFFERS OF SET.

8.0
8.0

GUARD & LUGGAGE.
SHELF.
11.2⅝
9.0
5.8

THIRD SMOKING  THIRD  THIRD SMOKING  SMOKING  THIRD SMOKING  5.1½

1.10
5.6

**Diagram 73**

EXTREME WIDTH.

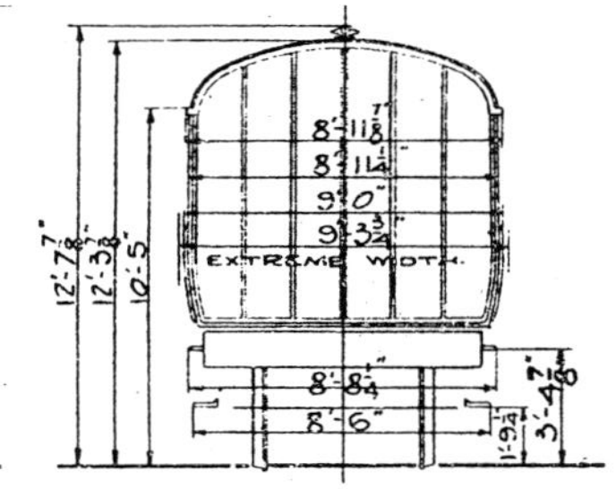

8.11⅞
8.11¼
9.0
9.3¾
8.8¼
8.6
10.5
12.2½

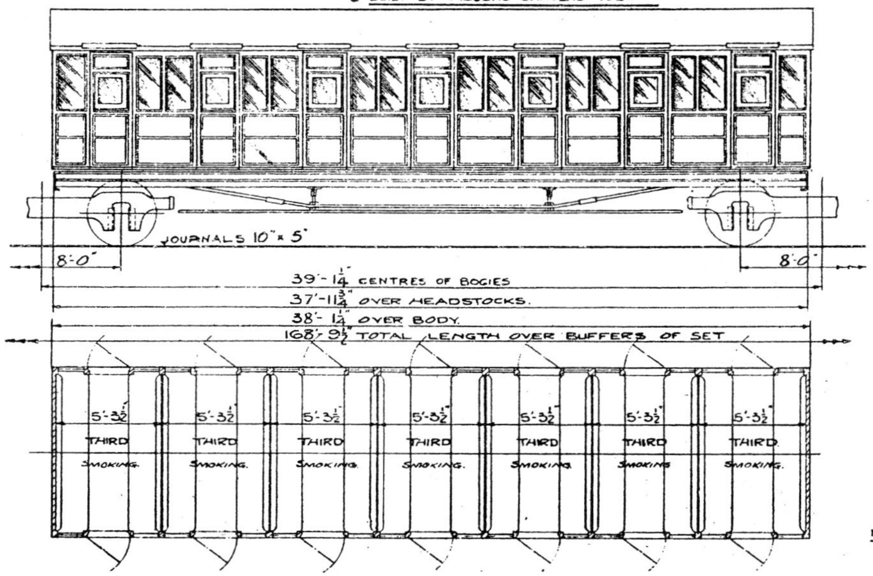

Note:- Seats with 8'6" Bogie weigh 83T.14c.

7 THIRD CLASS COMPARTMENTS.

SEATS FOR 84 THIRDS.

WEIGHT OF SET 81.16.3  T.C.G.  VACUUM BRAKE  ELECTRIC LIGHT

SEE DIAGRAM No 72 FOR No 1 OF QUADRUPLE SET.
SEE DIAGRAM No 74 FOR No 3 OF QUADRUPLE SET.
SEE DIAGRAM No 75 FOR No 4 OF QUADRUPLE SET.

Nos 47822, 47832, 47842, 47852. HAVE 8'6" BOGIES

2 BUILT BY MESSRS CRAVENS 1926

JOURNALS 10"× 5".

39.1¼ CENTRES OF BOGIES.
37.11¼ OVER HEADSTOCKS.
38.1¼ OVER BODY.
168.9½ TOTAL LENGTH OVER BUFFERS OF SET.

8.0
8.0

5.5½  THIRD  SMOKING  THIRD SMOKING  THIRD SMOKING  THIRD SMOKING  THIRD SMOKING  THIRD SMOKING  THIRD SMOKING

135

**Diagram 74A**

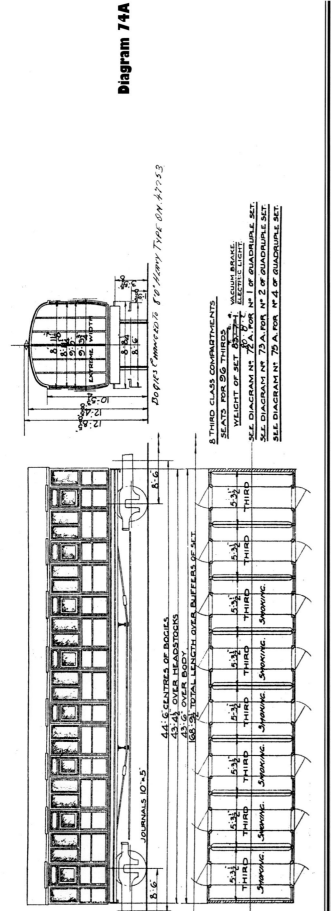

BOGIES CHANGED TO 8'-0"HEAVY TYPE ON N° 47753

8 THIRD CLASS COMPARTMENTS
SEATS FOR 96 THIRDS.
WEIGHT OF SET 83T.7c. VACUUM BRAKE.
ELECTRIC LIGHT.
SEE DIAGRAM N° 72 A. FOR N° 1 OF QUADRUPLE SET.
SEE DIAGRAM N° 73 A. FOR N° 2 OF QUADRUPLE SET.
SEE DIAGRAM N° 75 A. FOR N° 4 OF QUADRUPLE SET.

JOURNALS 10"×5"
44'-6" CENTRES OF BOGIES.
43'-4" OVER HEADSTOCKS.
43'-6" OVER BODY.
68'-9½" TOTAL LENGTH OVER BUFFERS OF SET.

8'-6"
5'-3½" THIRD · SMOKING. | 5'-3½" THIRD · SMOKING. | 5'-3½" THIRD · SMOKING. | 5'-3½" THIRD · SMOKING. | 5'-3½" THIRD · SMOKING. | 5'-3½" THIRD | 5'-3½" THIRD | 5'-3½" THIRD

**Diagram 75**

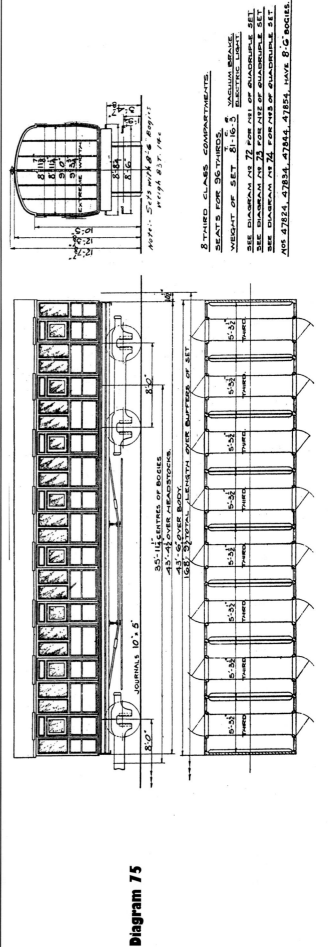

NOTE:- SETS WITH 8'-6" BOGIES WEIGH 83T. 15c.

8 THIRD CLASS COMPARTMENTS.
SEATS FOR 96 THIRDS.
WEIGHT OF SET 81-16-3. VACUUM BRAKE.
ELECTRIC LIGHT.
SEE DIAGRAM N° 72 FOR N° 1 OF QUADRUPLE SET
SEE DIAGRAM N° 73 FOR N° 2 OF QUADRUPLE SET
SEE DIAGRAM N° 74 FOR N° 3 OF QUADRUPLE SET
N° 47824, 47834, 47844, 47854, HAVE 8'-6" BOGIES.

JOURNALS 10"×5"
35'-11½" CENTRES OF BOGIES.
43'-4½" OVER HEADSTOCKS.
43'-6" OVER BODY.
68'-9½" TOTAL LENGTH OVER BUFFERS OF SET.

8'-0"
8'-0"

5'-5½" THIRD | 5'-5½" THIRD | 5'-5½" THIRD | 5'-5½" THIRD | 5'-5½" THIRD | 5'-5½" THIRD | 5'-5½" THIRD | 5'-5½" THIRD

| Diag No CBP | Order No | Compts/ seats | Built | Original number/ changes | 1943 numbers |
|---|---|---|---|---|---|
| **Built 1927 cont** | | | | | |
| 71* Composite (1st/3rd) 1927/8 | - | 3 3rd/ 4 1st :36/40 | MID | 47964/74/84/94 | 86191/5/9, 86203 |
| 70* Composite (1st/3rd) 1927/8 | - | 4 1st/ 3 3rd :40/36 | | 47963/73/83/93 | 86190/4/8, 86202 |
| 69* Second 1927/8 | - | 7: 84 | | 47962/72/82/92 | 86189/93/7, 86201 |
| 68* Brake second 1927/8 | - | 5: 60 | | 47961/71/81/91 | 86188/92/6, 86200 |
| **Built 1928** | | | | | |
| 72* Brake third 1928/9 | - | 5: 60 | MID | 47841/51 | 86292/6 |
| 73* Third | | 7: 84 | | 47842/52 | 86293/7 |
| 74* Third | | 8: 96 | | 47843/53 | 86294/8 |
| 75* Third | | 8: 96 | | 47844/54 | 86295/9 |
| 71* Composite (1st/3rd) 1928/9 | - | 3 3rd/ 4 1st :36/40 | MID | 47884/94 | 86183/7 |
| 70* Composite (1st/3rd) 1928/9 | - | 4 1st/ 3 3rd :40/36 | | 47883/93 | 86182/6 |
| 69* Second 1928/9 | - | 7: 84 | | 47882/92 | 86181/5 |
| 68* Brake second 1928/9 | - | 5: 60 | | 47881/91 | 86180/4 |
| **Built 1929** | | | | | |
| 72* Brake third 1928/9 | - | 5: 60 | CR | 47821/31 | 86284/8 |
| 73* Third | | 7: 84 | | 47822/32 | 86285/9 |
| 74* Third | | 8: 96 | | 47823/33 | 86286/90 |
| 75* Third | | 8: 96 | | 47824/34 | 86287/91 |
| 71* Composite (1st/3rd) 1928/9 | - | 3 3rd/ 4 1st :36/40 | CR | 47864/74 | 86175/9 |
| 70* Composite (1st/3rd) 1928/9 | - | 4 1st/ 3 3rd :40/36 | | 47863/73 | 86174/8 |
| 69* Second 1928/9 | - | 7: 84 | | 47862/72 | 86173/7 |
| 68* Brake second 1928/9 | - | 5: 60 | | 47861/71 | 86172/6 |
| 72A* Brake third 1928/9 | - | 5: 60 | ¶ | 47741/51/61/71 | 86340/4/8/52 |
| 73A* Third | | 7: 84 | | 47742/52/62/72 | 86341/5/9/53 |
| 74A* Third | | 8: 96 | | 47743/53/63/73 | 86342/6/50/4 |
| 75A* Third | | 8: 96 | | 47744/54/64/74 | 86343/7/51/5 |
| 71A* Composite (1st/3rd) 1929/30 | - | 3 3rd/ 4 1st :36/40 | ¶ | 47784/94/804/14 | 86231/5/9/43 |
| 70A* Composite (1st/3rd) 1929/30 | - | 4 1st/ 3 3rd :40/36 | | 47783/93/803/13 | 86230/4/8/42 |
| 69A* Second 1929/30 | - | 7: 84 | | 47782/92/802/12 | 86229/33/7/41 |
| 68A* Brake second 1929/30 | - | 5: 60 | | 47781/91/801/11 | 86228/32/6/40 |

¶ Two trains built by BHM, one each CR and M-C

## GE section quad arts

### DIAGRAMS 102, 103, 104, 105

These fourteen sets for the Liverpool St-Hertford East/Bishops Stortford service were built at York, and were regarded not as suburban trains, but as secondary passenger stock. They were built with the compartments to the standard dimensions of 7ft 6in in the first-class, and 6ft-6ft 2in in the second and third-class. Two coaches in the set were on 51ft underframes, the others shorter, the brake vehicle being of the same Diagram 105 that was used for the twin arts built for GN section outer suburban trains. Notice also that the brake second of the Hertford sets had a generous van space for handling parcels and mails traffic.

The Hertford quads led an uneventful life, working singly and in pairs. Other workings on this route were covered by six-coach sets of non-articulated stock, and by quint arts.

### LIST OF GE QUAD ART VEHICLES:

| Diag No CBP | Order No | Compts/ seats | Built | Original number/ changes | 1943 number |
|---|---|---|---|---|---|
| **Built 1929** | | | | | |
| 102 Brake second | 1928/9 | 264 | 3: 30 | YK | 62800-11 | 80014/8/22/6/30/4, 80038/42/6/50/4/8 |
| 103 Composite¶ | | | 4/2 : 40/20 | | 64000-11 | 80015/9/23/7/31/5, 80039/43/7/51/5/9 |
| 104 Third | | | 7: 70 | | 61800-11 | 80016/20/4/8/32/6, 80040/4/8/52/6/60 |
| 105* Third | | | 8: 80 | | 61812-23 | 80017/21/5/9/33/7, 80041/5/9/53/7/61 |
| 102 Brake second | 1929/30 | 334 | 3: 30 | YK | 62812/3 | 80062/6 |
| 103 Composite¶ | | | 4/2 : 40/20 | | 64012/3 | 80063/7 |
| 104 Third | | | 7: 70 | | 61824/5 | 80064/8 |
| 105* Third | | | 8: 80 | | 61826/7 | 80065/9 |

Air braked ¶The Dia 103 composites were first/ second-class, later all-third, brake seconds reclassified as brake thirds

| Diag No CBP | Order No | Compts/ seats | Built | Original number/ changes | 1943 number |
|---|---|---|---|---|---|
| **Built 1940** | | | | | |
| 104* Third | special | 1094 | 7: 70 | SF | 61800 | 80016 |
| | | Replacement body in quadruplet set – original damaged Ware | | | |
| **Built 1942** | | | | | |
| 102* (Brake third) | special | 1030 | 3: 30 | SF | 62804 | 80030 |
| | | New body, original DEA. | | | |

# Quintuplets

### DIAGRAMS 76-80, 81-85

The background to the decision to build these quint arts for the Enfield and Chingford services of the GE section has been mentioned already.

Generally, the quint arts followed many of the features of the GN section quad arts although the end windows of the brake vehicles were larger. Also, they were fitted with Westinghouse air brakes, the LNER having decided to retain the air brake for GE section suburban stock. Later units were mounted on the heavy 8ft type bogie rather than the 8ft 6in type initially used for the GN and GE London suburban trains. The later brakes (Diagram 85) had different side and end panels, and the guard's seat at the end. All the later vehicles (Diagrams 81-85) were slightly lower overall.

Two quint arts were used to form a ten-coach train for the principal Chingford and Enfield diagrams, but the quins were also used singly –

Top: **GE section quad art set 159, formed of Diagram 105 third 61820, Diagram 104 third 61808, Diagram 103 first/second composite 64008 and Diagram 102 brake second 62808. Eventually numbered 80049, 80048, 80047, 80046. A York photograph dated September 1929.**

Above: **The Hertford quad arts seemed to be shy photographically but here is a down Lea Valley train at Stratford in May 1931 behind 'D15/2' 4-4-0 No 8899. There are two leading ex-GER six-wheelers in front of the quad which has a Diagram 120 van to its rear.**

whereas the GN quads were not – on Chingford-Stratford, and Palace Gates and North Woolwich trains. There were also some workings for the sets between Liverpool St and Ilford.

Originally, the ten-coach trains were formed: BT + T + C + S + C + C + S + C + T + BT.

### LIST OF GE QUINT ART VEHICLES:

| Diag No CBP | Order No | Compts/ seats | Built | Original number/ changes | 1943 number |
|---|---|---|---|---|---|
| **Built 1925** | | | | | |
| 76 | 1924/5 | 4/3 | see | 63001/3/5/7/9/11, | 86396/401/6/11/6/21, |
| #(Composite) | | : 40/36 | below | 63013/5/7/9/21/3, | 86426/31/6/41/6/51, |
| | | | | 63025/7/9/31/3/5, | 86456/61/6/71/6/81, |
| | | | | 63037/9/41/3/5/7, | 86486/91/6/501/6/11, |
| | | | | 63049/51/3/5/7/9, | 86516/21/6/31/6/41, |
| | | | | 63061/3/5/7/9/71, | 86546/51/6/61/6/71, |
| | | | | 63073/5/7/9/81/3, | 86576/81/6/91/6/601, |
| | | | | 63085/7/9/91/3/5, | 86606/11/6/ — /26/31, |
| | | | | 63097/9/101/3/5/7, | 86636/41/6/51/6/61, |
| | | | | 63109/11/3/5 | 86666/71/6/81 |

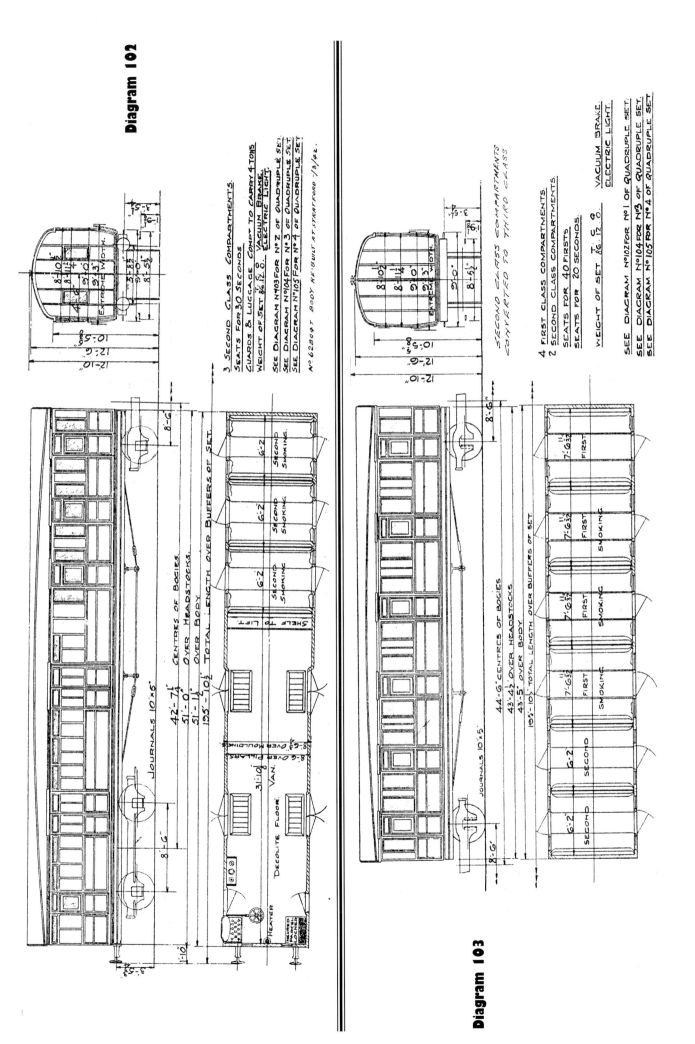

## Diagram 102

3 SECOND CLASS COMPARTMENTS.
SEATS FOR 30 SECONDS.
GUARDS & LUGGAGE COMPT TO CARRY 4 TONS
WEIGHT OF SET 86.12.0. VACUUM BRAKE.
ELECTRIC LIGHT.

SEE DIAGRAM Nº103 FOR Nº 2 OF QUADRUPLE SET.
SEE DIAGRAM Nº104 FOR Nº 3 OF QUADRUPLE SET.
SEE DIAGRAM Nº105 FOR Nº 4 OF QUADRUPLE SET.

Nº 62804 BODY RE-BUILT AT STRATFORD -/3/42.

## Diagram 103

SECOND CLASS COMPARTMENTS
CONVERTED TO THIRD CLASS

4 FIRST CLASS COMPARTMENTS.
2 SECOND CLASS COMPARTMENTS.

SEATS FOR 40 FIRSTS
SEATS FOR 20 SECONDS.

WEIGHT OF SET T.G. O.
86.12.0.

VACUUM BRAKE.
ELECTRIC LIGHT.

SEE DIAGRAM Nº102 FOR Nº 1 OF QUADRUPLE SET.
SEE DIAGRAM Nº104 FOR Nº 3 OF QUADRUPLE SET.
SEE DIAGRAM Nº105 FOR Nº 4 OF QUADRUPLE SET

# Diagram 104

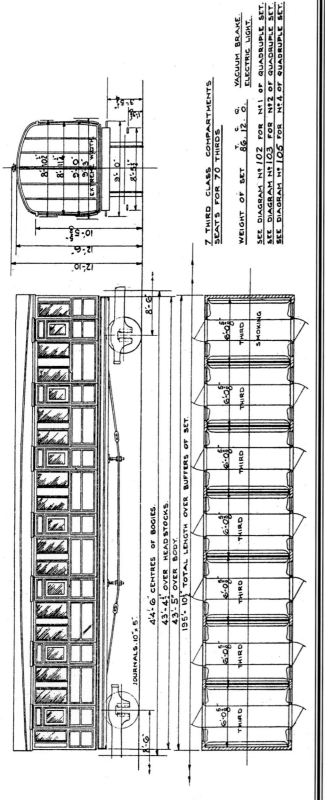

VACUUM BRAKE.
ELECTRIC LIGHT.

7 THIRD CLASS COMPARTMENTS
SEATS FOR 70 THIRDS

WEIGHT OF SET    T.C.G.  86.12.0.

SEE DIAGRAM Nº 102 FOR Nº1 OF QUADRUPLE SET.
SEE DIAGRAM Nº 103 FOR Nº2 OF QUADRUPLE SET.
SEE DIAGRAM Nº 105 FOR Nº4 OF QUADRUPLE SET.

| Diag No | CBP | Order No | Compts/ seats | Built | Original number/ changes | 1943 number |
|---|---|---|---|---|---|---|
| 77 (Second) | 1924/5 | - | 8: 96 | | 6501-58 | 86397/402/7/12/7/22, 86427/32/7/42/7/52, 86457/62/7/72/7/82, 86487/92/7/502/7/12, 86517/22/7/32/7/42, 86547/52/7/62/7/72, 86577/82/7/92/7/602, 86607/12/7/—/27/32, 86637/42/7/52/7/62, 86667/72/7/82 |
| 78 (Composite)¶ | 1924/5 | - | 4/4 : 48/48 | | 63000/2/4/6/8/10, 63012/4/6/8/20/2, 63024/6/8/30/2/4, 63036/8/40/2/4/6, 63048/50/2/4/6/8, 63060/2/4/6/8/70, 63072/4/6/8/80/2, 63084/6/8/90/2/4, 63096/8/100/2/4/6, 63108/10/2/4 | 86398/403/8/13/8/23, 86428/33/8/43/8/53, 86458/63/8/73/8/83, 86488/93/8/503/8/13, 86518/23/8/33/8/43, 86548/53/8/63/8/73, 86578/83/8/93/8/603, 86608/13/8/—/28/33, 86638/43/8/53/8/63, 86668/73/8/83 |
| 79 (Third) | 1924/5 | - | 8: 96 | | 60000-57 | 86399/404/9/14/9/24, 86429/34/9/44/9/54, 86459/64/9/74/9/84, 86489/94/9/504/9/14, 86519/24/9/34/9/44, 86549/54/9/64/9/74, 86579/84/9/94/9/604, 86609/14/9/—/29/34, 86639/44/9/54/9/64, 86669/74/9/84 |
| 80 (Brake third) | 1924/5 | - | 6: 72 | | 62000-57 | 86400/5/10/5/20/5, 86430/5/40/5/50/5, 86460/5/70/5/80/5, 86490/5/500/5/10/5, 86520/5/30/5/40/5, 86550/5/60/5/70/5, 86580/5/90/5/600/5, 86610/5/20/—/30/5, 86640/5/50/5/60/5, 86670/5/80/5 |

Builders:  CL Six trains — 63001-23 odd Nos; 6501-12; 63000-22 even Nos; 60000-11; 62000-11.

CR Five trains — 63025-43 odd Nos; 6513-22; 63024-42 even Nos; 60012-21; 62012-21.

HN Three trains — 63045-55 odd Nos; 6523-8; 63044-54 even Nos; 60022-7; 62022-7.

MET Seven trains — 63057-83 odd Nos; 6529-42; 63056-82 even Nos; 60028-41; 62028-41.

MID Five trains — 63085-103 odd Nos; 6543-52; 63084-102 even Nos; 60042-51; 62042-51.

RYP Three trains — 63105-15 odd Nos; 6553-8; 63104-14 even Nos; 60052-7; 62052-7.

Air-braked Into traffic with numbers in series 10362E- 10652E

# First/ second-class, later all-third ¶ Second/ third-class, later all-third.

## Built 1927

| Diag No | CBP | Order No | Compts/ seats | Built | Original number/ changes | 1943 number |
|---|---|---|---|---|---|---|
| 81* (Composite)# | 1927/8 | - | 4/3 : 40/36 | CL | 63120-3 | 86686/91/6/701 |
| 82* (Second) | 1927/8 | - | 8: 96 | | 6560/59/62/1 | 86687/92/7/702 |
| 83* (Composite)¶ | 1927/8 | - | 4/4 : 48/48 | | 63116-9 | 86688/93/8/703 |
| 84* (Third) | 1927/8 | - | 8: 96 | | 60058-61 | 86689/94/9/704 |
| 85* (Brake third) | 1927/8 | - | 6: 72 | | 62058-61 | 86690/5/700/5 |

Air braked  # First/second-class, later all-third ¶ Second/third-class, later all-third.

**Diagram 76**

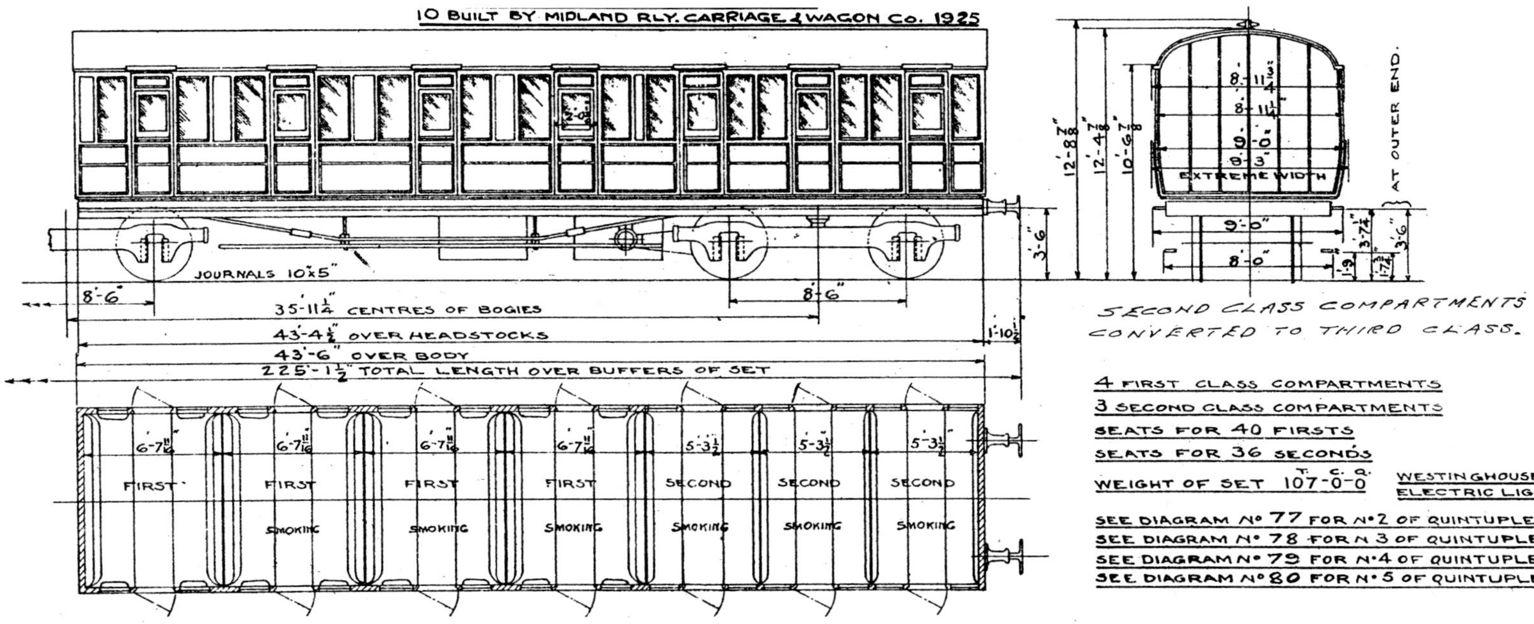
10 BUILT BY MIDLAND RLY. CARRIAGE & WAGON Co. 1925
JOURNALS 10"x5"
8'-6"
35'-11¼" CENTRES OF BOGIES
8'-6"
43'-4½" OVER HEADSTOCKS
43'-6" OVER BODY
1'-10½"
225'-1½" TOTAL LENGTH OVER BUFFERS OF SET
3'-6"
6'-7 11/16"
FIRST
FIRST
SMOKING
FIRST
SMOKING
FIRST
SMOKING
5'-3½"
SECOND
SMOKING
SECOND
SMOKING
SECOND
SMOKING
12'-8⅞"
12'-4 7/16"
10'-6 7/8"
8'-11¾"
8'-11½"
9'-0"
9'-3"
EXTREME WIDTH
9'-0"
8'-0"
3'-7¼"
1'-7¼"
1'-9"
3'-6"
AT OUTER END.

SECOND CLASS COMPARTMENTS CONVERTED TO THIRD CLASS.

4 FIRST CLASS COMPARTMENTS
3 SECOND CLASS COMPARTMENTS
SEATS FOR 40 FIRSTS
SEATS FOR 36 SECONDS
WEIGHT OF SET 107-0-0 (T. C. Q.)

WESTINGHOUSE BRAKE
ELECTRIC LIGHT

SEE DIAGRAM No 77 FOR No 2 OF QUINTUPLE SET
SEE DIAGRAM No 78 FOR No 3 OF QUINTUPLE SET
SEE DIAGRAM No 79 FOR No 4 OF QUINTUPLE SET
SEE DIAGRAM No 80 FOR No 5 OF QUINTUPLE SET

**Diagram 77**

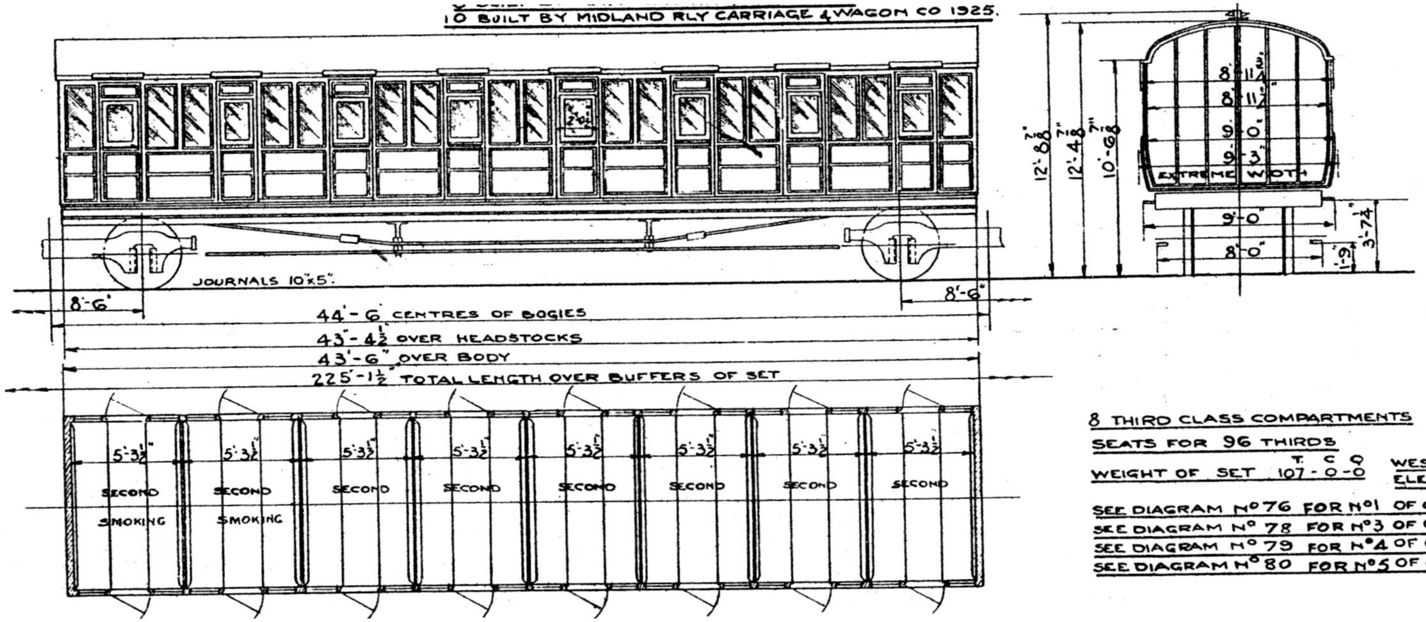
10 BUILT BY MIDLAND RLY CARRIAGE & WAGON CO 1925.
JOURNALS 10"x5".
8'-6"
8'-6"
44'-6" CENTRES OF BOGIES
43'-4½" OVER HEADSTOCKS
43'-6" OVER BODY
225'-1½" TOTAL LENGTH OVER BUFFERS OF SET
5'-3½"
SECOND
SMOKING
SECOND
SMOKING
SECOND
SECOND
SECOND
SECOND
SECOND
SECOND
12'-8⅞"
12'-4 7/8"
10'-6 7/8"
8'-11¾"
8'-11½"
9'-0"
9'-3"
EXTREME WIDTH
9'-0"
8'-0"
3'-7¼"
1'-9"

8 THIRD CLASS COMPARTMENTS
SEATS FOR 96 THIRDS
WEIGHT OF SET 107-0-0 (T. C. Q.)

WESTINGHOUSE BRAKE
ELECTRIC LIGHT

SEE DIAGRAM No 76 FOR No 1 OF QUINTUPLE SET
SEE DIAGRAM No 78 FOR No 3 OF QUINTUPLE SET
SEE DIAGRAM No 79 FOR No 4 OF QUINTUPLE SET
SEE DIAGRAM No 80 FOR No 5 OF QUINTUPLE SET

Top: **Clayton-built quint art brake third No 10352E, showing that these coaches were lined-out when new.**

Above: **Diagram 80 quint art brake second E86475E (built by Cravens in 1925, and formerly numbered in the 1xxxx series, later 62015). Part of set No 114B and photographed at Wood Street, Walthamstow, 1957.**

| Diag No CBP | Order No | Compts/ seats | Built | Original number/ changes | 1943 number |
|---|---|---|---|---|---|
| **Built 1929** | | | | | |
| 81* (Composite)# | 1928/9 - | 4/3 : 40/36 | CL | 63128-31/6-9 | 86706/11/6/21/6/31/6/41 |
| 82* (Second) | 1928/9 - | 8: 96 | | 6563-70 | 86707/12/7/22/7/32/7/42 |
| 83* (Composite)¶ | 1928/9 - | 4/4 : 48/48 | | 63124-7/32-5 | 86708/13/8/23/8/33/8/43 |
| 84* (Third) | 1928/9 - | 8: 96 | | 60062-9 | 86709/14/9/24/9/34/9/44 |
| 85* (Brake third) | 1928/9 - | 6: 72 | | 62062-9 | 86710/5/20/5/30/5/40/5 |

Air braked # First/second-class, later all-third ¶ Second/third-class, later all-third.

| Diag No CBP | Order No | Compts/ seats | Built | Original number/ changes | 1943 number |
|---|---|---|---|---|---|
| **Built 1930** | | | | | |
| 81* (Composite)# | 1930/1 - | 4/3 : 40/36 | M-C | 64051/3/5/7 | 86746/51/6/61 |
| 82* (Second) | 1930/1 - | 8: 96 | | 6571-4 | 86747/52/7/62 |
| 83* (Composite)¶ | 1930/1 - | 4/4 : 48/48 | | 64050/2/4/6 | 86748/53/8/63 |
| 84* (Third) | 1930/1 - | 8: 96 | | 60070-3 | 86749/54/9/64 |
| 85* (Brake third) | 1930/1 - | 6: 72 | | 62070-3 | 86750/5/60/5 |

Air braked # First/ second-class, later all-third ¶ Second/ third-class, later all-third.

| Diag No CBP | Order No | Compts/ seats | Built | Original number/ changes | 1943 number |
|---|---|---|---|---|---|
| **Built 1941** | | | | | |
| 76* (Composite) | special | 1022 | 4/3 : 40/36 | SF | 63067 | 86561 New body, original DEA. |
| **Built 1942** | | | | | |
| 85* (Brake third) | special | 1029 | 6: 72 | SF | 62066 | 86730 New body, original DEA. |

142

## Diagram 78

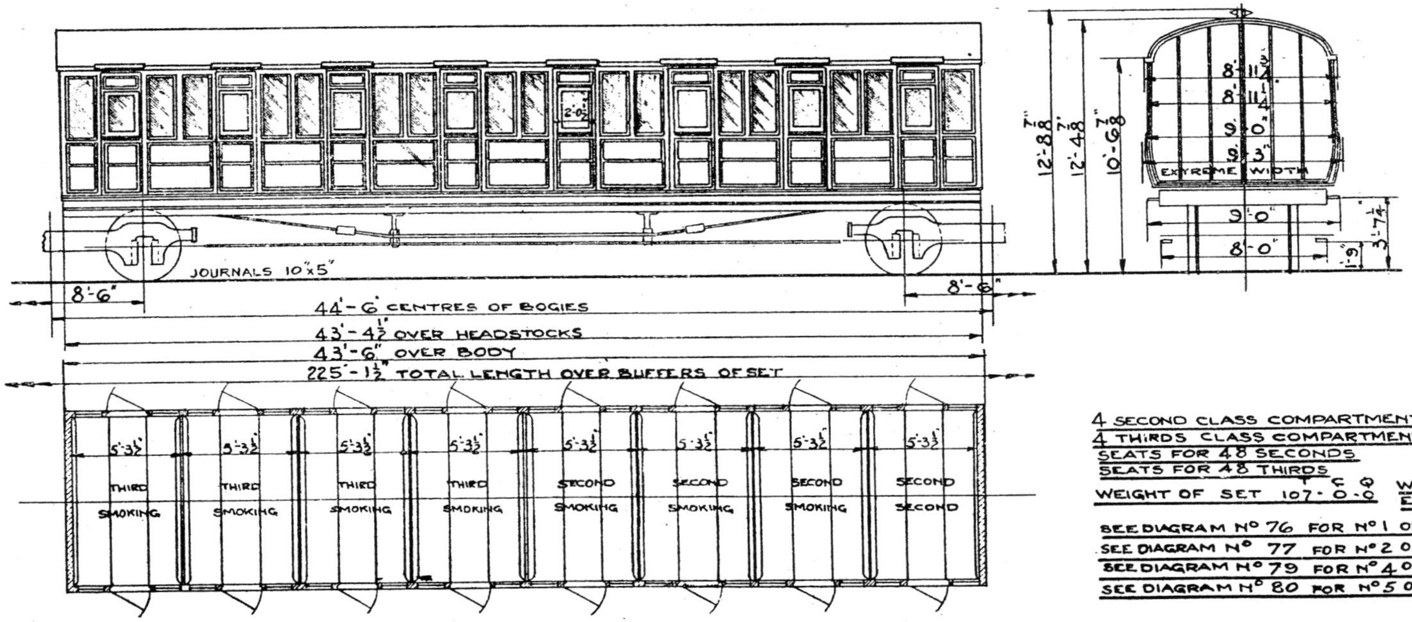

JOURNALS 10"x5"
8'-6"
8'-6"
44'-6" CENTRES OF BOGIES
43'-4½" OVER HEADSTOCKS
43'-6" OVER BODY
225'-1½" TOTAL LENGTH OVER BUFFERS OF SET
12'-8 7/8"
12'-4 7/8"
10'-6 7/8"
8'-11¾"
8'-11¼"
9'-0"
9'-3"
EXTREME WIDTH
9'-0"
8'-0"
3'-7¼"
1'-9"
5'-3½"
THIRD SMOKING
THIRD SMOKING
THIRD SMOKING
THIRD SMOKING
SECOND SMOKING
SECOND SMOKING
SECOND SMOKING
SECOND SECOND


4 SECOND CLASS COMPARTMENTS
4 THIRDS CLASS COMPARTMENTS
SEATS FOR 48 SECONDS
SEATS FOR 48 THIRDS
WEIGHT OF SET 107-0-0 (T C Q) — WESTINGHOUSE BRAKE, ELECTRIC LIGHT

SEE DIAGRAM Nº 76 FOR Nº 1 OF QUINTUPLE SET
SEE DIAGRAM Nº 77 FOR Nº 2 OF QUINTUPLE SET
SEE DIAGRAM Nº 79 FOR Nº 4 OF QUINTUPLE SET
SEE DIAGRAM Nº 80 FOR Nº 5 OF QUINTUPLE SET

## Diagram 79

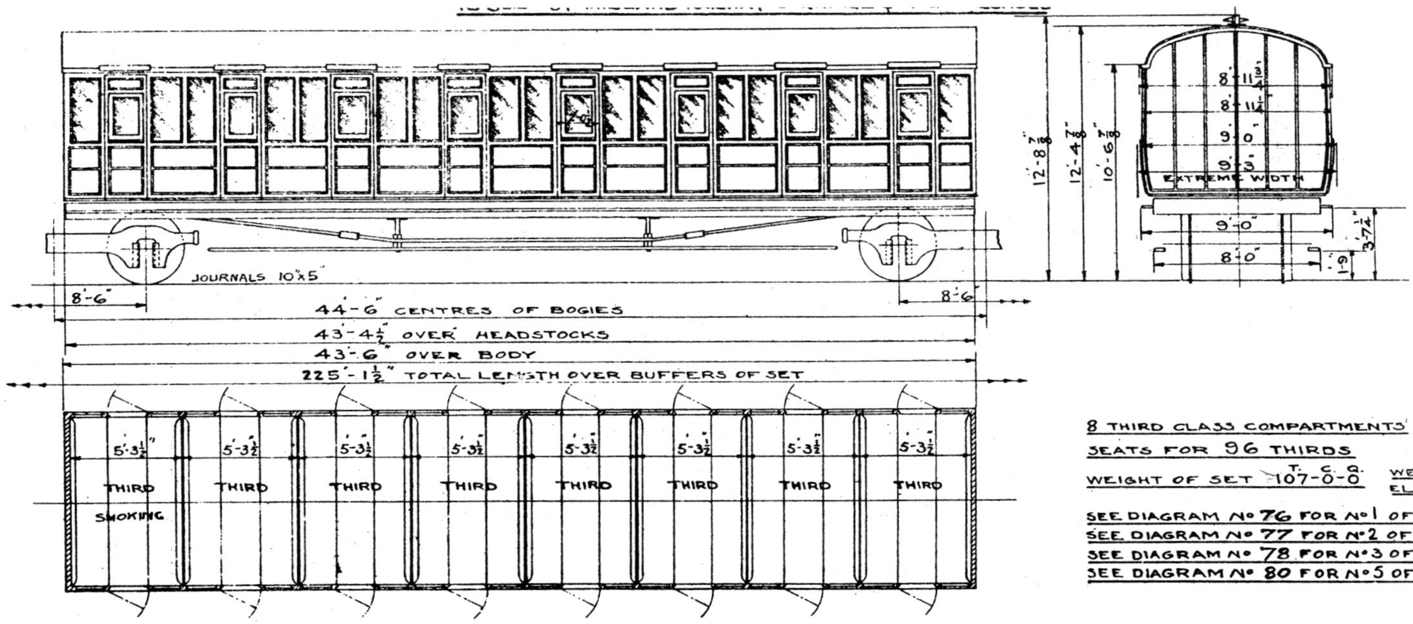

JOURNALS 10"x5"
8'-6"
8'-6"
44'-6" CENTRES OF BOGIES
43'-4½" OVER HEADSTOCKS
43'-6" OVER BODY
225'-1½" TOTAL LENGTH OVER BUFFERS OF SET
12'-8 7/16"
12'-4 7/16"
10'-6 7/16"
8'-11¾"
8'-11¼"
9'-0"
9'-3"
EXTREME WIDTH
9'-0"
8'-0"
3'-7¼"
1'-9"
5'-3½"
THIRD SMOKING
THIRD
THIRD
THIRD
THIRD
THIRD
THIRD
THIRD


8 THIRD CLASS COMPARTMENTS
SEATS FOR 96 THIRDS
WEIGHT OF SET 107-0-0 (T C Q) — WESTINGHOUSE BRAKE, ELECTRIC LIGHT

SEE DIAGRAM Nº 76 FOR Nº 1 OF QUINTUPLE SET
SEE DIAGRAM Nº 77 FOR Nº 2 OF QUINTUPLE SET
SEE DIAGRAM Nº 78 FOR Nº 3 OF QUINTUPLE SET
SEE DIAGRAM Nº 80 FOR Nº 5 OF QUINTUPLE SET

# Diagram 80

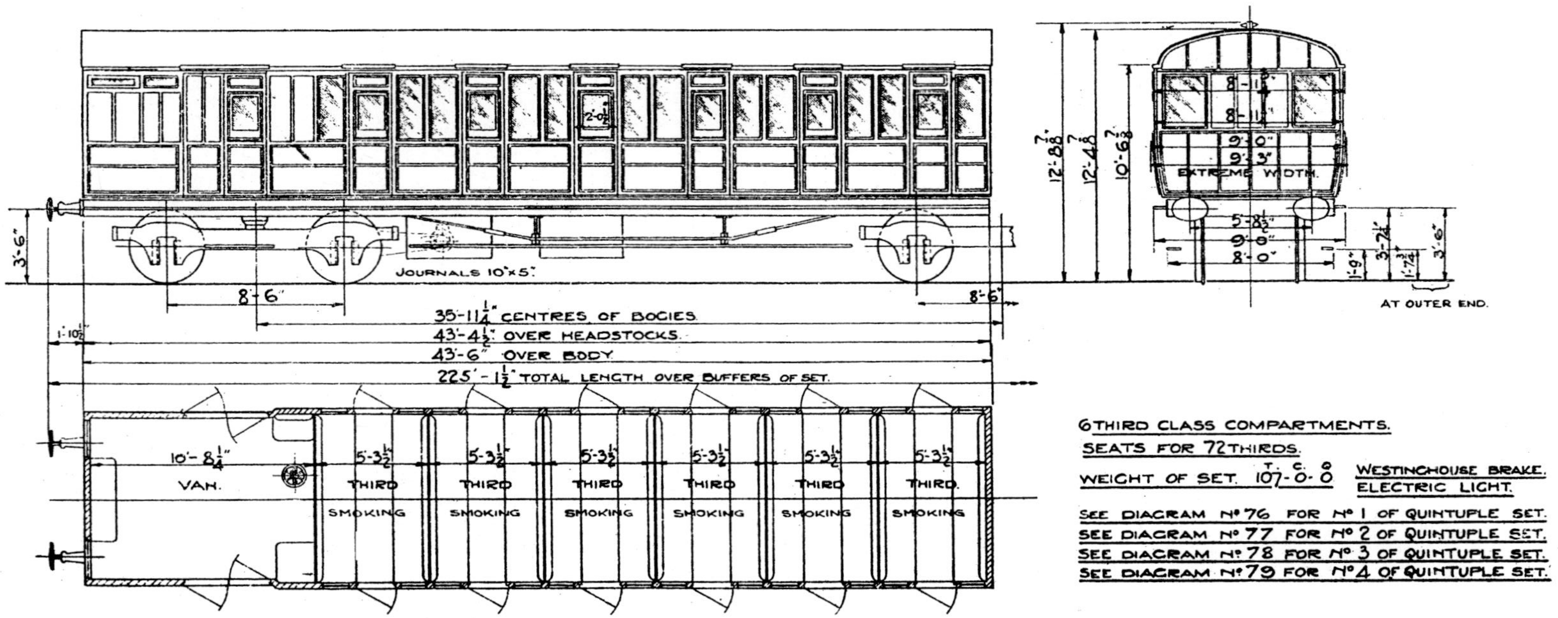

6 THIRD CLASS COMPARTMENTS.

SEATS FOR 72 THIRDS.

WEIGHT OF SET. T.C. & 107-0-0

WESTINGHOUSE BRAKE.
ELECTRIC LIGHT.

SEE DIAGRAM No 76 FOR No 1 OF QUINTUPLE SET.
SEE DIAGRAM No 77 FOR No 2 OF QUINTUPLE SET.
SEE DIAGRAM No 78 FOR No 3 OF QUINTUPLE SET.
SEE DIAGRAM No 79 FOR No 4 OF QUINTUPLE SET.

AT OUTER END.

EXTREME WIDTH.

35'-11¼" CENTRES OF BOGIES
43'-4½" OVER HEADSTOCKS
43'-6" OVER BODY
225'-1½" TOTAL LENGTH OVER BUFFERS OF SET.

JOURNALS 10×5".

THIRD SMOKING    THIRD SMOKING    THIRD SMOKING    THIRD SMOKING    THIRD SMOKING    THIRD SMOKING    VAN

5'-3½"

10'-8¼"

# Diagram 85

6 THIRD CLASS COMPARTMENTS.

SEATS FOR 72 THIRDS.

WEIGHT OF SET. T.C. & 107-0-0

WESTINGHOUSE BRAKE.
ELECTRIC LIGHT.

SEE DIAGRAM No 81 FOR No 1 OF QUINTUPLE SET.
SEE DIAGRAM No 82 FOR No 2 OF QUINTUPLE SET.
SEE DIAGRAM No 83 FOR No 3 OF QUINTUPLE SET.
SEE DIAGRAM No 84 FOR No 4 OF QUINTUPLE SET.

EXTREME WIDTH.

35'-11¼" CENTRES OF BOGIES.
43'-4½" OVER HEADSTOCKS.
43'-6" OVER BODY.
225'-0½" TOTAL LENGTH OVER BUFFERS OF SET.

THIRD SMOKING    THIRD SMOKING    THIRD SMOKING    THIRD SMOKING    THIRD SMOKING    THIRD SMOKING    VAN

5'-3½"

10'-8¼"

LOCKER    SEAT

8'-0"

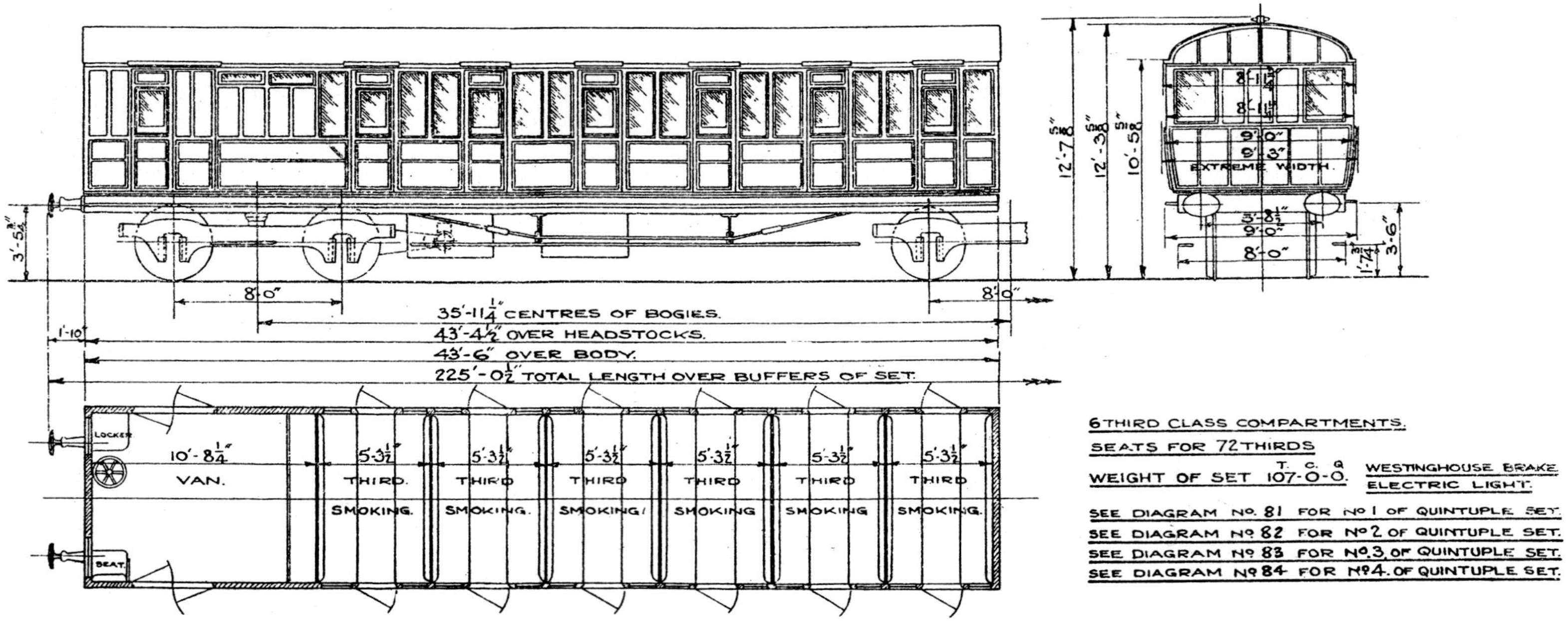

# CATERING VEHICLES

Inevitably, perhaps, the LNER followed the practices adopted for the East Coast main line services when it came to catering vehicles as the majority of such vehicles were employed on these prestigious services, and also those of the GN section.

No new catering vehicles had been built for the principal East Coast services for ten years. Two three-car sets, consisting of first-class dining car, kitchen car and third-class dining car had entered service on the 'Flying Scotsman' on the very eve of world war. The kitchen car was as nearly all-steel as had been possible, to make it as fireproof in view of the continued use of gas for cooking.

Gresley approached the problem of fire risk rather differently in 1921 with the Leeds quintuplet set in which the kitchen equipment was all-electric. The vehicles themselves were of conventional teak bodies on steel underframes. Both these developments – the three-car sets of the 'Flying Scotsman', and the evolution of electric cooking equipments – were influences on the policy to be adopted for catering vehicles by the newly formed LNER. Three authorities were involved in the specification and operation of catering vehicles: the Superintendents and Passenger Managers for each of the Areas or sections, the chief mechanical engineer's department, and, not least, the Hotels Department.

An indication of the LNER's first thoughts for standard restaurant car designs came with the deliberations leading to conclusion of the 1924 Carriage Building Programme. Priority was accorded to the construction of new restaurant cars for the 'Flying Scotsman', and other Anglo-Scottish trains.

The first proposals considered at a meeting held in York in November 1923 were for a repeat of the 1914 three-car sets, and alternatively for the well-tested East Coast combination of a restaurant/kitchen first, paired with a third-class restaurant pantry car. Objections to the three-car sets were that they would be costly, and would increase train weight; the two-car formation presented the disadvantages of noise and cooking smells arising from the combination of kitchen and dining facilities in one vehicle. The CME's representative at that York meeting came up with a third option, that of a triplet restaurant car.

To this, the objections were that if one vehicle was stopped for attention, then three vehicles were out of traffic. As first proposed, the triplet was offered with either gas or electric cooking equipment. The Hotels Department's preference was for electric cooking, and during the discussion it was noted that this option would increase the cost of a triplet by £1,500 on the likely building cost of £8,500. That was not all. If triplet restaurant cars were chosen, it was expected that there would have to be spare sets – one held at Kings Cross and one at Edinburgh Waverley. In the event, only one spare set was provided, and five triplets were included in the 1924/5 Programme.

Within a month, it had been decided to build the triplet restaurant cars, each dining car having two saloons: one for smoking, the other for non-smokers. The design was prepared by Doncaster where the triplets were to be built. The cooking equipment would be all-electric, the SPMs having been convinced as a result of a trial of an electric car between Kings Cross and Darlington and back in late November 1923. No record of the vehicle used is given, but surely it must have been the GNR quintuplet of 1921 as none other was available. Special dispensation would have had to be given for its operation north of Doncaster.

The other catering vehicles featuring in the 1924 programme were for the GE section Continental boat trains, for a Newcastle-Oxford and return working, and for the Newcastle-Swansea express which was to receive a complete set of new coaches. The new cars were to be 65ft in length and of three types: first-class, composite and third-class. In addition, there were to be restaurant pantry cars, similar in layout to those in East Coast service, the pantry serving as additional kitchen space to the main restaurant car although without cooking ranges and ovens.

Gresley and Bulleid were present at the January 1924 meeting of the three authorities mentioned above when the policy for catering vehicles was agreed. It was found that the restaurant cars would have to be built on the 60ft underframe, as agreement to the use of the greater length was not forthcoming. The types of cars were confirmed but it was thought that there was no requirement for a composite car. When it came to fitting out the cars, it was agreed that floors would be covered in rubber sheeting, that glass louvres would be fitted to the saloon windows of restaurant cars and those open thirds designated for dining use. Dining cars would be fitted out with net racks, and provision for hand luggage would be made under, and between, seats.

The main types of restaurant cars that would serve the LNER were established at this meeting: restaurant/kitchen first; restaurant/kitchen third; triplet restaurant car set; pantry third-class car.

During 1924, there were the first thoughts of tea cars, capable of serving light refreshments from a pantry. The only available vehicles were vestibuled twins with pantries built by the GNR during World War I, and these were introduced on Hull-Liverpool services in 1924/5, in competition with the LMS service which also offered tea cars. This experiment proved unprofitable, but it had spurred plans to convert some vestibule thirds to pantry cars. The ex-GNR cars displaced from the Liverpool service were then used between York and Swindon. It would be 1932 before the question of tea or buffet cars was again raised.

First-class restaurant cars built under the 1924 CBP had their seats upholstered in leather. This was not to the liking of the passenger managers who preferred green cloth or tapestry but they were overruled by the chief general manager. Rubber flooring was found to be unsatisfactory for restaurant cars, and was replaced from 1928 by carpeting in first-class cars, and by carpet restricted to the aisle only, and laid over lino, in the third-class.

In July 1926, the general policy on restaurant cars was reviewed. At the time, there were 126 restaurant cars, 35 pantry thirds and the two tea car twins in LNER stock. Ninety-two cars were in regular service, and no less than 34 were spare, or used for private charters. The standard types of restaurant cars in use were:

| | |
|---|---|
| Restaurant/kitchen first | Working with open thirds or pantry thirds. Drawing No 4673N. |
| Pantry third | Working with adjacent first-class restaurant car. Drawing 4675N. |
| Triplet set | For important services with heavy and regular patronage such as the two pairs of principal East Coast day trains (and the 8am Newcastle-Kings Cross and 5.30pm return) which received triplets in 1928. Drawing No 4580N. |

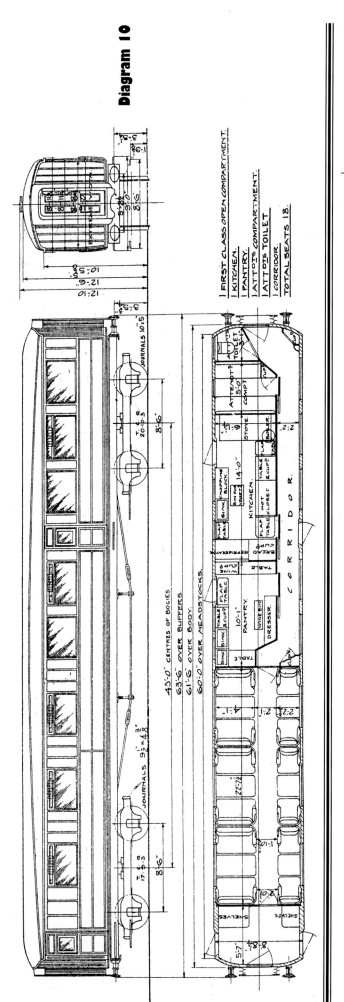

**Diagram 10**

1 FIRST CLASS OPEN COMPARTMENT.
1 KITCHEN.
1 PANTRY.
1 ATTDTS COMPARTMENT.
1 ATTDTS TOILET.
1 CORRIDOR.
TOTAL SEATS 18.

43'-0" CENTRES OF BOGIES
63'-6" OVER BUFFERS.
61'-6" OVER BODY.
60'-0" OVER HEADSTOCKS.

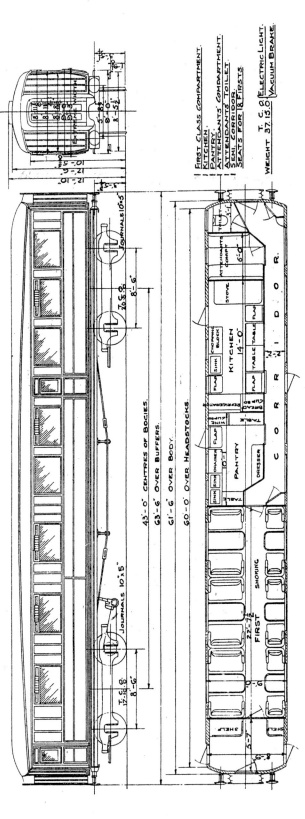

**Diagram 10A**

1 FIRST CLASS COMPARTMENT.
1 KITCHEN.
1 PANTRY.
1 ATTENDANTS' COMPARTMENT.
1 ATTENDANTS' TOILET.
1 SEMI CORRIDOR.
SEATS FOR 18 FIRSTS.

T. C. O. ELECTRIC LIGHT.
WEIGHT 37. 15. 0. VACUUM BRAKE.

43'-0" CENTRES OF BOGIES.
63'-6" OVER BUFFERS.
61'-6" OVER BODY.
60'-0" OVER HEADSTOCKS.

This Diagram 10C car, latterly No 9009 and originally No 51770 built Doncaster 1928, was nearing the end of its days when photographed in departmental use in 1966. Note that it still carries the BR maroon livery with crest, applied in the late 1950s.

For further consideration were other types of cars: a restaurant third, for use with an open third in general service, or for third-class excursion trains, and a composite restaurant car. The former already existed (Drawing 4674N), and had been built in the 1924 programme, but no design was available for the latter type which had been rejected for the 1924 programme.

New designs for restaurant cars were approved for the 1926/7 CBP: a restaurant first, and a pantry third. This was as the result of the decision to introduce electrically equipped cars, the decision being accompanied by the Board's approval of investment in charging points at a number of locations such as Newcastle, Liverpool Street and Parkeston Quay, Harrogate, Marylebone, Manchester London Road and Ardwick, Manchester Central, and Aberdeen.

Although the electrically equipped cars were able to charge their batteries when running from axle-driven generators, the supply was usually insufficient to meet the maximum demand from the ovens, grills and boiler. As a result, some food was pre-cooked, and at the carriage sidings, or on arrival at the departure station, the car was plugged into the charging point – usually for not less than two hours. This allowed the batteries to be charged, the ovens and grills preheated and for some cooking to proceed. The use of the on-board equipment required some skill on the part of the chef who had to keep a close watch on the ammeter which indicated the maximum current available, and he had to juggle with the combination of current available from the shore supply, and the limited capacity of the batteries.

At a meeting held at Kings Cross in December 1927, it was decided that electric cooking equipment would be adopted in restaurant cars ordered in the 1929 programme, and that they would be built to the 9ft 3in width, subject to acceptance of a report from the loading gauge committee. The extra width had been adopted for the new triplet sets built for East Coast service in 1928. These included the two sets with the special Louis XIV interiors.

A later third-class restaurant/kitchen car design was introduced with the car built for the Leeds-Glasgow service under the 1930/1 building programme.

From 1932, the LNER introduced buffet cars on a variety of services. At first there were conversions from existing open third coaches, and pre-Grouping vehicles of GN, GC and NE design at that. The exception was the Diagram 27A open third converted to Diagram 185, and described in this section.

# Restaurant cars

## First-class: (RF), or either class/unclassed: (RU)

### DIAGRAM 10, 10A, 10B, 10C, 11

There were two basic designs: one (Diagrams 10/10A/10B/10C) with a single saloon, seating 18 diners, the other (Diagram 11), with two saloons (smoking and non-smoking) seating 30. The increased dining space in the latter was achieved by omitting the attendant's compartment, and by reducing the size of the pantry, and the kitchen.

The variants of Diagram 10 followed the changes in practice, Diagram 10 being the 9ft width, gas cooking equipment type; 10A, the 9ft 3in width type, also with gas cooking and built for the Continental boat trains, 10B, the 9ft 3in width type for general service, with gas cooking, and 10C, the electric cooking equipment version of 10B. Diagram 10 had an end lobby with serving shelves whereas in Diagrams 10B and 10C there was no more than the usual vestibule space, and the space saved as a result enabled the pantry to be made larger than in Diagram 10 cars.

Of the early vehicles, Dia 10 No 22251 was built for the Newcastle-Oxford working of the through Bournemouth service, and the three GE cars were used between Liverpool St and Parkeston Quay. In time, they were replaced by all-electric cars and then transferred to the NEA under the 1935/6 building programme.

The 1927/8 CBP included eight single restaurant cars and, of these, Dia 10C car No 43040 was allocated to a Kings Cross-Harrogate working, to/from Leeds only. The series of Dia 10C cars for the GC section were put into new sets of vestibuled stock for the Marylebone-Manchester, and Bradford expresses; electric charging equipment was

# Diagram 10B

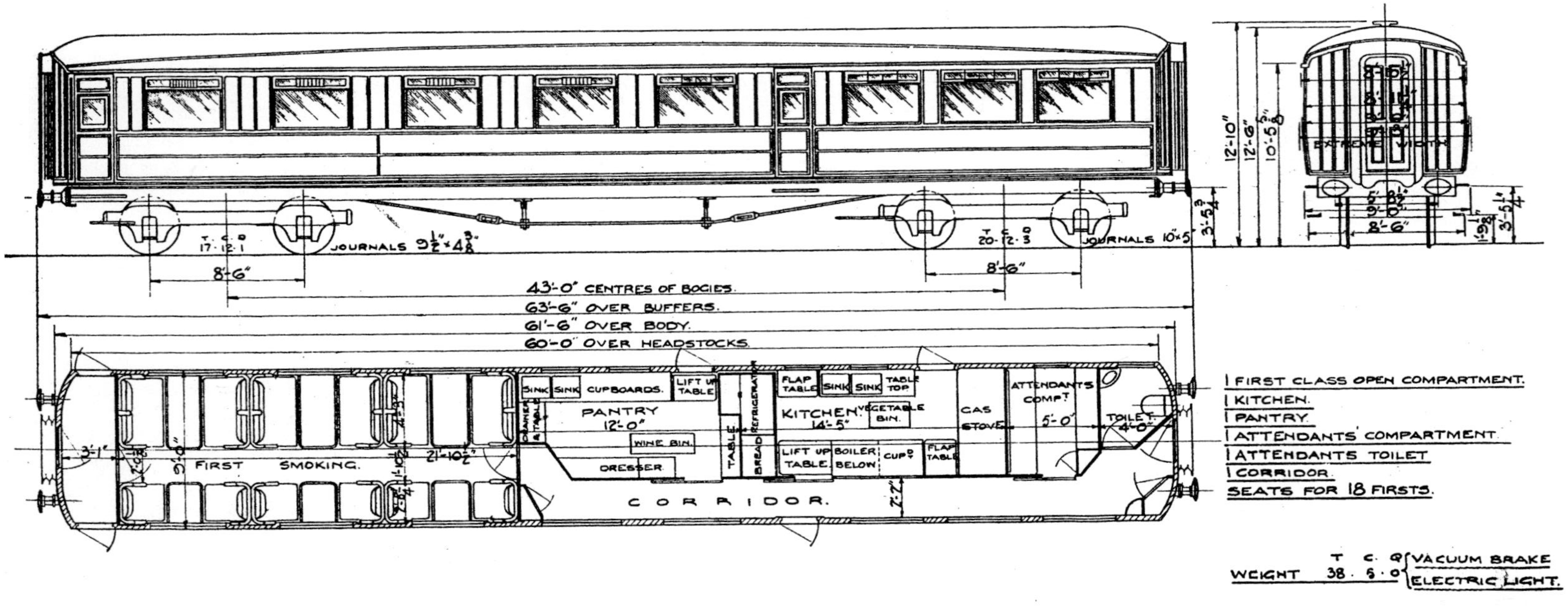

FIRST CLASS OPEN COMPARTMENT.
KITCHEN.
PANTRY.
ATTENDANTS COMPARTMENT
ATTENDANTS TOILET
CORRIDOR
SEATS FOR 18 FIRSTS.

T. C. Q. {VACUUM BRAKE
WEIGHT 38. 6. 0. {ELECTRIC LIGHT.

43'-0" CENTRES OF BOGIES.
63'-6" OVER BUFFERS.
61'-6" OVER BODY.
60'-0" OVER HEADSTOCKS.

CORRIDOR.

PANTRY
12'-0"

KITCHEN/VEGETABLE
14'-5"

ATTENDANTS
COMP'T
5'-0"

FIRST SMOKING.

# Diagram 10C

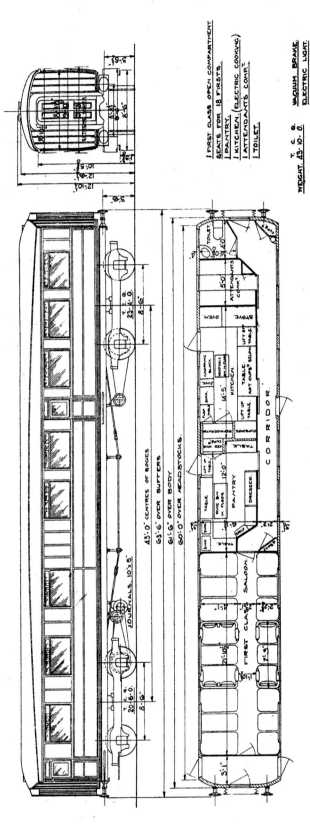

FIRST CLASS OPEN COMPARTMENT.
SEATS FOR 18 FIRSTS.
PANTRY.
KITCHEN (ELECTRIC COOKING)
ATTENDANTS COMPT.
1 TOILET.

T. C. Q.           VACUUM BRAKE.
WEIGHT 43. 10. 0.   ELECTRIC LIGHT.

43'-0" CENTRES OF BOGIES.
63'-6" OVER BUFFERS.
61'-6" OVER BODY.
60'-0" OVER HEADSTOCKS.

CORRIDOR.

PANTRY
12'-0"

KITCHEN
14'-5"

ATTENDANTS
COMPT.
5'-0"

FIRST CLASS SALOON.

148

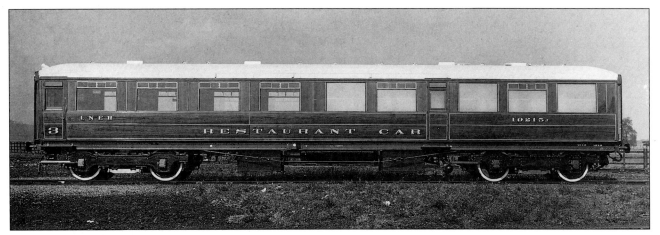

Diagram 16 car No 10215J (built Doncaster 1925, later No 1225, and rebuilt in BR days. Note that the window ventilators are unpainted. The windows to the corridor side have caught the light and are not actually of obscured glass. The four, ceiling-mounted extractor vans to the saloon and kitchen show up clearly.

duly installed at terminal points. These cars were paired with open thirds to Diagram 27A, the latter serving as third-class dining accommodation.

The three GE section cars were used on Continental boat trains, as were those in the 1928/9 programme. One of the 1929-built gas-equipped cars was subsequently transferred to the North Eastern Area for use on excursion trains composed of cream and green Tourist stock, and was repainted to match. It was intended for the longer distance excursions on which full meal service was required, something that was beyond the capability of the Tourist stock buffet cars. With the decision to build all-electric restaurant cars, Gresley was loath to construct new gas-equipped catering vehicles although there were isolated examples. After a review of the needs of the NEA for gas-fitted cars to work in long-distance excursions on journeys serving locations without charging points, it was decided to transfer gas-fitted cars from the GE section, and replace them by new all-electric cars.

One of the two Diagram 10C East Coast cars was allocated to the 4pm Kings Cross-Newcastle and 10.35am return, paired with a pantry car.

Nearly all the LNER restaurant cars were built at Doncaster Works, notable exceptions being the contractor-built Dia 10C cars for the Cromer sets. These were the first electric or LNER restaurant cars to work on the Norwich expresses and they worked with open thirds which the GE section regarded as restaurant cars, and they were originally lettered as such.

In 1928, the chief general manager considered that the SSA restaurant cars working to Aberdeen and Glasgow were not altogether satisfactory and compared unfavourably with those operated by the LMS. His solution was that new triplets should be built for East Coast stock, to work through to both cities from Kings Cross, and on the Aberdeen service they would displace older cars to other services. The through working of triplets to Aberdeen was short-lived.

In the 1929/30 Programme, the SSA had asked for two cars of Diagram 11 to cover the 12noon Glasgow-Newcastle and 5.44pm return, and the 9.50am Aberdeen-Edinburgh and 2.14pm return, in each case paired with Dia 27A open thirds. The Area gained a new car, as a result of the loss of an older vehicle working in the 12noon Edinburgh-St Pancras when this train was derailed at Carlisle in January 1931. The two cars in the 1930/1 Programme were to work from Glasgow-Newcastle in winter, and through to Leeds (and back) in summer. Following a review of the Area's requirements in 1934, the two cars to Dia 11 were ordered for Edinburgh-Aberdeen workings.

The unclassed Dia 11 No 42782 was ordered under the 1932 building programme. It was one of the coaches affected by the suspension of all new coach construction by the LNER during 1932, and remained partly completed until its completion was authorised in June 1933. This type of vehicle was used to provide dining facilities between Kings Cross and York on the down 'Highlandman', and also on the down 'Aberdonian'.

During World War 2, all ten Dia 11 restaurant cars were chosen for use as kitchen cars to serve in ambulance trains which were taken across the Channel between August and November 1944. Three of these spent several years abroad, and on return were extensively rebuilt in BR days to become restaurant cafeteria cars.

## LIST OF FIRST-CLASS OR UNCLASSED RESTAURANT CARS:

| Diag No CBP | Order No | Compts/ seats | Built | Original number/ changes | 1943 number | |
|---|---|---|---|---|---|---|
| **Built 1925** | | | | | | |
| 10* | 1924/5 71 | 1† 18 | DR | 22251 | 9001 | §§ |
| 10A* | 1924/5 59 | 1† 18 | SF | 10211E (676) [2865] | 9002 | §§ Continental set |
| | 60 | | | 10212E (677) [2866] | 9003 | §§ Continental set |
| | | | | Transfers 1935, became unclassed. | | |
| 10A* | 1925/6 120 | 1† 18 | DR | 681 (2867) | 9000 | §§ Transferred 1935, became unclassed |
| **Built 1928** | | | | | | |
| 10C* | 1927/8 196 | 1† 18 | DR | 43040, 51770/1 | 9008-10 | |
| **Built 1929** | | | | | | |
| 10B* | 1927/8 197 | 1† 18 | YK | 678-80 (21474¶, 31929, 680) | 9004-6 | §§ ¶ unclassed Transfers 1934/39 |
| 10C* | 1927/8 196 | 1† 18 | DR | 51772/3 | 9011/2 | |
| | 1928/9 260 | | | 51774/5 | 9013/4 | |
| | | | | 682/3 | 9017/8 | |
| | | | | 42969 | 9007 | |
| | | | | 1222/3 | 9019/20 | |
| | | | MET | 6119/20 (651/2) | 9015/6 | Cromer sets |
| 11* (unclassed) | 1929/30 306 | 2† 30 | DR | 43041 | | |

Converted for use in ambulance train 1943/4 and served overseas. Not returned until 1953 when it was rebuilt as a restaurant cafeteria car M9217E.

| | | | | | | |
|---|---|---|---|---|---|---|
| **Built 1930** | | | | | | |
| 11* | 1929/30 320 | 2† 30 | DR | 31922/3 | 9023/4 | |
| **Built 1931** | | | | | | |
| 11* (unclassed) | 1930/1 390 425 | 2† 30 | DR | 31924/6 31935 | 9025/ — 9027 | Accident replacement for former M & NB car W/O Carlisle 1931 |
| | 391 | | | 42783 | | |

Nos 31924/6/35, 42783 converted for use in ambulance trains 1943/4. Nos 31924/35 returned to service but Nos 31926 and 42783 served overseas and were not returned until 1953, and then rebuilt as restaurant cafeteria cars, M9215/6E.

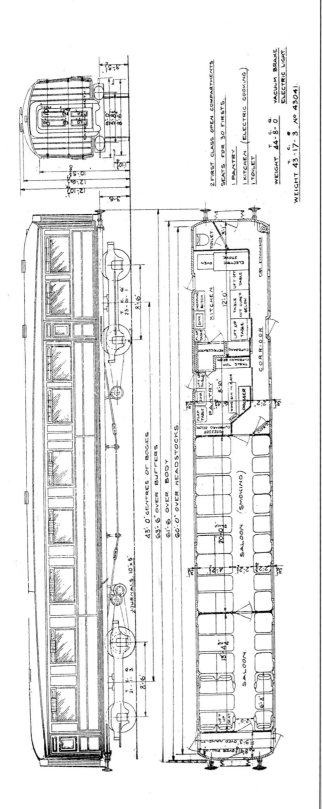

**Diagram 11**

2 FIRST CLASS OPEN COMPARTMENTS
SEATS FOR 30 FIRSTS.
1 PANTRY
1 KITCHEN (ELECTRIC COOKING)
1 TOILET

T.C.G.
WEIGHT 44-8-0  VACUUM BRAKE
T.C.R.  ELECTRIC LIGHT.
WEIGHT 43-17-3 Nº 43041.

43'·0" CENTRES OF BOGIES
63'·6" OVER BUFFERS
61'·6" OVER BODY
60'·0" OVER HEADSTOCKS

KITCHEN

CORRIDOR

PANTRY

SALOON (SMOKING)

SALOON

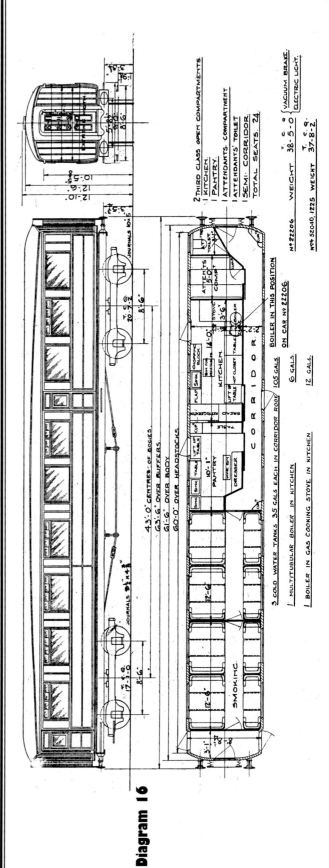

**Diagram 16**

2 THIRD CLASS OPEN COMPARTMENTS
1 KITCHEN.
1 PANTRY.
1 ATTENDANTS COMPARTMENT
1 ATTENDANTS' TOILET
1 SEMI-CORRIDOR
TOTAL SEATS 24.

Nº 22206  WEIGHT 38-5-0  T.C.G. VACUUM BRAKE.
Nºs 52040, 1225 WEIGHT 37-8-2 T.C.R.  ELECTRIC LIGHT.

43'·0" CENTRES OF BOGIES.
63'·6" OVER BUFFERS.
61'·6" OVER BODY.
60'·0" OVER HEADSTOCKS.

ATTENDANTS
COMPT

KITCHEN

PANTRY

CORRIDOR

SMOKING.

BOILER IN THIS POSITION
ON CAR Nº 22206.

3 COLD WATER TANKS 35 GALS EACH IN CORRIDOR ROOF 105 GALS
1 MULTITUBULAR BOILER IN KITCHEN  6 GALS.
1 BOILER IN GAS COOKING STOVE IN KITCHEN  12 GALS.

**Diagram 145**

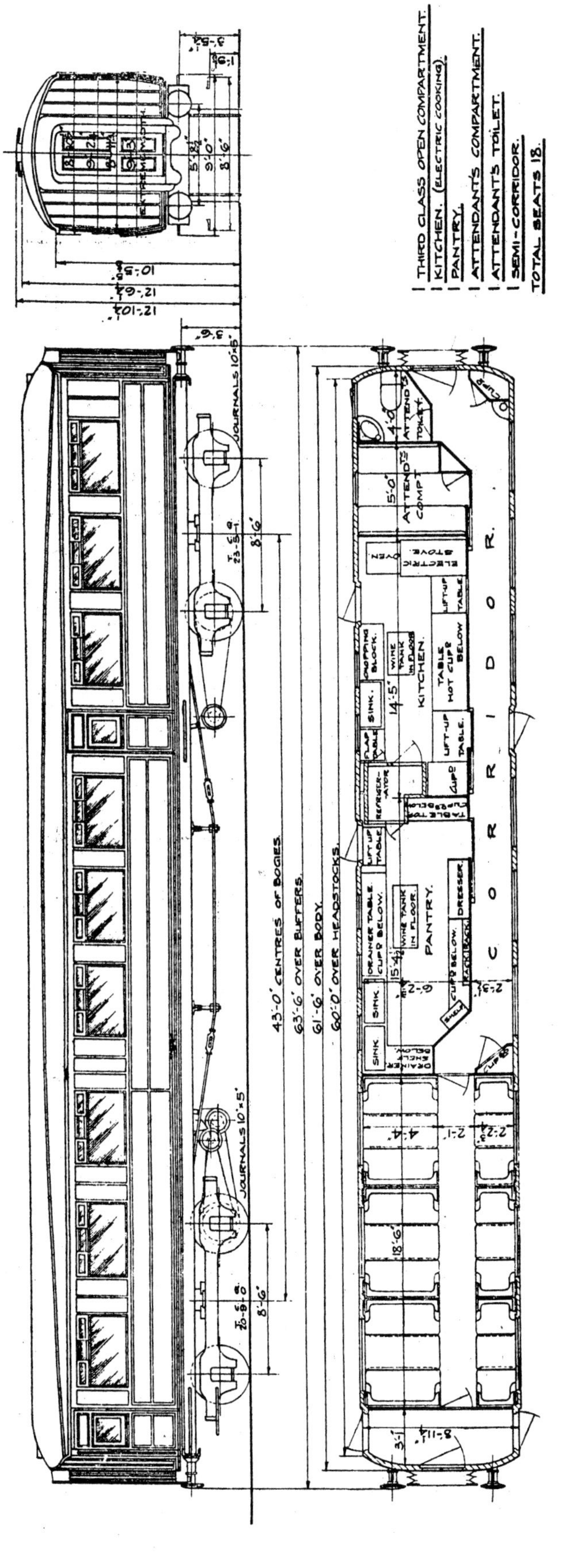
THIRD CLASS OPEN COMPARTMENT.
KITCHEN. (ELECTRIC COOKING).
PANTRY.
ATTENDANT'S COMPARTMENT.
ATTENDANT'S TOILET.
SEMI-CORRIDOR.
TOTAL SEATS 18.
43'-0" CENTRES OF BOGIES
63'-6" OVER BUFFERS
61'-6" OVER BODY
60'-0" OVER HEADSTOCKS
CORRIDOR
KITCHEN
PANTRY

*Built 1934*

| | | | | | | |
|---|---|---|---|---|---|---|
| 11* (first-class) | 1934 | 539 | 2† 30 | DR | 31868, 31902 | 9021/2 |
| (unclassed) | 524 | | | DR | 42782 | 9029 |

The following vehicles were allocated to Scottish Region stock after 1949, and the number prefixed by SC: 9005, 9021-5/7.

## Third-class: (RT)

### DIAGRAM 16, 145

As first-class passengers were always likely to be provided with dining facilities, a third-class car with kitchen was likely to find less favour. Of the 1925 cars, the NEA example was built for use in the Newcastle-Swansea service, routed via Banbury and Cheltenham. The two East Coast cars were ordered for a Newcastle-Glasgow working but one was transferred to the NEA after a relatively short time, and moved again to the GC section. No 1225 remained in East Coast stock.

Possibly they were at a loose end. Nos 1225 and 52040 were chosen for use in ambulance trains. No 1225 was in the process of being converted to a pharmacy car when the order for the ambulance train was cancelled. All three Diagram 16 cars were chosen in 1953 for conversion as kitchen/buffet cars, this work being undertaken at York Works.

The single car built in 1930 was one of a set of new vehicles introduced on the Leeds-Glasgow express as from 16 February 1931. It worked with a semi-open first on one side, and an open third on the other. The crew served breakfast, lunch, tea and dinner during the 555-mile round trip.

### LIST OF THIRD-CLASS RESTAURANT CARS:

| Diag No | CBP | Order No | Compts/ seats | Built | Original number/ changes | 1943 number | |
|---|---|---|---|---|---|---|---|
| *Built 1925* | | | | | | | |
| 16 | 1924/5 | 72 | 2† 24 | DR | 10213Y (22206) | 9063 | §§ |
| | | | | | 10214J | 9064 | §§ |
| | | | | | (1224) [22265] To NEA 1928 then 52040 – 1931 | | |
| | | | | | 10215J (1225) | 1225 | §§ |

Nos 1225 and 52040 selected for ambulance train use; No 1225 not used.

All three cars were converted as kitchen buffet cars in October 1953 and retained their numbers, No 1225 being allocated to the London Midland Region as M1225E. Classified (R)KB.

*Built 1930*

| | | | | | | | |
|---|---|---|---|---|---|---|---|
| 145 | 1930/1 | 392 | 1† 18 | DR | 22650 | 9093 | Leeds-Glasgow set |

## Pantry thirds: (RTP)

### DIAGRAM 15, 112

This was a type really only popular with the East Coast and GN section operators. The vehicle was effectively an open third with a pantry which had storage cupboards, a hot plate and a sink. Its main purpose was to relieve the work carried out in the kitchen of the adjoining restaurant car.

On the GN section, an RTP was used in such workings as the Harrogate portion of the 1.40pm Kings Cross-York, and in the 4pm ex-Kings Cross. The East Coast cars were employed chiefly on relief Anglo-Scottish expresses; one duty in postwar days involved the inclusion of a couple of cars in an overnight train with those postwar sleeping cars that lacked attendant's compartments. With the rapid decline in demand for full meals in the early postwar years, there were very few duties which justified the use of an RTP in addition to a restaurant/kitchen car.

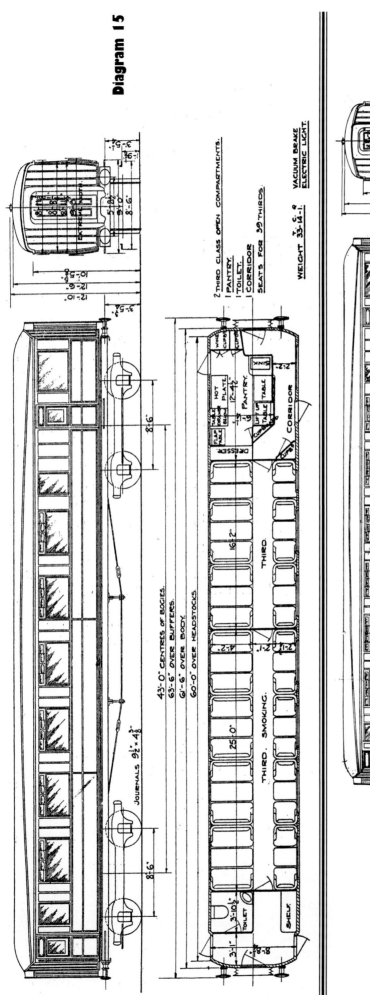

**Diagram 15**

JOURNALS 9½ × 4⅞

43'-0" CENTRES OF BOGIES.
63'-6" OVER BUFFERS.
61'-6" OVER BODY.
60'-0" OVER HEADSTOCKS.

THIRD. SMOKING.

2 THIRD CLASS OPEN COMPARTMENTS.
1 PANTRY.
1 TOILET.
1 CORRIDOR.
SEATS FOR 39 THIRDS.

VACUUM BRAKE
ELECTRIC LIGHT.

WEIGHT T. C. Q.
33-14-1.

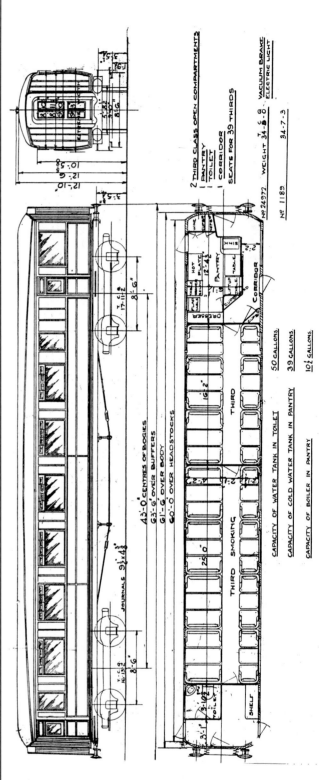

**Diagram 112**

JOURNALS 9½ × 4⅞

43'-0" CENTRES OF BOGIES.
63'-6" OVER BUFFERS.
61'-6" OVER BODY.
60'-0" OVER HEADSTOCKS.

THIRD SMOKING.

THIRD

2 THIRD CLASS OPEN COMPARTMENTS.
1 PANTRY.
1 TOILET.
1 CORRIDOR.
SEATS FOR 39 THIRDS.

No 24972    WEIGHT 34-8-0.    VACUUM BRAKE
ELECTRIC LIGHT.

No 1189    34-7-3.

CAPACITY OF WATER TANK IN TOILET    50 GALLONS.

CAPACITY OF COLD WATER TANK IN PANTRY    39 GALLONS.

CAPACITY OF BOILER IN PANTRY    10½ GALLONS.

152

The solitary Diagram 145 car No 22650 (built Doncaster 1930, and 9093 under the 1943 renumbering), apart from being a car with electric cooking, reveals one or two changes as compared with the 1925 vehicle. There is a single smoking saloon only, non-smoking diners occupying the open third which ran next to this car in the formation of the Leeds-Glasgow train.

## LIST OF THIRD-CLASS PANTRY CARS:

| Diag No CBP | Order No | Compts/ seats | Built | Original number/ changes | 1943 number | |
|---|---|---|---|---|---|---|
| **Built 1925** | | | | | | |
| 15 | 1924/5 73 | 2† 39 | DR | 1257 (2331) | 9061 | Trans 1937 |
| | | | | 1258 | 9062 | |
| **Built 1928** | | | | | | |
| 112* | 1927/8 198 | 2† 39 | YK | 42972 | 9066 | |
| **Built 1929** | | | | | | |
| 112* | 1929/30 261 | 2† 39 | DR | 1189 (42998) | 9067 | Transferred 1940 |

## Buffet car: (RB)

### DIAGRAM 185

The LNER's first buffet cars were were glorified tea – or beer – cars that were conversions of Great Northern open thirds and they were introduced on the Kings Cross-Cambridge service in 1932. On Sundays,

they were employed on excursion trains and in their early days close attention was paid to the use made of them, and their performance generally. Before long, it was appreciated that there was scope for a buffet car which had the equal ability of being able to serve less elaborate meals than the those featuring in the table d'hôte menu offered on regular services, and of being employed for long-distance excursion trains. Two conversions of ex-NER open thirds were approved in 1932, and during the next year it was decided to embark on a programme to introduce buffet cars on services previously without catering facilities.

In March 1934, it was agreed to convert a Diagram 27A open third into a buffet car to replace the restaurant car previously used on the 12noon Newcastle-York and 6.15pm return. The vehicle chosen was No 22314, and somewhat unusually for LNER practice the conversion was allocated a new Diagram number.

| Diag No CBP | Order No | Compts/ seats | Built | Original number/ changes | 1943 number |
|---|---|---|---|---|---|
| **Converted 1934** | | | | | |
| 185 | - - | 1† 24 | YK | 22314 | 9154 |

Converted from Dia 27A open third, built 1930

Diagram 15 car No 1257 (built Doncaster 1925, later No 2331, and 9061 under the 1943 renumbering). The pantry is at the left-hand end in this photograph. The vehicle carries a shopping date of October 1925, by which time application of the 1xxxx series numbers had been abandoned.

Interior of the first-class saloon in one of the 1924 triplet restaurant cars. This exhibits the standard features of the early LNER restaurant cars: the buffalo hide (green) upholstery, mahogany panelling and parcel racks in polished brass. The floor is covered in rubber sheeting but this did not prove satisfactory. At the time, LNER publicity described the cars as 'Keynote - simplicity'.

## Triplet restaurant cars: (RTS)

### DIAGRAM 12, 12A, 12B, 13, 14, 14A

The background to the choice in early 1924 of triplet restaurant car sets for the principal East Coast trains has already been referred to.

The sets themselves were relatively straightforward, the vehicles being to the 9ft body width. The outer coaches were purely dining saloons, divided, as usual, into smoking and non-smoking saloons. Their underframes were 54ft 5¼in length. The kitchen car was a short vehicle on an underframe just under 41ft in length, and the set as a whole measured 155ft 7in over the buffers. Heavy-type bogies were used throughout, the articulation bogies having 10in x 5in journals. Electric power was derived from two 7.2kW dynamos which were suspended from the underframe, and belt-driven from the axles. Electric charging points were installed at Edinburgh Waverley in preparation for their use.

Subsequent changes were few. Mechanical refrigeration plants and ice cream cabinets were added to all five sets after 1927. There was some swapping of bogies, the Metro heavy type being used on more than one set.

Until further triplets arrived in 1928, the five triplets were employed in the two train sets for the 'Flying Scotsman', in the two train sets allocated to the afternoon Scotsmen, and one triplet was the spare. In later days, the Louis XIV sets were the usual choice for the 'Flying Scotsman', and the older triplets then took their turn in the other sets, or were held as spares. One was allocated to the 8am Newcastle-Kings Cross and 5.30pm (later 5.45pm ) return on which the demand for meal service was second only to the 'Flying Scotsman'.

By 1939, with the arrival of new triplet sets, as many as three of the 1924 sets were used on trains such as the 'Norseman' or regarded as spares.

Two of the 1928 triplets were very similar to those of 1924, except

that the dining cars were built to the 9ft 3in body width. As the doors of the kitchen car could not be recessed, to keep within the permitted overall width the body width of this vehicle remained 9ft. The dining saloons were very similar in all respects to their predecessors. The other two 1928 triplets were the special Louis XIV cars mentioned below.

With the arrival of the new batch of triplets in the summer of 1928, two sets were provided for the 'Flying Scotsman', scheduled to run non-stop between Kings Cross and Edinburgh, two for the summer-only relief 'Flying Scotsman', two for the afternoon Scotsmen, with one triplet as spare for the East Coast allocation.

In addition, a set was used on the Newcastle working just described, and the GN section allocated set worked in the 7.50am Leeds-Kings Cross 'Breakfast Flyer', and 1.30pm return. These two diagrams were also allocated a back-up triplet.

### LOUIS XIV RESTAURANT CARS DIAGRAMS 13, 14, 14A

The extra triplet sets in the 1927/8 building programme were ordered presumably in anticipation of the introduction of non-stop running between Kings Cross-Edinburgh by the 'Flying Scotsman' as from the summer of 1928. Accordingly, it was decided that restaurant cars of a distinctive character should be specified, particularly as the journey time could not be reduced from the overall 8¼ hours agreed with the LMS, and competition rested with the provision of attractive on-board facilities.

The original intention was that the stock forming the northbound non-stop would work out and back to Aberdeen, and a charging point was duly installed at Aberdeen. Another set would run through to Glasgow, and so charging facilities were installed at Glasgow Queen Street and Cowlairs. This plan did not prove possible so far as working to Aberdeen was concerned, in view of the need to accommodate staff layovers. During the summer of 1928, however, the special sets were used on an altered working through to Aberdeen although the armchairs took unkindly to the curvature of the track north of Edinburgh, and passengers tended to become unseated! There were also complaints at the lack of parcel racks for passengers joining at Edinburgh for destinations to the north. The result was that the Louis XIV sets were transferred to the 9.50am Kings Cross-Glasgow, and the next day's 8.55am up, until they resumed duty on the 'Flying Scotsman' to/from Edinburgh, as from October 1928. The Louis XIV sets continued to be used in the summer non-stop until the 1939 season when they were replaced by newly-built triplets, and were then transferred to the relief 'Flying Scotsman'.

Although referred to as the 'Louis XIV' sets, only the first-class saloons were radically different, and the interior decor consultant used by Gresley was Sir Charles Allom. In place of polished woodwork, the interior of the dining saloon had a painted finish throughout, in tones of soft-blue and stone. The decor featured elaborate mouldings in the French style, and the overall intention was to create the ambience of a restaurant on terra firma. This was achieved by raising the cornice line to create a feeling of spaciousness, and accordingly the usual hat racks were dispensed with; instead, there was a small wardrobe for hanging garments. In place of table lamps, concealed lighting was provided behind translucent curtain pelmets, and these were supplemented by shaded lamps in the ceiling. The finishing touch was the use of individual loose chairs, arranged 2 + 1 and accommodating the same number of diners as in the conventional cars. The third-class cars had a less ornate decor treatment, and the seating was of the normal bench type.

## LIST OF TRIPLET RESTAURANT CARS:

| Diag No | CBP | Order No | Compts/ seats | Built | Original number/ changes | 1943 number |
|---|---|---|---|---|---|---|
| **Built 1924** | | | | | | |
| 12 (restaurant first) | 1924/5 | 33 | 2† 36 | DR | 6431J/41J/51J/61J/71J (16431/41/51/61/71) | 1401/4/7/10/3 |
| 13* (kitchen car) | | | - | | 6432J/42J/52J/62J/72J (16432/42/52/62/72) | 1402/5/8/11/4 |
| 14 (restaurant third) | | | 2† 42 | | 6433J/43J/53J/63J/73J (16433/43/53/63/73) | 1403/6/9/12/5 |

6441-3J were deliberately derailed during the General Strike at Cramlington in May 1926 but not badly damaged

| Diag No | CBP | Order No | Compts/ seats | Built | Original number/ changes | 1943 number |
|---|---|---|---|---|---|---|
| **Built 1928** | | | | | | |
| 12B* (restaurant first) | 1927/8 | 199 | 2† 36 | DR | 46191 | 9052 |
| 13* (kitchen car) | | | - | | 46192 | 9053 |
| 14A* (restaurant third) | | | 2† 42 | | 46193 | 9054 |
| 12A (restaurant first) | 1927/8 | 199 | 2† 36 | DR | 16481/91 | 1416/9 |
| 13* (kitchen car) | | | - | | 16482/92 | 1417/20 |
| 14A (restaurant third) | | | 2† 42 | | 16483/93 | 1418/21 |

16481-3, 16491-3 were the White Allom cars 1419-21 W/O Goswick 1947

| Diag No | CBP | Order No | Compts/ seats | Built | Original number/ changes | 1943 number |
|---|---|---|---|---|---|---|
| 12B* (restaurant first) | 1928/9 | 262 | 2† 36 | DR | 16501/11 | 1422/5 |
| 13* (kitchen car) | | | - | | 16502/12 | 1423/6 |
| 14A* (restaurant third) | | | 2† 42 | | 16503/13 | 1424/7 |

Under the 1943 renumbering scheme the East Coast triplets were allocated – in order from 1923-8 building – the numbers 9031-51, 9055-60. Only the former GN section vehicles, 46191-3, carried 90xx numbers.

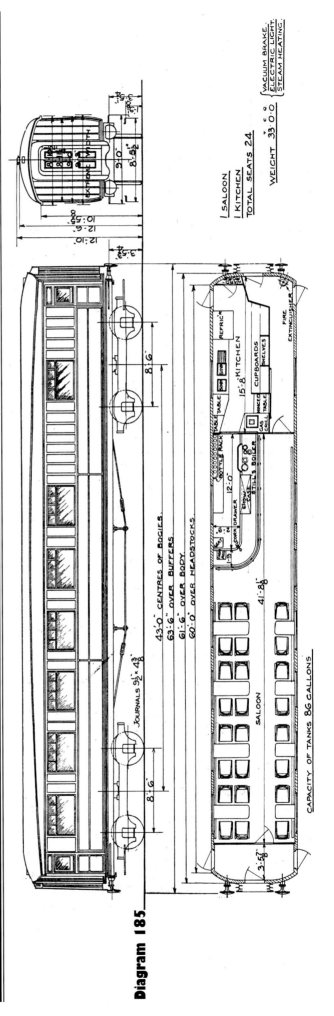

Diagram 185

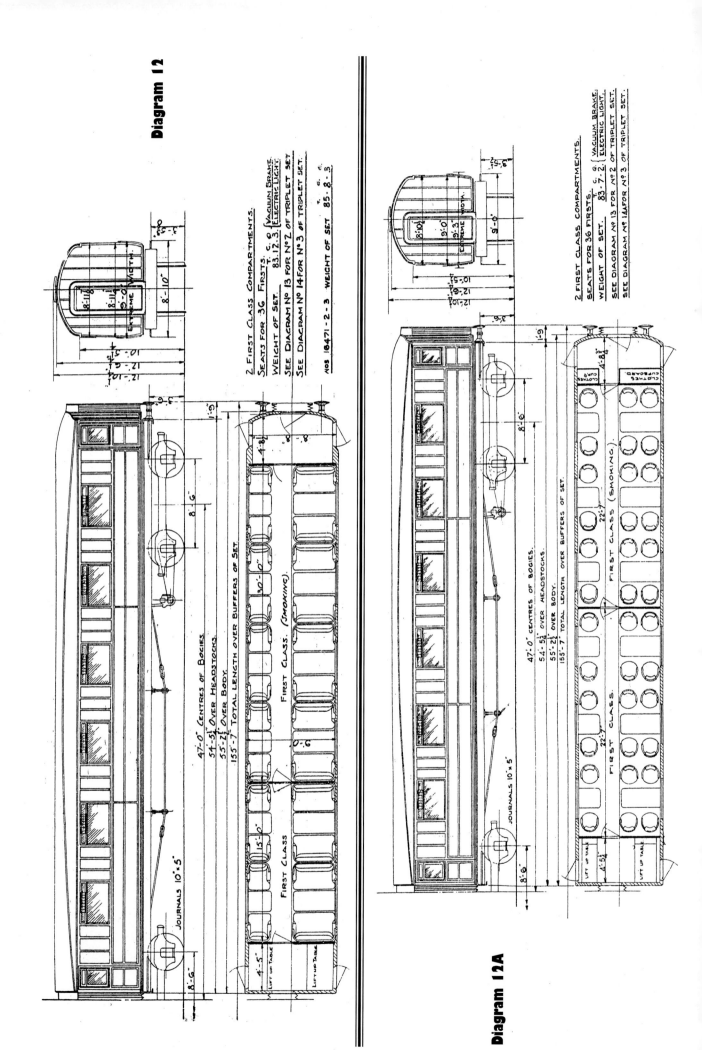

**Diagram 12**

2 FIRST CLASS COMPARTMENTS.
SEATS FOR 36 FIRSTS. C. P. ( VACUUM BRAKE
WEIGHT OF SET. 83.12.3. ( ELECTRIC LIGHT.
SEE DIAGRAM Nº 13 FOR Nº2 OF TRIPLET SET.
SEE DIAGRAM Nº 14 FOR Nº 3 OF TRIPLET SET.

NOS 16471 - 2 - 3   WEIGHT OF SET   85 . 8 . 3

47'-0" CENTRES OF BOGIES.
54-5¼" OVER HEADSTOCKS.
55'-2½" OVER BODY.
155'-7" TOTAL LENGTH OVER BUFFERS OF SET.

FIRST CLASS (SMOKING).

FIRST CLASS

JOURNALS 10"×5"

**Diagram 12A**

2 FIRST CLASS COMPARTMENTS.
SEATS FOR 36 FIRSTS. C. P. ( VACUUM BRAKE.
WEIGHT OF SET.   83.7.2. ( ELECTRIC LIGHT.
SEE DIAGRAM Nº 13 FOR Nº 2 OF TRIPLET SET.
SEE DIAGRAM Nº 14 FOR Nº 3 OF TRIPLET SET.

47'-0" CENTRES OF BOGIES.
54-5¼" OVER HEADSTOCKS.
55'-2½" OVER BODY.
155'-7" TOTAL LENGTH OVER BUFFERS OF SET.

FIRST CLASS (SMOKING).

FIRST CLASS.

CLOTHES CUPBOARD.

LIFT UP TABLE

JOURNALS 10"×5"

**Diagram 13**

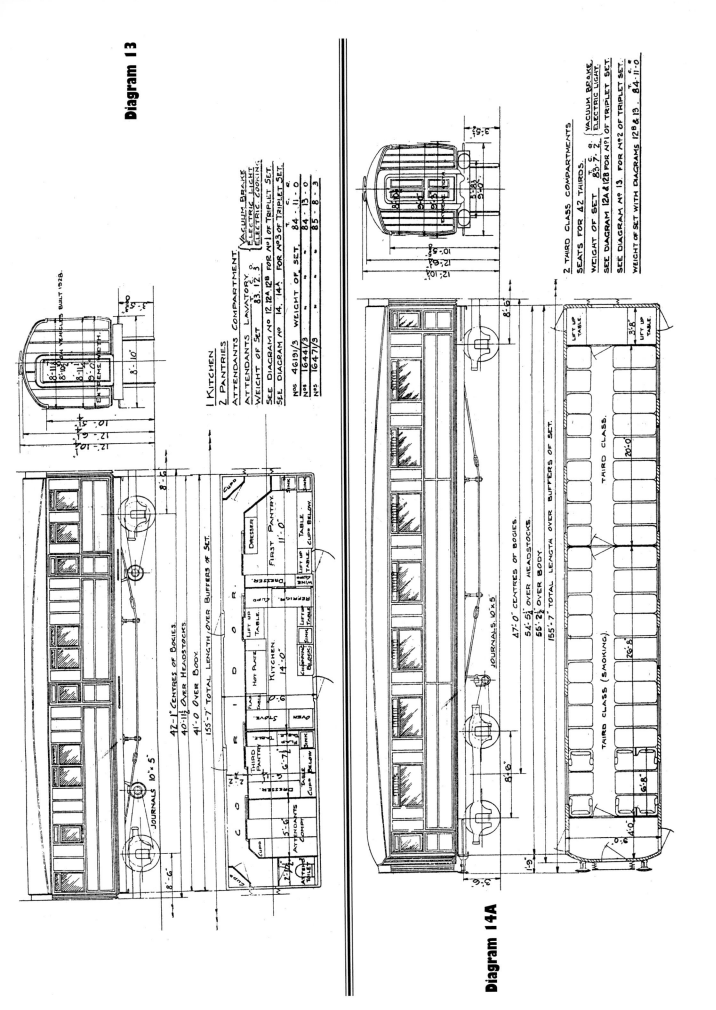

ON VEHICLES BUILT 1928.

**EXTREME WIDTH.**

1 KITCHEN
2 PANTRIES
ATTENDANTS COMPARTMENT.
ATTENDANTS LAVATORY.  [VACUUM BRAKE / ELECTRIC LIGHT / ELECTRIC COOKING.

WEIGHT OF SET    83. 12. 3 9

SEE DIAGRAM Nº 12. 12A.12B FOR Nº1 OF TRIPLET SET.
SEE DIAGRAM Nº 14. 14A. FOR Nº3 OF TRIPLET SET.

| | | | |
|---|---|---|---|
| Nºs 4619I/3 | WEIGHT OF SET. | 84. 11. 0 |
| Nº 16441/3 | " " | 84. 13. 0 |
| Nº 16471/3 | " " | 85. 8. 3 |

CUP⁰

FIRST PANTRY.  11'-0"
DRESSER
LIFT UP TABLE.
TABLE
CUPS BELOW.
SINK
SINK

WINE
REFRIG⁰R
CUP⁰
DRESSER
LIFT UP TABLE.

KITCHEN.  14'-0"
HOT PLATE
FLAP TABLE
STOVE
CHIPPING BLOCKS
SINK

THIRD PANTRY 9'-7½"
OVEN
LIFT UP TABLE
SINK

DRESSER
TABLE CUPS BELOW

ATTENDANTS COMP⁰T 5'-6"
ATTEND⁰ TOILET

CUP⁰

C O R R I D O R.

JOURNALS 10" x 5"

8'-6"

42'-1" CENTRES OF BOGIES.
40'-11½" OVER HEADSTOCKS.
41'-0" OVER BODY.
155'-7" TOTAL LENGTH OVER BUFFERS OF SET.

---

**Diagram 14A**

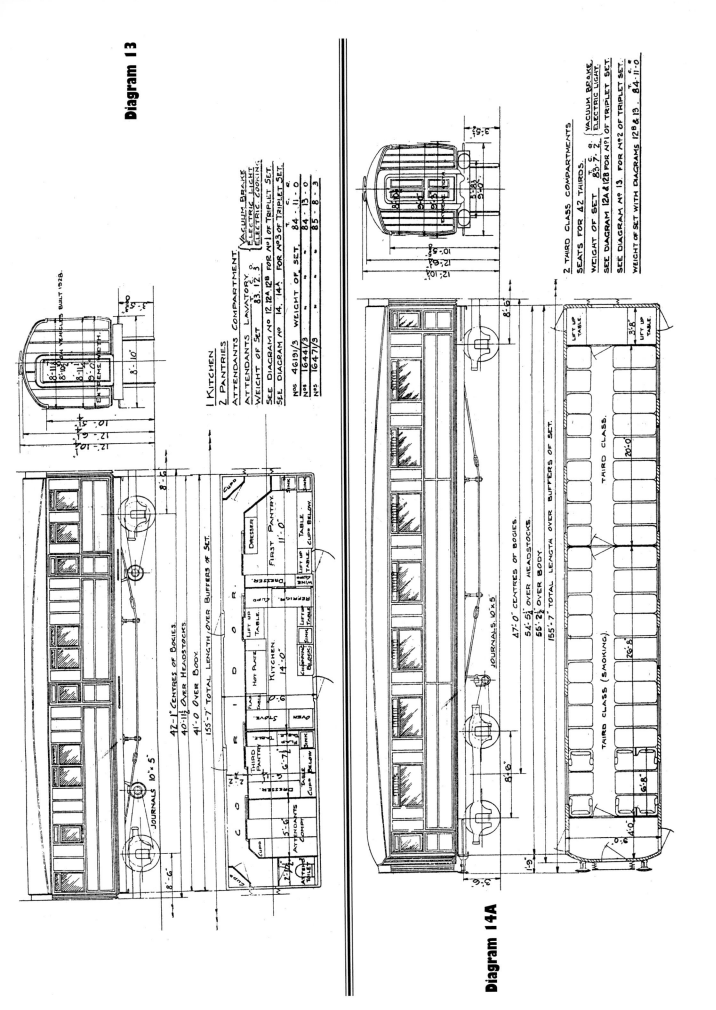

JOURNALS 10" x 5"

8'-6"

47'-0" CENTRES OF BOGIES.
54'-5½" OVER HEADSTOCKS.
55'-2½" OVER BODY.
155'-7" TOTAL LENGTH OVER BUFFERS OF SET.

LIFT UP TABLE.

THIRD CLASS.  20'-0"

LIFT UP TABLE.  3'-8"

THIRD CLASS (SMOKING).  26'-8"

6'-8"
4'-0"

2 THIRD CLASS COMPARTMENTS
SEATS FOR 42 THIRDS.
WEIGHT OF SET   83. 7. 2  [T. C. 8. / VACUUM BRAKE / ELECTRIC LIGHT.
SEE DIAGRAM 12A & 12B FOR Nº1 OF TRIPLET SET.
SEE DIAGRAM Nº 13. FOR Nº2 OF TRIPLET SET.
WEIGHT OF SET WITH DIAGRAMS 12B & 13.  84. 11. 0 T. C. 8.

# SLEEPING CARS

The LNER operated sleeping car services on the East Coast route, and jointly with the LMS between St Pancras and Edinburgh, via the Settle & Carlisle line and the Waverley Route.

Until 1914/5, there were two overnight trains in winter each way between Kings Cross and Scotland, at 8pm and 11.30pm down, and 10.50pm and 11.15pm up from Edinburgh. These offered East Coast Joint Stock sleeping cars between Kings Cross and Aberdeen, Inverness, Fort William, Glasgow, Perth, and Dundee and return (except the Dundee car which ran one way only). There was also the Kings Cross to Newcastle sleeping car service which had been operated by Great Northern/North Eastern Joint Stock.

The Anglo-Scottish trains were duplicated – sometimes triplicated – during the peak period which extended from May to October inclusive. By the last year before Grouping, there had been one or two changes, principally that the 8pm left earlier, at 7.30pm or thereabouts, and that the 11.30pm departed Kings Cross an hour or so earlier. Sleeping berths were provided only for the first-class, and third-class accommodation was seated only. Where first-class berths and third-class compartments were provided in one coach, it was referred to as a Sleeping Composite.

The superintendents and passenger managers of the constituent companies forming the LNER were concerned at the state of the East Coast stock when meeting six weeks or so before Grouping was effected. They were concerned that there should be a thorough renovation of East Coast stock which, it was alleged, 'had got into such a bad state that strong complaints are being received from the travelling public.' Early in 1923, the Traffic Committee went so far as to say that 'it is stated that the (West Coast) sleeping car accommodation is now much better than the East Coast'.

Of the sleeping cars inherited by the LNER, the most recent example was a twin first, completed in 1922, while the other elliptical roofed cars dated from 1907-10, these having been variously modified from

1920, some being converted to all first-class cars and others given replacement underframes. There were 32 clerestory cars and, while in 1923 it was agreed that four were to be condemned, the remainder were to be refurbished. As for the two former Midland & North British Joint Stock sleeping cars used on the St Pancras–Edinburgh service, these were described in 1927 as of 'a very old pattern and have given rise to complaints from passengers...' Their refurbishment was not considered worthwhile, and it was agreed that they should be replaced by two cars to LMS design. In 1928 the joint stock was disbanded, and in due course a replacement sleeping composite was built by the LNER for the Southern Scottish Area which had taken over responsibility for running the service on the Company's part; this vehicle is not described in this book as it appeared after the admittedly arbitrary cut-off date of 1931 for new designs.

The 1923 Carriage Building Programme of the LNER not surprisingly included new sleeping cars. Doncaster was to build two twin first-class cars similar to that built in 1922 and to this pre-Grouping design, listed as East Coast Diagram 68. York would build six first-class cars similar in general outline to those built before 1914, and listed as East Coast Diagram 64B. Later this type was allocated LNER Diagram 17. Justification for the new cars was that three cars were required for the newly introduced Aberdeen-Penzance service while three would be allocated to the new Kings Cross-Inverness via Aberdeen service. The sleeping cars between Aberdeen and Penzance lasted no longer than May 1924.

The 1924/5 Programme continued the renewal of the sleeping car fleet, with the construction of 11 first-class sleeping cars and five sleeping composites. These cars were regarded as second in importance only to re-equipment of the 'Flying Scotsman'. Some of the firsts were originally to be twins but it was then decided that there was insufficient traffic to justify the twin vehicles, except to Newcastle. The sleeper composites are shown as being required for the Aberdeen-Penzance service for which full first-class cars had been built in the 1923 Programme and which, in any case, ceased running almost before these

Diagram 17 car No 10197J (built Doncaster, 1924, but carrying a shopping date of 3 January 1925). These cars were generally similar to those built for the ECJS before World War I. This vehicle later became No 1237.

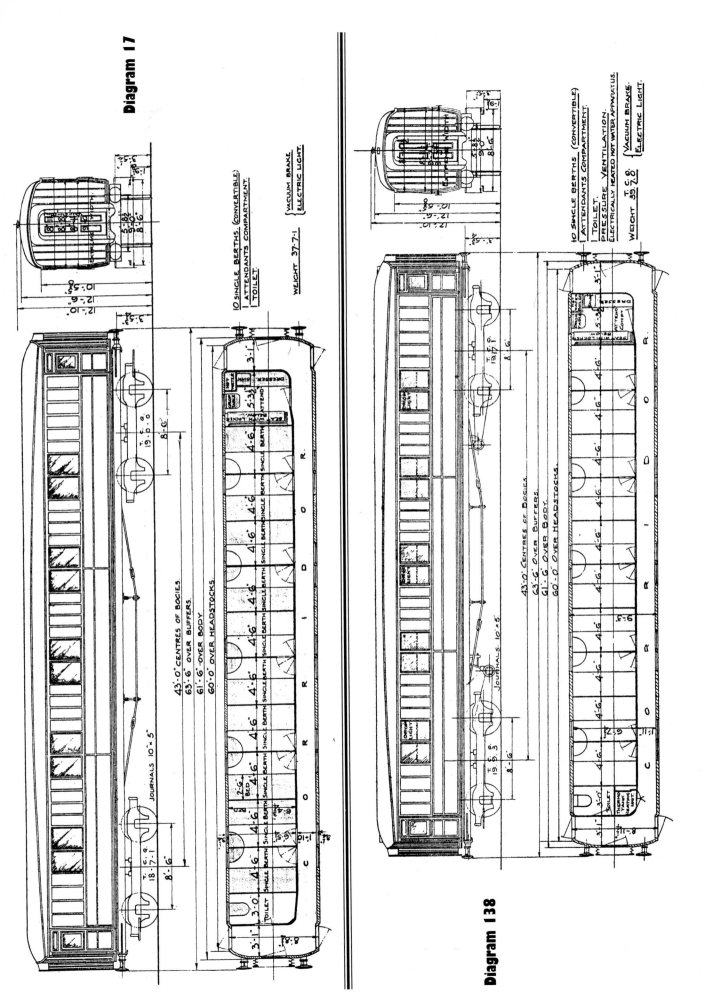

**Diagram 17**

10 SINGLE BERTHS. (CONVERTIBLE)
ATTENDANTS COMPARTMENT.
TOILET.

WEIGHT 37-7-1 { VACUUM BRAKE
ELECTRIC LIGHT.

43'·0" CENTRES OF BOGIES.
63'·6" OVER BUFFERS.
61'·6" OVER BODY.
60'·0" OVER HEADSTOCKS.

JOURNALS 10"× 5"

**Diagram 138**

10 SINGLE BERTHS (CONVERTIBLE)
ATTENDANTS COMPARTMENT.
TOILET.
PRESSURE VENTILATION.
ELECTRICALLY HEATED HOT WATER APPARATUS.

WEIGHT 39-7-0 { VACUUM BRAKE
ELECTRIC LIGHT.

43'·0" CENTRES OF BOGIES.
63'·6" OVER BUFFERS.
61'·6" OVER BODY.
60'·0" OVER HEADSTOCKS.

JOURNALS. 10"× 5"

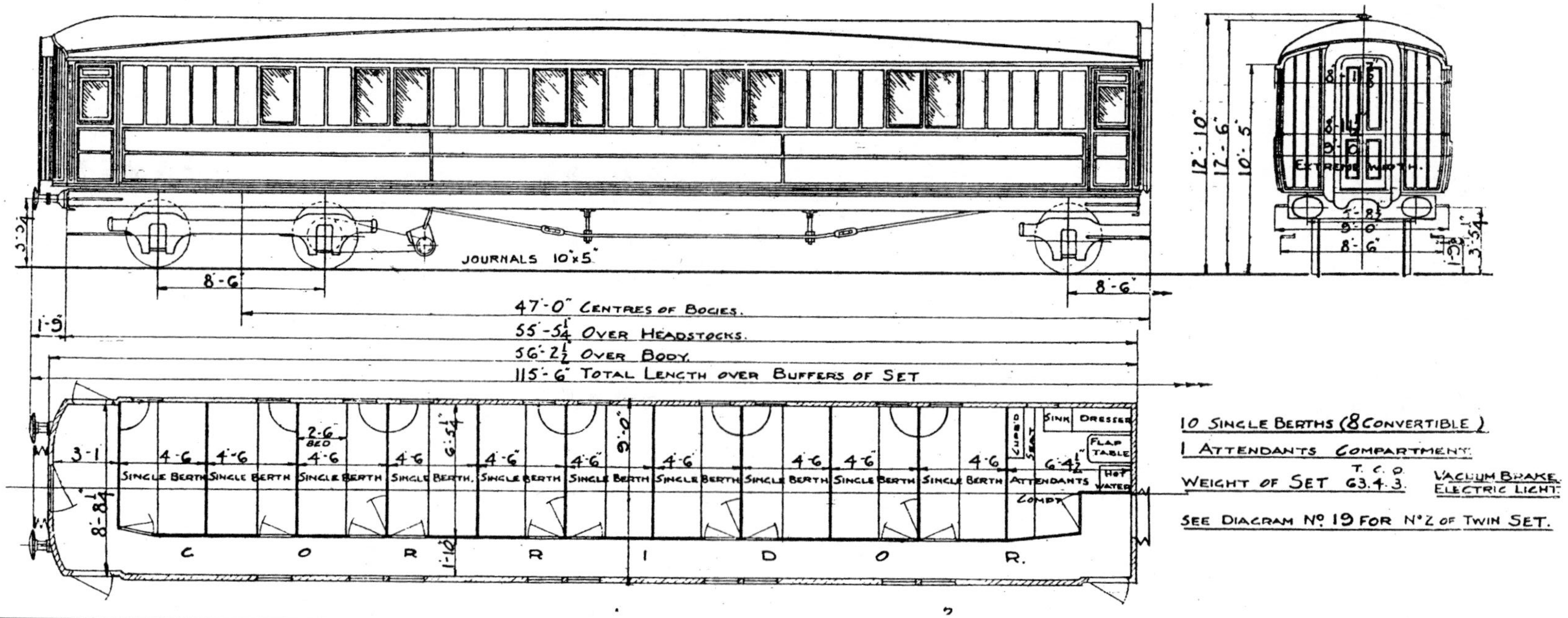

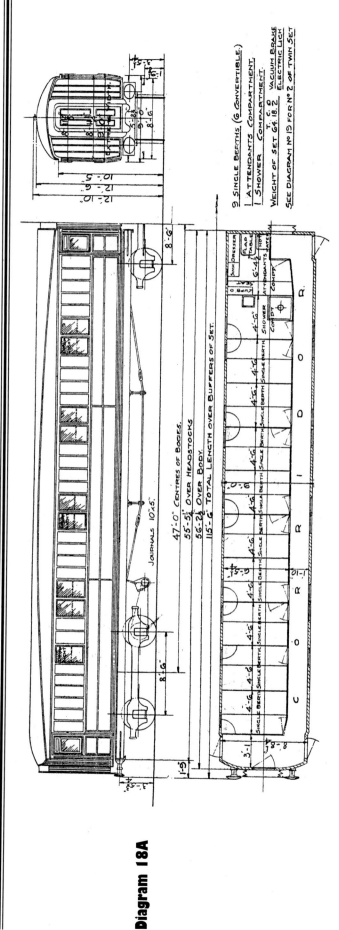

JOURNALS 10"x5"
47'-0" CENTRES OF BOGIES.
55'-5¼" OVER HEADSTOCKS.
56'-2½" OVER BODY.
115'-6" TOTAL LENGTH OVER BUFFERS OF SET
SINGLE BERTH
ATTENDANTS COMPT
SINK DRESSER
FLAP TABLE
HOT WATER
C O R R I D O R.
EXTREME WIDTH
10 SINGLE BERTHS (8 CONVERTIBLE)
1 ATTENDANTS COMPARTMENT
WEIGHT OF SET T. C. Q. 63.4.3.
VACUUM BRAKE. ELECTRIC LIGHT.
SEE DIAGRAM Nº 19 FOR Nº 2 OF TWIN SET.

## Diagram 18

JOURNALS 10"x5".
47'-0" CENTRES OF BOGIES.
55'-5¼" OVER HEADSTOCKS
56'-2½" OVER BODY.
115'-6" TOTAL LENGTH OVER BUFFERS OF SET.
SINGLE BERTH
SHOWER COMPT
ATTENDANTS COMPT
SINK DRESSER
FLAP TABLE
HOT WATER
C O R R I D O R.
EXTREME WIDTH
9 SINGLE BERTHS (6 CONVERTIBLE.)
1 ATTENDANTS COMPARTMENT.
1 SHOWER COMPARTMENT.
WEIGHT OF SET T. C. Q. 64.18.2
VACUUM BRAKE ELECTRIC LIGHT
SEE DIAGRAM Nº 19 FOR Nº 2 OF TWIN SET

## Diagram 18A

The impressive appearance of a Diagram 18/19 twin first (built Doncaster, 1926). In this photograph, the left hand of the pair is No 1205 (Diagram 19), seen from the corridor side, and No 1204 is on the right-hand. No 1204 was later altered to include a shower compartment.

composite cars were delivered. Replacements continued in the 1925 Programme, too, namely four first-class single cars, three twin firsts and five sleeping composites.

There was progress towards the introduction of third-class sleeping (ie, lying-down) accommodation in the 1925 Programme. Discussion between the East Coast and West Coast authorities regarding the provision of proper third-class accommodation on overnight Anglo-Scottish trains had taken place at intervals, at least as early as 1906. The conclusion was that it would be undesirable to run third-class sleeping cars, no doubt because the railways feared that their provision would extract revenue from the profitable first-class sleeping car operations. The case for building third-class sleeping cars was aired by the LNER's passenger managers in 1923 and, having heard their objections, the chief general manager proposed the construction of six-compartment convertible third-class coaches offering passengers a rug and pillow as bedding, in which there would be four berths per compartment by night, and ordinary third-class seating by day. Thirty-one cars would be required, to replace the same number of ordinary vestibuled thirds in East Coast service.

In the end, the proposal was dropped early in 1925, and not until May 1928 was there a decision to proceed with the construction of 16 third-class sleeping cars. These were put into service in September 1928, at the same time as third-class cars were also introduced by the LMS and GWR, but on each railway only on those trains which already had first-class sleeping cars. The third-class cars (referred to as 'convertible' sleeping cars) were considered as an 'entirely additional travelling facility', in the eyes of the LNER Finance Committee and their construction was charged to the Company's Capital Account; the subsequent order was dealt with in the same way.

Public reaction to the new facility had been such that approval was sought for 19 more third-class cars (in two batches) in advance of the 1929/30 Programme so that they would be ready for the 1929 summer season. These, to Diagram 109, were to the increased 9ft 3in width, with recessed doors at each end. In place of four additional cars, the third-class sitting compartments in the Diagram 20 cars were converted to the same standard as the full third-class sleeping cars. These altered cars were used on the Kings Cross–Inverness services via Forres and via Carr Bridge, and for the Perth service. One of the convertible thirds was reported in 1930 as still being on loan to the SSA for use on the Edinburgh–St Pancras service.

The next development was logical in that ten third-class sleeping cars were included in the 1930/1 Programme which had proper mattresses for the berths, but still lacked full bedding and washing facilities in the compartments. To drawings approved in February 1931, these were the first LNER standard coaches on the 65ft underframe, approval having been granted in late 1929 for the introduction on the company's main lines of coaching stock to a maximum length of 67ft.

Great care was taken to maintain and improve the standards of the first-class cars in the fleet. An East Coast Joint Stock car had been fitted with an pioneering Stone's pressure ventilation system as early as 1907 or so. In 1929, Thermotank supplied a full ventilation and heating system using warmed or cooled air for installation in a Diagram 17 car. At the same time, electric water heaters were installed in two Diagram 17 cars, rather than the gas heating previously employed.

These new developments were combined in four prestigious Diagram 138 cars put into service during 1930. With their special interior decor and fittings, they marked the progression to a much higher standard of accommodation on East Coast expresses generally, and their introduction coincided with the production of the 'Super First' day coaches mentioned elsewhere in the book. In 1930, a shower compartment was fitted in place of a berth in one body of the Diagram 18/19 twin firsts, and this additional luxury was extended to later first-class cars.

The first-class and sleeping composite sleeping cars were maintained by Doncaster Works, and the third-class convertible and non-convertible cars by York Works. Between September/October, and the following April/May each of the LNER's sleeping cars was programmed for shopping including lifting and varnishing.

# First-class: (SLF)

### DIAGRAM 17

These cars had ten single berths, an attendant's compartment and a lavatory, and they ran on the heavy type standard bogie. Their exterior design differed from that of the pre-Grouping cars in that there were large windows on the corridor side. The interiors featured the simplicity in favour with Gresley at the time, with mahogany for much of the interior panelling, offset by white enamel. Care was taken to group the controls for heating and lighting so that they could be oper-

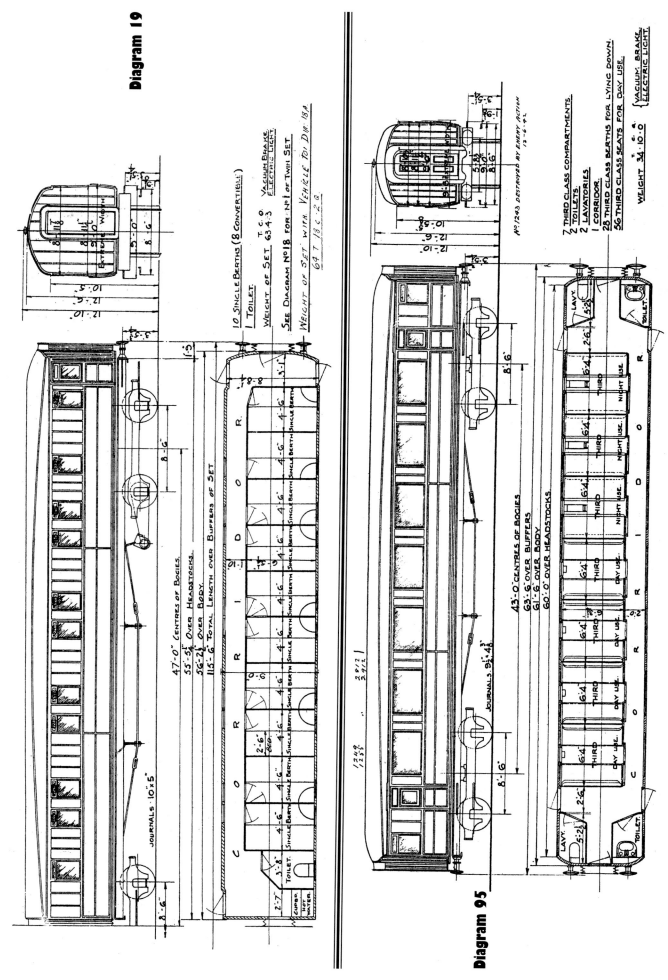

**Diagram 19**

10 SINGLE BERTHS (8 CONVERTIBLE)
1 TOILET.
WEIGHT OF SET 63.4.3 } T.C.O. VACUUM BRAKE ELECTRIC LIGHT
SEE DIAGRAM N°18 FOR N°1 OF TWIN SET
WEIGHT OF SET WITH VEHICLE FOR DIA.18A.
64 T 13 C 2 Q

EXTREME WIDTH
10'·0"
12'·6"
12'·10"

47'·0" CENTRES OF BOGIES.
55'·5½" OVER HEADSTOCKS.
56'·2½" OVER BODY.
115'·6" TOTAL LENGTH OVER BUFFERS OF SET

JOURNALS 10"×5"

TOILET. SINGLE BERTH SINGLE BERTH SINGLE BERTH SINGLE BERTH SINGLE BERTH SINGLE BERTH SINGLE BERTH SINGLE BERTH SINGLE BERTH SINGLE BERTH TOILET.
CUPBD. HOT WATER.

CORRIDOR

**Diagram 95**

43'·0" CENTRES OF BOGIES.
63'·6" OVER BUFFERS.
61'·6" OVER BODY.
60'·0" OVER HEADSTOCKS.

JOURNALS 9"×4½"

N°1243 DESTROYED BY ENEMY ACTION 13·6·41.

7 THIRD CLASS COMPARTMENTS.
2 TOILETS
2 LAVATORIES
1 CORRIDOR.
28 THIRD CLASS BERTHS FOR LYING DOWN.
56 THIRD CLASS SEATS FOR DAY USE.
WEIGHT 34·10·0 } T.C.6. VACUUM BRAKE ELECTRIC LIGHT.

LAV. TOILET.
THIRD NIGHT USE. THIRD NIGHT USE. THIRD NIGHT USE. THIRD DAY USE. THIRD DAY USE. THIRD DAY USE. THIRD DAY USE.

CORRIDOR

162

By its very nature, the design for the third-class convertible sleeping cars favoured the restriction of bodyside doors to the ends only. The resultant vehicle was not only mechanically stronger but aesthetically more pleasing, as demonstrated by Diagram 95 car No 1241 (built York, 1928). This shows the corridor side of what was basically a vestibuled third. These were to the 9ft width, and the later Diagram 109 cars had recessed doors.

The photograph shows some of the underframe lettering/designations: the stars, to show operating staff where they could 'pull the strings' to destroy the vacuum and so release the brakes, and at the right-hand end the shopping details. In this case, the details are: 'P 9-8-28' and 'V 5-9-28', representing the dates of painting and of varnishing the vehicle. The unusual month's gap is explained by the incidence of the works' holiday. These cars were introduced to traffic on 24 September 1928. Other designations included W to denote the location of the Westinghouse air fitting, and L to denote the date that the vehicle had last been lifted.

ated by a passenger lying in bed. There were supplies of hot and cold water to the basins, the hot water being generated by a Still's gas-fired boiler in the attendant's compartment.

Various subsequent changes were made. Nos 1317-9 were fitted with electric water heaters in 1929, and No 1261 was effectively the prototype for the Thermotank heating and ventilating system fitted from new in first-class cars from 1930. From late 1942, at least seven Diagram 17 cars were temporarily converted with two-tier berths in each of the end compartments, for use on Newcastle and Aberdeen-Kings Cross services.

## DIAGRAM 138

These cars were designed so that, if required, the single-berth compartments could be converted into five double berths, as there was a communicating door between each berth. In addition to the installation of Thermotank ventilation and heating, the interiors were specially finished. Waring & Gillow was responsible for the interior decor and furnishings of one pair of cars, White Allom for the other pair. The Waring & Gillow interior had glossy and shaded blue paintwork, in Art Deco style while the other consultant's scheme harked back to earlier themes and made use of panelling painted a bluish green, with mouldings picked out in a biscuit shade.

The distinctive decor of these cars was reportedly not to the liking of some passengers, and the SPMs' committee went on record to say that it would be preferable to revert to mahogany panelling and lacquered brass fittings. Their plea went unanswered, and the Art Deco style of the 1930 pair furnished by Waring's was adopted for later first-

class cars with the difference that Rexine was used to avoid the scuffing to paintwork that had been experienced.

The arrival of these cars enabled the earliest of the ECJS elliptical-roofed sleeping cars to be withdrawn.

## LIST OF FIRST-CLASS NON-ARTICULATED SLEEPING CARS:

| Diag No CBP | Order No | Compts/ berths | Built | Original number/ changes | 1943 number | |
|---|---|---|---|---|---|---|
| **Built 1924** | | | | | | |
| 17* | 1924/5 | 37 | 10: 10 | DR | 10194-7J (1147/9, 1235/7) | 1147/9, 1235/7 EC Dia 64B |
| **Built 1925** | | | | | | |
| 17* | 1924/5 | 37 | 10: 10 | DR | 10198-201J (1238/61/8/9) 1208-10 | 1208-10/38 1261/8/9 EC Dia 64B |
| **Built 1927** | | | | | | |
| 17* | 1925/6 | 118 | 10 : 10 | DR | 1316-9 | 1316-9 |
| **Built 1930** | | | | | | |
| 138 | 1930/1 | 361 | 10: 10 | DR | 1152-5 | 1152-5 |

# Twin first-class: (SLFT)

## DIAGRAMS 18, 18A AND 19

These cars could accommodate 20 passengers in the twin bodies which had one attendant's compartment. Fourteen of the berths could be converted to double berths. Compared with two single 20-berth cars with a combined weight of 74¾ tons, the twins weighed in at 63¼ tons, demonstrating well the advantages offered by articulation.

In September 1930 it was agreed that a shower bath should be fitted in place of a sleeping berth in car No 1204 of twin Nos 1204/5. This involved the installation of water-raising equipment, including a compressor, and a frame-mounted water tank. The vehicle worked on alternate nights on the 10.35pm Kings Cross-Edinburgh, and 10.50pm return. A charge of 1/- was made for use of the shower.

Usual employment for these cars in prewar days was on the 10.35pm Kings Cross-Edinburgh, and 11pm return, and the 10.45pm Newcastle, and 11pm return working.

Six SLFTs were in storage at the end of World War 2.

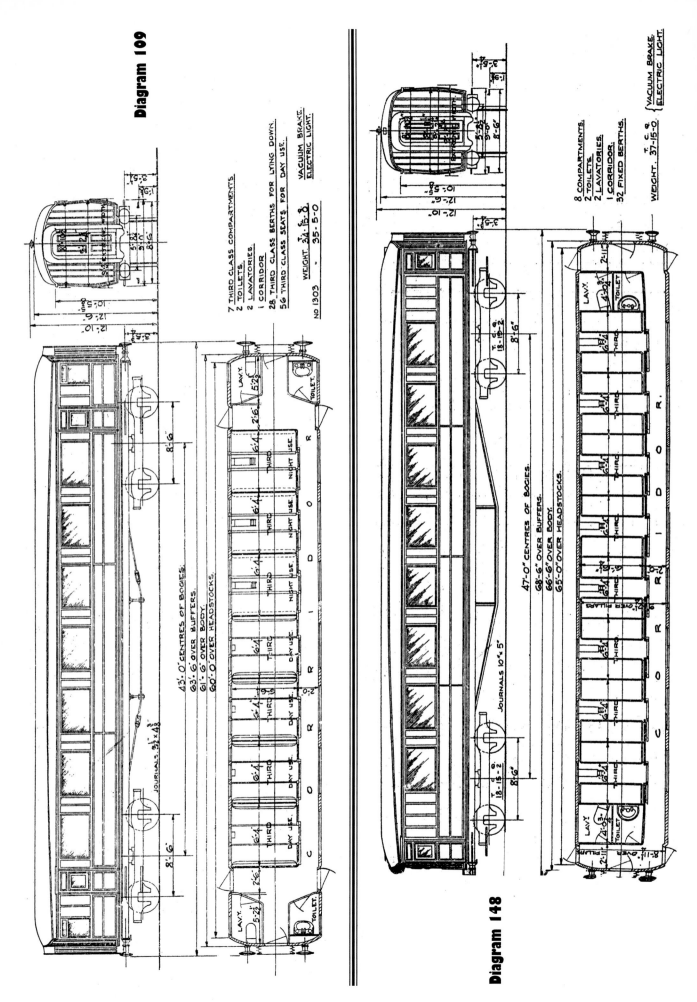

**Diagram 109**

7 THIRD CLASS COMPARTMENTS
2 TOILETS.
2 LAVATORIES.
1 CORRIDOR
28 THIRD CLASS BERTHS FOR LYING DOWN.
56 THIRD CLASS SEATS FOR DAY USE.

VACUUM BRAKE.
ELECTRIC LIGHT.
WEIGHT. 34-15-8.
" 35-5-0

No 1303

43'-0" CENTRES OF BOGIES.
63'-6" OVER BUFFERS.
61'-6" OVER BODY.
60'-0" OVER HEADSTOCKS.

JOURNALS 3½" × 4¾"

**Diagram 148**

8 COMPARTMENTS.
2 TOILETS.
2 LAVATORIES.
1 CORRIDOR.
32 FIXED BERTHS.

T. C. 8.
WEIGHT. 37-15-0.

VACUUM BRAKE.
ELECTRIC LIGHT.

47'-0" CENTRES OF BOGIES.
68'-6" OVER BUFFERS.
66'-6" OVER BODY.
65'-0" OVER HEADSTOCKS.

JOURNALS 10" × 5"

**Diagram 20**

**LIST OF TWIN FIRST-CLASS SLEEPING CARS:**

| Diag No | CBP | Order No | Compts/ berths | Built | Original/ number/ | 1943 number |
|---|---|---|---|---|---|---|
| **Built 1926** | | | | | | |
| 18 | 1925/6 | 122 | 10: 10 | DR | 1202/33 | 1202/33 |
| 18A | | | 9 : 9 | | 1204 | 1204 With shower bath |
| 19 | | | 10: 10 | | 1203/5/34 | 1203/5/34 |
| | | | Twins formed: 1202/3, 1204/5, 1233/4 | | | |

# Third-class: (SLT)

## DIAGRAM 95

As already mentioned, the introduction of third-class sleeping cars allowed passengers to lie down at night, rather than sit upright or slump in their seats. The compartment was converted for night use by pulling out the seats, and by lowering hinged bed frames to create the upper berths. Access to the upper berths was by means of steps. Passengers paid a supplement of 6/- for journeys within England, or 7/- for Anglo-Scottish journeys, and for which they were provided with a pillow and a rug. The coaches each had seven compartments, with separate wcs and washrooms at each end.

As from 24 September 1928, these third-class convertible cars were introduced on the 7.30pm from Kings Cross, running to Aberdeen and Inverness; on the 10.25pm to Glasgow; 10.35pm to Edinburgh, and 10.45pm to Newcastle. An East Coast car (No 1290, as at 1931/32) was loaned to provide a service on the 9.15pm St Pancras-Edinburgh, and 9.55pm return. By 1937, a car of either Diagram 95 or 109 type was included in the 1.5am Kings Cross-Newcastle, working forward from Newcastle in order to serve intermediate stations to Edinburgh, and also in the 'Highlandman' to/from Fort William.

From the point of view of the design developments with coaches, the Diagram 95 vehicles are significant for being the first LNER vestibuled stock to have entry at the vestibules only, without compartment-side doors. On the corridor side there were seven large windows.

## DIAGRAM 109

These followed the design of Diagram 95 except that the clearance for the operation of 9ft 3in width coaches allowed the bodies to be built to the increased width, with recessed doors, the extra 3in being used to provide more spacious seating/berths.

At first, the convertible thirds were used on scheduled services only, but from 1931 it was agreed jointly by the LNER and LMS that both companies would use such vehicles on Anglo-Scottish excursion trains. The Diagram 95 and 109 cars were regarded as interchangeable.

In 1939, the future of the fleet of 45 convertible cars was discussed and the general feeling was that as they were incapable of modification to non-convertible sleeping cars they should be altered to day coaches only, and transferred to the Areas. In their place, new non-convertible cars would be built. The war intervened before any decisions were made.

Seventeen cars of Diagrams 95 and 109 were converted for use in ambulance trains during World War 2 while six were held in storage on the LNER at the end of the war.

In 1946, the Big Four companies and the Railway Clearing House made moves towards producing a new type of non-convertible third-class sleeping car. An all-line car did not materialise, and instead the LNER proceeded with its unique design of an interlocking berth third-class car.

As at 1951, there were 13 vehicles of Diagram 95 in service, and 29 of Diagram 109. Until 1953, six remained abroad, and on repatriation were heavily converted to produce restaurant cafeteria cars of a new design.

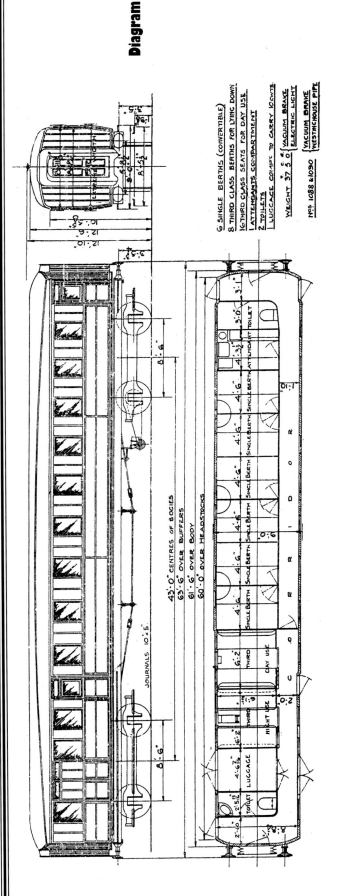

6 SINGLE BERTHS (CONVERTIBLE)
8 THIRD CLASS BERTHS FOR LYING DOWN
16 THIRD CLASS SEATS FOR DAY USE.
ATTENDANTS COMPARTMENT
2 TOILETS
LUGGAGE COMPT TO CARRY 10 CWTS
WEIGHT 37.5.0
Nos 1288 & 1290
VACUUM BRAKE
ELECTRIC LIGHT
VACUUM BRAKE
WESTINGHOUSE PIPE

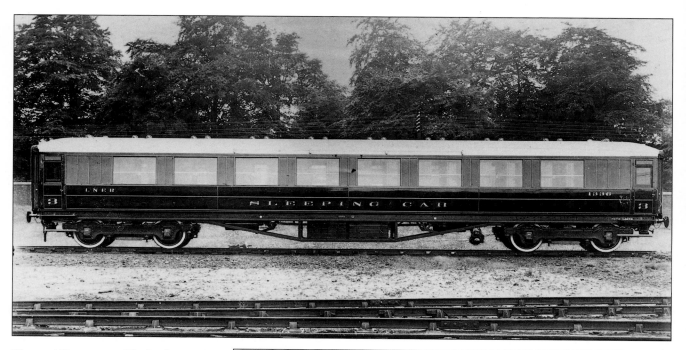

Diagram 148 non-convertible sleeping car No 1336 (built York, 1931). Although the large corridor-side windows were retained, the corridor partition of the compartment did not have a clear-glass window, so as to ensure greater privacy now that passengers were able to retire at night to fixed berths with proper mattresses.

## DIAGRAM 148

These 65ft non-convertible, 32-berth sleeping cars were built on the 65ft underframe which was the first to be used for standard stock. Angle-iron trussing replaced the previous bar trussing with turn-buckle adjustment. One improvement in passenger comfort was that the corridors were heated. The interior finish comprised polished teak panelling and white paint.

The form of these cars was the subject of discussion during November 1931, and possibly they had been intended to be convertible as it was now said that they would be 'non-convertible' and lettered 'Sleeping Car'. They were introduced on the 7.30pm Kings Cross-Aberdeen (two cars), 10.25pm Dundee (one car), 10.35pm Edinburgh (two cars) and 10.45pm Newcastle (two cars). Their introduction had the effect of releasing ten (day) vestibule thirds for transfer to the Areas.

## LIST OF THIRD-CLASS CONVERTIBLE AND NON-CONVERTIBLE SLEEPING CARS:

| Diag No | CBP | Order No | Compts/ berths/seats | Built | Original/1943 number/ |
|---|---|---|---|---|---|
| *Convertible sleeping cars* | | | | | |
| *Built 1928* | | | | | |
| 95 | 1928/9 | 278 | 7: 28/56 | YK | 1241-56 | 1241/4/5/6/9/52-6 ambulance train use WW2 1243 DEA |

After 1948 Nos 1242/7 remained as sleeper thirds, as did Nos 1248/50/1 which became 1519/26/7. Nos 1252-4 returned from wartime use as 1528-30. No 1245 was scrapped. Nos 1241/4/6/9/55/6 were rebuilt as restaurant cafeteria cars in 1954 as M 9209-14E.

## LIST OF SLEEPER COMPOSITE CARS:

| Diag No No | CBP /third-class seats | Order | First-class berths | Built | Original number/ changes | Postwar numbers§ |
|---|---|---|---|---|---|---|
| **Built 1925** | | | | | | |
| 20* | 1924/5 | 52 | 6 berths / 2 3rd compts: 16¶ | DR | 10205-9J (1088-92) ¶ conv to provide eight sleeping berths/16 seats in 1929 | 1707-10/39 |
| **Built 1926** | | | | | | |
| 20* | 1925/6 | 121 | 6 berths / 2 3rd compts: 16¶ | DR | 1093-7 ¶ conv to provide eight sleeping berths/16 seats in 1929 | 1776, 1848/89/–, 1097 |

§ Renumbering seems to have been undertaken to clear the 10xx series for postwar steel-panelled stock built for East Coast service in 1947-9.

| | | | | | | |
|---|---|---|---|---|---|---|
| **Built 1929** | | | | | | |
| 109* | 1929/30 | 287 | 7: 28/56 | YK | 1270-2/6-84 | |
| | | 307 | | YK | 1285-91 | |
| **Built 1930** | | | | | | |
| 109* | 1930/1 | 356 | 7: 28/56 | YK | 1296-1305 | |
| ***Non-convertible sleeping cars*** | | | | | | |
| **Built 1931** | | | | | | |
| 148 | 1931/2 | 426 | 8: 32 | YK | 1336-44/6 | |

# Composite: (SLC)

## DIAGRAM 20

As built, these cars had six first-class berths convertible to double berths, two third-class compartments seating 16, and a locker compartment. In rebuilt form, the third-class compartments had hinged top bedframes and accommodation for eight recumbent passengers by night, and a nominal 16 seats by day.

The original justification for these cars has been mentioned, and the fact that they were used on the Kings Cross-Inverness and Perth services in their altered form. By 1935, they were usually employed as the through Lossiemouth car in the 'Aberdonian', in the Inverness via Forres portion of the 'Highlandman' (returning empty to Perth in the up direction), and as the Darlington car in the 1.5am Newcastle, returning empty during the day to London.

Nine remained in use in 1951.

# SPECIAL VEHICLES – mainly East Coast but some odd men out

As we have seen, providing the reader accepts that 'standard' was something of a relative term in the days before jig-built rolling stock, and when coaches received something like ten coats of varnish before they were sent out to face the world, the coaching stock produced under the aegis of H. N. Gresley was 'standard'. As always, it is the exceptions that prove interesting. There is no real logic to the inclusion of the various diagrams appearing in this section, except that they do not fit easily elsewhere!

## The 'Toilet thirds'

### DIAGRAM 23A

When Diagram 23 vestibule thirds Nos 1007/12 entered service in November 1924, as 10026J and 10031J, there was nothing to distinguish them from their fellows. The decision to run the main portion of the 'Flying Scotsman' non-stop between Kings Cross and Edinburgh as from May 1928 was kept a secret as close as possible to the introduction of the service so as to avoid the LMS coming up with a 'spoiler'. In March 1928, the formations were agreed for the principal day East Coast trains during the coming summer. The main concern was to decide on sets to run with the new triplet restaurant cars as from 9 July 1928, the start of the 'main' season.

Four sets of coaches – sets Nos 1-4 – were earmarked. The existing Nos 1/2 sets were to run on the 'Flying Scotsman' from April-July 1928, having been shopped from Doncaster and York in the March of that year; they were then to be replaced by newly formed sets Nos 1/2. The vehicles from the earlier sets Nos 1/2 were then held as replacements, and for strengthening the new sets Nos 1/2. Most of these coaches were fitted with lavatory water tanks of greater capacity – with non-stop running there was no chance to top up the tanks en route – the seating was reupholstered, and shades fitted to the lights in compartments and corridors. At this stage, there was no mention of any on-train novelties.

The East Coast premier vehicles were always a cut above the rest in that there were small refinements such as hassocks in the first-class compartments, roller towels in the lavatories, and train attendants to look after the passengers. In 1926, the East Coast travelling inspector of the time, a young man earmarked as a potential high-flyer for LNER management, suggested that a special vehicle with toilets for the use of female passengers, and with hairdressing accommodation, should be provided on important passenger trains. The idea was firmly stamped on at the time, but duly materialised in 1928 for the summer non-stop running of the 'Flying Scotsman'. In his paper delivered to the I Loco E, Newsome says that the scheme for the conversion of one of the coaches to provide a ladies' retiring room and a hairdressing saloon was prepared at Kings Cross in April 1928. This seems to suggest that the idea was taken up by Wedgwood and Gresley over the heads of the passenger managers who were so against the suggestion in 1926.

The converted vehicles featured in press accounts of the non-stop 'Flying Scotsman', and in September 1928 they were reported to be in service although the official records are a little ambiguous as to when they actually entered service. Thirds Nos 1007/12 were altered by stripping three of the compartments. One provided space for a ladies' toilet compartment with dressing table, armchair, full-length mirror and washbasin. All this was fitted into just over 7½ft! Not that the hairdressing saloon was very much bigger, and that included a chair, washbasin and showcase. These two facilities accounted for the space formerly occupied

by 2½ compartments, the remainder of the third compartment becoming a coupé, to serve as a waiting-room for the hairdressing saloon. The side doors of the three former compartments were made fast, and the compartment-side windows were given frosted glass while the quarterlight between the second and third compartment was panelled over. An additional water tank was provided, too. An illuminated sign indicated if the hairdressing salon was engaged.

The hairdressing service was initially contracted out but there were complaints from passengers of extortionate charges so that the LNER Hotels Department stepped in and took over the service which was offered to men and women alike. In addition, the summer 1928 non-stops featured a travelling news vendor selling newspapers, magazines and books. This service lost money but was reintroduced the next summer, with the newspapers being sold by the train attendant.

The Toilet Thirds, as they were somewhat unimaginatively, if not quaintly, known by LNER management proved to be a success. For the summer 1932 service, when the journey time of the non-stop 'Flying Scotsman' was at last reduced, to 7½ hours, the Toilet Thirds offered another novelty. The two compartments at the other end of the coaches to the existing special facilities were stripped and replaced by a cocktail bar, of suitably modish design, and with bar stools and chairs. The barman served drinks only, and it was found that the facility did not abstract revenue from the restaurant cars. From 1934, the cocktail bars were redesignated as buffets, by then probably because their range of refreshments had been extended. The 'Northern Belle' cruise trains were introduced by the LNER during the summer of 1933 and, for each season up to and including 1939, one of the Toilet Thirds was borrowed from the 'Flying Scotsman', to be replaced by a former GNR saloon coach also fitted with a cocktail bar.

Nos 1007/12 remained in the 'Flying Scotsman' sets until the entry into service of the 1938 sets built for these trains. For a further year, the Toilet Thirds continued in East Coast stock, but it was then decided that No 1012 should be converted as a full-length buffet-lounge car, and No 1007 returned to traffic as a full third. The war intervened but sometime before 1945 both coaches were converted to full thirds and redesignated Diagram 23.

| Diag No | CBP | Order No | Compartments /seats | Number as converted | 1943 number |
|---------|-----|----------|---------------------|---------------------|-------------|

**Built 1924** as Diagram 23, converted with ladies' retiring-room and hairdressing saloon on Diagram 23A, 1928, and cocktail bar added, 1932

| | | | | | |
|---------|-----|----------|---------------------|---------------------|-------------|
| 23A | - | - | 3: 21 | - | 1007/12 | 12109/10 |

Reverted to Dia 23, some time after 1939

## 'Super Firsts' (FK)

### DIAGRAMS 139, 147

The introduction of the regular non-stop running by the 'Flying Scotsman', and the provision of special on-board facilities, not to mention the use of stock with retrimmed upholstery to the latest designs, was a product of the competitive atmosphere which existed between the LMS and LNER for Anglo-Scottish traffic. During 1928, the LMS had introduced some opulent lounge brakes and semi-open firsts for use in the 'Royal Scot', and although these were not apparently very popular with passengers, their appearance must have given food for thought for the LNER. The sets for the 1928 'Flying Scotsman', Louis XIV restaurant cars

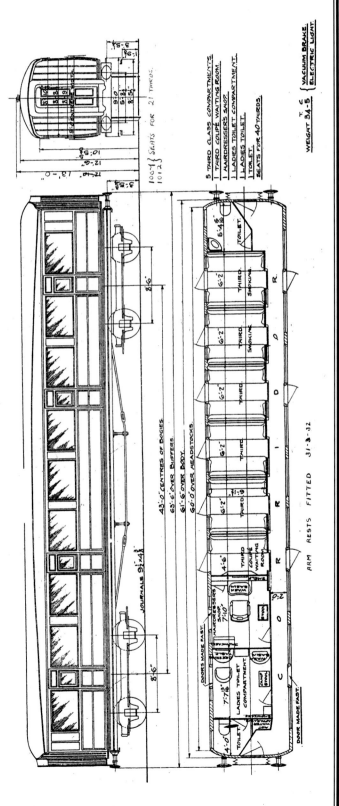

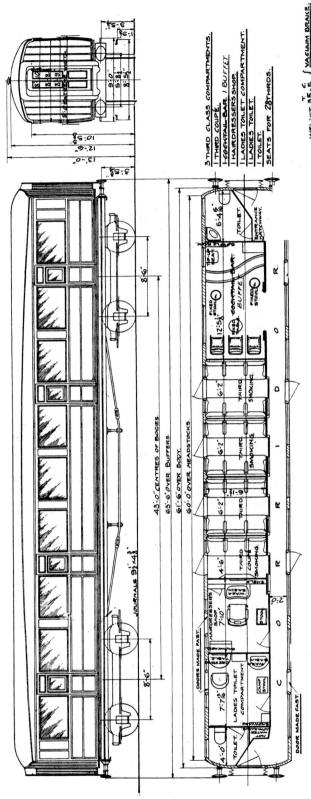

**Diagram 23A**

showing the original conversion, with a hairdressing salon/ladies' retiring room

The plan of the additional cocktail bar/buffet of 1932.

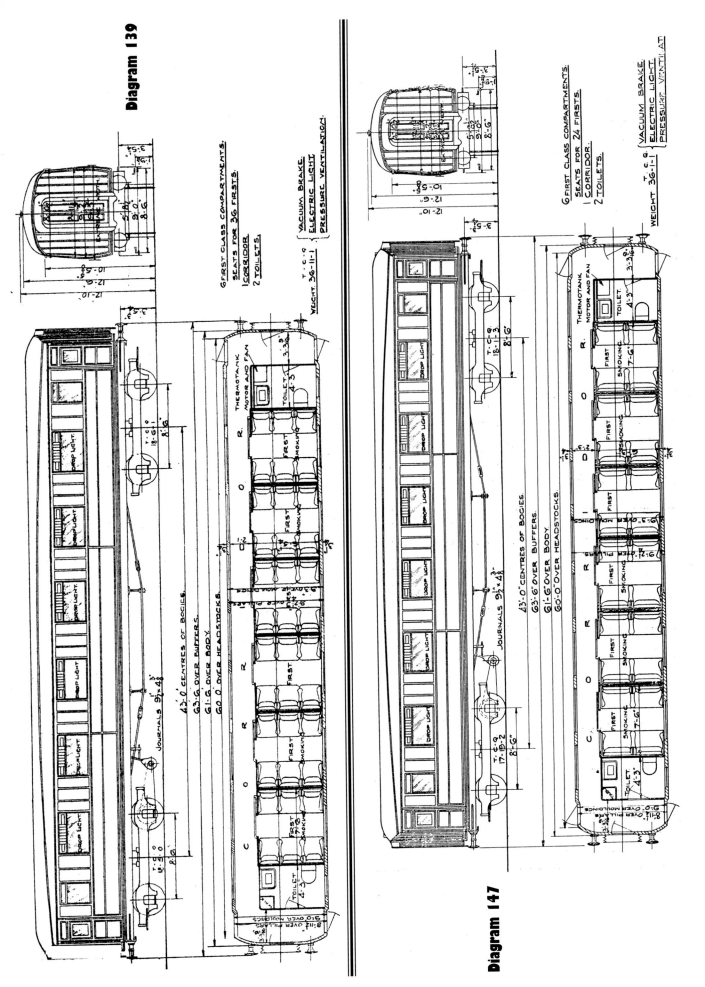

**Diagram 139**

6 FIRST CLASS COMPARTMENTS.
SEATS FOR 36 FIRSTS.
1 CORRIDOR
2 TOILETS.

VACUUM BRAKE.
ELECTRIC LIGHT.
PRESSURE VENTILATION.

WEIGHT. 36-11-1 } T.C.Q.

**Diagram 147**

6 FIRST CLASS COMPARTMENTS.
SEATS FOR 24 FIRSTS.
1 CORRIDOR.
2 TOILETS.

VACUUM BRAKE.
ELECTRIC LIGHT.
PRESSURE VENTILAT

WEIGHT 36-1-1 } T.C.Q.

Above: **Diagram 147 first No 1135 as built (Doncaster, 1931). It later became 54751, and then 11065 under the 1943 renumbering).**

Left: **A Diagram 28 open third, by now relegated to departmental use as a ballast brake and stripped of gangways, but demonstrating the different profile of these all-steel vehicles and the distinctively recessed windows.**

and Toilet thirds excepted, consisted of standard stock which had been in service for four years or so and, indeed, the vestibule firsts were the oldest vehicles in the sets.

A drawing of what became known as a 'Super First' was examined by the superintendents and passenger managers in January 1929 when it was agreed that new first-class coaches for the Anglo-Scottish services should be to this design. One proposal provided for a vehicle seating 42 passengers, with a single lavatory positioned amidships. This layout was rejected, with the request that first-class vestibule coaches must have two lavatories, and that the new stock should be built to the 9ft 3in width. Gresley's reaction was to point out that, if built to increased width, the coaches would be able to have end doors only. The end-door layout had already appeared in the third-class convertible sleeping cars put into traffic from 1928. Two of the new first-class coaches were included in the 1930/1 CBP, for inclusion in the sets for the 'Flying Scotsman' which also was to receive other new stock.

The new vehicles were Nos 1132/3 (Diagram 139) and they went into service on the '10 o'clocks' during the summer of 1930. Apart from the installation of pressure ventilation, there were a number of innovations with the interior decor which had pastel and shaded paint finishes above the waist line, the upholstery being continued up to this level. Each compartment had a large window, and these were originally of the drop-type, able to be opened but also with louvre ventilators; these windows were later sealed. The press gave the vehicles some attention, on account of the Vita-glass used for the main compartment windows: this was supposed to let through health-giving rays from the sunlight but was claimed to block ultraviolet emissions. The windows had curtains with pelmets, and all interior metal fittings were chromium-plated. The three-a-side seating originally comprised winged armchairs, the angle of the seats and backs being adjustable. Four footstools were provided in each compartment, the ambience being completed by an attractive rug and carpeting in the corridors which, for probably the first time, had heating. Cocoa-fibre mats were provided in the vestibules. The lavatories were improved in design and larger than usual, and featured terrazzo flooring.

The Thermotank type of pressure ventilation was fitted, with outlet vents for warmed or cooled air in the compartments, and with control over the quantity of air supplied, and its temperature.

Sadly, initial passenger reaction was far from favourable, and the vehicles received two-a-side seating late in 1930, 'as per the stock on the West Coast' read the instruction. Consequently, the next pair of 'Super Firsts' were built with two-a-side seating.

These next two coaches were No 1134/5 (Diagram 147) which perpetuated the innovations of the earlier 'Super Firsts' although two-a-side seating was fitted from the start. As far as the pressure ventilation was concerned, these coaches lacked under-seat heating and, as pre-heating of the coach tended to drain the batteries or prove inadequate, steam heating was fitted early in 1932.

It was decided to build one of the 'Super Firsts' for use on the 8am Newcastle-Kings Cross and 5.30pm return, and this was included in the 1931/2 Building Programme. In the autumn of 1930, very soon after approval of this programme, it was agreed that 32 'end-door' coaches with 'wide side lights' (ie without compartment side doors and their accompanying quarterlights) should be built for main line services 'in view of the improved stock which the LMS is using on important services'. The 'Super Firsts' may have had their problems when new, but they served as the prototypes of the vastly more attractive end-door designs of vestibuled coaches which were built for premier services by the LNER from 1932.

Nos 1132/3 were included in sets Nos 1/2 for the summer 1931 'Flying Scotsman', and 1134/5 in the sets for the relief 'Scotsman'. In April 1932, all four coaches were fitted with wiring to receive radio/record-player transmissions relayed from the brake coach in the sets used on the afternoon Scotsmen which usually included Nos 1134/5. By 1937, all four coaches were regarded as replacement vehicles for more recent end-door firsts, and Nos 1132/3, always perhaps the less popular, were transferred under the 1938 CBP to the GC section for use on principal trains from Marylebone.

During World War 2, the seating was altered to three-a-side and the Thermotank pressure ventilation equipment was taken out of use.

## LIST OF 'SUPER FIRSTS' (FKLs):

| Diag No | CBP Order No | Compts/ seats | Built | Original number/ changes | 1943 number | |
|---|---|---|---|---|---|---|
| **Built 1930** | | | | | | |
| 139 | 1930/1 357 | 6: 36¶ | DR | 1132/3 | 11048/9 | PV |
| | | ¶ 24 seats from late 1930, 36 seats from 1943 | | | | |
| **Built 1931** | | | | | | |
| 147 | 1930/1 357 | 6: 24¶ | DR | 1134/5 | 11064/5 | PV |
| | | ¶ Later 36 seats | | (54750/1) | | Trans 1939 |
| | | | | 11064 W/O Goswick 1947 | | |

# All-steel coaches and vans

Although some people's impression may be that Gresley was a traditionalist who perpetuated teak-bodied coaches to the point of their obsolescence, he was well-aware of the merits and demerits of other materials for use in coaching stock. As early as 1914, Gresley had proposed to the Great Northern Railway's locomotive committee that an all-steel coach should be built as an experiment. The idea was lost amid the preparations for World War 1, but once the LNER had met its most pressing needs for the renewal of stock, the first all-steel vehicles were put into service from 1927. As the company's workshops were unable at that time to handle the construction of all-steel stock, the orders were placed with contractors although Gresley also said that the railway wished to assist the steel industry which was one of its main customers. Timber was becoming expensive.

Speaking to a railway lecture and debating society in 1928, at the time that the last of the all-steel coaches and vans were going into service, Gresley pointed out that because British railways – and presumably he was thinking of the operators rather than engineers – were wedded to the idea that all coaches should have compartment-side doors, it was impossible to introduce the sort of all-steel coaches that has gone into service in the USA, and on the CF du Nord, in France. Admittedly, earlier steel coaches had tended to be noisy. Although all-steel coaches were heavier and more expensive than their composite teak/steel equivalents, the advantages were that they would last longer than the teak-bodied stock, and could be painted with cellulose paints. Corrosion was an obvious hazard and to combat this the all-steel stock had an air space between the outer and inner lining of the body. In practice, the vehicles seem not to have suffered much from corrosion, other than in the end panels of the vans, and the lower panels of the doors. Gresley was recorded as saying in 1937 that the all-steel stock had involved higher maintenance but he offered no evidence.

Two types of all-steel vehicle were put in service by the LNER during 1927/8, and the contracts were placed with two builders: Metropolitan Carriage Wagon & Finance Co of Saltley, Birmingham, and Cammell-Laird & Co Ltd of Nottingham. The two firms were soon to merge to form Metropolitan-Cammell.

## DIAGRAM 28

The design for these open thirds followed that of the teak-bodied Diagram 27 fairly closely. Their overall dimensions were the same, but the tumblehome sides of the all-steel bodies were to a different profile, with the result that there were some restrictions on their operation, most notably on the Southern Railway. The external appearance varied to the extent that the windows had radiussed corners instead of being square as with the teak-bodied stock. The exteriors were painted with a grained, lined out and varnished finish to resemble the standard varnished teak livery. The interiors were arranged with three saloons, with 2 + 2 seating, and with one lavatory.

The Diagram 28 coaches seemed mostly to be used in excursion sets, but were also employed as dining cars on the GC section, despite their 2 + 2 seating.

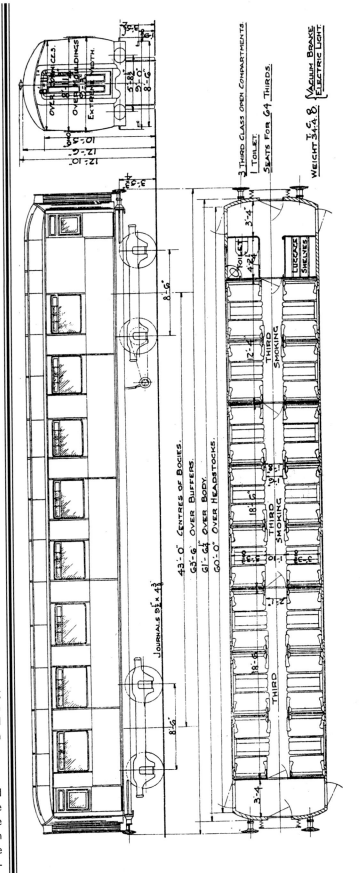

**Diagram 28**

Top: Diagram 45 all-steel full brake No 170 (built Cammell-Laird, 1927, and withdrawn before renumbering under the 1943 scheme). The effect of the ersatz teak livery is somewhat less than convincing. Note the inside solebar 8ft bogies fitted.

Above: No 3801Y (later 23801), one of the pair of Diagram 26 open thirds, formerly intended or used as an ambulance car, and turned out by Stratford Works for the North Eastern Area.

## LIST OF ALL-STEEL OPEN THIRDS (TOVs):

| Diag No CBP | Order No | Compts/ seats | Built | Original number/ changes | 1943 number |
|---|---|---|---|---|---|
| **Built 1927** | | | | | |
| 28 | 1926/7 | - 3† 64 | MET | 42463/4/6/72/6 | 12223-7 |
| | 1927/8 | | | 42481/2/9/90 | 12228-31 |
| | 1926/7 | | | 5529-33 | 12232-6 |
| **Built 1928** | | | | | |
| 28 | 1927/8 | - 3† 64 | MET | 5534-40 | 12237-43 |

The following vehicles were allocated to Scottish Region stock after 1949, and the number prefixed by SC: 12232/3.

## DIAGRAM 45

The Cammell-Laird built brake vans were the more novel in that the design prepared by the contractor had no underframe trussing. Otherwise the outline followed that of the standard 61ft 6in teak bodied full brakes.

Early in 1928 it was noted that Nos 163-76 were allocated to the principal East Coast sets, or held as spares, and they remained on top-link work until at least 1937.

## LIST OF ALL-STEEL PASSENGER BRAKE VANS (Bs):

| Diag No CBP | Order No | Compts/ seats | Built | Original number/ changes | 1943 number |
|---|---|---|---|---|---|
| **Built 1927** | | | | | |
| 45 | 1926/7 | - - | CM | 163-170 | 70039-45/— |
| | | | | | 170 W/O Goswick 1947 |
| **Built 1928** | | | | | |
| 45 | 1926/7 | - - | CM | 35, 37 | 70036/7 |
| | | | | 6700 | 70038 |
| | | | | 171-93 | 70047-69 |

# Open thirds: (TOV)

## DIAGRAM 26

The two coaches to this Diagram have no business to be in a book dealing with LNER standard stock. However, because they were put into traffic in 1924, and later allocated an LNER Diagram, they cannot be ignored.

A number of the pre-Grouping railways built ambulance coaches for the war effort in the last years of World War I, particularly after the entry of the United States into the war. These vehicles seemed to have been deliberately constructed to the same standards and outlines as contemporary vestibuled passenger stock. Some indeed were unfinished or unused at the end of hostilities, and subsequently went into service as passenger coaches. Fourteen ex-ambulance cars of GER design went into traffic as ordinary coaches in 1923 on the LNER.

In the case of the Great Eastern Railway, a number of ambulance train vehicles were still on hand at Grouping, some having been built in 1918, others having been converted for ambulance train use from coaches. Some of the vehicles returned from war use had bodies that were beyond repair or infected and, as seems to have been the case with the two coaches to Diagram 26, they received new bodies to the style in vogue with the company. Some 54ft ward cars from ambulance trains were converted to open thirds at Stratford Works in 1923, and these were similar to the Diagram 26 coaches.

As was the practice in the 1924 CBP, stock for the North Eastern Area, other than for a set train, was built with dual braking, and this was the case with Nos 23801/2.

| Diag No CBP | Order No | Compts/ seats | Built | Original number | 1943 number | |
|---|---|---|---|---|---|---|
| 26 | 1924 | - 2† 42 | SF | 23801/2 | 23801/2 | Dual braked as built |

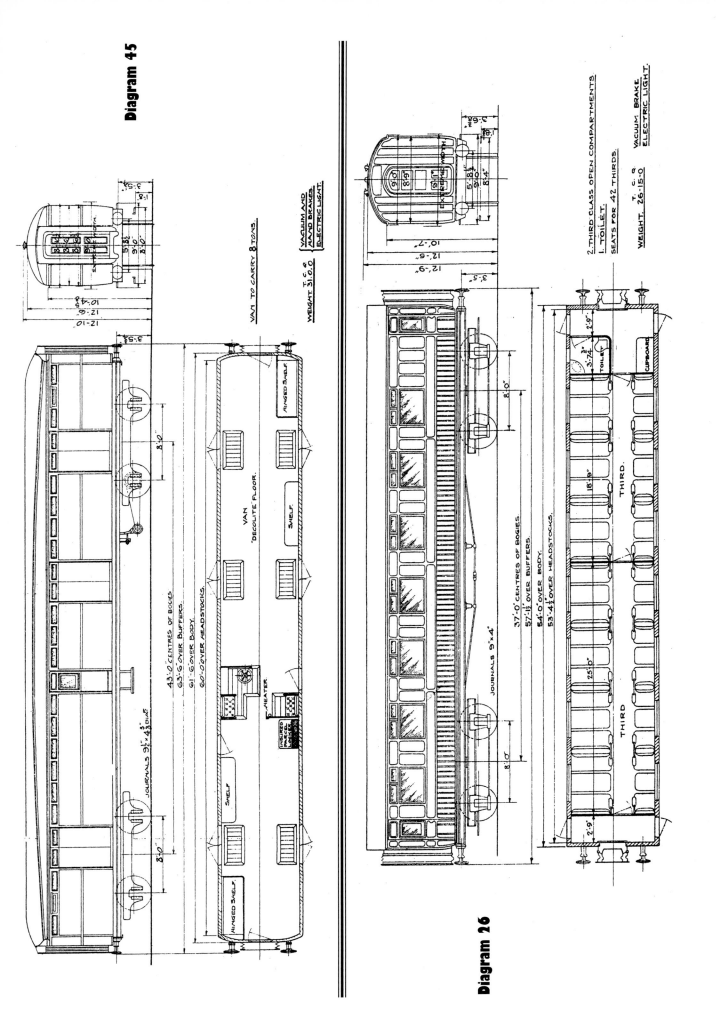

**Diagram 45**

EXTREME WIDTH

10'-4"
12'-6"
12'-10"

5'-8½"
9'-0"
8'-0"

3'-5½"

JOURNALS 9½" x 4⅜" DIAM

43'-0" CENTRES OF BOGIES.
63'-6" OVER BUFFERS.
61'-0" OVER BODY.
60'-0" OVER HEADSTOCKS.

8'-0"

8'-0"

3'-5½"

HINGED SHELF.

VAN
'DECOLITE' FLOOR.

SHELF.

HEATER.

INSURED PARCEL LOCKER.

SHELF.

HINGED SHELF.

VAN TO CARRY 8 TONS.

T. C. Q    VACUUM AND
WEIGHT 31.0.0   HAND BRAKES.
ELECTRIC LIGHT.

**Diagram 26**

EXTREME WIDTH

9'-0"
8'-8"
9'-0"
8'-4"

5'-8½"
9'-0"
8'-4"

10'-7"
12'-5"
12'-9"

3'-5½"

JOURNALS 9" x 4"

37'-0" CENTRES OF BOGIES.
57'-1½" OVER BUFFERS.
54'-0" OVER BODY.
53'-4½" OVER HEADSTOCKS.

8'-0"

8'-0"

2'-9"

3"
3'-7¾"

TOILET

CUPBOARD.

18'-9"

THIRD.

25'-0"

THIRD.

2'-9"

2. THIRD CLASS OPEN COMPARTMENTS
1. TOILET.
SEATS FOR 42 THIRDS.

T. C. Q    VACUUM BRAKE
WEIGHT 26.15.0   ELECTRIC LIGHT.

# NON-PASSENGER STOCK

The standard designs of coaching stock finalised in November/December 1923 included bogie brake vans on 51ft and 60ft underframes, with or without gangways. The two drawings without gangways were Darlington Nos 11995/6, for 51ft and 60ft underframes, but the latter type was never built. The principal designs used by the Company were to drawings Nos 12008/10, the former for a 60ft underframe vestibuled type, the latter for a 51ft underframe type.

Although it was logical that the non-vestibuled vans should be on a 51ft underframe, and with screw couplings, the GE section's 'special requirements', in particular at Liverpool St, meant that a vestibuled 52ft 6in van was specified although relatively few were built. The GE section also received 61ft 6in vans, as well as a number of older less than 61ft vans transferred from East Coast stock.

The bodies of the 60ft and 51ft underframe vestibuled vans followed many of the features of the elliptical roofed vans built for ECJS and GNR service from 1906. The differences were that they had neither their prominent guard's duckets, and side lamps, nor the roof skylights, but instead there were shallow glass lights at cant-rail level. Three pairs of hinged doors were provided each side on the 60ft vans – the ECJS vans tended to have sliding doors – there was a single guard's door each side, and Decolite patented flooring. The 51ft vans had just two pairs of doors each side.

At first, the GNR pressed steel 8ft wheelbase bogie with inside sole-bars were used for all vans. Possibly these were examples recovered from Gresley GNR and ECJS coaches which received compound bolster bogies during the early 1920s. Later the single bolster, outside solebar bogies with 10in x 5in journals were used for the 61ft 6in vans, with the result that a higher payload could be carried.

Non-standard bogie vans resulted from a decision to reuse the underframes of former ECJS and GN/NE sleeping cars while those built at Dukinfield on Diagram 44 possibly used the underframes from GCR-built ambulance cars purchased by the LNER from France in 1923. Similarly, some four-wheeled vans were built using the underframes of GNR Howlden period four-wheelers in 1933, and again in 1935. The carriage building programmes tended to show the brake vans as straight replacements for vehicles either being condemned, or transferred to other

Areas, often noting that four or six-wheeled vans, or non-vestibuled vans were being displaced in favour of vestibuled, bogied vehicles. The numbered East Coast sets were allocated vans, and these are shown in the formations listed in the Appendix. The all-steel full brakes are described in the section dealing with special vehicles.

The LNER was never very keen on non-bogie vans, but some four-wheeled vans were built, although the North Eastern Area's plan to specify six-wheeled vans in the 1925/6 CBP was by all accounts overruled by the chief general manager. Also, four-wheeled milk vans were constructed in 1927, and these and the contemporary vans were in the passenger stock series. The miscellaneous collection of covered carriage trucks, horseboxes and cattle vans were regarded as non-common user, and they are not described in this book.

Last, but certainly not least, are the TPO vans, of which just three were built before 1930, and these alone are covered in this book.

## Vestibuled brake vans: (BV)

### 61ft 6in – DIAGRAMS 43, 113, 245, 260

Diagram 43 vehicles were produced from 1924-8, and had a payload of eight tons. Diagram 113 was very similar, except that there was a guard's ducket on the right-hand side of the body. Some of these vans had 10in x 5in journals, and an increased payload of 10 tons. The type was supplanted by the steel panelled Diagram 198 which was built from 1935, but subsequently Diagram 245 with teak panelling was introduced.

Two Diagram 113 vans were converted to cinema cars from 1935/6-42 but in this state they are not described in this book.

Diagram 245 was generally as Diagram 113, and teak panelled, and vans to this design were built from 1938-43. They were principally intended for racing pigeon traffic, and were fitted with shelves along each side of the interior to accommodate the pigeon baskets. The racing pigeon federations insisted on vestibuled, electrically-lit vans as in those days the owners travelled throughout with the pigeons on their journey for release. Payload, 10 tons.

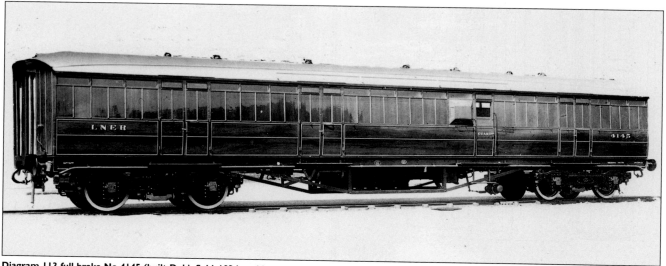

Diagram 113 full brake No 4145 (built Dukinfield, 1934, and became 70169 under the 1943 renumbering).

## Diagram 43

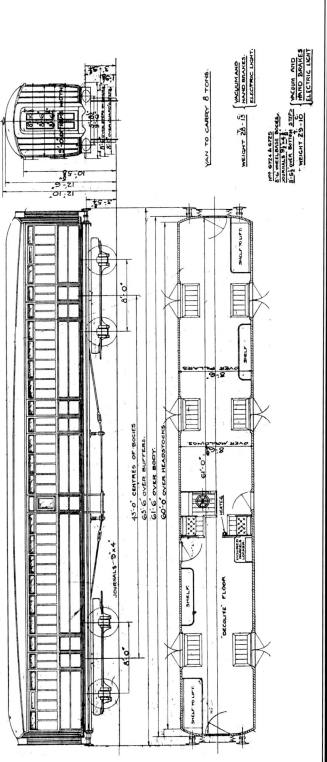

45'-0" CENTRES OF BOGIES.

63'-6" OVER BUFFERS.

61'-6" OVER BODY.

60'-0" OVER HEADSTOCKS.

JOURNALS—9"x4".

6'-0"

8'-6" OVER PILLARS.

61'-0" OVER MOULDINGS.

"DECOLITE" FLOOR.

SHELF

HEATER.

MOUNTED PARCELS LOCKER

SHELF TO LIFT.

SHELF TO LIFT

VAN TO CARRY 8 TONS.

WEIGHT 28-15 { VACUUM AND HAND BRAKES. ELECTRIC LIGHT.

Nos 6724 & 6725
8'-6" WHEELBASE BOGIES.
JOURNALS 9"x4".
8'-5½" OVER BOTTOM STEP
WEIGHT 29-10 { T. C. VACUUM AND HAND BRAKES ELECTRIC LIGHT

---

## Diagram 113

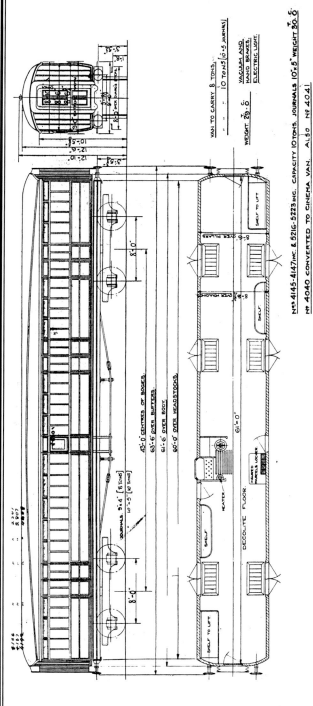

45'-0" CENTRES OF BOGIES.

63'-6" OVER BUFFERS.

61'-6" OVER BODY.

60'-0" OVER HEADSTOCKS.

JOURNALS 9"x4" [8 TONS]
10"x5" [10 TONS]

8'-0"

61'-0"

8'-6" OVER PILLARS.

8'-0" OVER MOULDINGS.

"DECOLITE" FLOOR.

SHELF

HEATER.

HEATED PARCELS LOCKER

SHELF TO LIFT.

SHELF TO LIFT

VAN TO CARRY 8 TONS, ...... { ..... 10 TON 5 (10·5 JOURNALS)

WEIGHT 29-0 { T. C. VACUUM AND HAND BRAKES. ELECTRIC LIGHT.

Nos 4145-4147 INC. & 5216-5223 INC. CAPACITY 10 TONS. JOURNALS 10"x5" WEIGHT 30-0

No 4040 CONVERTED TO CINEMA VAN. ALSO No 4041

**Diagram 245**

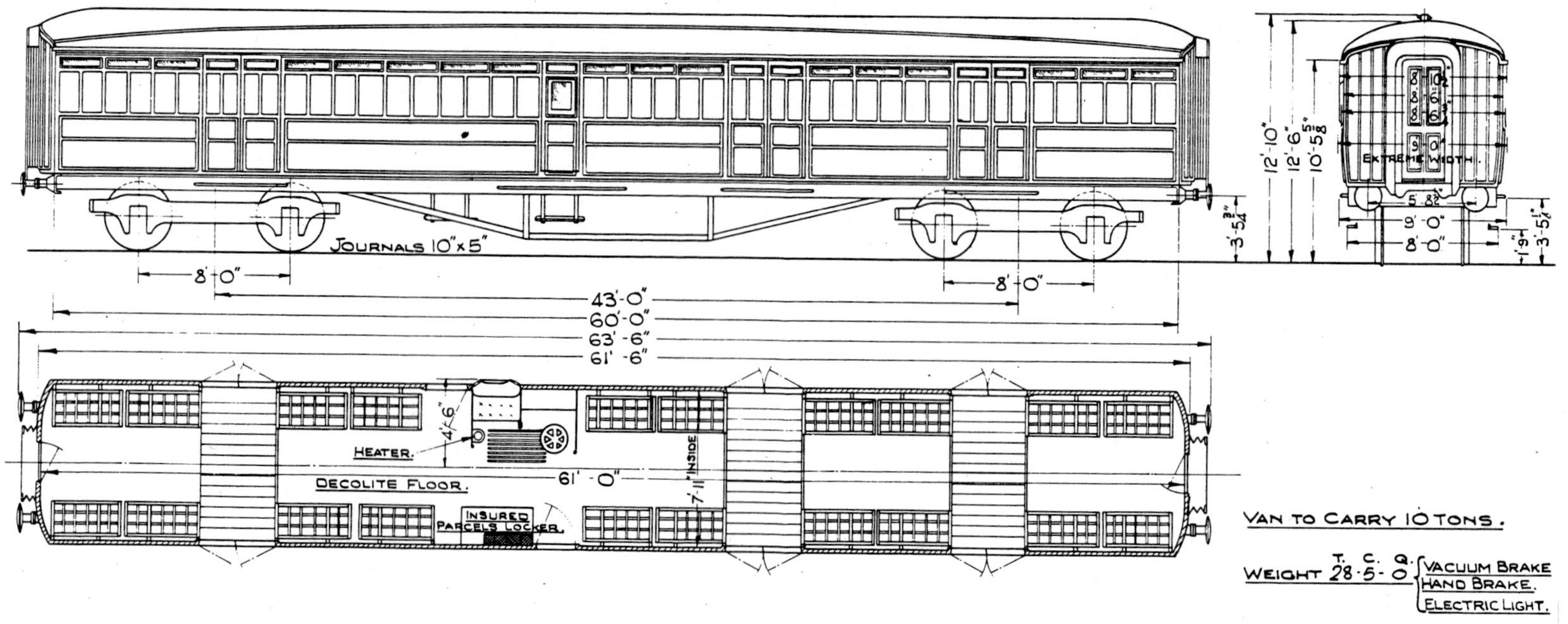

VAN TO CARRY 10 TONS.

WEIGHT 28·5·0 { VACUUM BRAKE
                HAND BRAKE.
                ELECTRIC LIGHT.

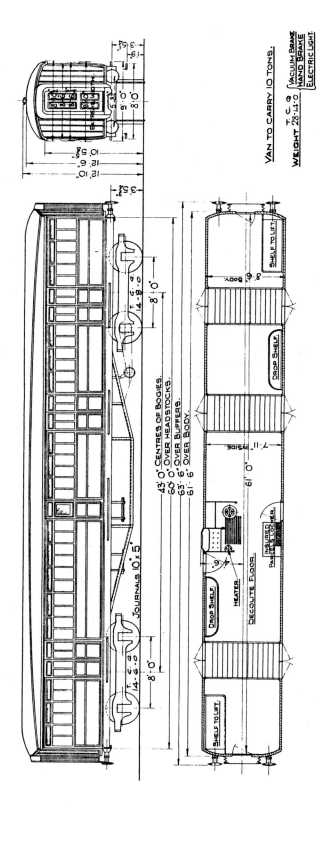

**Diagram 260**

VAN TO CARRY 10 TONS.

WEIGHT 28·14·0 { VACUUM BRAKE
                 HAND BRAKE
                 ELECTRIC LIGHT.

Diagram 245 full brake No E70765E (built York, 1943) is seen in the final condition for many of these vans, in BR's all-blue livery with white lettering. At Inverness, March 1974. Intended as a full brake but actually turned out as a ward car for a World War 2 ambulance train.

Again, there was something of a confusion during World War 2, in that a new Diagram, 315, was issued to cover vans to 9ft width, but with steel panelling. Later these were shown as Diagram 245.

Somewhat confusingly, Diagram 260 included vans with either steel, or with teak panelling, and these differed from Diagram 245 as the body was to an overall width of 8ft 11½in.

It is possible that some of this confusion arises from the fact that the bogie brakes served as ward cars in World War 2 ambulance trains and, indeed, were the largest single group of vehicles converted, the LNER supplying 70 ward cars, 21 of which were converted from Diag 198 brake vans. Although there is no confirmation it would appear that the Diag 245 and 260 vehicles (70740-67) included some actually completed as ward cars.

In May 1945, the LNER's Emergency Board of Directors approved the fitting of partitions in 352 vestibuled brake vans. No 70499 (Diagram 245) was the first to receive the guard's enclosure which made the guard's life more comfortable. In that connection, a number of vans were also fitted with coal stoves to heat the interior.

## LIST OF PASSENGER BRAKE VANS (Bs):

| Diag No CBP | Order No | Built | Original number/ changes | 1943 number | |
|---|---|---|---|---|---|
| **Built 1924** | | | | | |
| 43* | 1924/5 | 43 | YK | 10233-9J (140[5270]/1-146) | 70017/20/ — /2-5 |
| **Built 1925** | | | | | |
| 43* | 1924/5 | 59 | SF | 6724 | 70018 |
| | | 60 | | 10246E (6725) | 70019 | Continental boat sets |
| **Built 1926** | | | | | |
| 43* | 1924/5 | 67 | YK | 160-162 | 70026-8 |
| | | | | 7135-7 | 70000-2 |
| | | | | (342-4) | | Transferred 1928/9 CBP |
| **Built 1928** | | | | | |
| 43* | 1927/8 | 203 | DR | 4184-90 | 70003-9 |
| | | | | 5201-7 | 70010-6 |
| **Built 1929** | | | | | |
| 113* | 1928/9 | 265 | DR | 5208-12 | 70176-80 |
| | | | | 149 | 70193 |
| | | 266 | YK | 5213/4 | 70181/2 |
| | | | | 4028/34/40/1/59, | 70160-4, |
| | | | | 4171/9/92/3 | 70172-5 | 4040/1 converted to cinema cars |
| **Built 1930** | | | | | |
| 113* | 1930/1 | 363 | DR | 117/8 | 70191/2 |
| **Built 1931** | | | | | |
| 113* | 1930/1 | 395 | DR | 4136-9 | 70165-8 |
| **Built 1932** | | | | | |
| 113* | 1931/2 | 450 | DK | 5219/20 | 70186/7 |

| Diag No CBP | | | | Original number/ changes | 1943 number | |
|---|---|---|---|---|---|---|
| **Built 1933** | | | | | | |
| 113* | 1933 | 496 | DK | 5216-8/21-3 | 70183-5/8-90 | |
| **Built 1934** | | | | | | |
| 113* | 1934 | 573 | DK | 4145-7 | 70169-71 | |
| **Built 1938** | | | | | | |
| 245* | 1937 | 777 | YK | 2426-39 | 70412-25 | |
| | | | | 4233-47 | 70456-70 | |
| | 1938 | 870 | | 4213-20 | 70448-55 | |
| **Built 1939** | | | | | | |
| 245* | 1937 | 777 | YK | 4248-53 | 70471-6 | |
| | | | | 5274-80 | 70499-70505 | |
| | 1938 | 870 | | 5281-3 | 70506-8 | |
| | special | 878 | | 1011 | 70514 | Accident replacement |
| **Built 1943** | | | | | | |
| 245* | 1940 | 1073 | YK | 70740/50-66 | 70752 W/O Ilford 1944 70753 W/O | |
| 260* | 1940 | 1059 -1061 | YK | 70741-9/67 | | |

## NON-STANDARD LENGTHS
These vestibuled vans all followed the general outline of the Diagram 43 and 113 vans, but were built on different length underframes.

### DIAGRAM 44
Possibly these were built on the underframes of former GCR-built ambulance train vehicles, a number of which were purchased by the LNER from a contractor.

### DIAGRAM 111, 154, 282
These were built for the GE section, to match the vestibuled coaches also on the 51ft underframe. They ran on the 8ft wheelbase bogie, and the payload was restricted to eight tons. Diagrams 154/282 had a guard's ducket, and there were also minor dimensional changes with these diagrams as compared with Diagram 111.

### DIAGRAM 207 58ft 6in
### AND DIAGRAM 208 56ft 6in
The cost of the combined 1935/6 carriage building programme was such that the chief accountant put pressure on all concerned to save money on new construction. As a result, the underframes of four condemned sleeping cars built for the ECJS and GN/NE Joint stock were used for new vans, otherwise virtually identical to the standard length vehicles.

## LIST OF PASSENGER BRAKE VANS (Bs):

| Diag No CBP | Order No | Built | Original number/ changes | 1943 number |
|---|---|---|---|---|
| **Built 1926** | | | | |
| 44 | 1925/6 119 | DK | 153-9 | 70029-35 |
| **Built 1928** | | | | |
| 111* | 1927/8 204 | YK | 6739-48 | 70145-54 |
| **Built 1930** | | | | |
| 111* | 1929/30 321 | DR | 6749-53 | 70155-9 |
| **Built 1932** | | | | |
| 154 | 1930/1 394 | YK | 6754-63 | 70280-9 |
| **Built 1935** | | | | |
| 207 | 1935/6 573 | DR | 4197 | 70396 |
| 208 | 1935/6 573 | DR | 4194-6 | 70397-9 |

Nos 4197. 4194-6 on recovered underframes from sleeping cars Nos 1410, 1146/8/51 — see text.

| | | | | |
|---|---|---|---|---|
| **Built 1938** | | | | |
| 282 | 1937 778 | YK | 6785-90/7 | 70554-60 |

**Diagram 44**

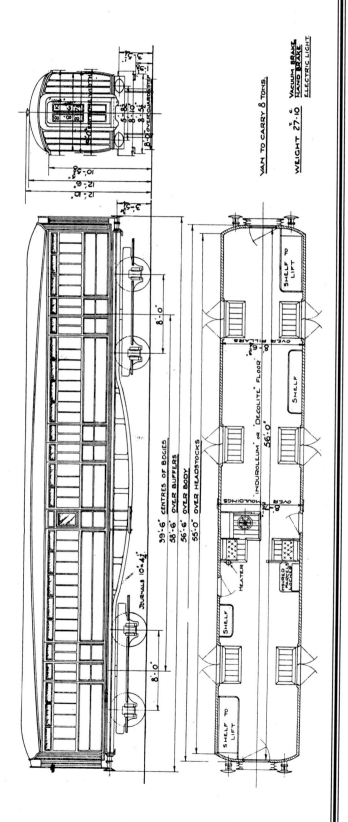

JOURNALS 10'-4"

39'-6" CENTRES OF BOGIES
58'-6" OVER BUFFERS
56'-6" OVER BODY
55'-0" OVER HEADSTOCKS

8'-0"

"INLAIDLINOLEUM" or "DECOLITE" FLOOR

56'-0"

OVER MOULDINGS

8'-6" OVER PILLARS

SHELF TO LIFT

SHELF

SHELF

HEATER

INSURED PARCELS LOCKER

SHELF TO LIFT

SHELF TO LIFT

VAN TO CARRY 8 TONS.

T. C.
WEIGHT 27·10

VACUUM BRAKE
HAND BRAKE
ELECTRIC LIGHT

---

**Diagram 111**

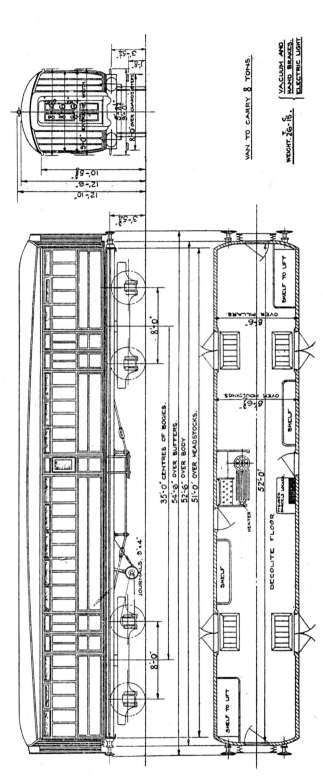

JOURNALS. 9'-4"

35'-0" CENTRES OF BOGIES.
54'-6" OVER BUFFERS
52'-6" OVER BODY
51'-0" OVER HEADSTOCKS.

8'-0"

8'-6" OVER PILLARS

8'-6" OVER MOULDINGS

DECOLITE FLOOR

52'-0"

SHELF TO LIFT

SHELF

HEATER

INSURED PARCELS LOCKER

SHELF

SHELF TO LIFT

VAN TO CARRY 8 TONS.

T. C.
WEIGHT 26·15.

VACUUM AND
HAND BRAKES.
ELECTRIC LIGHT

**Diagram 154**

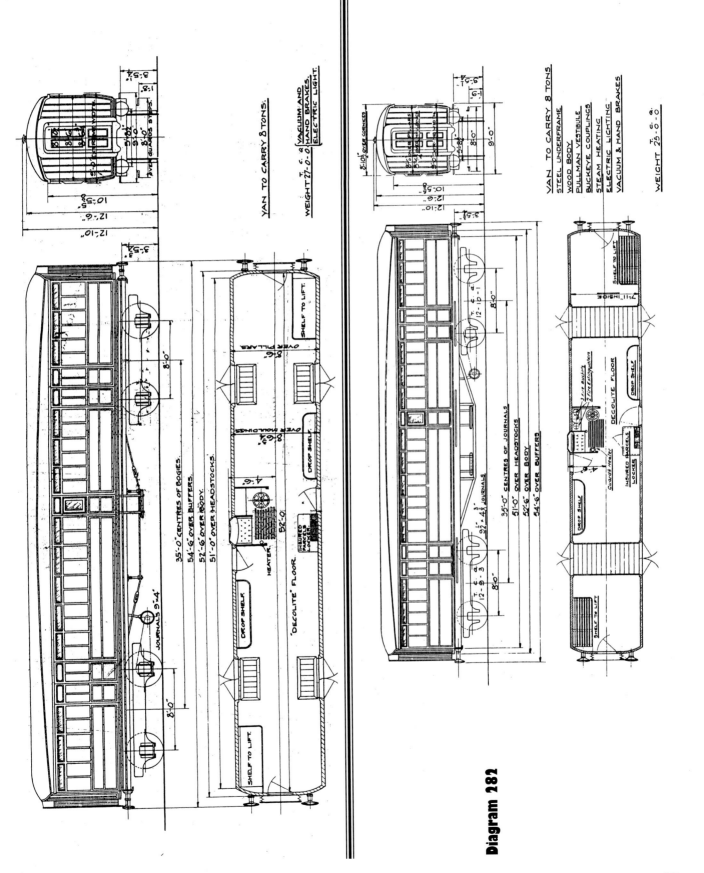

VAN TO CARRY 8 TONS.

T.C.B. @ VACUUM AND
WEIGHT 27-0-0. HAND BRAKES.
ELECTRIC LIGHT.

35'-0" CENTRES OF BOGIES.
54'-6" OVER BUFFERS.
52'-6" OVER BODY.
51'-0" OVER HEADSTOCKS.

JOURNALS 9"×4".

8'-6" OVER PILLARS.

8'-6" OVER MOULDINGS.

52'-0"

SHELF TO LIFT.

DROP SHELF

"DECOLITE" FLOOR

HEATER

INSURED PARCELS LOCKERS

**Diagram 282**

35'-0" CENTRES OF JOURNALS
51'-0" OVER HEADSTOCKS
52'-6" OVER BODY
54'-6" OVER BUFFERS

VAN TO CARRY 8 TONS

STEEL UNDERFRAME
WOOD BODY
PULLMAN VESTIBULE
BUCKEYE COUPLINGS
STEAM HEATING
ELECTRIC LIGHTING
VACUUM & HAND BRAKES

T.C.B.
WEIGHT 25-0-0

SHELF TO LIFT.

DECOLITE FLOOR

DROP SHELF

Guards Heater

INSURED PARCELS LOCKERS

7'-11" INSIDE

179

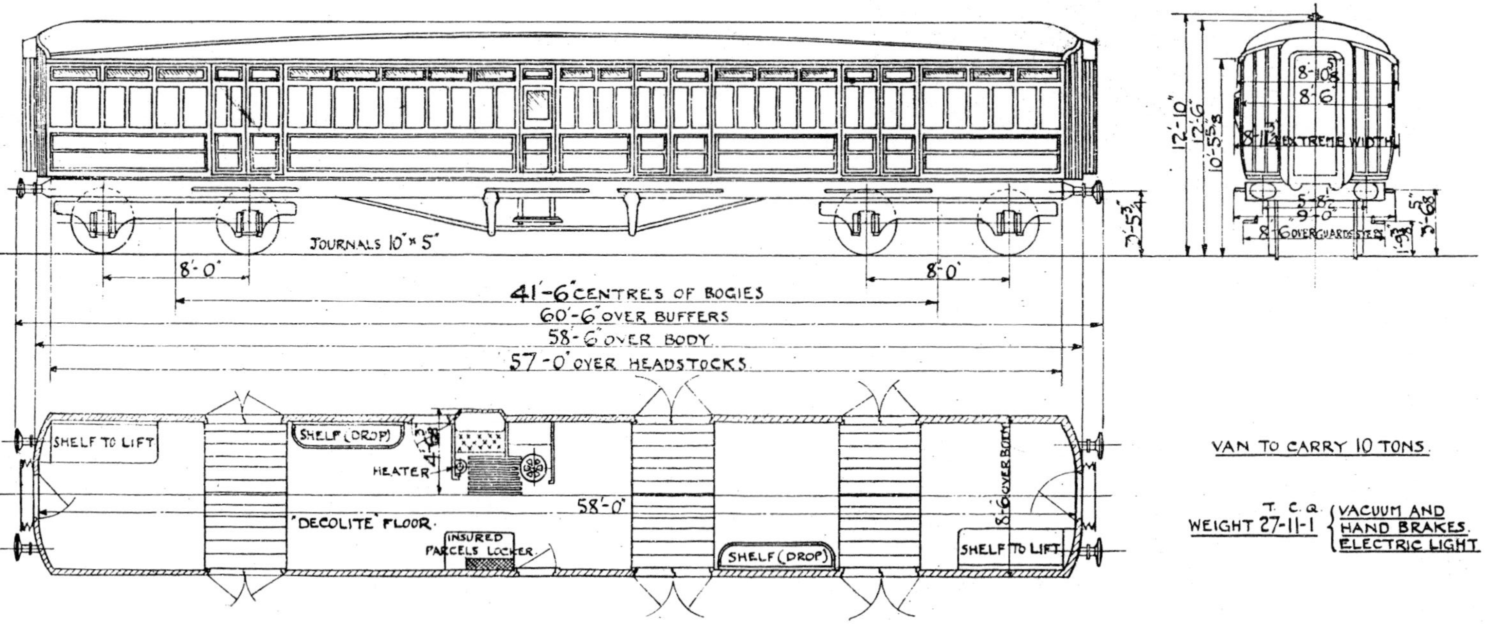

**Diagram 207**

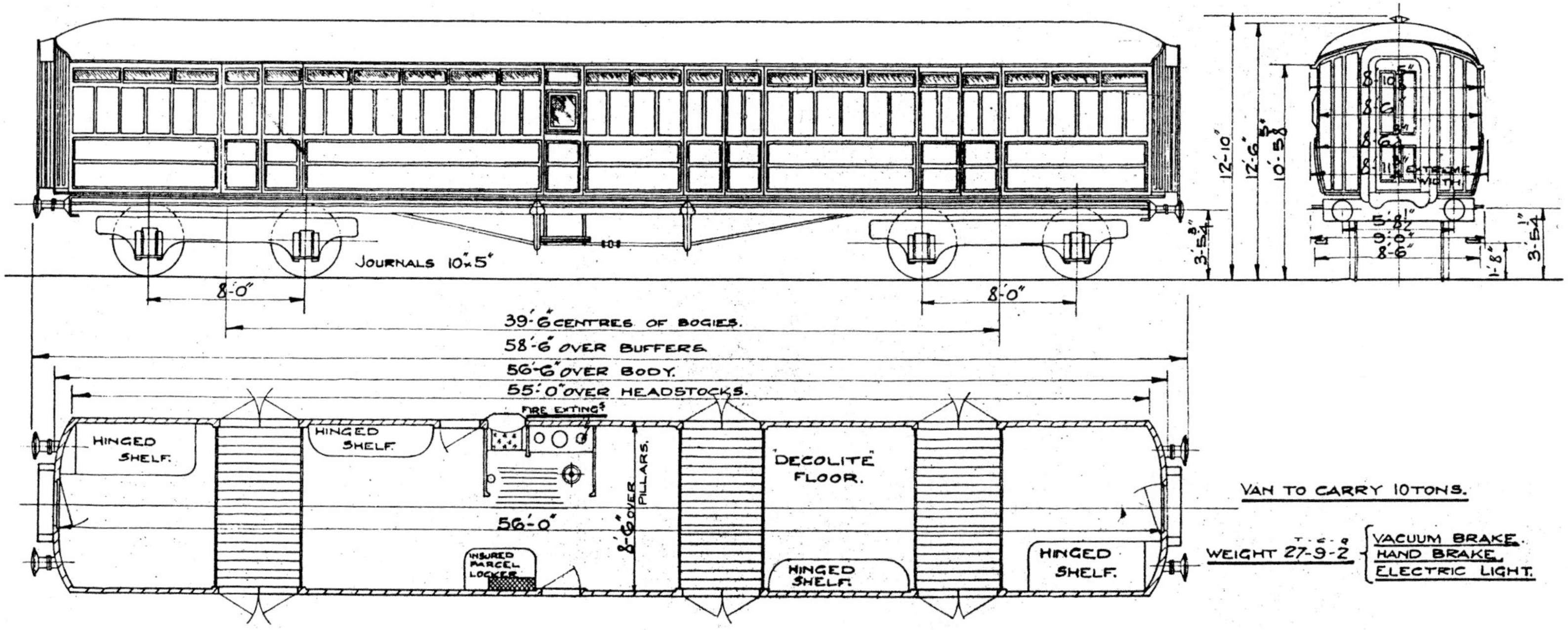

VAN TO CARRY 10 TONS.

T.C.Q. VACUUM AND
WEIGHT 27-11-1 HAND BRAKES
ELECTRIC LIGHT

41'-6" CENTRES OF BOGIES
60'-6" OVER BUFFERS
58'-0" OVER BODY
57'-0" OVER HEADSTOCKS

JOURNALS 10" × 5"

8'-0"

58'-0"

SHELF TO LIFT
SHELF (DROP)
HEATER
"DECOLITE" FLOOR.
INSURED PARCELS LOCKER
OVER BODY
SHELF TO LIFT
SHELF (DROP)

**Diagram 208**

VAN TO CARRY 10 TONS.

T.C.Q. VACUUM BRAKE
WEIGHT 27-9-2 HAND BRAKE.
ELECTRIC LIGHT.

39'-6" CENTRES OF BOGIES.
58'-6" OVER BUFFERS.
56'-6" OVER BODY.
55'-0" OVER HEADSTOCKS.

JOURNALS 10×5"

8'-0"

56'-0"

8'-6" OVER PILLARS.

HINGED SHELF.
HINGED SHELF.
FIRE EXTING?
HEATED PARCEL LOCKER
"DECOLITE" FLOOR.
HINGED SHELF.
HINGED SHELF.

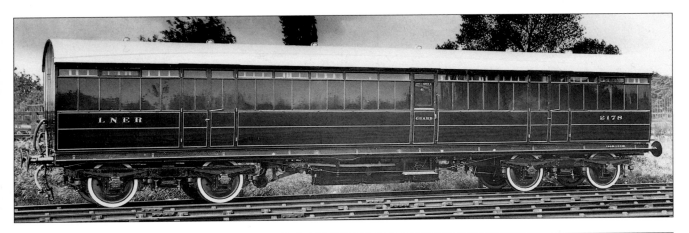

# Non-vestibuled brake vans: (B) and pigeon vans: (P)

### DIAGRAMS 67, 129, 284, 357

These were all on the 51ft underframe, and were principally built for the GE section, earlier examples being dual-fitted. Diagrams 129 and 284 had a guard's ducket, and 129 was built for racing pigeon traffic, the interior of these vans having shelves to accommodate the baskets.

Van 70561 of Diagram 284 was converted to a stowage van in replacement of an earlier vehicle destroyed in the Gidea Park accident of January 1947. The conversion involved the fitting of offset gangways, and two pairs of sliding doors on each side, and was coded Diagram 357. Diagram 129 van No 70268 was rebuilt as a PO tender in the early 1950s.

### LIST OF PASSENGER BRAKE VANS (Bs) OR PIGEON VANS (Ps):

| Diag No | CBP | Order No | Built | Original number/ changes | 1943 number | |
|---------|-----|----------|-------|--------------------------|-------------|---|
| **Built 1926** | | | | | | |
| 67* | 1925/6 | 126 | DK | 31, 6686-90 ≠ | 70070-5 | |
| **Built 1927** | | | | | | |
| 67* | 1925/6 | 126 | DK | 6691-3 | 70076-8 | ≠ |
| **Built 1928** | | | | | | |
| 129* | 1927/8 | 213 | YK | 2178/99, 2246, 2306 | 70251-4 | ≠ |
| **Built 1931** | | | | | | |
| 129* | 1930/1 | 400 | DR | 6764-83 70268 to TPO tender | 70255-74 | |

Top: **Diagram 129 full brake No 2178 (built York, 1928, and later 70251)** was one of just four built for other than the Great Eastern section. It was dual fitted as built.

Above: **Diagram 129 full brake E70276E (built York, 1938, and originally No 6791). At Kittybrewster, May 1966.**

| Diag No | CBP | Order No | Built | Original number/ changes | 1943 number | |
|---------|-----|----------|-------|--------------------------|-------------|---|
| **Built 1937** | | | | | | |
| 129* | special | 749 | YK | 6784 | 70275 | |
| **Built 1938** | | | | | | |
| 129* | special | 788 | YK | 6791 | 70276 | |
| **Built 1939** | | | | | | |
| 284* | 1938 | 871 | YK | 6792-6 | 70561¶/ 2/3/ — /4 | 6795 W/O |
| | | | | 70561 converted in 1949 to a PO stowage van, to Dia 357 | | |

# Four-wheel brake vans: (BY)

### DIAGRAM 120, 170, 176, 177

Once again, the GE section managed to specify a non-standard type, despite the fact that the LNER generally was not keen on building non-bogie passenger full brake stock!

A number of four-wheel vans built under the 1933 programme used the underframes of Howlden suburban coaches, no less than 200 of these having been withdrawn at the end of 1932.

### LIST OF FOUR-WHEEL PASSENGER BRAKE VANS (BYs):

| Diag No | CBP | Order No | Built | Original number/ changes | 1943 number | |
|---------|-----|----------|-------|--------------------------|-------------|---|
| **Built 1928** | | | | | | |
| 120* | 1927/8 | 212/225 267 | SF | 6801-14 6815-29 | 70194-70207 70208-22 | ≠ |

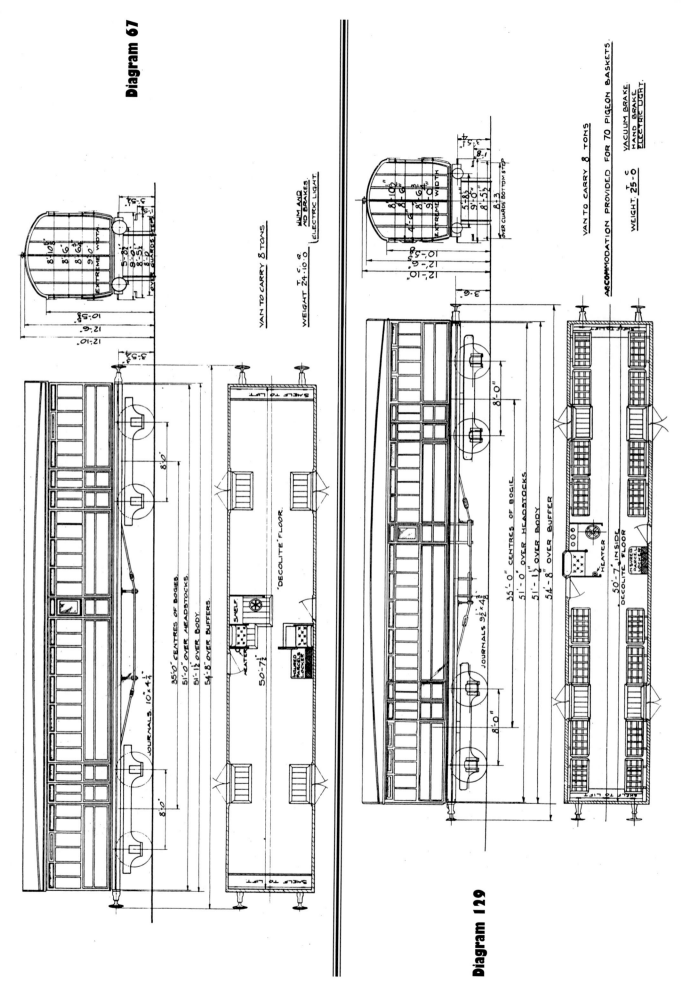

**Diagram 67**

EXTREME WIDTH

8'·10⅝"
8'·6"
8'·6¾"
9'·0"

10'·5⅝"
12'·6"
12'·10"

OVER GUARD STEPS

VAN TO CARRY 8 TONS

W/M AND AVO BRAKES
(ELECTRIC LIGHT)

T. C. G.
WEIGHT 24·10·0

JOURNALS. 10" × 4¼"

35'·0" CENTRES OF BOGIES
51'·0" OVER HEADSTOCKS
51'·1½" OVER BODY
54'·8" OVER BUFFERS

'DECOLITE' FLOOR.

SHELF TO LIFT

SHELF

HEATER

FLOORED PARCEL LOCKER

50'·7½"

SHELF TO LIFT

**Diagram 129**

EXTREME WIDTH

8'·10½"
8'·6"
8'·6¾"
9'·0"
4'·6"

5'·8⅝"
9'·0"
8'·5¾"
8'·3
OVER GUARDS BOTTOM STEP

10'·5⅝"
12'·6"
12'·10"

3'·6"

VAN TO CARRY 8 TONS

ACCOMMODATION PROVIDED FOR 70 PIGEON BASKETS.

VACUUM BRAKE
HAND BRAKE
ELECTRIC LIGHT.

T C
WEIGHT 25·0

JOURNALS 9½" × 4¾"

8'·0"

35'·0" CENTRES OF BOGIE
51'·0" OVER HEADSTOCKS
51'·1½" OVER BODY
54'·8" OVER BUFFER

8'·0"

HEATER

FLOORED PARCEL LOCKER

50'·7½" INSIDE
DECOLITE FLOOR

SHELF TO LIFT

SHELF TO LIFT

# Diagram 284

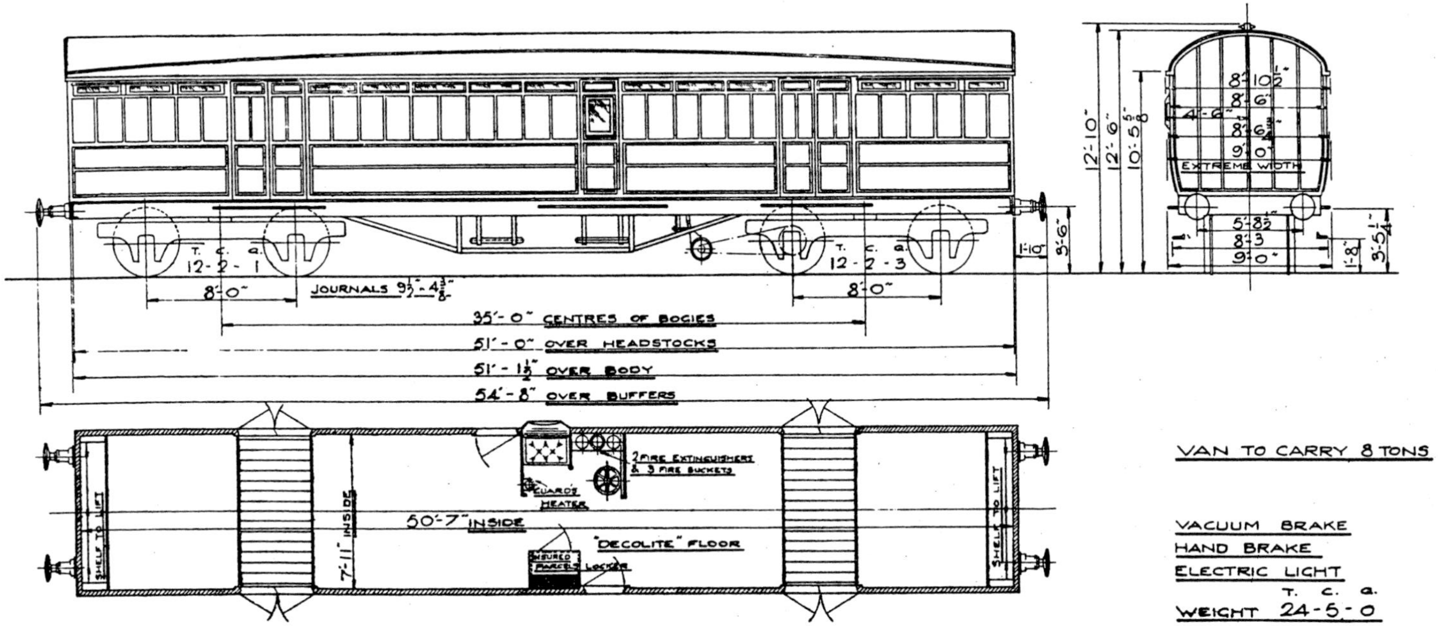

VAN TO CARRY 8 TONS

VACUUM BRAKE
HAND BRAKE
ELECTRIC LIGHT
T. C. a.
WEIGHT 24·5·0

35'-0" CENTRES OF BOGIES
51'-0" OVER HEADSTOCKS
51'-1½" OVER BODY
54'-8" OVER BUFFERS

JOURNALS 9½ x 4⅛"

T. C. a.
12'-2·3"
8'-0"

T. C. a.
12'-2·1"
8'-0"

9'·6"
10'·1"

EXTREME WIDTH
12'-10"
12'-6"
10'-5⅝"

10'·2"
8'·8"
9'·6"
6'·6"
4'·6"

5'-8½"
8'·3"
9'·0"

9'·6"

50'-7" INSIDE

"DECOLITE" FLOOR

2 PASS EXTINGUISHERS
& 3 FIRE BUCKETS

DONDROL
HEATER

SHELF TO LIFT

7'-11" INSIDE

# Diagram 357

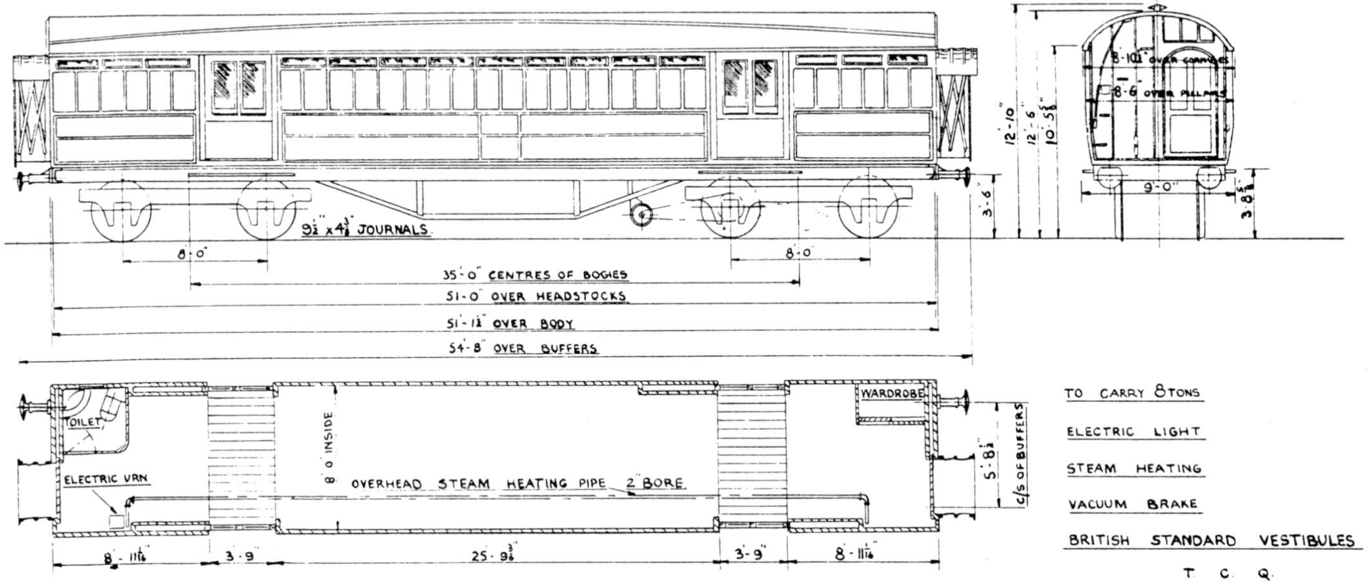

TO CARRY 8 TONS
ELECTRIC LIGHT
STEAM HEATING
VACUUM BRAKE
BRITISH STANDARD VESTIBULES
T. C. Q.
WEIGHT - 24·0·0

35'-0" CENTRES OF BOGIES
51'-0" OVER HEADSTOCKS
51'-1½" OVER BODY
54'-8" OVER BUFFERS

9½" x 4½" JOURNALS

8'-0"
8'-0"

3'-6"
12'-10"
12'-6"
10'-5½"

8'-10"
8'-6" OVER PILLAR
9'-0"

3'·6"

WARDROBE

C/S OF BUFFERS
5'-8½"

3'-9"
8'-11½"

OVERHEAD STEAM HEATING PIPE 2" BORE

8'-0" INSIDE

25'-9¾"

TOILET
ELECTRIC VRN

8'-11½"
3'-9"

WATER TANK CAPACITY - 39 GALLONS

**Diagram 120**

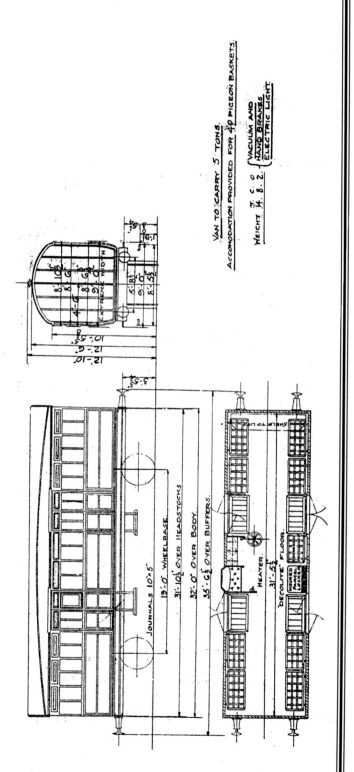

VAN TO CARRY 5 TONS.
ACCOMMODATION PROVIDED FOR 40 PIGEON BASKETS.
WEIGHT 14. 8. 2. {VACUUM AND HAND BRAKES ELECTRIC LIGHT.

JOURNALS 10"×5".
19'-0" WHEELBASE.
31'-10½" OVER HEADSTOCKS.
32'-0" OVER BODY.
35'-6½" OVER BUFFERS.

EXTREME WIDTH.
10'-5½"
12'-6"
12'-10"

HEATER.
'DECOLITE' FLOOR.
31'-5½"

**Diagram 170**

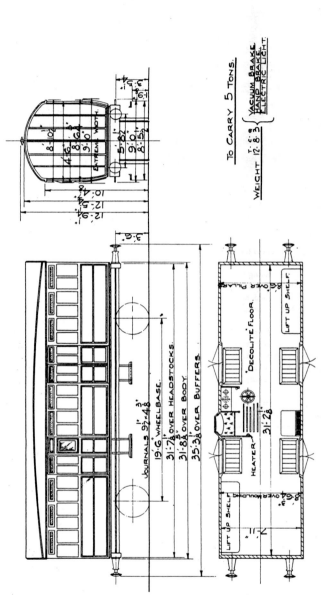

TO CARRY 5 TONS.
WEIGHT 12. 8. 3. {VACUUM BRAKE HAND BRAKE ELECTRIC LIGHT.

JOURNALS 9½"×4⅞".
19'-6" WHEELBASE.
31'-7½" OVER HEADSTOCKS.
31'-8½" OVER BODY.
35'-3½" OVER BUFFERS.

EXTREME WIDTH.
10'-4½"
12'-0½"
12'-6"

LIFT UP SHELF.
'DECOLITE' FLOOR.
HEATER.
31'-2½"

Above: **Diagram 120 brake van No 6820** (built Stratford, 1928, and No 70213 under the 1943 numbering). These were dual fitted as built.

Right: **A Diagram 120 van, No 70229** (built Stratford, 1929 as 6837) is behind the 'N2' 0-6-2T No 9550 in this picture of the 4.35pm Nottingham Victoria-Mansfield leaving Bulwell Common on 9 August 1947. Next the van is a North Eastern Diagram 178 non-vestibuled third, then an LNER lavatory composite, an NBR vestibuled coach and an NER brake.

Below right: **Diagram 120 van, classified BYP by BR, E70221E** (built Stratford 1928, as 6828). Branded 'on loan Easingwold Light Railway' and photographed at Easingwold, 1957. XP branding to denote its clearance to run on passenger trains.

Below: **The net and traductor arm side of Diagram 131 TPO van No 2339** (built York, 1929). Later 6132, it became 70279 under the 1943 scheme).

**Diagram 176**

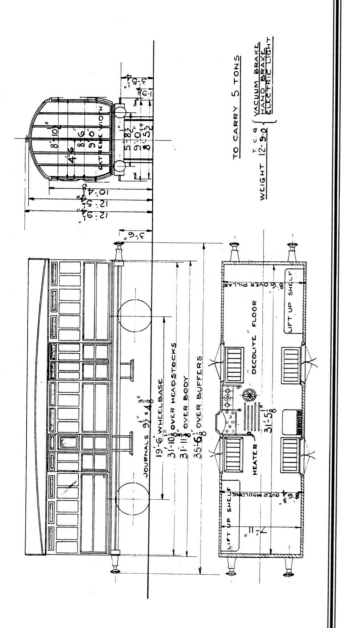

TO CARRY 5 TONS.

T.C.Q. { VACUUM BRAKE
WEIGHT 12-9-0 { HAND BRAKE
{ ELECTRIC LIGHT

**Diagram 177**

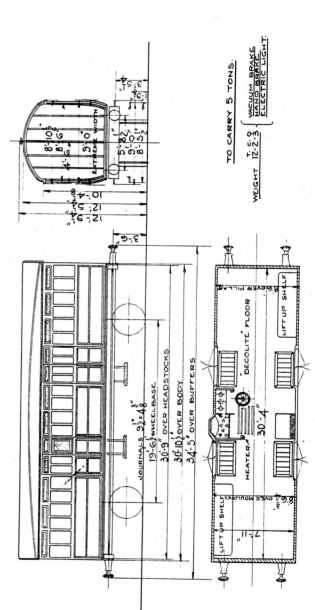

TO CARRY 5 TONS.

T.C.Q. { VACUUM BRAKE
WEIGHT 12-2-3 { HAND BRAKE
{ ELECTRIC LIGHT.

**Diagram 86**

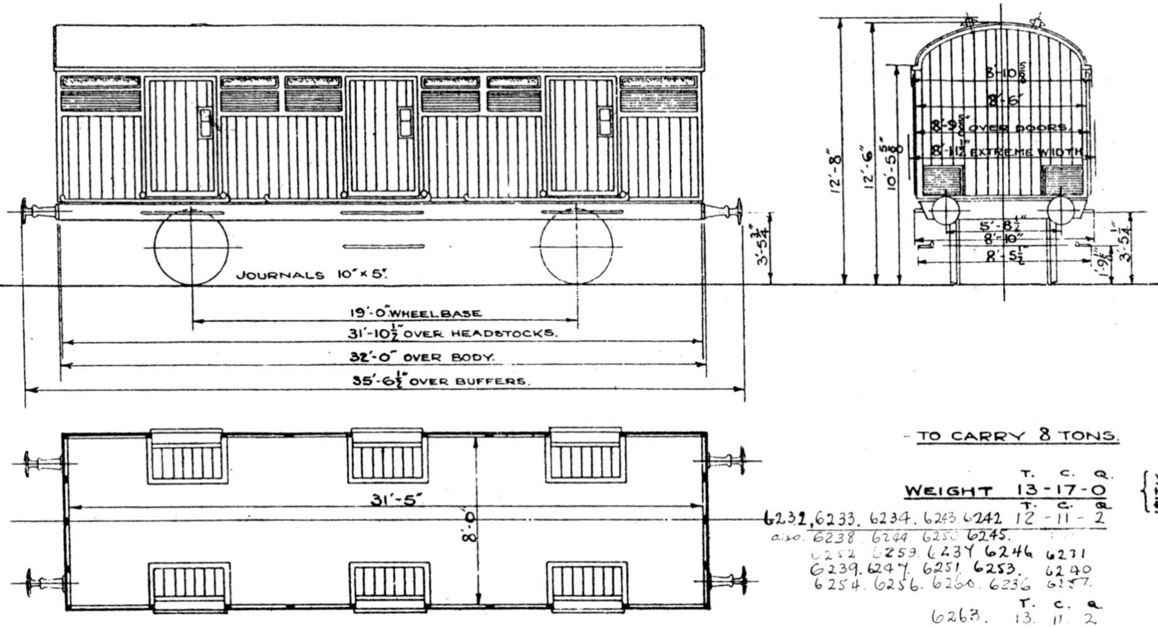

12'-8"
12'-6"
10'-5"(min)

8'-6"
8'-11½"EXTREME WIDTH
8'-9"OVER DOORS.

3'-5¼"
1'-6½"
5'-8½"
8'-6"
8'-5½"

JOURNALS 10"x 5'
19'-0"WHEELBASE.
31'-10½"OVER HEADSTOCKS.
32'-0"OVER BODY.
35'-6½"OVER BUFFERS.

8'-0"
31'-5'

VACUUM AND HAND LEVER BRAKE.
ELECTRIC LIGHT.
Oil Lamps.

—TO CARRY 8 TONS.

T. C. Q.
WEIGHT 13-17-0

WEIGHT 13-17-0    12-11-2

6232, 6233, 6234, 6243, 6242, 6245.
also  6238  6244  6250  6245.
6242  6259  6243  6246  6271
6239, 6247  6251  6253  6240
6254  6256  6260  6232  6257.
T. C. Q.
6263.  13  11  2

**Diagram 87**

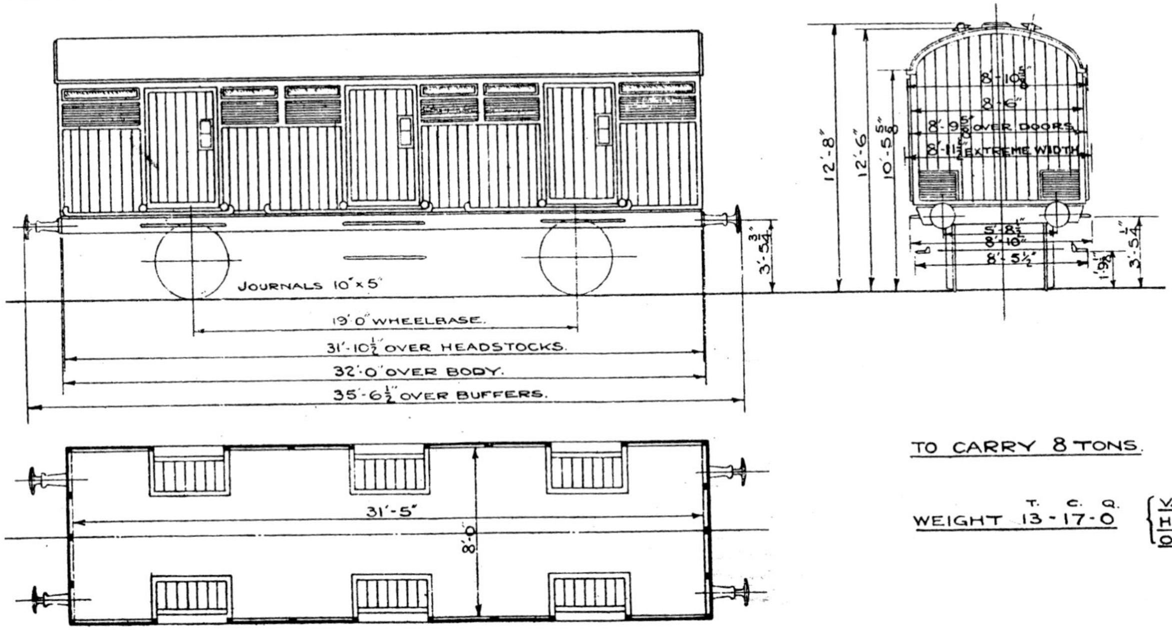

12'-8"
12'-6"
10'-5"(min)

8'-6"
8'-10½"
8'-9"OVER DOORS.
8'-11"EXTREME WIDTH

3'-5¼"
1'-6½"
5'-8½"
8'-6"

3'-5¼"

JOURNALS 10"x 5'
19'-0"WHEELBASE.
31'-10½"OVER HEADSTOCKS.
32'-0"OVER BODY.
35'-6½"OVER BUFFERS.

8'-0"
31'-5'

VACUUM AND HAND LEVER BRAKE.
OIL LIGHTING.

TO CARRY 8 TONS.

T. C. Q.
WEIGHT 13-17-0

187

**Diagram 131**

**Built 1929**

| | | | | | | | |
|---|---|---|---|---|---|---|---|
| 120* | 1928/9 | 267 | SF | 6830-9 | 70223/ — /4-31 | 6831 DEA | |
| | 1929/30 | 325 | YK | 6840-7/8 (772), | 70232-4/ — /5/6/ — /7, ≠ | | |
| | | | | 6850 | 70246/40 | | |

**Built 1930**

| | | | | | | | |
|---|---|---|---|---|---|---|---|
| 120* | 1929/30 | 325 | YK | 6849, | 70239 | ≠ | |
| | | | | 6851-4 (773-6) | 70247/8/ — /50 | ≠ | |
| | | | | 767-71 | 70241-5 | ≠ | |

**Built 1933**

| | | | | | |
|---|---|---|---|---|---|
| 170* | 1933 | 499 | DR | 5228-45 | 70304-21 |
| 176 | 1933 | 499 | DR | 4140-4 | 70328-32 |
| | | | | 5224-7 | 70333/4/ — /6 |
| 177 | 1933 | 499 | DR | 5246-9 | 70337-40 |

Diags 170/6/7 — underframes from GNR Howlden passenger stock

**Built 1935**

| | | | | | |
|---|---|---|---|---|---|
| 170* | 1934 | 635 | DR | 5255-60 | 70322-7 |

---

# Milk and general vans: (M)

### DIAGRAMS 86, 87

The Diagram 86 general purpose vans were somewhat outside the usual run of LNER vehicles, and again were specified by the GE section which had originally asked for six-wheeled vehicles.

The milk vans were built for the GE section, but one commentator avers that they were used for the Northallerton-Finsbury Park traffic, loaded with milk churns consigned from stations on the line to Leyburn and beyond.

| Diag No | CBP | Order No | Built | Original number/changes | 1943 number | |
|---|---|---|---|---|---|---|
| **Built 1926** | | | | | | |
| 86* | 1925/6 | 125 | SF | 6231-52 | 70079-70100 | ≠ |
| **Built 1927** | | | | | | |
| 86* | 1925/6 | 125 | SF | 6253-82 | 70101-30 | ≠ |
| 87 | 1926/7 | 160 | SF | 6283-96 | — /70132-6/ — /8-44 | |

---

# TPO van: (POS)

These were the first LNER design mail vans, and had a distinctive appearance in order to maximise their interior space, at the same time staying within an overall width of 8ft 6in in the period before 9ft 3in width vehicles were cleared for general running over the East Coast main line.

The three vans were built for the North Eastern TPO, the 8.25pm from Kings Cross, and its return working, and were fitted with mail bag delivery brackets and a pick-up net on one side, the interior having a lavatory, wardrobe and overhead steam pipes for heating.

In 1932, pressure from the Post Office resulted in agreement by the LNER to convert the most recent gas-lit TPO vans to electric lighting, and to construct new vans to replace the oldest vehicles. The new arrivals allowed the 1929 vans to be transferred to the GE section, for use on the Liverpool Street-Peterborough working. The delivery and collection equipment of the three vans was removed as it was not required on this service.

### DIAGRAM 131

| Diag No | CBP | Order No | Built | Original number/changes | 1943 number |
|---|---|---|---|---|---|
| **Built 1929** | | | | | |
| 131 | 1927/8 | 279 | YK | 2260/86, 2339 | 70277-9 |
| | | | | (6130-2) | Trans 1933 |

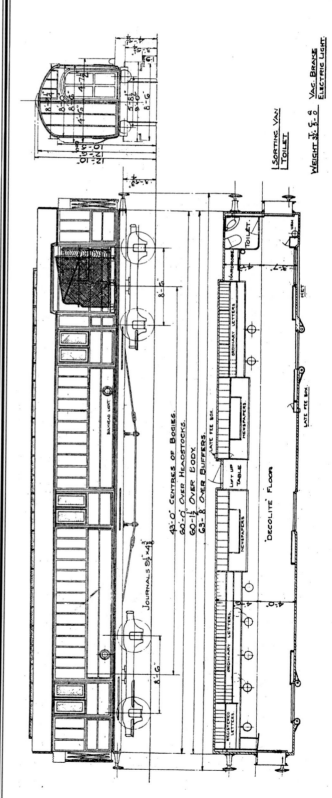

# APPENDIX

## Appendix 1

### AN EAST COAST INSPECTOR AT WORK

It is tempting to think that all was shipshape and Bristol-fashion in the past, and that all trains ran on time in the days when East Coast trains had gleaming Pacifics at the head of polished Gresley teak-panelled carriages. We have little in the way of actual evidence, other than reminiscences and sometimes these can be too golden to be true.

We do however have an interesting and professional perspective on East Coast expresses – which as far as the LNER was concerned were the crème de la crème – from an East Coast Inspector. The Inspector's job was to keep a careful eye on standards of operation, adherence to established practice, and instances where performance, staff, vehicles and passenger facilities were the cause for comment. These Inspectors had been a feature of East Coast operations before 1914 but, in LNER and BR days, the appointment was generally short-term and the man

chosen was a Traffic Apprentice or the like; in the case of the years before 1939 they tended to be one of the 'Bell Boys', chosen by Mr R. Bell, one of the LNER's Assistant General Managers, and regarded as 'bright, young men' for the future.

L. W. (Lance) Ibbotson was an East Coast Inspector and he went on to become a senior manager in BR. Some Inspectors might have chosen to pull their punches when it came to producing reports on the East Coast trains they rode on and observed. His report was entirely concerned with the East Coast daytime and nighttime expresses, as well as the principal Kings Cross-Newcastle trains and the Leeds-Glasgow express.

Mr Ibbotson's report is the only one that the author has encountered which was the subject of discussion by the Superintendents and Passenger Managers of the LNER at their monthly meetings. They were not particularly pleased at what he had to say and prepared their defences accordingly.

At least 16 coaches, newly renovated by Doncaster and York Works and ready to form prestige East Coast sets for the summer service, make an appreciable load for 'J3' 0-6-0 No 4151 and 'C2' Atlantic No 3981 as they pull away southwards from Grantham on 2 June 1934. Next to the engines is one of the 1924 triplet restaurant car sets.

The report has survived in the archives of the Scottish Record Office and extracts are included here to give the reader a little more of the atmosphere behind the figures and records of the carriages themselves. It was addressed to the Superintendents and Passenger Managers and was considered first at their meeting of 24 April 1933. Some of the issues raised by the Report struck home, and were discussed at subsequent meetings, action having been taken in the meantime. Now to its observations and recommendations which have been selected (and edited) for their relevance to some of the features described elsewhere in the book.

**Lighting** – Did not meet a single case of faulty lighting. Train Attendants turned off lights in compartments – why? 'Dim' light in first-class sleeping cars so dim as to be invisible.

**Heating** – For most part quite adequate, especially in restaurant cars. With steam heating the back of a long train may rarely be hot enough on a cold day. Carriages heated with electricity do not seem very successful, except on long runs with few stops.* New type of first-class carriage in which the heating apparatus is almost beyond reproach. The heating of corridors goes a long way to achieve this result.† Window fastenings on corridor side not keeping shut.§ Very large number of cases where lavatory water is cold.

* He was referring to Diagram 7 composite No 1063. † He was referring to the 'Super Firsts' of Diagrams 139 and 147, and later. § End-door type vehicles not described in this book.

**Cleaning** – Standard of cleaning reasonably high – but should eliminate all ledges which are dust-traps. Sleeping cars which I inspected were often very dirty. This applies especially to the first-class and, more especially, those starting from Edinburgh. Not cleaned under carpets – woodwork rarely polished.

On some trains there are special carriage cleaners – in my opinion they should be replaced by Train Attendants.

Passengers complain about lavatory cleanliness and smell.

**Accommodation** – For the most part, the accommodation was in excess of passengers travelling. Not uncommon for a train to run with two third-class passengers to compartments. One or two cases where first-class accommodation is not sufficient. This seems to indicate a lack of flexibility in stock arrangements. One lavatory in three should be reserved for ladies.

**Catering** – Cooking of food and service are invariably excellent, meals invariably served hot. One point where complaints are justified – that is price. All meals very expensive, especially from the third-class passengers' point of view. Costs should be reduced – and less should be charged for 'short' menus.

## OBSERVATIONS ON PARTICULAR TRAINS

**10am from Edinburgh** – On 24 February 1933, the train was two hours or more late. Heating always good, cleaning patchy. New third-class carriages with three-a-side seating very popular.

**10am from Kings Cross** – On 24 February 1933, this train was also two hours or more late. Accommodation not so well used. On 7 March 1933, cleaning was none too good – the restaurant car had previous day's crumbs still apparent.

**1.20pm from Kings Cross** – Heating not too good. The restaurant car was 'very messy' after lunch. Third-class considerably in excess of requirements. Front parcels van never well used.

**2.5pm from Edinburgh** – Food on this train had left Kings Cross the previous day. Meat served out by chef's hands. Marshalling and accommodation a problem – short of first-class and vans marshalled all over the train and introducing a smell of fish. On 14 February 1933, the Perth composite was 'exceedingly ancient' No 1240.

**8.15am from Newcastle** – Asked for rugs to be put out on one day because of inadequate heating. Suggest that rugs should be available at stations.

**7.30pm Kings Cross-Aberdeen** – Accommodation for non-sleeping car passengers considerably in excess of requirements, composite carriage for each destination served by this train which is unnecessary.

**8.55am Leeds-Glasgow** – Seating accommodation again more than ample, especially after leaving Newcastle. Could be lightened by providing a brake third in place of the front brake first and cut-out the third marshalled in front of the Sheffield composite. Heating only moderate except restaurant cars – windows in sliding doors would not stay up.

**5.10pm Edinburgh-Leeds** (actually the return working of the Leeds-Glasgow) – Thirty-one third-class passengers between Edinburgh and Newcastle, of which four had dinner.

At the time, Train Attendants were provided only on the up and down 'Flying Scotsman' and the 1.20pm Kings Cross-Edinburgh and 2.5pm return

The Report is piece number BR/LNE/8/328 in the Scottish Record Office, Edinburgh.

| The Superintendents and Passenger Managers commented on Mr Ibbotson's Report and its specific criticisms as follows: | |
| --- | --- |
| Day trains – 'Generous accommodation' | Train formations reviewed, not possible to base criticisms on 'isolated journeys'. |
| Night trains – 'Generous accommodation' | Unwise to reduce through portions. |
| Sleeping car lighting | Dim lights are satisfactory |
| Lights turned off unnecessarily | Agree. Attendants to be instructed. |
| Steam heating inadequacies | Constantly receiving attention of the CME. |
| Electric heating not satisfactory | One coach only electrically heated – works on 8.25pm Kings Cross-Edinburgh and 7.50pm up New type of first has electric *and* steam heating |
| Problems with window fastenings in new first-class carriages | Cause for complaint, receiving the attention of the CME. |
| Drop windows on corridor side of new carriages will not remain closed | Being dealt with by CME. |
| Lavatories marked for ladies | Don't agree |
| Smell from lavatories | Deodorisers to be placed in lavatories |
| Elimination of ledges | Called to the attention of the CME. |
| Sleeping cars dirty | Position not as bad as suggested. |
| Restaurant cars have crumbs | Agree that small carpet-sweeper should be provided in restaurant cars. |
| Catering suggestions | Passed to Hotels Department |
| Replace carriage cleaners by train attendants | They do more cleaning and more thoroughly than attendants. |

# Appendix 2

## EAST COAST SETS FROM 1924-31

The newly formed LNER regarded as one of its priorities the construction of four new sets of coaches for the 'Flying Scotsman' and the Afternoon Scotsmen (the 1.15pm Kings Cross-Edinburgh Waverley, and 1.45pm return). The first of these sets entered service on 1 October 1924. In addition, there were two sets of former East Coast Joint Stock vehicles, dating from 1914, and with some later vehicles. All six sets were referred to as sets Nos 1-6, and each coach was branded on the solebars. J Set 1, 2, 3, 4, 5, 6, as appropriate.

The four 1924 sets were formed of the standard LNER vestibuled coach types, and included triplet restaurant car sets. The coaches were maintained at York Works, with the exception of the triplets which were dealt with by Doncaster Works. The vehicles in the sets were renovated during the winter months when they were lifted, washed and revarnished, with other attention as appropriate.

For the introduction of non-stop running by the 'Flying Scotsman' in the summer of 1928, Gresley proposed the formation of sets for the 'Flying Scotsman' as follows:

**Set No 1:** BTKL 1055 (Dia 40); TKL 1005 (Dia 23); CKL 1061 (Dia 7); RC Triplet 16451-3; FKL 1196 (ECJS Dia 59); TKL 1006 (Dia 23); TKL 1007 (Dia 23); TKL 1008 (Dia 23); B 177 (Dia 45)

**Set No 2:** BTKL 1056 (Dia 40); TKL 1009 (Dia 23); CKL 1062 (Dia 7); RC Triplet 16471-3; FKL 1353 (ECJS Dia 59); TKL 1010 (Dia 23); TKL 1011 (Dia 23); TKL 1012 (Dia 23); B 178 (Dia 45)

The two sets were scheduled to go to the shops by March 1928, and to return to traffic as complete sets the following month. In this case, the individual coaches were not only shopped as usual, but most were fitted with larger capacity water tanks, all were retrimmed, and one or two other changes were made. After receipt from the works, the complete trains were marshalled into formations at Hornsey.

Sets Nos 3/4 were made up for the relief to the 'Flying Scotsman':

**Set No 3:** BTKL 112 (Dia 40); CG 1072 (Dia 8); B 167 (Dia 45); TKL 1048 (Dia 23); TKL 1049 (Dia 23); RT 1193 (ECJS Dia 29A); RK 1213 (ECJS Dia 80A); RF 1191 (ECJS Dia 75A); CKL 151 (Dia 7); CKL 154 (Dia 7); BTKL 139 (Dia 40)

**Set No 4:** BTKL 113 (Dia 40); CG 1074 (Dia 8); B 168 (Dia 45); TKL 1050 (Dia 23); TKL 1051 (Dia 23); RT 1192 (ECJS Dia 29A); RK 1212 (ECJS Dia 80A); RF 1190 (ECJS Dia 75A); CKL 156 (Dia 7); CKL 157 (Dia 7); BTKL 140 (Dia 40)

These vehicles were to be sent for shopping by 11 April 1928, and were expected to re-enter traffic on 27 April 1928.

To run with the new triplets built in 1928, two other sets were to be available for 9 July 1928. The proposed sets were:

BTKL 1057 (Dia 40); TKL 1000 (Dia 23); CKL 1065 (Dia 7); new RC Triplet; FKL 187* (ECJS Dia 59); TKL 1001 (Dia 23); TKL 1002 (Dia 23); TKL 1003 (Dia 23); B 192 (Dia 45)

BTKL 1058 (Dia 40); TKL 1014 (Dia 23); CKL 1066 (Dia 7); new RC Triplet; FKL 1123* (ECJS Dia 59); TKL 1015 (Dia 23); TKL 1016 (Dia 23); TKL 1017 (Dia 23); B 193 (Dia 45)

* These coaches were previously in sets Nos 5/6, used on the afternoon Scotsmen, and were replaced by 1927-built Dia 2 firsts, Nos 1130/1.

These newly formed sets would displace sets Nos 1/2, the vehicles from which would then become strengthening and replacement coaches for the four East Coast sets, except that the triplet RCs would go to sets Nos 3/4.

Vehicles to form two new sets for the '10 o'clocks' were included in the 1930/1 CBP. The intention was that 14 of the Dia 23 thirds, the Dia 2 firsts Nos 1130/1, Dia 40 brake thirds 112/3, Dia 7 composites Nos 154/5, and a

couple of older vehicles would be transferred to the Areas in due course.

The winter renovation of stock was based on a schedule by which the stock went into works in January/February 1931, for outshopping at the end of March.

### SETS 1/2 – 4 MAY – 5 JULY 1931

**Set No 1:** BTKL 1055 (Dia 40); CKL 162 (Dia 7); CG 1072 (Dia 8); Toilet Third 1007 (Dia 23A); TKL 1042 (Dia 23); RC triplet 16451-3; FKL 1196 (ECJS Dia 59); CG 1073 (Dia 8); TKL 1029 (Dia 23); B 177 (Dia 45); BCKL 1078 (Dia 34)

**Set No 2:** BTKL 1056 (Dia 40); CKL 163 (Dia 7); CG 1074 (Dia 8); Toilet Third 1012 (Dia 23A); TKL 1030 (Dia 23); RC triplet 16471-3; FKL 1353 (ECJS Dia 59); CG 1075 (Dia 8); TKL 1031 (Dia 23); B 178 (Dia 45); BCKL 1079 (Dia 34)

### SETS 1/2 – FROM 6 JULY 1931

**Set No 1:** BTKL 1160 (Dia 114); TKL 1114 (Dia 115); CKL 1259† (Dia 137); TKL 1115 (Dia 115); Toilet third 1007 (Dia 23A); RC triplet 16481-3†; FK 1132 (Dia 139); TKL 1116 (Dia 115); B 117† (Dia 113)

**Set No 2:** BTKL 1161 (Dia 114); TKL 1117 (Dia 115); CKL 1260† (Dia 137); TKL 1118 (Dia 115); Toilet third 1012 (Dia 23A); RC triplet 16491-3†; FK 1133 (Dia 139); TKL 1119 (Dia 115); B 118† (Dia 113)

† Maintained by Doncaster Works

With the entry into traffic of the 'new' Sets 1/2, vehicles from the former sets 1/2 were then held for strengthening regular sets. Note the range of 9ft 3in width coaches in the 'new' sets, to Diagrams 113, 114, 115, 137, and the 'Super Firsts' on Diagram 139.

SETS 3/4 – for the relief 10.5am down 'Flying Scotsman' and return workings from 6 July 1931:

**Set No 3:** CG 1292 (Dia 116); B 166 (Dia 45); TKL 1018 (Dia 23); TKL 1019 (Dia 23); TKL 1020 (Dia 23); RC Triplet 16501-3; FKL 1134 (Dia 147); CKL 151 (Dia 7); BTKL 114 (Dia 40); TKL 1032 (Dia 23); BTKL 1059 (Dia 40); BCKL 1080 (Dia 34)

**Set No 4:** CG 1293 (Dia 116); B 167 (Dia 45); TKL 1035 (Dia 23); TKL 1036 (Dia 23); TKL 1040 (Dia 23); RC Triplet 16511-3; FKL 1135 (Dia 147); CKL 156 (Dia 7); BTKL 115 (Dia 40); TKL 1041 (Dia 23); BTKL 1060 (Dia 40); BCKL 1081 (Dia 34)

Note the appearance in both sets of the 'Super Firsts' on Diagram 147.

SETS 5/6 – for the afternoon Scotsmen from 4 May 1931:

**Set No 5:** BCKL 1076 (Dia 34); B 190 (Dia 45); TKL 1021 (Dia 23); CG 1067 (Dia 8); TKL 1022 (Dia 23); TKL 1023 (Dia 23); RC Triplet 16431-3; B 149 (Dia 113); BTKL 142 (Dia 40)

**Set No 6:** BCKL 1077 (Dia 34); B 191 (Dia 45); TKL 1024 (Dia 23); CG 1068 (Dia 8); TKL 1025 (Dia 23); TKL 1026 (Dia 23); RC Triplet 16461-3; B 160 (Dia 43); BTKL 143 (Dia 40)

The strengthening vehicles available from 6 July 1931 were:

RC Triplets: 16451-3; 16471-3
FKLs (ECJS Dia 59): 1196; 1353
CKLs: 157/8/62/3/83 (Dia 7); 1065 (Dia 7)
CGs: 1072-5 (Dia 8); 1294 (Dia 116)
BCKLs (Dia 34): 1078/9/82-5
TKLs (Dia 23): 1027-31/3/4/7-9/42/3
BTKLs (Dia 40): 138; 145-8/50; 1055/6
and a number of all-steel vans to Diagram 45

# ACKNOWLEDGEMENTS

I N preparing this book, reference was made as much as possible to original sources. The custodians of the major archives relating to LNER carriages are the Public Record Office, Kew, the Scottish Record Office, Edinburgh and the National Railway Museum. The staffs at Kew and at Edinburgh were always ready to provide the material requested and it was a pleasure to work at either location. Similarly, too, at the National Railway Museum where in particular I would like to thank Phil Atkins, the Librarian. Mike Blakemore was also most helpful during his time at the Museum.

Norman Newsome whose paper, *The Development of LNER Carriage and Wagon Design*, was first read before the Institution of Locomotive Engineers on 10 March 1948, has been as always most helpful in the preparation of this work.

For help in various ways, first I would like to express my especial gratitude to Chris Bishop for his interest in the project, and for his care in reading the manuscript and proofs and for pinpointing items for attention and improvement. I am also most grateful to Bryan Dawes; Michael Brooks (for the loan of historical material); Richard Casserley for making available photographs from his own collection and that of his father and, indeed, for much other invaluable information; Robert Humm (for the loan of illustrative material); John Lloyd; David Lowther, David Percival and John Watling, the last-named for some much-valued material on the numbering of GER stock. I would like to include a special 'thank you' to Brian Stephenson for allowing me access to Rail Archive Stephenson, for his interest, and care in making available some excellent prints for reproduction in this book.

As usual, I would like to thank my family, Carol, Edmund and Georgia for their interest and patience, and for their many helpful suggestions and unstinting interest.

## REFERENCES

The principal sources of reference were those held at the PRO, in particular the LNER Board Minutes, the minutes of the Joint Meeting of the Locomotive and Traffic Committee, the minutes of the Traffic Committee and the minutes of the meetings of the Superintendents and Passenger Managers, in each case during the LNER period, or in the case of the SPM meeting, from 1921. There are a number of LNER Secretarial papers held at Kew covering diverse subjects, as well as those of the former Hotels Executive of the British Transport Commission, to which reference has been made. Also of value are the rule books and sectional appendices held at the PRO. At the Scottish Record Office there are various files which do not appear elsewhere and which cast much useful light on East Coast and LNER matters.

At the National Railway Museum, quite the most interesting fresh material on hand were the instructions issued by the Chief Mechanical Engineers of the LNER from 1923-1948 relating to carriage and wagon matters.

Finally, many useful references have come from study of the following journals: *The Engineer, The LNER Magazine, The Locomotive Magazine, the Railway Engineer, The Railway Gazette, The Railway Magazine, The Railway Observer, Railway World and Trains Illustrated.*

## PHOTOGRAPHIC CREDITS

The following photographs are reproduced by courtesy of the respective photographers or owners of collections:
*Rail Archive Stephenson:*
T. G. Hepburn - p 4; p 5; p 13; p 14 (bottom); p 34 (below); p (centre); p 73; p 185 (right); p 189. F. R. Hebron - p 7. J. P. Wilson - p 9 (both); p 192. D. M. C. Hepburne-Scott - p (bottom). *Colling Turner/Photomatic* - p 69 (top); p 122. J. F. *Davies/Photomatic* - p 115 (lower). *G. R. Grigs/Photomatic* - p 80 (top); p 101 (top); p 115 (top); p 138 (lower). *W. M. Rogerson/Photomatic* - p 83; p 88.
H. C. Casserley/courtesy R. M. Casserley p 20; p 36; p 40 (lower); p 46 (upper); p 48 (upper); p 52; p 57 (lower); p 65 (centre); p 70; p 75 (top); (top); p 86 (lower); p 91 (top); p 95; p 99 (lower); p 101 (bottom); p 111; p 124; p 134 (both); p 142 (lower); p 177; p 185 (below right).
R. M. Casserley p 59 (bottom); p 77 (centre); p 91 (lower); p 105 (lower).
J. F. Henton p 101 (centre).
*L&GRP* - C. J. L. Romanes p 12.
*David Lowther:* p 147; p 170 (lower).
*National Railway Museum:*
p 11 (top and bottom); p 14 (top); p 15; p 22 (lower); 29 (both); p 34 (top and above); p 38; p 40 (top); p 41 (lower); p 44; p 46 (lower); p 48 (lower); p 55 (top and above); p 57 (top); p 65 (top and bottom); p 80 (lower); p 86 (lower); p 10 (top); p 116; p 138 (top); p 153 (top); p 161; p 163; p 166; p 170 (top); p 172 (both); p 174; p 181 (top); p 185 (top).
David Percival: p 41 (top); p 55 (bottom); p 63; p 72; p 75 (bottom); p 77 (bottom); p 181 (lower).
*By courtesy of Robert Humm Collection* p 17 (top); p 22 (upper); p 25; p 34 (bottom); p 59 (top); p 69 (bottom); p 99 (top); p 149; p 153 (bottom); p 158.

**Away from Netherfield & Colwick station goes a Grantham-Nottingham train on 3 March 1957, headed by 'L1' 2-6-4T No 67800. The train comprises a couple of postwar non-vestibuled coaches, but the last vehicle is appropriately a teak bodied non-vestibuled Diagram 246 brake third described in this book.**